Springer Series on Asian Criminology and Criminal Justice Research

Series Editor
Jianhong Liu, Faculty of Social Sciences & Humanities
University of Macau Department of Sociology
Taipa, Macao, Macao

The series publishes both theoretical and empirical work along several themes in Asian Criminology, with a focus on research-level monographs and edited volumes. It aims to cover 4 main themes: the elaborations and adaptations of research models and established theories (established mainly by Western scholarship) to Asian contexts; an introduction of innovative concepts, theories and policies originating in Asian societies to Western audiences; and in-depth studies of particular Asian countries, as they reflect local traditions and cultures one hand, and a general understanding of criminal behavior or criminal justice, on the other. It will feature authors from any country of origin doing research about or pertaining to Asian countries.

The series encourages submissions of both quantitative and qualitative research approaches, as well as mixed methods and comparative approaches, with a focus on studies using rigorous methods and presenting new research results. It will be of interest to researchers in criminology and criminal justice, as well as related fields such as sociology, demography and international studies.

Sudhir Krishnaswamy • Renuka Sane
Ajay Shah • Varsha Aithala
Editors

Crime Victimisation in India

 Springer

Editors
Sudhir Krishnaswamy
National Law School of India University
Bengaluru, Karnataka, India

Ajay Shah
NIPFP and xKDR Forum
Mumbai, Maharashtra, India

Renuka Sane
NIPFP and xKDR Forum and Jindal
Global University
Sonipat, Haryana, India

Varsha Aithala
National Law School of India University
Bengaluru, Karnataka, India

ISSN 2522-5545   ISSN 2522-5553   (electronic)
Springer Series on Asian Criminology and Criminal Justice Research
ISBN 978-3-031-12250-7   ISBN 978-3-031-12251-4   (eBook)
https://doi.org/10.1007/978-3-031-12251-4

This Springer imprint is published by the registered company Springer Nature Switzerland AG
The registered company address is: Gewerbestrasse 11, 6330 Cham, Switzerland

Contents

About the Editors

Sudhir Krishnaswamy is Vice-Chancellor, Director of online and hybrid programs, and Professor of Law at the National Law School of India University, Bengaluru. He teaches political philosophy and politics in India, research methodology, constitutional law, law and justice, and legal system reform. His main areas of interest are constitutional law, legal system reform, legal theory, intellectual property law, and administrative law. He has written on a wide range of topics, including Indian constitutional law, intellectual property law, and judicial corruption.

He is also the co-founder and trustee of the Centre for Law and Policy Research. Previously, he was the Director of the School of Policy and Governance, and Professor of Law and Politics at Azim Premji University, Bengaluru. He was also the Dr. B.R. Ambedkar Visiting Professor of Indian Constitutional Law at Columbia Law School. He has been a teaching fellow in law at Pembroke College at Oxford University, an Assistant Professor at the National Law School of India University, and Professor at the West Bengal National University of Juridical Sciences. He has taught law at universities in Australia, the UK, and the USA.

A Rhodes Scholar and graduate of the University of Oxford, he has earlier worked with the Prime Minister's Committee on Infrastructure, Planning Commission, and the Kasturi Rangan Expert Committee on Bangalore Governance. He is also the only Indian member of Facebook's social media oversight board.

He has a Doctor of Philosophy in Law and a Bachelor of Civil Laws degree from the University of Oxford and a Bachelor of Arts and Law (Honors) degree from the National Law School of India University, Bengaluru.

Renuka Sane is Associate Professor at the National Institute of Public Finance and Policy. Her research interests lie in household finance, credit and bankruptcy, pensions, and the regulatory state.

She was a member of the research team of the Bankruptcy Legislative Reforms Commission on individual insolvency. She is also a member of the Pension Advisory Committee of the Pension Fund Regulatory Development Authority, and a member of the working group on personal insolvency at the Insolvency and Bankruptcy Board of India.

She has a PhD in Economics from the University of New South Wales and holds an MA in Economics from Mumbai University.

Ajay Shah studied at IIT, Bombay and USC, Los Angeles. He has held positions at the Centre for Monitoring Indian Economy (CMIE), Indira Gandhi Institute for Development Research (IGIDR), Department of Economic Affairs at the Ministry of Finance, and National Institute for Public Finance and Policy (NIPFP).

He is now part of xKDR Forum and Jindal Global University. His research is at the intersection of economics, law, and public administration.

His second book, co-authored with Vijay Kelkar, *In service of the republic: The art and science of economic policy*, featured in Bloomberg's global "2020 Best Books on Business and Leadership." His work can be accessed on his home page (http://www.mayin.org/ajayshah).

Varsha Aithala is a Dr. N R Madhava Menon Doctoral Scholar (2020–2023) and guest faculty at the National Law School of India University, Bengaluru. Her doctoral thesis examines the role of private capital in Indian legal system reform. Her research interests span the areas of contract law, corporate law, legal system reform, legal education, and the legal profession. She was a research fellow and visiting faculty at Azim Premji University, Bengaluru, where she offered courses on private law and legal system reform.

She has more than 10 years of extensive experience in corporate and commercial laws and has specialized in international and domestic private equity and venture capital investment transactions.

She has a Master of Corporate Law degree from the University of Cambridge and a Bachelor of Arts and Law (Honors) degree from Nalsar University of Law, Hyderabad.

Chapter 1
Crime Victimisation Surveys in Indian Criminal Justice System Reform

Renuka Sane and Ajay Shah

1 The Criminal Justice System in the Larger Context of State Building

The state is defined as a community that achieves and maintains a monopoly on physical force in a given territory. State building consists of creating conditions under which residents do not inflict violence upon one another. In the jargon of public economics, the personal safety of citizens is a "public good." It satisfies the two tests for a public good: it is *non-rival* (your consumption of safety does not diminish my safety) and *non-excludable* (we cannot exclude a newborn child from the blanket of safety) (Kelkar & Shah, 2019). Hence, personal safety of residents is a legitimate goal for the state.

We are grateful to Sudhir Krishnaswamy and Varsha Aithala who invited us to participate in their research project on crime victimisation surveys. Our thinking on this was greatly shaped by our collaborators for the IDFC Institute crime victimisation survey work (2017), where we worked with Reuben Abraham, Pradnya Saravade, Neha Sinha, Avanti Durani and Rithika Kumar, the CHRI crime victimisation survey work (2015) where we worked with Maja Daruvala, Devika Prasad and Devyani Srivastava. We also thank Rajiv Mehrishi and Nandkumar Saravade for extensive conversations on these questions.

R. Sane
NIPFP and xKDR Forum and Jindal Global University, Sonipat, Haryana, India

A. Shah (✉)
NIPFP and xKDR Forum, Mumbai, Maharashtra, India
e-mail: ajayshah@mayin.org

The criminal justice system is unusually important, from the viewpoint of both economics and politics:

- In the political system, if individuals are not safe when organising political activities, the foundational concept of democracy—free competition between rival political parties—breaks down.
- In the economic system, if individuals are not safe when conducting business activities and imposing competitive pressure upon rivals, the foundational concept of capitalism—free competition between rival firms—breaks down.

In both aspects (politics or economics), remarkably modest levels of violence are required, in order to induce fear through a threat of violence. Once violence is a feasible strategy for some individuals, even on a small scale, this gives a decline in competitive conditions in politics and economics.

In politics and in economics, the hallmark of competitive conditions is close elections and the lack of domination by one party, or one firm in the marketplace. These yardsticks are only meaningful under free and fair conditions. Once violence is in the picture, these yardsticks are no longer a sufficient condition for ascertaining that healthy competition is in fray.

As an example, if one firm has 34% market share and another firm has 32% market share, the interpretation changes sharply when the former firm deploys violence upon the other. If competition in the market is free and fair, then it is reasonable to think that the two firms have similar levels of productivity. If, however, one of the two firms is gaining an upper edge through the use of violence (delivered either through private persons or through employees of the state), then it is likely that this firm has rough parity on market share but significantly inferior levels of productivity.

The personal safety of residents is also linked to freedom of speech. Violence or the threats of violence can be directed against persons who present uncomfortable facts and arguments into the public domain, thus inducing a chilling effect, and hampering both the political and economic life of a country.

For these reasons, protecting residents against internal violence is a fundamental aspect of every successful state. Personal safety is of enormous intrinsic value: high levels of safety directly generate welfare. Safety fosters exploration of the world, by the individual, under conditions of freedom, which is a purpose of human existence. The intertwined feedback loops of capitalism and freedom are founded in an environment of unquestioned personal safety. Conversely, when safety is under threat, it is not clear that political and economic freedom induces positive feedback loops upon each other. Every state aspiring for high capabilities builds institutional capacity to pursue the goal of the safety of residents. This is a combination of addressing external threats, which are addressed through a combination of international relations and military capabilities, and internal threats, which requires the criminal justice system (CJS).

2 Building the Criminal Justice System

The criminal justice system (CJS) is the institutional infrastructure that ensures safety of citizens. It consists of laws, courts, public prosecutors, police and prisons. In India, there are foundational flaws in each of these elements, and across many decades, a process of improvement has not commenced.[1] A research community is required, which is able to understand the full landscape of the CJS, and undertake the rational process of identifying problems, developing a strategic sense of the required changes, and working on the practical aspects of the small improvements which are made every day. A small process of thinking about courts has begun in India, but on the remaining elements there is a weak landscape (Datta et al., 2019; Saravade, 2015b; Shah, 2012).

As with many other fields, one strand of the Indian policy discourse on CJS reform consists of technological solutionism. This assigns supremacy to building computer equipment and associated monitoring mechanisms over the people such as mass surveillance using video cameras. However, as has been seen with many other fields in India, the human behaviour of the individuals that make up the state is shaped by incentives, and a more fundamental transformation of organisations, process manuals, power and incentives is required (Datta & Shah, 2015). Computer technology can be a part of a useful reform process, but a digital-first approach is generally unsuitable.

In the CJS, in particular, there is a greater danger of a digital-first approach inducing intrusions into the privacy of individuals and tilting the balance of power away from individuals and into the hands of state organisations (Bailey et al., 2018). Computer technology can be a useful element of a sophisticated reform programme, but such a reform programme needs to be primarily rooted in modifying the nature of state power and the incentives of self-interested state functionaries.[2] The first step in such a reform programme is that of establishing basic measurement of the functioning of the system.

3 The Role of Measurement

In most areas of public policy, it is useful to think in terms of a three-stage process:

---

[1] For example, see Bhandari (2016), Parsheera (2015), Saravade (2015a), and Saravade and Sane (2013).

[2] For an analogy from the world of business, consider transformative "Business Process Re-engineering" (BPR). BPR projects have repeatedly generated large improvements in productivity. All BPR projects involve computer technology. However, BPR projects are led by the top management and primarily reshape organisation design, incentives and processes. A great deal of computer engineering is an implementation pathway. If the computer engineering were present, but the top management were not absorbed in a more fundamental reshaping of the organisation design, the technology transformation by itself would not sufficiently reinvent the firm.

Inputs

We start at the inputs, a design of government, which maps into recruitment of personnel, purchases of goods and services, and their deployment into operation of exerting coercive force upon society, through a certain set of process manuals. The inputs are ultimately grounded in a theory of change about the nature of the world and the value of such state intervention. As an example, in the field of education, the inputs are teachers recruited and school buildings built.

Outputs

The functionaries go about their process manuals and produce certain proximate outputs. As an example, in the field of education, the outputs are students enrolled and hours of teaching delivered.

Outcomes

Finally, there is the desired impact upon society, the outcome. As an example, in the field of education, the outcome is the change in knowledge of children.[3]

Such an approach generates insights into whether the present strategy of inputs and outcomes is able to generate the desired outcomes. The education bureaucracy may like to count the number of teachers recruited, the number of schools built, the number of children enrolled and the pass rate of students in the official examination system. However, what matters most in measurement is finding a random sample of 15-year-olds and administering an internationally comparable test (the OECD PISA) upon them, to judge the knowledge of science and mathematics in these students.

This approach to outcomes measurement readily lends itself to bang-for-the-buck measures. As an example, in the field of education, it is easy to measure the per pupil expense ("PPE"). In the Indian case, over a period of the last 20 years, the PPE has risen greatly while the outcomes have essentially not changed at all. This helps question the theory of change that has shaped the existing design of inputs.

Similarly, in the field of bankruptcy, Shah and Thomas, 2017, define inputs as the laws and the institutional infrastructure required for the bankruptcy process to work, outputs as the transactions that go through the system, and outcomes as recovery rates, and broader growth in the credit markets.

---

[3] See http://www.asercentre.org/Learning/Trends/-/p/375.html for the measurement of educational outcomes by ASER.

In the case of policing, inputs would be policemen or public prosecutors hired, and police stations or jails built. Outputs may be measured from within the MIS of the police. This would include measures such as the number of cases filed, the number of cases where prosecution in court commenced, the success rate in achieving conviction and the crime rate (as measured in the MIS of the police). The outcomes would be a citizen-centric view of law and order. They are the ultimate output that we seek to deliver. They consist of three things: (a) the actual incidence of crime as reported by the people (and not as counted in the MIS of the police), (b) trust in the policing system and (c) perception of safety that enables freedom in behaviour.

There is quite a bit of knowledge, internationally, on how some of this measurement is done. For an array of standardised crimes (e.g., theft of a car), a random sample of households is asked questions:

1. In the last 1 year, have you or your immediate family experienced this crime?
2. If you did, did you go to the police and was it a satisfactory experience?
3. If, hypothetically, you were to experience this crime in the future, would you go to the police?

The advantage of this household survey-based measurement is that it avoids the infirmities of the MIS systems within the police. If households prefer to not file an FIR, or if filing FIRs is difficult, then crime events would not show up in the police MIS systems. In contrast, household survey-based measurement generates direct evidence of the outcome.

An important element of all public goods problems lies in "coping costs." For example, when the electricity supply is bad, we buy voltage stabilisers or generators. It is, hence, important to measure the adaptations and distortions of behaviour of households that are caused by the prospective fear of crime. This would include questions such as:

1. How much are you spending for security-related services?
2. At what time in the evening do you feel it is unsafe for your teenage daughter to be out alone?

A good state of law and order is one where households lead an unencumbered life, where they do not suffer from costs of coping. The decision of a resident to engage in economic activity or political activity should not be shaped by the threat of violence that might be encountered.

The measurement of crime as seen from citizens versus the measurement of crime as seen in the official police MIS will throw up some discrepancies which are also interesting. They portray the unwillingness of citizens to go to the police. Our first task is to establish our statistical system. This requires ongoing measurement through two tracks: (a) internal MIS of the police and (b) survey-based measurement of outcomes.

4   Crime Victimisation Surveys in India

In India, small-scale city-based surveys measuring crime have been conducted since the 1980s. These include surveys that studied causes of victimisation, or the perception of the citizens by police and lawyers in the 1980s (Krishna et al., 1981; Rajan & Krishna, 1981). The first crime victims survey, with a sample of 1000 respondents, took place in 1992: International Crime (Victim) Survey in Bombay (ICS Bombay). This was followed by surveys in four cities of Tamil Nadu—Madurai, Coimbatore, Trichy, and Chennai, in 2001 (Chockalingam, 2003). In 2007 and 2008, a survey was conducted in Rajasthan that also asked questions on non-reporting of crime (Banerjee et al., 2021). This survey showed that 1.7% of individuals were victims of a crime in the prior year and that 5.9% of households had at least one member who was a victim of a crime. Theft was the most common type of crime (37.9% of all the reported crimes), followed by burglary (16.6%) and assault (12%).[4]

In 2015 and 2017, there were two large-scale crime victimisation surveys conducted by the CHRI (Project Vishwas Setu) and the IDFC Institute (SATARC), respectively. The former surveyed 5850 households in Mumbai and 4950 households in Delhi while the latter surveyed in Chennai and Bangalore in addition to Mumbai and Delhi. Both surveys broadly asked three kinds of questions:

1. Was the respondent a victim of a crime in the last 1 year? (such as theft, house break-in, sexual harassment, assault, criminal intimidation, unnatural death and missing persons)
2. Did the respondent report this to the police? Did the police respond appropriately? If the households chose to not report to the police, what were their reasons?
3. Do households feel safe in their neighbourhoods? Or in public transport? At different times of the day?

Both these surveys were focused on urban regions. The Karnataka Crime Victimization Survey (KVCS), 2018–2019, moved this forward to the full state of Karnataka thus allowing a better understanding of both urban and rural regions in the state. The KCVS also expanded the range of crimes to include public order offences like rioting, arson and unlawful assembly, and offences committed by government officials like bribery and abuse of power.

Another important survey is the Status of Policing in India Reports (SPIR) in 2018 and 2019, which not only measured the perception on the incidence of crime but also measured the perceptions and response of the police personnel. This is interesting as it gives us a perspective on how those manning the system look at

---

[4] Another source of information on incidence of crime have been surveys such as the India Human Development Survey (IHDS) and the National Family Health Survey (NFHS)—though strictly not about measuring crime—they provide an indicator of some kinds of crimes experienced by survey respondents.

crime, and their role in ensuring safety. It also helps us understand the "how" and "why" behind the crime.

There are some similarities as well as differences in what one learns from the three crime vicitimisation surveys. The KCVS, for example, reports a crime victimisation rate of 30%, that is nearly double that reported by the CHRI survey. This may be associated with much greater crime rates in rural India. The SPIR finds that people's perceptions of crime differ greatly from the actual number of reported crimes in the same region—states that have the highest reported crime (such as Kerala) have the lowest perception of crime.

All four surveys have similar findings on reporting behaviour of victims of crimes—that is, there is large-scale under-reporting of crime. The process of reporting, and dealing with the system, is one of the prime reasons why people do not wish to deal with the police. The surveys also point to under-reporting by the police—when households do make it to the police station, they often are not able to register an FIR, reinforcing the reluctance to go in the first place. The KCVS survey points out that this is not uniform across complaints—registering property offences is easier than offences against the body and law. The SPIR survey also points to heterogeneity in the ability to register cases—the situation gets progressively worse for economically or socially vulnerable groups.

Despite these gaps, people's perception of the police is better than what one would have imagined. The surveys three CVS surveys show that around 50% of the victims are satisfied with the police response. However, as the SPIR points out, this overall satisfaction does not, at the same time, diminish the fear of the police.

The surveys also find that a large number of households feel "safe" in their neighbourhoods in cities such as Chennai, Bangalore, and in the state of Karnataka. Mumbai also does reasonably well. Delhi, however, fares poorly on the perception of safety with more than half the respondents saying that crime is a serious problem.

5 The Way Forward

The criminal justice system is a core public good. The ultimate goal of state building in a liberal democracy is that the safety of residents should be unquestioned, which would create conditions for creativity and leadership. This calls for a high prioritisation of the elements of the criminal justice system.

One of the first steps towards this aspiration is the measurement of how the system works, and where and why it fails. This can help understand the correlations between other aspects of society—such as employment, education, and prosperity—with those of crime. Such an understanding then lays the foundation for devising solutions. For example, one solution that is often talked of to reduce crime is to improve the quality of streetlights in public places. A regular measurement system also helps in evaluating whether policy actions are leading to the desired result. In the streetlight example, it would be useful to know what impact did the lights have on incidence of crime? Did they help as we had expected them to? If not, why did they not help. This can help policymakers do course correction before it is too late. There are two areas where we can make tangible progress in measuring the CJS.

1. *Reported crime data*: Improving the quality of measurement should begin with the data capture of registration of complaints and FIRs at the police station. As we have seen from survey evidence, there is a big gap between actual crime and registered crime. This gap needs to be reduced so that crime records can become more reliable. In India, the logistics of crime measurement are also problematic; in that, crime is recorded at the police station and then aggregated at the district and state level. If the data flows through the various layers are filled with leakages, then even if the reporting improves at the station level, the aggregate statistics at the district, state and national level, will be beset with errors.

   There are two responses that are important. First, recording of data at the level of the police station should be given priority and should not be left as a "residual" duty for a relatively junior constable. These data need to be captured digitally, and the data entry staff needs to be trained through a detailed process manual on the process of classification of crime as well as entering the records. This will help with achieving consistency of data across the country, and reconciling records as the data becomes more aggregated.

2. *Survey data*: Beyond official data, there is a need to measure household interactions with the criminal justice system. As discussed earlier, welfare of citizens is the ultimate outcome of the criminal justice system. The surveys discussed in this paper are an important start to more systematic, comprehensive and continuous measurement of citizen experience with crime and the CJS. For the survey data to be credible, it needs to be conducted by independent groups (such as the role played by ASER in education). The existence of such survey data will allow researchers to build a literature on the causes and consequences of crime.

   A critical component of such measurement is the existence of "panel data," which provides repeated measurements on individuals across time. This makes it possible for us to understand how crime trends and safety perceptions have evolved over time. It also helps to study how changes in social or economic conditions of individuals affect crime relative to changes in macro-economic conditions, or changes in policy.

   An example of how research on crime and safety is a study of women's labour force participation. A unique problem that is faced in India is the lack of women's labour force participation (LFP). Indian women's LFP is at 21%, which is one of the lowest rates in the world. In Bangladesh, it is 36%; in Sri Lanka, it is 34%; in Pakistan, it is 22%; and in China, it is 61%.[5] A great research effort is underway, where economists, sociologists and anthropologists are deciphering the sources of the low women's LFP in India. It is likely that low levels of personal safety constitute one important constraint which is holding women back. If we are able to understand this constraint better and improve conditions of safety,

---

[5] See https://data.worldbank.org/indicator/SL.TLF.CACT.FE.ZS

we would have a large impact upon women's LFP (which is an important objective in and of itself) and upon GDP.

Once a measurement system is in place, it should be used as an input into policy-making. Measurement is also important in that it makes available "local knowledge" that can lead to a programme of reform based on the state of personal safety and conditions in each location. For example, if evidence points to certain parts of India faring worse on crime and safety perceptions, then resources can be targeted towards those regions. The police departments in each region can design responses based on the problems in their jurisdictions. Similarly, if it emerges that there is a systematic pattern in when crimes occur, or on the kinds of victims that get targeted, then policy can be designed to tackle such crime. The research literature on the criminal justice system in India is in its early stages, as is the feedback from research into policymaking. Improvements in measurement should be the catalyst in making this transformation.

6 Conclusion

Most elements of the Indian state work poorly. The CJS is a particularly important element of the state, as personal safety is an essential precondition for the intertwined working of democratic politics and the market economy. In the sequencing of the elements that will make the Republic of India a mature market economy located in a liberal democracy, one of the highest priorities should be the establishment of a capable CJS, the interlinked institutional apparatus of laws, courts, police, public prosecutors and prisons.

Measurement of crime through FIR is limited (as the police exercise discretion on what FIRs are filed, victims may choose to not report crimes, and the process of capturing and the releasing the statistics is limited), Crime victimisation surveys, carried out on a household panel, can create important new knowledge about crime rates, the perceptions about the police in the eyes of the people and the extent to which the lives of the people are distorted owing to the fear of crime.

Such data would be enormously influential. It would help measure the causes and consequences of changes to personal safety, assess the progress (or lack thereof) about this foundational public good and support better decision-making at the leadership of the institutions that make up the CJS.

Early work on building CVS datasets in India has begun. Many of the papers in this book report on these experiences. There is a complex agenda for CJS reform, that is an essential element of India's journey in the days to come. Building high-quality CVS data is a precondition for progress on the overall agenda of CJS reform.

References

Bailey, R., Bhandari, V., Parsheera, S., & Rahman, F. (2018). *Use of personal data by intelligence and law enforcement agencies (tech. rep.).* NIPFP.

Banerjee, A., Chattopadhyay, R., Duflo, E., Keniston, D., & Singh, N. (2021). Improving police performance in Rajasthan, India: Experimental evidence on incentives, managerial autonomy, and training. *American Economic Journal: Economic Policy, 13*(1), 36–66. https://doi.org/10.1257/pol.20190664

Bhandari, V. (2016). Pretrial detention in India: An examination of the causes and possible solutions. *Asian Journal of Criminology, 11*, 83–110. https://link.springer.com/article/10.1007/s11417-015-9218-x

Chockalingham, K. (2003). *Criminal victimization in four major cities in Southern India. Forum on Crime and Society.* United Nations Office on Drugs; Crime.

Datta, P., & Shah, A. (2015). *How to make courts work?* The Leap Blog, 22 February 2015. https://blog.theleapjournal.org/2015/02/how-to-make-courts-work.html

Datta, P., Hans, M., Mishra, M., Patnaik, I., Regy, P., Roy, S., Sapatnekar, S., Shah, A., Singh, A. P., & Sundaresan, S. (2019). *How to modernise the working of Courts and Tribunals in India.* NIPFP Working Paper no 258. https://www.nipfp.org.in/media/medialibrary/2019/03/WP%5C2019%5C258.pdf

Kelkar, V., & Shah, A. (2019). *In service of the republic: The art and science of economic policy.* Penguin Allen Lane. http://www.mayin.org/ajayshah/books/isotr2019.html

Krishna, K. P., Iqbal, M., & Khan, M. Z. (1981). Police – Community relations – A study in images. *Indian Journal of Criminology, 9*(1), 14–22.

Parsheera, S. (2015). *Reforms of prosecution in the Indian criminal justice system.* The Leap Blog, 7 May 2015. https://blog.theleapjournal.org/2015/05/reforms-of-prosecution-in-indian.html

Rajan, V. N., & Krishna, K. P. (1981). *Victims of homicide.* Institute of Criminology and Forensic Science. https://www.ojp.gov/pdffiles1/Digitization/84653NCJRS.pdf

Saravade, N. (2015a). *Reinventing the criminal justice system (Part 1 of 2).* The Leap Blog, 11 March 2015. https://blog.theleapjournal.org/2015/03/reinventing-criminal-justice-system.html

Saravade, N. (2015b). *Reinventing the criminal justice system (Part 2 of 2).* The Leap Blog, 20 March 2015. https://blog.theleapjournal.org/2015/03/reinventing-criminal-justice-system20.html

Saravade, P., & Sane, R. (2013). *What ails the police?* The Leap Blog, 12 May 2013. https://blog.theleapjournal.org/2013/05/what-ails-police.html

Shah, A. (2012). *Law and order: How to go from outrage to action.* The Leap Blog, 23 December 2012. https://blog.theleapjournal.org/2012/12/law-and-order-how-to-go-from-outrage-to.html

Shah, A., & Thomas, S. (2017). *The Indian bankruptcy reform: The state of the art, 2017.* The Leap Blog, 13 July 2017. https://blog.theleapjournal.org/2017/07/the-indian-bankruptcy-reform-state-of.html

Chapter 2
Crime Victimization and Safety Perception Survey: Delhi and Mumbai

Devyani Srivastava and Devika Prasad

1 Introduction

The Commonwealth Human Rights Initiative (CHRI) commissioned[1] a crime victimization and safety perception survey in the cities of Delhi and Mumbai in 2014 to collect data on incidence of crime, features of the crime(s) experienced, households' reporting to the police, satisfaction levels with the police response, and perceptions of safety. At the time of its publication in 2015, this was the first known systematic attempt to record the actual crime experience of residents in both Delhi and Mumbai. While crime victimization surveys have long been recognized world over for their usefulness in measuring crime and informing policing and public safety priorities, India is yet to adopt this as a regular practice. In this light, this chapter identifies the unique insights that can be gained through such surveys to shape better-informed policies and decision-making on policing, crime prevention strategies, and public safety. It further attempts to share reflections on lessons learnt with regard to the survey methodology and the field experience while administering the survey. It is hoped this will contribute to the scholarship around crime victimization surveys emanating from India, as well as provide critical reflections and learning from this holistic survey effort to propel and strengthen both governmental and local surveys across the country.

---

[1] Nielson India Pvt. Ltd. administered the survey, prepared the statistical analysis, and provided preliminary drafts of the survey report.

D. Srivastava (✉) · D. Prasad
Commonwealth Human Rights Initiative, New Delhi, India
e-mail: devyani@humanrightsinitiative.org

S. Krishnaswamy et al. (eds.), *Crime Victimisation in India*, Springer Series on Asian Criminology and Criminal Justice Research,
https://doi.org/10.1007/978-3-031-12251-4_2

The need for periodic crime victimization surveys is linked to envisioning better policing—a key area of intervention for CHRI. In India, the police are endemically under-resourced. It is imperative to allocate funds and personnel wisely. To do this, using a variety of techniques and processes to know where crime is occurring, where the public feels unsafe, and gaps between crime incidence and reported crime, can help the police to make informed decisions about crime prevention and reduction strategies, as well as public outreach initiatives. While existing crime statistics, such as those collected by the National Crime Records Bureau (NCRB), can give some insight into crime trends, these data are not comprehensive. NCRB data rely on crime reported at police stations, and not all incidents of crime are reported. Further, if not all police stations send data—whether because they lack the personnel, digital records systems or other resources to do so—even some reported crime will be missing from the official statistics.

Such gaps grow wider when we consider the urban-rural divide. An additional, and even more concerning, problem revolves around accusations of "burking"—or, police refusal to register reported crimes due to pressure to keep the crime rate low.

Each of these limitations, though they may not all be equally widespread, means that NCRB data provide an incomplete picture. It certainly does not capture unreported crime, public satisfaction with the police, or the public's perceptions of safety. Periodic public surveys are the only reliable medium to collect this information. These can assess most accurately where, when, and to whom crime is occurring. In the United Kingdom and numerous other countries, crime victimization surveys are undertaken to estimate the difference between the official crime rate, and the actual experience and reporting of crime. Through such surveys, it is possible to ask why individuals did not report crimes to the police, as well as assess the public's overall safety perception. In these ways, these surveys provide the most holistic picture of crime incidence and experience, quantitative assessments of public satisfaction levels with the police first response, and safety perceptions.

In addition, crime victimization survey findings can help identify the resource needs of the police. Findings would be able to show what resources are needed, and where, to meet the public's safety needs. Using these data, the police and government can frame budgetary/resource/human resource allocations to match the demands and needs of public safety.

Lastly, these surveys can also act as tools for police accountability, particularly as they can measure how many reported complaints the police actually register, or not. Police delay or refusal to register complaints into FIRs is a denial of access to justice right at the gateway of the legal system. In India, refusal to register complaints of specific offences is a punishable offence under the Indian Penal Code and some special laws. Surveys provide a quantum of unregistered complaints, giving police leadership, and departments as a whole, data from which to consider taking measures to prevent refusal, and enforce accountability systemically.

CHRI's survey was administered in Delhi and Mumbai. The two metropolitan cities were selected for their large, diverse populations as well as for their unique policing characteristics. Both stand out as having the largest police strength among urban police departments.

Another significant factor was that Delhi Police and Mumbai Police are both police commissionerates and thereby vest greater operational autonomy with the police leadership at the city level than non-commissionerates. Due to this, it was felt that there may be a greater chance of pick-up by the police leadership of the findings of a crime victimization survey and prompt faster systemic responses. Finally, potential replicability was another reason to hone in on two cities, with the rationale that police organizations, particularly smaller and mid-sized ones, could more easily draw lessons from city-level survey experiences than larger state-level surveys.

The survey focused on seven cognizable crime categories—theft, assault, house break-in, sexual harassment, criminal intimidation, un-natural death, and missing persons. We chose these seven because they are broad crime categories that occur frequently, and because when most of them are reported, the police must register them by filing a First Information Report (FIR) and initiate investigation.

> Criminal law in India categorizes crimes as either cognizable or non-cognizable. Cognizable offences are serious crimes defined under Section 2(c) of the Code of Criminal Procedure, 1973 (CrPC) in accordance with the First Schedule of the CrPC, or any other relevant law in force. For cognizable crimes, the police have the authority to arrest without a warrant and start an investigation without the permission of a Judicial Magistrate. Non-cognizable offences and cases, defined in Section 2(l) are less serious.
>
> A First Information Report is a written document prepared by the police when they receive information about the alleged commission of a cognizable offence. It is only after the FIR is registered at the police station that the police can start the investigation into the occurrence.

"Missing persons" itself is not a criminal offence. When a person is reported missing, the police enter the details in designated registers in the police station and immediately initiate investigation to determine whether a crime has occurred, for instance, murder or kidnapping. A complaint or First Information Report (FIR) is registered only when evidence or reasonable suspicion of any criminal activity related to the missing person is found. To note, the police must follow different procedures when a child is reported missing.

Among sexual crimes codified in Indian law, CHRI decided to cover only the offence of sexual harassment in the Indian Penal Code (IPC).[2] Sexual harassment is defined in Section 354A of the IPC as follows:

1. A man committing any of the following acts-

    (i) Physical contact and advances involving unwelcome and explicit sexual overtures; or
    (ii) A demand or request for sexual favours; or
    (iii) Showing pornography against the will of a woman; or
    (iv) Making sexually coloured remarks,

shall be guilty of the offence of sexual harassment.

---

[2] This is distinct from sexual harassment in the workplace which is defined in a separate law.

It is important to note that sexual harassment has been codified in the IPC as gender-specific—only men can be perpetrators and only women can be victims. The first three acts contained in the Section are punishable with rigorous imprisonment which may extend to 3 years, or with fine, or with both. Making "sexually coloured remarks" is punishable with a maximum prison term of 1 year, or fine, or both.

We also sought to survey how the experience of households facing might differ by socio-economic profiles and therefore selected samples of high-, mid-, and low-income households.

Overall, the survey covered 4950 households in Delhi and 5850 households in Mumbai. The survey was conducted in July–August 2015; households were

Non-inclusion of Rape and Sexual Assault against Children
While designing the survey, we decided to exclude the offences of rape or sexual offences against children. This is mainly due to the recognized limitations and difficulties in seeking to capture the experience of rape or other sexual offences *as part of* an omnibus crime survey. A panel of experts constituted by the US government to look at the issue of measuring rape and sexual assault as part of their National Crime Victimisation Survey highlighted at least four major obstacles.[3] These include a high degree of error in sampling with greater difficulty in ensuring a credible sample size of rape and sexual assault victims through the household sampling; the difficulties created in seeking to measure rape in the context of crime due to the fear of information being disclosed to the police; stricter requirements of privacy which an omnibus survey may not be able to ensure; and the use of ambiguous terms in the questionnaire which may not yield accurate results. The panel went on to recommend an independent survey—separate from the National Crime Victimisation Survey—for measuring rape and sexual assault.

CHRI shared similar concerns. As in any context, surveying women and children in India on sexual assault requires base knowledge of the law at least in terms of the offence, nuance, and sensitivity. More so with the expansion of the definition of rape in law in 2013, an accurate measure of a victim's experience would require the right questions to be asked around specific acts that took place in the course of the alleged assault, and the circumstances on consent. Interacting with women would have to be mindful of the deep stigma associated with admitting, or even just saying "rape," for many, and how to be able to address these in designing and administering a survey that is seeking objective answers to direct questions on crime experience and reporting. The age-appropriate language to be used with children is another issue and necessary factor of the readiness and orientation of the survey team. We were also mindful of the psychological impact it may have on survivors. Perhaps even

(continued)

---

[3] National Research Council (2014).

sensitively framed questions on rape can trigger trauma, fear, and apprehension. The questioning itself requires an extremely sensitive approach, including dealing with issues that may arise as a result of it. Another serious concern was the high probability of the perpetrator being within the family and the crime itself occurring within the home. Concern on this is backed by official crime statistics, which consistently reveals that a large proportion of reported rape cases are where the victim knows the offender. In 2019, for instance, the victim knew the offender in 94.2% of the reported rape cases in that year.

There were practical limitations tied to the apprehensions above. When CHRI conducted the pilot, the surveying team reported just how difficult it was to seek privacy while speaking with women within the household, and how difficult it was even to capture sexual offences such as sexual harassment and stalking. Including rape would necessitate a team comprising only of women, and conducting rigorous training both on skills and on legal provisions.

For these reasons, we felt that the level of expertise involved in this was neither feasible with the available resources, nor appropriate.

We strongly recommend that offences like rape require their own specialized surveys, and they should not be lumped together with other crime categories. They will require very carefully crafted methodology that takes into account the trauma and fear that survivors may experience. The household survey methodology is not at all suitable in surveys focused on sexual assault as it can trigger trauma for women and children and cause tensions within families/households.

surveyed based on their experiences in the preceding 12-month period (July 2014 to June 2015).

2 CHRI 2015 Survey: Sampling and Survey Methodology

The survey was administered at the household level in Delhi and Mumbai and covered all districts/zones in the cities. It included households, both owned and rented, among low-income, mid-income, and high-income categories and sought to distinguish the experience of recent migrants to the city against long term residents. The survey was confined to adult members only and did not extend to crimes experienced by minors. Only female adult members of the household were asked questions relating to sexual harassment.

Survey Structure

The survey covered four subjects:

I. Crime Incidence (Part A)

   The objective here was to estimate the incidence of seven crime categories: theft, assault, house break-in, sexual harassment, criminal intimidation, unnatural death, and missing persons. These were chosen as they represent a broad cross section of crimes that occur frequently.

II. Crime Characteristics (Part B)

   This component focused on understanding the characteristics of the crime committed such as sub-categories of crime, where and when it was committed, who was the perpetrator and if s/he was known to the victim.

III. Crime Reporting and Police Response (Part C)

   Part C focused on the reporting behavior of the victim, whether the crime was reported to the police and the experience thereof, and if the crime was not reported, the reasons thereof.

IV. Perception of Safety (Part D)

   This component addressed how safe respondents felt in their neighbourhoods, as well as in city travel.

The complete survey is presented in Annexure 1. The survey exercise was conducted in July–August 2015 and asked households to answer the questions based on their experiences in the preceding 12-month period (July 2014 to June 2015).

Sampling

The study follows a multi-stage sampling design, similar to that used in India's National Sample Survey,[4] the US Census Bureau Surveys,[5] and numerous others.

We sought to reliably estimate the rate of crime incidence at the police zone level. Delhi at the time was divided into 11 administrative police zones and Mumbai into 13. At a 95% confidence level and 5% margin of error, the required sample size is 384 for each zone.

Given the lack of reliable data on the true crime rate in either city, we decided to keep a buffer of 15% at the zone level, and the sample size was set at 450 households per zone. This gave an overall sample size of 4950 households in Delhi and 5850 households in Mumbai.

In the first stage of selecting geographical areas from which we would draw a sample of households, we used stratified random sampling to choose three census wards[6] within each police zone. All wards in each zone were first assigned to an income stratum,[7] based on whether a majority of households in the ward were high-,

---

[4] *For example,* Ministry of Statistics and Programme Implementation (2015).

[5] *For example,* Murphy (2008).

[6] Wards that fell into two or more police zones were excluded for the purposes of this study.

mid-, or low-income.[8] Thereafter, one ward from each stratum was randomly selected from every zone.

In the absence of information on the exact number of households in each zone according to income level, an equal number of households were sampled from each stratum in each police zone. With 450 sample households from each zone, this translated into 150 households[9] per sample ward.

In the second stage, each selected ward was subdivided into one-square kilometre grids.[10] We excluded from selection any grids that had a different income level than that which was dominant in the ward. For example, in a high-income ward, mid- and low-income grids were omitted and random selection was performed only on high-income grids.[11] We chose 3 of these in each ward.

In the third stage, within each grid we selected a random starting point from which surveyors went continuously household to household until reaching our quota of 50, in order to meet the target of 150 households per ward. While the random walk and quota methods can be subject to limitations,[12] these sampling procedures have been successfully used in numerous studies. Given the expense of completing a full household listing in each grid, it was determined that this procedure would best meet the objectives of the study within time and resource constraints.

---

[7] Income level served as the basis for the stratification; though it would be ideal to adjust strata for other parameters as well, budgetary constraints prohibited this. Income nevertheless does have strong correlations with other socio-economic parameters. Because crime incidence is likely to vary based on income and other socio-economic factors, we hoped this stratification would give insight into how households of different income levels are affected by crime.

[8] The Nielsen Neighbourhood Skyline (NSL) database was used to identify the income level of each ward. NSL provides a profile of household socio-economic demographics at the neighbourhood level for the top 57 cities in India. It includes information on income, savings, and expenditure of the households living in the neighbourhood, in addition to providing details on road networks, markets, connectivity parameters, etc. High income was defined as a majority of households earning Rs 1 million or more per year, mid-income as Rs 0.3–1 million per year, and low-income as less than Rs 0.3 million per year. The geographical units discussed here generally track those defined by municipal boundaries.

[9] With sampling spread across 11 police zones in Delhi and 13 in Mumbai, the sample size for each income strata is representative at (a) the city level with 3% margin of error at 95% confidence level and (b) at the zone level with 8% margin of error at 95% confidence level.

[10] This division was based on Nielsen's Cell Grid Geo-spatial Database. This database is based on semi-automated algorithms employing Small Area Statistics and Geo-spatial Analytics techniques to disaggregate socio-economic data for a given geographic area into a grid consisting of cells, each having an area approximately 1 sq. km. The database includes economic, demographic, infrastructure, and land cover data for every cell.

[11] Given the desire to determine statistical validity at the zone level, as well as cost and time constraints, we employed stratified sampling at the ward level. To ensure that grids appropriately represented the income level stratification of the ward as a whole, it was necessary to guarantee homogeneity of income level in the selection of grids. Admittedly, this imposes the limitation that the study would not capture whether the crime profile of heterogeneous localities differed from homogeneous ones.

[12] Anthony G. Turner, United Nations Secretariat Statistics Division (2003), as on 20 December 2015. For more details on various procedures for conducting random walks, see generally Juergen H.P. Hoffmeye-Zlotnik (2003). Out of the zone level sample of 450, 150 were to be drawn from each of three income strata, with 50 from each grid. A floor of 30 crime-affected households per zone was set. Had 30 households not been reached in this initial sweep, we would have increased the number of households surveyed by 50 until meeting that quota.

Survey Administration

Nielson's field interviewers administered the survey in both the cities. The training of the interviewers involved a dedicated session with the CHRI team on legal provisions relating to the selected crimes, procedures for reporting and registration of crime, and an overview of the duties of the police in ensuring public safety. The interviewers were given background notes and checklists to explain legal provisions, including the ingredients of each crime with a focus on sexual offences brought in following criminal law amendments in 2013; differences between cognizable and non-cognizable offences; differences in the procedure for reporting and registering a complaint and a First Information Report; safeguards for women in reporting a crime; and other relevant special provisions pertaining to missing persons.

A pilot was carried out covering 100 households each in Delhi and Mumbai. The pilot highlighted several challenges the interviewers faced in accessing households. Many families expressed hesitation to talk to the survey team, or participate in the survey because it related to crimes and their experience with the police. Some among those that had experienced crime were fearful that the information being collected would get reported to the police. To instil confidence in the independence and credibility of the survey process, CHRI provided an authorization letter to the survey teams with contact details of relevant persons within the organization. The conduct of the survey would have been improved through more stringent checks of completed survey forms throughout the duration of the surveys.

Part A of the survey, which addressed demographic characteristics and whether households were affected by crime, was administered to each of the households identified in the process outlined above.

Parts B and C addressed characteristics of crime, such as where and when crime occurred, and victims' experiences when reporting to the police.[13] These parts were administered to all of the crime-affected households identified in Part A; this resulted in a total of 647 households in Delhi (13% of sample households) and 927 (15% of sample households) in Mumbai.

As there was no a priori information on incidence of any of the 7 crimes, it was not possible to set a quota for the individual crimes. Theft turned out to be the most common crime (506 incidents in Delhi and 746 in Mumbai), while in both cities fewer than 100 households were victims of each of the other six crimes. Consequently,

---

[13] With regard to police response, the questionnaire contained several questions with multiple or nuanced answers, such as on cases of missing persons, or knowing whether the police properly registered a First Information Report. While CHRI provided background on law and criminal procedure, it was a challenge for the surveyors (who are not subject experts) to frame clarifying questions when needed. This may have resulted in some flaws in the findings presented here, even though they faithfully represent the answers given by respondents. One additional benefit, then, of the government undertaking routine crime victimization surveys would be to better train surveyors and build capacity to get more accurate answers, and preserve such institutional knowledge and practice over time. With this kind of robust data, the findings would best be able to help the police and government make decisions about deployment, training, and resource allocation, among others.

the analysis of reporting behaviour or police response in this section can be considered to be representative only at the city level and for all 7 crimes taken together.

Part D assessed the safety perception of residents in Delhi and Mumbai. To attain reliability at the city level, the sample size was set at 3025 respondent households in Delhi and 3575 households in Mumbai. Statistically, the sample size is representative at the city level at 95% confidence level and 2% margin of error. With 11 police zones in Delhi and 13 in Mumbai, this results in 275 samples per police zone.[14]

City-level representativeness of the safety perception of crime-affected households at a 95% confidence level and 5% margin of error would require 384 sample households. As such, analysis of the safety perception of crime-affected households will be representative at the city level as long as the crime incidence rate in Delhi and Mumbai is greater than 12.59% and 10.74%, respectively.[15]

With no a priori information on the actual rate of incidence of crime, it was decided to administer Part D to all crime-affected households. Thus, assuming X^Z to be the number of crime-affected households in a police zone (and X^W to be the number of crime-affected households in a ward), $275-X^Z$ would be the number of non-victim households sampled per zone ($90-X^W$ per ward). With this design, the city-level sample would be representative of the perception of non-victim households at a 95% confidence level and 3% margin of error even if the incidence of crime exceeds 25%.

A brief demographic profile of our sample is shown below Table 2.1:

Weights

The absence of a household sampling frame and lack of information on crime incidence or reporting behaviour across geographic or socio-economic factors, even at the city level, did not allow computation of household-level weights. We attempted a limited city-level weight computation based only on the number of households according to income, for which city-level information was available (Table 2.2).

The same was used for estimating the city-level projection of the number of households affected by crime. However, the same was not used at subsequent levels when estimating reporting incidence, as the number of households in each income strata who had reported crime to the police fell below 384 per strata (the minimum required sample size for a city-level representation at 95% confidence level and 5% margin of error). This statistically constrained the computation of a city-level weighted ratio for crime reporting behaviour.

---

[14] The analysis at the zone level will be representative at 95% confidence level with 6% margin of error.

[15] This was computed by dividing 384 (the minimum required sample size for city level representation) by the respective city sample sizes: 3025 in Delhi and 3575 in Mumbai. Ex post, the ratios were computed to be 13% (15%) in Delhi (Mumbai).

Table 2.1 Demographic profile of the sample of CHRI 2015 survey

		Part A: crime incidence		Parts B and C: crime characteristics, reporting, and police response		Part D: perception of Safety	
		Delhi	Mumbai	Delhi	Mumbai	Delhi	Mumbai
Total in sample		4990	6036	647	927	3035	3658
Income level of households	Low	1657	2029	239	371	1013	1214
	Medium	1667	1999	248	317	1003	1243
	High	1666	2008	160	239	1019	1201
Gender of respondent	Male	2290	4030	275	620	1335	2410
	Female	2700	2006	372	307	1700	1248
Length of residency	Greater than 5 years in city	4631	5893	605	900	2810	3561
	Greater than 5 years at current address	3820	5322	521	804	2316	3204

Source: Crime Victimization Survey, CHRI, 2015

Table 2.2 City-level weights computation for the CHRI 2015 survey

City	Annual household earning	Population			Sample			Weight
		No. of households (2014–15; in '000)	% of households in each strata		No. of households in sample	% of households in each strata		
Mumbai	<Rs 3 lakh (Low)	1285	44%		1657	33%		1.34
	Rs 3–10 lakh (Mid)	807	28%		1667	33%		0.83
	>Rs 10 lakh (High)	802	28%		1666	33%		0.83
	Total	2894	100%		4990	100%		
Delhi	<Rs 3 lakh (Low)	2037	54%		2029	34%		1.62
	Rs 3–10 lakh (Mid)	833	22%		1999	33%		0.67
	>Rs 10 lakh (High)	874	23%		2008	33%		0.70
	Total	3744	100%		6036	100%		

Source: Crime Victimization Survey, CHRI, 2015

3   Key Findings

The findings of the survey are presented below under the following heads: (1). Crime incidence and characteristics; (2) demographic profile of victimized households; (3) crime reporting and police response; and (4) overall safety perceptions.

Crime Incidence and Characteristics

The survey explored households' experience of the selected crimes over a period of 1 year (July 2014–June 2015) in both Delhi and Mumbai. Specifically, it sought to measure the types of crimes most frequently experienced, the socio-economic profile of the victimized households, and patterns, if any, of when and how the selected crimes took place. The main findings are as follows:

Each Crime Was Experienced at Least Once in Both Delhi and Mumbai

Overall, 705 of the households surveyed in Delhi (14.13%) and 994 (16.47%) in Mumbai faced one of the seven crime categories addressed in the survey. Some of them fell victim to crime more than once, though the proportion was relatively small (Table 2.3).

Table 2.3 Crime-wise percentage of households affected by crime

Crime	City	No. of households surveyed	No. of households affected by crime	% of households affected
Assault	Delhi	4990	51	1.02%
	Mumbai	6036	98	1.62%
Criminal Intimidation	Delhi	4990	17	0.34%
	Mumbai	6036	31	0.51%
House Break-in	Delhi	4990	51	1.02%
	Mumbai	6036	65	1.08%
Missing Persons	Delhi	4990	1	0.02%
	Mumbai	6036	3	0.05%
Sexual Harassment	Delhi	2700	75	2.78%
	Mumbai	2006	39	1.94%
Theft	Delhi	4990	506	10.14%
	Mumbai	6036	746	12.36%
Un-natural Death	Delhi	4990	4	0.08%
	Mumbai	6036	12	0.20%
Total	**Delhi**	**4990**	**705**	**14.13%**
	Mumbai	**6036**	**994**	**16.47%**

Source: Crime Victimization Survey, CHRI, 2015

Theft Was the Most Frequently Experienced Crime in Both Cities

Theft emerged as the most frequently experienced of the seven crimes surveyed in both Delhi and Mumbai. 10.14% of households in Delhi (506) and 12.36% of households in Mumbai (746) had been victimized by theft in the period covered. Of these, nearly 20% of households in Delhi (100) and 14% in Mumbai (106) had been victims of theft multiple times. As such, the total number of instances of theft reported by the respondents was 650 and 874, respectively, in each city (Table 2.4).

In both cities, theft of a cell phone was the most common form of theft followed by theft of luggage and theft of wallet, purse, or cash (Fig. 2.1). One notable finding is that households in Delhi were victims of car theft much more so than those surveyed in Mumbai. Car thefts accounted for 10% of theft cases in Delhi, compared to only 1% in Mumbai.

These findings match official crime data reported by the National Crime Records Bureau (NCRB). In 2014, theft constituted 51% of total cognizable crimes registered in Delhi, and 25% in Mumbai, representing the highest proportion of registered crimes in both cities.[16] The NCRB data also bears out that auto theft cases are

Table 2.4 Crime category as a percentage of total crime cases

Crime type	Delhi			Mumbai		
	Households affected by crime	Cases of crime experienced	Cases of crime by category as a % of total crime cases	Households affected by crime	Cases of crime experienced	Cases of crime by category as a % of total crime cases
Assault	51	51	5.97%	98	101	8.92%
Criminal Intimidation	17	17	1.99%	31	31	2.74%
House Break-in	51	51	5.97%	65	66	5.83%
Missing Persons	1	1	0.12%	3	3	0.27%
Sexual Harassment	75	80	9.37%	39	45	3.98%
Theft	506	650	76.11%	746	874	77.21%
Un-natural Death	4	4	0.47%	12	12	1.06%
Overall	**705**	**854**		**994**	**1132**	

Source: Crime Victimization Survey, CHRI, 2015

---

[16] National Crime Records Bureau, Ministry of Home Affairs (2014), *Crime in India 2014*, Table 2.2.

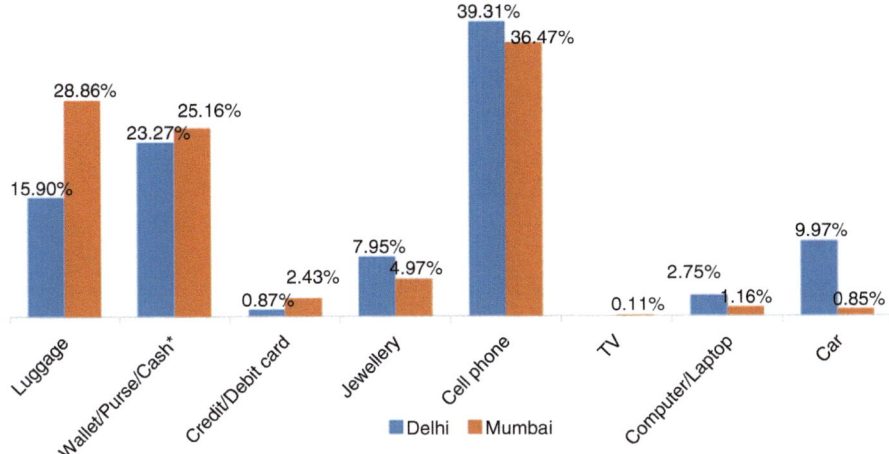

Cash and wallet/purse were separate answer categories in the survey, and are shown tallied together here because they frequently occurred together.

Source: CHRI Survey, CHRI, 2015

Fig. 2.1 Composition of theft crime

higher in Delhi as compared to Mumbai with over 21,000 cases registered in Delhi in 2014 and less than 4000 in Mumbai.[17]

Further, a common trend across both cities is that a greater number of households belonging to low-income and mid-income categories experienced theft than those in the high-income category (Table 2.5). Of the households that experienced crime only once in the period covered, 39% in Delhi and 38% in Mumbai belonged to low-income, as compared to 25% and 28% of high-income households, respectively. When it comes to households that experienced theft more than once, there is a notable difference between the two cities. While in Delhi, the majority of the households that experienced theft more than once belonged to mid-income (49%), in Mumbai, majority (42%) belonged to low-income households.

Experience of Assault Slightly More in Mumbai than Delhi

Around 1% of victimized households in both cities had experienced a form of assault in the year covered (Table 2.3). In Mumbai, physical assault cases constituted nearly 9% of the total crime cases covered by the survey, making it the second most commonly experienced crime in the city after theft (Table 2.4). In Delhi, the assault cases constituted about 6%, amounting to the third most experienced crime following theft and sexual harassment. Two-thirds of assault cases in Delhi and

---

[17] National Crime Records Bureau, Ministry of Home Affairs (2014), *Crime in India 2014,* Table 2.2.

Table 2.5 Households affected by theft according to income level

City	No. of thefts experienced	No. of households			
		Total	Low-income	Mid-income	High-income
Delhi	One	406	157	147	102
			39%	36%	25%
	Two or more	100	28	49	23
			28%	49%	23%
Mumbai	One	640	245	216	179
			38%	34%	28%
	Two or more	106	44	33	29
			42%	31%	27%

Source: Crime Victimization Survey, CHRI, 2015

Table 2.6 Composition of assault crimes

	Delhi	Mumbai
No. of households surveyed	4990	6036
No. of households affected by assault	51	98
% of households affected by assault	1.02%	1.62%
Composition of assault crimes		
Grabbed/shoved/slapped/beat	63.93%	88.52%
Attack by throwing rocks/ bottles	3.28%	4.92%
Attack with a gun or a knife	3.28%	3.28%
Attack with any other dangerous object	4.92%	1.64%
Attack in any other way	24.59%	1.64%

Source: Crime Victimization Survey, CHRI, 2015

four-fifths of those in Mumbai involved grabbing, shoving, slapping, or beating. The categories of attacks with dangerous objects, including guns and knives, accounted for just over 11% of cases in Delhi and just under 10% in Mumbai (Table 2.6). However, whereas 6 in 10 cases of assault in Mumbai involved a sole assailant, 7 in 10 cases in Delhi had multiple perpetrators.

The two cities somewhat differed in terms of time and place of occurrence of assault cases. 60% of the assault cases in Delhi happened in the 12 PM–6 PM period and location wise were primarily divided between residential (33%) and open areas/ streets (45%). Incidences of assault in Mumbai, on the other hand, mostly took place in the open areas (61%) during the day time (6 AM–6 PM accounted for 71%) (Table 2.7).

Table 2.7 Place and time of assault crime cases

	Delhi					Mumbai				
	Place of assault	12 am to 6 am	6 am to 12 pm	12 pm to 6 pm	6 pm to 12 am	*Overall*	12 am to 6 am	6 am to 12 pm	12 pm to 6 pm	6 pm to 12 am
Assault										
Residential area	33%	3%	2%	22%	5%	15%	1%	4%	6%	3%
Work place	14%	2%	2%	10%	0%	6%	0%	6%	0%	0%
Commercial place	3%	0%	2%	2%	0%	11%	2%	4%	4%	0%
Open area/ on the streets	45%	2%	5%	24%	14%	61%	3%	6%	35%	16%
Public transport	5%	2%	2%	2%	0%	7%	3%	3%	1%	0%
Time bracket share in total assault		9%	12%	60%	19%		10%	24%	47%	19%

Source: Crime Victimization Survey, CHRI, 2015

Sexual Harassment Instances Were Higher in Delhi than in Mumbai

The questions on sexual harassment were framed based on the definition in Section 354A, IPC.

The survey questionnaire posed the following acts as sexual harassment only to adult women respondents:

Passing of lewd or unwelcome sexual comments;
Continuously stared at in a lewd or threatening manner;
Followed by men till you were scared or uncomfortable;
Touched indecently, groped, pinched; and
Unwanted messages through SMS/e-mail/social media/internet/or telephone calls.

Questions relating to sexual harassment were administered only when a female adult member of the household was responding to the survey.

Focused training sessions were conducted as part of the preparatory training of the surveyors to explain the ingredients of sexual harassment as defined under the law. The sessions also explained terms used in the questionnaire such as "unwelcome" and "lewd" sexual comments and provided a few examples to illustrate. The intention was to make sure the entire survey team, not just the field surveyors, understood the ambit of the crime of sexual harassment, and that full efforts were made at all levels to ensure an accurate measure of the crime.

Table 2.8 Composition of sexual harassment crime

	Delhi	Mumbai
No. of households surveyed	4990	6036
No. of households affected by sexual harassment	75	39
% of households affected by assault	2.78%	1.94%
Composition of sexual harassment crimes		
Passed lewd or unwelcome sexual comments	75.94%	56.72%
Continuously stared at in a lewd or threatening manner	18.72%	20.90%
Followed by men till you were scared or uncomfortable	3.74%	10.45%
Touched indecently/groped/pinched	1.60%	11.94%

Source: Crime Victimization Survey, CHRI, 2015

There were 1700 female respondents in Delhi and 1248 in Mumbai. Of these households, 75 (over 4%) in Delhi and 39 (over 3%) in Mumbai shared that a female member of the household was a victim of sexual harassment over the previous year.

Indeed, in Delhi 1 in 11 cases of all crime incidents were sexual harassment, compared to 1 in 25 in Mumbai. Of sexual harassment cases, 94% in Delhi fell into the categories of staring or passing lewd comments. However, almost a quarter of cases in Mumbai involved either indecent touching or groping, or being followed by men (Table 2.8). Following theft, sexual harassment of female adult members emerged as the second most experienced crime in Delhi.

Offender Not Known to the Victim in Most of the Crimes Covered

For assault and criminal intimidation cases in both Delhi and Mumbai, victims recognized perpetrator(s) by name or sight in just over two-thirds of cases. A significant difference can be seen between the two cities, however, when it comes to sexual harassment cases. While most of the victims of sexual harassment in Delhi knew the perpetrator by sight, in almost 9 out of 10 cases in Mumbai, the victim did not know the perpetrator. Most cases of sexual harassment in Mumbai took place on public transport or commercial places.[18] These two trends together suggest that many perpetrators take advantage of a perceived anonymity of public spaces to harass women. This also gives guidance for the police response—in Mumbai, the police can step up its presence and patrolling in the areas that are prone to cases of sexual harassment; in Delhi, where perpetrators are largely known to victims, the police can work in partnership with NGOs to reach both victim and perpetrators and devise the appropriate strategies (Table 2.9).

---

[18] The lack of a similar trend in Delhi could be tied to the fact that many individuals reported that they avoided public transport and felt unsafe earlier in the evening more so than respondents in Mumbai (see Section III).

Table 2.9 Cases where offenders were known to victim

Crime category	Cases of crime	At least one known by name	At least one known by sight	Did not know offender	Did not see the offender
	No.s	% of cases of crime[a]			
Delhi					
Assault	51	35.3%	33.3%	35.3%	13.7%
Sexual Harassment	80	1.25%	60%	38.8%	1.3%
Criminal Intimidation	17	47.1%	41.2%	11.8%	11.8%
Mumbai					
Assault	101	27.7%	31.7%	35.6%	10.9%
Sexual Harassment	45	2.2%	11.1%	86.7%	2.2%
Criminal Intimidation	31	35.5%	29.0%	32.3%	6.5%

Source: Crime Victimization Survey, CHRI, 2015
[a]May exceed 100% in case of multiple perpetrators with differing identification status

Demographic Profile of Affected Households

High-Income Households Less Affected by Crime Compared to Low-Income Households

Overall, the survey shows that high-income households are less affected by crime compared to low-income households (Table 2.10). In Mumbai, the percentage of households affected by crime gradually decreased while moving up the income ladder. Though high-income households in Delhi were somewhat less affected by crime than the other two income categories, the percentage of crime-affected households was comparable between mid- and low-income brackets.

Experience of Crime Comparable across Religion, Caste, Mother Tongue, and Period of Stay in City

Of the households surveyed in both cities, over 85% were Hindu and 7–8.5% were Muslim. The rates of crime victimization among these groups were comparable.[19] Similarly, the rate of crime victimization for the SC/ST community (constituting 14% of sample in Delhi and 12% in Mumbai) was also comparable to non-SC/ST households in both cities. We asked respondents whether they had been living in the city for less than 5 years, to see whether recent migrants were affected by crime

---

[19] As stated in the methodology, sample sizes below that used to determine a representative size at the city or police zone levels must be treated with caution, and not used to make generalizations. This analysis is shown for comparative purposes within our survey and to demonstrate potential findings of a large-scale survey.

Table 2.10 Percentage of sample households affected by crime across income classes

City	Income class	Sample households in each income class	Households affected by crime	% of sample households affected by crime
Delhi	Low	1013	239	23.59%
	Medium	1003	248	24.73%
	High	1019	160	15.7%
Mumbai	Low	1214	371	30.56%
	Medium	1243	317	25.5%
	High	1201	239	19.9%

Source: Crime Victimization Survey, CHRI, 2015

differently than long-term residents. However, recent migrants constituted a very small portion of the sample: 7% in Delhi and 2% in Mumbai. Based on this data, there was no notable difference between the two groups.

Yet, those who do not speak the primary language of the city they live in seem to be more vulnerable to crime, particularly when it comes to non-Hindi speakers in Delhi. One must be cautious in drawing conclusions from a small sample size, yet it stands to reason those migrants who struggle to communicate in the local language would be at a relatively greater risk of crime as a result of their lack of knowledge of the city, and difficulty communicating due to language barriers (Table 2.11).

Crime Reporting and Police Response

Low and Inconsistent Rate of Reporting Crimes to the Police

Overall, less than 50% of the households who experienced crime in both cities reported it to the police, with Mumbai showing lower reporting at 41.8% than Delhi at 46.8%. There is, however, significant variation across crime categories in terms of rate of reporting:

- Un-natural death and missing persons cases have a high reporting rate at 75% and 100%, respectively, in both cities;
- Reporting of assault and criminal intimidation was higher in Delhi at nearly 55% and 47% as compared to 25% and 22%, respectively, in Mumbai whereas reporting of house break-in was higher in Mumbai at 60% as compared to Delhi at 35%;
- Reporting of sexual harassment was higher in Mumbai at 11% as compared to 7.5% in Delhi (Table 2.12).[20]

---

[20] Please note that the offence of sexual harassment (Section 354A) was added to the Indian Penal Code only in 2013 by the Criminal Law (Amendment) Act 2013. Before this, Section 354 punished "outraging the modesty of a woman," which applied only to routine incidents of molestation.

Table 2.11 Impact of demographic characteristics on victimization and reporting behaviour

City	City sample household size	Religion/ caste/period of stay/mother tongue	Households in each income class		Sample crime victim households	Sample crime-affected households reporting crime
	No.		No.	% of city sample household	% of sample household	% of crime victim households
Religion						
Delhi	4990	Hindu	4381	87.80%	13.10%	44.43%
		Muslim	348	6.97%	13.22%	36.96%
		Christian	43	0.86%	4.65%	50.00%
		Sikh	212	4.25%	10.85%	47.83%
		Other	6	0.12%	33.33%	50.00%
Mumbai	6036	Hindu	5341	88.49%	15.22%	42.44%
		Muslim	520	8.61%	15.96%	43.37%
		Christian	64	1.06%	25.00%	25.00%
		Sikh	32	0.53%	18.75%	66.67%
		Other	79	1.31%	11.39%	33.33%
Caste						
Delhi	4990	Non-SC/ST	4275	85.67%	13.01%	45.14%
		SC/ST	715	14.33%	12.73%	37.36%
Mumbai	6036	Non-SC/ST	5308	87.94%	15.49%	42.70%
		SC/ST	728	12.06%	14.42%	39.05%
Period of stay in city						
Delhi	4990	≤3 years	204	4.09%	9.80%	50.00%
		4–5 years	155	3.11%	14.19%	22.73%
		>5 years	4631	92.81%	13.06%	44.63%
Mumbai	6036	≤3 years	59	0.98%	18.64%	27.27%
		4–5 years	84	1.39%	19.05%	37.50%
		>5 years	5893	97.63%	15.27%	42.56%
Mother tongue						
Delhi	4990	Hindi	4732	94.83%	12.49%	44.16%
		Non-Hindi	258	5.17%	21.71%	42.86%
Mumbai	6036	Marathi	2869	47.53%	14.15%	43.10%
		Non-Marathi	3167	52.47%	16.45%	41.65%
		Hindi	*2290*	*37.94%*	*16.77%*	*41.15%*
		Gujarati	*416*	*6.89%*	*15.38%*	*48.44%*
		Others	*461*	*7.64%*	*15.84%*	*38.36%*

Source: Crime Victimization Survey, CHRI, 2015

Table 2.12 Households reporting crimes to police

City	Crime	Cases of crime experienced No.	Households reporting crimes to police No.	% of cases of crime
Delhi	Theft	650	336	51.70%
	Assault	51	28	54.90%
	House Break-in	51	18	35.30%
	Sexual Harassment	80	6	7.50%
	Criminal Intimidation	17	8	47.10%
	Un-natural Death	4	3	75.00%
	Missing Persons	1	1	100.00%
	Overall	854	400	46.80%
Mumbai	Theft	874	383	43.80%
	Assault	101	26	25.70%
	House Break-in	66	40	60.60%
	Sexual Harassment	45	5	11.10%
	Criminal Intimidation	31	7	22.60%
	Un-natural Death	12	9	75.00%
	Missing Persons	3	3	100.00%
	Overall	1132	473	41.80%

Source: Crime Victimization Survey, CHRI, 2015

Table 2.13 Cases of theft reported to the police

Crime subcategory	Delhi Total cases in sample No.	Reported to police No.	% of sample cases	Mumbai Total cases in sample No.	Reported to police No.	% of sample cases
Luggage	103	47	45.63%	234	80	34.19%
Wallet/Purse	59	27	45.76%	161	52	32.30%
Credit/Debit card	6	4	66.67%	23	12	52.17%
Jewellery	54	38	70.37%	47	34	72.34%
Cell phone	246	119	48.37%	328	156	47.56%
TV	0	0	0%	1	0	0.00%
Computer/ Laptop	17	16	94.12%	11	7	63.64%
Cash	98	44	44.90%	61	35	57.38%
Car	67	41	61.19%	8	7	87.50%

Source: Crime Victimization Survey, CHRI, 2015

There is further variation within the sub-categories of each crime. Among theft cases, for example, in both cities less than half of the incidents of cell phone and luggage theft were reported to the police. Theft of high value items like jewellery, computers or laptops, and cars resulted in a higher rate of reporting to the police. This may be due to the utilitarian concern that claiming insurance for these items often requires showing a copy of the FIR registered by police, as in the case of insurance claims for vehicle theft (Table 2.13).

Table 2.14 Cases of sexual harassment reported to police

Crime sub-category[a]	Delhi			Mumbai		
	Total cases in sample	Reported		Total cases in sample	Reported	
	No.	No.	%	No.	No.	%
Passed lewd or unwelcome sexual comments	68	3	4.41%	22	5	22.73%
Continuously stared at in a lewd or threatening manner	4	1	25.00%	10	0	0.00%
Followed by men till you were scared or uncomfortable	5	1	20.00%	5	0	0.00%
Touched indecently/groped/pinched	3	1	33.33%	8	0	0.00%
Total	80	6	7.5%	45	5	11.10%

Source: Crime Victimization Survey, CHRI, 2015
[a]The survey also included a sub-category on receiving inappropriate or unwanted phone calls or text messages, but in this survey no respondents selected that option as an answer

In stark contrast, even serious cases of sexual harassment involving being touched or groped or being followed were not reported in most of the cases in both cities (Table 2.14).

Unreported crime amounts to crime that remains unaddressed and unresolved. A major benefit of public crime surveys is that they provide a reliable measure of the volume of crime experienced, but unreported, along with important markers of the types of crimes that usually go unreported, profile of such victims, characteristics of such crimes, and reasons for not reporting. Proactive police departments can use this information to initiate crime prevention and targeted community policing programmes.

Given the small sample of households that had experienced crime, and within that sample, of those that had reported victimization to the police, CHRI's survey was unable to discern clear patterns in terms of the impact of socio-economic profile of victims on their interaction with the police. A larger survey, or disaggregated smaller surveys, would be able to throw light on details such as the differences in levels of reporting of crime experienced by caste, gender, religion, educational background and income levels, the differences in reasons for not reporting across different social groups, and the differences in the experience of reporting to the police based on these factors.

(continued)

In fact, a national public survey carried out in 2018 across India found that socio-economic profiles have a significant bearing on people's experience with the police.[21] For instance, the survey found that higher income groups, and those with higher education such as college educated and above, were twice more likely to seek the police's help, than the poor and people who are not literate.[22] Among vulnerable sections, it found that Muslims reported a higher rate of contact with the police than Scheduled Castes, Scheduled Tribes and Other Backward Classes.[23] At the same time, it also noted an important variation: that while higher income groups are more likely to contact the police for loss of goods or documents, the poor were more likely to report complaints of domestic violence and family disputes.

Measuring such differences can be tremendously helpful in understanding and addressing gaps found in the relationship between the police and different sections of society through targeted reform measures in police administration, training, supervision, accountability, as well as in informing trust building exercises with communities as required.

Victims of Crime Are Reluctant to Engage with the Criminal Justice System

For respondents, the primary reason for not reporting crimes centred on the fear of being caught in complex or bureaucratic police and court systems (Table 2.15). People also often reported that they felt that there was little evidence of the crime, or that the police would not be able to do anything about the incident. A significant number said they did not report the crime for fear of retaliation.

Responses reveal that many victims envision reporting to the police, and possibly proceeding with a criminal case, as daunting and burdensome. They also perceive little gain in going to the police, as they believe there is little evidence and the police will not be able to take steps to hold perpetrators accountable.

While these trends stay consistent across crime categories, particular reasons for not reporting are more emphasized in some kinds of crime. For example, of the 80 households in Delhi that experienced sexual harassment, 74 of them did not go to the police. Of these, 52 said they did not want to get stuck in police or court matters. In Mumbai, there were 45 cases of sexual harassment, 40 of which went unreported. Twenty-six said they did not report out of fear of retaliation.

Particularly in cases of sexual harassment, the data clearly indicate exceedingly low levels of reporting while incidence is relatively high in both cities. The reasons

---

[21] Common Cause and Lokniti—Centre for the Study of Developing Societies (2018)

[22] Ibid. pg.35.

[23] Ibid., pg.36.

Table 2.15 Reasons cited for not reporting crime (as a percentage of total unreported cases)[a]

City	Delhi		Mumbai	
	Number of cases	As % of crime not reported	Number of cases	As % of crime not reported
No. of crimes not reported	454		659	
Fear of retaliation	38	8%	100	15%
Lack of evidence	150	33%	138	21%
Didn't know where to report	24	5%	23	3%
Didn't know any of the helpline numbers	8	2%	9	1%
Did not think the police would entertain your complaint	88	19%	69	10%
Did not think the police would be able to do anything about the case	67	15%	112	17%
Family matters do not need to be reported	16	4%	85	13%
Did not want to get stuck in police/court matters	216	48% %%	242	37%
Scared to go to the police station	22	5%	81	12%

Source: Crime Victimization Survey, CHRI, 2015
[a]Sum exceeds 100% as respondents could select multiple options

for low reporting cited above immediately signal the need for further targeted study. To be sure, visible and active efforts must be made by the police, strengthened by partnering with NGOs, to hold mass awareness programmes to educate women that sexual harassment is now a crime they can complain of, the process to make a complaint, and assure them of their safety in this process.

To increase women's confidence to report these cases, it may also be beneficial to formalize the role of NGOs in providing public education as well as training police in gender sensitization so that they can respond to reported cases of sexual harassment appropriately. Government can make it mandatory for all modes of public transport—autos, taxis, buses, trains/metro—to prominently display the numbers of the police control room and women's helpline number(s). Acting on women's safety requires a response to low reporting. The detailed reasons for the gap between the experience of sexual harassment and reporting must be identified first (Table 2.16).

Less than Half of the Cases Reported to the Police Were Registered

Taking all crimes together, in both cities less than half of the cases reported to the police by the respondents had their complaint registered as a First Information Report (FIR). Given that only half of all crimes experienced were reported in the first place, this means only a quarter of crimes experienced were registered.

Table 2.16 Reasons cited for not reporting crime, according to crime category (as a percentage)

Crime category	Did not want to get stuck in police/ court matters		Lack of evidence		Did not think the police would entertain your complaint		Did not think the police would be able to do anything about the case	
	Delhi	Mumbai	Delhi	Mumbai	Delhi	Mumbai	Delhi	Mumbai
Theft	65%	69%	85%	75%	85%	71%	54%	71%
Assault	6%	12%	1%	13%	2%	10%	18%	12%
House Break-in	3%	7%	11%	4%	8%	4%	10%	5%
Sexual Harassment	24%	6%	2%	5%	3%	7%	13%	6%
Criminal Intimidation	1%	4%	1%	1%	0%	6%	4%	5%
Un-natural Death	0%	1%	0%	1%	1%	1%	0%	1%
Missing Persons	0%	0%	0%	0%	0%	0%	0%	0%

Source: Crime Victimization Survey, CHRI, 2015

In terms of sexual harassment, none of the six cases reported in Delhi[24] and only two of the five cases in Mumbai led to an FIR being filed. This is particularly concerning in light of the fact that only 7.5% of households in Delhi and 11.1% of those in Mumbai who had faced sexual harassment reported the incident to the police.

As Table 2.17 below shows, half or less of households who reported thefts, assaults, or break-ins answered that FIRs were filed in their cases. Only in cases of un-natural death was FIR registration consistently high; however, none of the missing persons cases in Mumbai were registered.[25]

Within sub-categories of crime, there are also differences in the proportion of reported cases that had FIRs registered. For instance, FIRs were filed for 37% of reported cell phone thefts in Delhi and 45% of those in Mumbai.

Cases of car theft had a relatively better rate of FIR registration, probably due to insurance requirements.[26] Reports of theft of other high value items like computer or laptop and jewellery also were more likely to be registered. Notably, the types of theft showing a high rate of FIR registration in general were also more commonly reported in the first place (Table 2.18).

Police failure and refusal to register reported cognizable offences violate the procedure established under Indian law. Section 154 of the Code of Criminal Procedure that governs the registration of crimes makes it mandatory on the police

---

[24] In Delhi, this low rate of FIR registration in sexual harassment cases also casts doubt on the purported success of initiatives like *Operation Shistachar* (Express News Service, 2015) by the Delhi Police. The high number of individuals detained under this operation is also worrying.

[25] This may be because no cognizable offence was made out.

[26] Because of the high number of car thefts in Delhi, the Delhi Police encourages and facilitates electronic filing of FIRs in these cases.

Table 2.17 FIR registered—number and as a percentage of crimes reported to police

City	Crime category	Crime cases	Crimes reported to police	FIR Registered No.	FIR Registered % of crime reported
Delhi	Overall	854	400	195	48.75%
Mumbai	Overall	1132	473	229	48.41%
Delhi	Theft	650	336	169	50.30%
	Assault	51	28	12	42.86%
	House Break-in	51	18	9	50.00%
	Sexual Harassment	80	6	0	0.00%
	Criminal Intimidation	17	8	1	12.50%
	Un-natural Death	4	3	3	100.00%
	Missing Persons	1	1	1	100.00%
Mumbai	Theft	874	383	187	48.83%
	Assault	101	26	12	46.15%
	House Break-in	66	40	19	47.50%
	Sexual Harassment	45	5	2	40.00%
	Criminal Intimidation	31	7	2	28.57%
	Un-natural Death	12	9	7	77.78%
	Missing Persons	3	3	0	0.00%

Source: Crime Victimization Survey, CHRI, 2015

Table 2.18 FIR registered in cases of theft—number and as a percentage of theft cases reported to police

	Delhi			Mumbai		
		FIR registered			FIR registered	
Item stolen	No. of cases reported to police	No.	% of cases reported	No. of cases reported to police	No.	% of cases reported
Luggage	47	26	55.32%	80	43	53.75%
Wallet/Purse	27	15	55.56%	52	24	46.15%
Credit/Debit card	4	1	25.00%	12	5	41.67%
Jewellery	38	26	68.42%	34	13	38.24%
Cell phone	119	44	36.97%	156	70	44.87%
Computer/Laptop	16	10	62.50%	7	6	85.71%
Cash	44	21	47.73%	35	21	60.00%
Car	41	26	63.41%	7	5	71.43%

Source: Crime Victimization Survey, CHRI, 2015

to register complaints, or information they receive, alleging the commission of a cognizable offence in the form of a First Information Report. The Supreme Court in a landmark judgement delivered in 2014 has further reiterated this mandatory duty of the police.[27] In this judgement, the apex Court asserted that under Section 154, CrPC, the police is duty bound to register an FIR so long as the information

---

[27] Lalita Kumari versus Government of Uttar Pradesh & Ors, AIR 2014 SC 187.

discloses the commission of a cognizable offence and cannot question the credibility or reasonableness of the information received. At this stage, the police are not empowered to carry out any inquiry, commonly referred to as preliminary inquiry, to ascertain whether the information received is genuine or not, except for a very limited category of cases. In case the police refuse to register a case, they violate their legal duty.

Anyone aggrieved by police refusal to register their complaint as an FIR can either send a written complaint to the district Superintendent of Police (police officer in charge of the district) who can order the officer-in-charge of the concerned police station to register the FIR where the information discloses the commission of a cognizable offence.[28] An aggrieved person may also approach the Judicial Magistrate with a complaint seeking an order to the police to register the FIR and begin investigation. In addition to these legal remedies, the Criminal Law (Amendment) Act 2013 inserted another important remedy, which was codified as Section 166A(c) of the Indian Penal Code.[29] This section makes the failure to register an FIR under Section 154 of the CrPC for specified sexual offences (rape, assault, trafficking and acid throwing related offences) as a punishable offence in itself with up to 2 years prison term and a fine. With this, a complaint can be filed against the police officer for refusing to register a complaint of the specified sexual offences.[30]

Despite the clear legal requirement, non-registration of reported crimes remains widely prevalent in India. The 2018 national survey on the state of policing in India referenced above found that 24 per cent of those who approached the police to register a complaint were unable to do so.[31] Crime reported, but not registered by the police, will fail to be investigated and thereby remains unaddressed. As official crime data collate only those cases that the police register and allow to enter the system, public surveys are a crucial, and potentially the sole, source of information for measuring the extent of non-registration. Additionally, once again, they also reveal significant patterns such as the demographic profile of those most affected, different reasons/factors put forward by the police in refusing to register, and the different forms of harassment meted out to complainants. The 2018 survey for instance threw up that those in rural areas are relatively more likely to report success in filing complaint/FIR than those in urban areas. It also revealed that the police persuading the

---

[28] Section 154(3), Code of Criminal Procedure, 1973.

[29] Section 156 (3), Code of Criminal Procedure, 1973.

[30] For more information on legal remedies available in instances of police failure to register complaints alleging sexual offences, see the booklet titled *Police Registration of Sexual Offences: A Guide on Procedures and Holding Police Accountable*, Commonwealth Human Rights Initiative and Association for Advocacy and Legal Initiatives (2020).

[31] Common Cause and Lokniti—Centre for the Study of Developing Societies (2018)

complainant to resolve the matter or arrive at a compromise is a major reason behind their failure to register. Proactive police departments can use this data to review factors that explain the differences as well as the gaps found in police behaviour.

Only Half of Those Who Reported Crime to the Police Were Satisfied with the Police Response

For those households who reported crime, roughly 36% in Delhi and 51% in Mumbai said they were satisfied with the police response (Table 2.19). Satisfaction varies across the subcategories of crime in both cities. Notably, satisfaction was the lowest for sexual harassment cases in Delhi whereas in Mumbai, house break-in cases recorded the lowest satisfaction.

The reasons for dissatisfaction mainly included delay and/or refusal to register an FIR, rude behaviour while registering an FIR, and attempting to dissuade the complainant from filing an FIR. On sexual harassment, at least 60% of respondents both in Delhi and in Mumbai attributed their dissatisfaction with the police to refusal to register FIR (Table 2.20). Among those who said they were dissatisfied with the police response, most answered that this was on account of delay and/or refusal to register an FIR, rude behaviour while registering an FIR, and attempting to dissuade the complainant from filing an FIR.

Table 2.19 Satisfaction with police response

City	Crime category	Cases of crime	Crimes reported	Satisfied with police response	
				Count	%
Delhi	Overall	854	400	145	36.25%
Mumbai	Overall	1132	473	242	51.16%
Delhi	Theft	650	336	125	37.20%
	Assault	51	28	12	42.86%
	House Break-in	51	18	4	22.22%
	Sexual Harassment	80	6	1	16.67%
	Criminal Intimidation	17	8	2	25.00%
	Un-natural Death	4	3	1	33.33%
	Missing Persons	1	1		0.00%
Mumbai	Theft	874	383	200	52.22%
	Assault	101	26	15	57.69%
	House Break-in	66	40	14	35.00%
	Sexual Harassment	45	5	2	40.00%
	Criminal Intimidation	31	7	5	71.43%
	Un-natural Death	12	9	4	44.44%
	Missing Persons	3	3	2	66.67%

Source: Crime Victimization Survey, CHRI, 2015

Table 2.20 Reasons cited for dissatisfaction—as a percentage of those dissatisfied with police response

City	Crime category	Crimes reported No.s	Rude/ impolite	Refused to register FIR	Put me at fault and tried to persuade me not to register	Asked for a bribe	Took a long time to register FIR	PCR van took an hour or more	Did not help injured persons
			% of crime reported						
Delhi	Overall	255	41.18%	27.84%	18.82%	5.1%	31.37%	5.49%	3.53%
	Theft	211	41.23%	24.64%	20.38%	5.21%	32.7%	5.21%	4.27%
	Assault	16	31.25%	25%	0%	6.25%	43.75%	6.25%	0%
	House Break-in	14	50%	57.14%	7.14%	7.14%	7.14%	14.29%	0%
	Sexual Harass-ment	5	20%	60%	0%	0%	0%	0%	0%
	Criminal Intimida-tion	6	33.33%	33.33%	50%	0%	33.33%	0%	0%
	Un-natu-ral Death	2	100%	50%	50%	0%	50%	0%	0%
	Missing Persons	1	100%	100%	0%	0%	0%	0%	0%
Mumbai	Overall	231	43.29%	43.29%	29.87%	19.05%	41.13%	17.75%	16.02%
	Theft	183	46.99%	45.9%	33.88%	22.95%	42.08%	21.31%	20.22%
	Assault	11	54.55%	27.27%	54.55%	0%	36.36%	9.09%	0%
	House Break-in	26	19.23%	38.46%	0%	7.69%	34.62%	3.85%	0%
	Sexual Harass-ment	3	0%	66.67%	0%	0%	66.67%	0%	0%
	Criminal Intimida-tion	2	50%	0%	50%	0%	0%	0%	0%
	Un-natu-ral Death	5	20%	20%	0%	0%	60%	0%	0%
	Missing Persons	1	100%	0%	0%	0%	0%	0%	0%

Source: Crime Victimization Survey, CHRI, 2015

Even out of those who said they were satisfied, overall, with how the police responded, comparatively few[32] answered that the reasons for their satisfaction included that the police: "explained the action they will take"; "arrived without delay"; and "acted fast" (Table 2.21).

---

[32] Respondents were able to choose more than one reason for why they were satisfied by the police response. Therefore, these numbers are not lower simply because respondents chose other reasons.

Table 2.21 Reasons cited for satisfaction—as a percentage of those satisfied with police response

City	Crime category	Number satisfied with police No.	Listened carefully	Registered my complaint correctly	Registered my complaint without delay	Explained the action they will take	Arrived without delay	Acted fast
			As a percentage of those satisfied with the police response					
Delhi	Overall	145	51.03%	53.79%	33.79%	8.97%	4.14%	8.28%
	Theft	125	49.6%	54.40%	32.80%	6.4%	0.8%	6.4%
	Assault	12	66.67%	66.67%	50%	33.33%	33.33%	16.67%
	House Break-in	4	25%	50%	25%	0%	0%	0%
	Sexual Harassment	1	100%	0%	0%	0%	0%	100%
	Criminal Intimidation	2	50%	0%	50%	0%	0%	50%
	Un-natural Death	1	100%	0%	0%	100%	100%	0%
	Missing Persons	0	–	–	–	–	–	–
Mumbai	Overall	242	53.72%	48.76%	32.23%	27.69%	19.01%	19.42%
	Theft	200	54%	48.5%	31.5%	26.5%	18.5%	20.00%
	Assault	15	40%	46.67%	13.33%	33.33%	13.33%	20.00%
	House Break-in	14	92.86%	57.14%	64.29%	57.14%	35.71%	14.29%
	Sexual Harassment	2	100%	50%	50%	0%	0%	0.00%
	Criminal Intimidation	5	20%	60%	0%	20%	0%	0.00%
	Un-natural Death	4	0%	25%	25%	0%	50%	25.00%
	Missing Persons	2	0%	50%	100%	0%	0%	50.00%

Source: Crime Victimization Survey, CHRI, 2015

There were also few respondents who answered that the police arrived without delay or acted fast. Such reasons may not have been applicable to all cases; for example, those who reported crime at a police station after the crime occurred would not be expected to answer that the police arrived without delay. However, these responses could also reflect issues on the ground, such as lack of police personnel and PCR vans. This is yet another instance where data help identify the questions that need to be answered, rather than providing an answer to all questions.

Perceptions of Safety

Residents of Mumbai Perceive the Police More Positively than Delhi Residents

More than two-thirds of those in Mumbai answered that they perceive the police in a positive light, though just under half of Delhi respondents did (Table 2.22). In both cities, the perception is consistent across income levels without any significant variation (Table 2.23). It should also be noted that just over a fifth of respondents in both cities answered that they viewed the police in neither a positive nor negative light.

Respondents Most Feared Falling Victim to Theft, Assault, or Sexual Harassment

Fear of theft seems universal across the two cities. Fewer people are fearful of assault and un-natural death in Delhi compared to Mumbai.

Table 2.22 Overall perception on local police (% of final sample households)

City	Total households	Very positive	Positive	Neutral	Negative	Very negative
Delhi	3035	2%	40%	22%	32%	3%
Mumbai	3659	19%	45%	22%	13%	1%

Source: Crime Victimization Survey, CHRI, 2015

Table 2.23 Satisfaction with police—by income class

City	Income category	Very positive	Positive	Neutral	Negative	Very negative
Delhi	Low	4%	34%	21%	36%	5%
	Medium	1%	41%	21%	35%	2%
	High	2%	46%	25%	25%	1%
Mumbai	Low	17%	47%	25%	11%	1%
	Medium	20%	47%	22%	10%	1%
	High	20%	42%	20%	17%	2%

Source: Crime Victimization Survey, CHRI, 2015

Table 2.24 Crimes people fear most of falling victim to (% of sample respondents)[a]

City	Theft	Assault	Un-natural death	Sexual crime	Criminal intimidation
Delhi	86%	16%	5%	17%	2%
Mumbai	77%	26%	13%	4%	3%

Source: Crime Victimization Survey, CHRI, 2015
[a]Respondents could choose more than one option. As such, the sum of these percentages exceeds 100%

Around a quarter of the Mumbai respondents listed assault as their second strongest fear. This is possibly shaped by actual experiences. Around 6% of sample households in Delhi experienced assault in the previous year, in Mumbai, the proportion was higher at roughly 10%. Public perceptions of safety, inevitably influenced by media reporting and other information in the public domain, also play a role in shaping individual fears. This is most evident in Delhi, where 17% of households answered that they were worried about sexual harassment.

Delhi's actual experience of sexual harassment was roughly one percentage point higher than that in Mumbai (Table 2.24). However, given Delhi's long-standing reputation as unsafe for women, the aftermath of the Jyoti Singh Pandey gangrape case in 2012 and the resulting heightened coverage of women's safety issues, the fear of sexual crime has likely become much more acute in Delhi.

Households in Delhi Begin Feeling Unsafe, Even in Their Own Neighbourhoods, Earlier in the Evening than Those in Mumbai

Respondents in Mumbai felt considerably less fearful of crime in their neighbourhoods relative to respondents in Delhi, though the safety perception among those in Mumbai was only marginally better than Delhiites. One possible reason is that, as shown above, around half of crimes in Delhi were committed in and around residential areas, whereas the rate of crime in residential areas in Mumbai was significantly lower, at 30%. In both cities, the vast majority of households reported feeling safe in their neighbourhoods during the daytime. Female respondents felt as safe as their male counterparts in their neighbourhood during daytime in both the cities.

When it comes to travelling beyond the immediate neighbourhood, there is a clear difference in safety perception based on gender. Whereas only 7% of respondents would be worried for a lone male member staying away from home beyond 8 pm in Delhi, 52% would worry for a lone female member of the household at the same hour of the night (Tables 2.25, 2.26, and 2.27).

Travel at Night Is Considered More Unsafe in Delhi than in Mumbai

In Delhi, the pattern of heightened safety concerns at night-time extends to the perceived safety of travelling in the evening. 45% of Delhiites (compared to just under 14% in Mumbai) start to worry about their safety while travelling by public transport after 9 pm.

Table 2.25 Do you feel safe walking around in the neighbourhood during the day

City			Yes		No		Don't know	
	Gender	No. of respondents	No.	%	No.	%	No.	%
Delhi	Male	1335	1147	85.92%	148	11.09%	40	3%
Delhi	Female	1700	1430	84.12%	210	12.35%	60	3.53%
Delhi	Overall	3035	2577	84.91%	358	11.80%	100	3.29%
Mumbai	Male	2410	1950	80.91%	204	8.46%	256	10.62%
Mumbai	Female	1248	1059	84.86%	110	8.81%	79	6.33%
Mumbai	Overall	3658	3009	82.26%	314	8.58%	335	9.16%

Source: Crime Victimization Survey, CHRI, 2015

Table 2.26 At what time in the evening would one stop feeling safe walking around alone in neighbourhood

City	Gender	Always feel safe	After 7 PM	After 8 PM	After 9 PM	After 10 PM	After 11 PM	After Midnight
Delhi	Male	2%	13%	20%	20%	28%	15%	3%
	Female	1%	9%	16%	29%	31%	13%	2%
	Overall	1%	10%	18%	25%	30%	14%	2%
Mumbai	Male	14%	7%	3%	5%	17%	33%	22%
	Female	8%	5%	4%	8%	19%	39%	17%
	Overall	12%	6%	3%	6%	17%	35%	20%

Source: Crime Victimization Survey, CHRI, 2015

Table 2.27 What time would one start worrying about safety of an adult male/female household member who is out alone at night

	City	After 7 PM	After 8 PM	After 9 PM	After 10 PM	After 11 PM	After Midnight	Would not worry
Male Member of household	Delhi	1%	6%	24%	33%	33%	2%	1%
	Mumbai	1%	4%	8%	18%	39%	20%	10%
Female Member of household	Delhi	21%	31%	32%	13%	2%	0%	0%
	Mumbai	6%	11%	16%	25%	29%	8%	5%

Source: Crime Victimization Survey, CHRI, 2015

Similarly, whereas 22% of respondents in Mumbai would feel unsafe using their own transportation to move around the city beyond 10 PM, the ratio jumps to 68% in Delhi. However, a significant gender difference regarding safety perception for travel at night did not emerge (Tables 2.28 and 2.29).

Table 2.28 At what time in the evening would one stop feeling safe travelling in public transport?

City	Gender	After 7 PM	After 8 PM	After 9 PM	After 10 PM	After 11 PM	After Midnight	Would not worry
Delhi	Male	2%	13%	32%	32%	19%	1%	1%
	Female	2%	18%	24%	33%	22%	1%	0%
	Overall	2%	16%	27%	33%	21%	1%	1%
Mumbai	Male	5%	2%	7%	19%	33%	23%	11%
	Female	3%	4%	9%	22%	41%	17%	4%
	Overall	4%	3%	7%	20%	36%	21%	9%

Source: Crime Victimization Survey, CHRI, 2015

Table 2.29 At what time in the evening would one stop feeling safe while travelling in personal transport?*

City	Gender	Always feel safe	After 7 PM	After 8 PM	After 9 PM	After 10 PM	After 11 PM	After midnight
Delhi	Male	3%	2%	6%	16%	39%	33%	3%
	Female	2%	2%	6%	17%	48%	22%	2%
	Overall	2%	2%	6%	16%	44%	27%	3%
Mumbai	Male	15%	1%	1%	8%	12%	31%	19%
	Female	7%	1%	2%	7%	15%	35%	15%
	Overall	13%	1%	1%	7%	13%	32%	17%

*Note: 67% (52%) of responding households in Delhi (Mumbai) owned two wheelers at the time of survey. Car ownership was 31% (15%) among Delhi (Mumbai) respondent households. However, the question was asked to all respondents irrespective of whether they owned a vehicle
Source: Crime Victimization Survey, CHRI, 2015

4 Learning and Way Forward

Public crime victimization surveys provide information on crime and safety concerns in society that is crucial for effective policy and operational responses. They are the medium by which the experiences and perceptions of the public can be collated, analysed, and examined to inform policy and state responses to crime and public safety. Importantly, the data amassed can *only* be gathered through these surveys; the existing collation and reporting of data and statistics overseen by the National Crime Records Bureau cannot capture these crucial data points. Regular crime victimization surveys would be a necessary, and immensely valuable, counterpart to the existing official statistics.

To begin with, such surveys generate data that enable police departments and governments to know the real incidence of crime experienced by members of the public. A singularly unique aspect of such surveys, as exemplified by this pilot initiative, is their ability to identify the proportion of crime experienced that goes unreported. For CHRI, unearthing this data was a major motivation for conducting the survey. This survey itself shows a rate of unreported crime of over 50% in both Delhi and Mumbai. There is no other method by which the government could gather information on such crimes. Should this finding be borne out by a larger study, it would carry serious implications for the scale of response needed from both the police and government.

Further, even without attempting to generalize the results, this survey points to important information (as well as areas of future research) on experiences of crime, the location and timing of crimes, and how crime affects migrants, different income classes, vulnerable groups and women. Moreover, the survey tells us how the police initially respond to crime, and how satisfied the public is with this response; all based on the direct opinions and/or lived experiences of ordinary households. General safety perceptions also show how safe, or unsafe, the public feels—a measure that will not be revealed without a survey. All this helps understand the nature of crime better, and allows police and policymakers to implement crime reduction strategies and policies where they can make the most impact. As crime reduction strategies become more focused and targeted, a natural progression would be to evaluate police performance against these; such a step would help address the current lack of systems or processes for regular police performance evaluation.

Crime surveys will be most effective when carried out regularly, at fixed intervals (preferably annually), and across the full jurisdiction of any police organization. Year on year tracking will throw up patterns in the changing nature of crime, experiences of crime, and relating to victims. Similarly, tracking the levels of reporting to the police will provide a consistent measure of the level of public confidence in the legal system in general, and in the police specifically. The information gathered can help assess the extent to which crime reduction strategies are working on the ground, and help shape suitable corrective measures.

A dilemma faced was deciding the crimes to be covered in the survey. Being the first survey of this scale, the consensus was to stick to crimes commonly reported to and registered by the police to allow comparison with official crime statistics. While it would be important to ensure a core set of crime categories are included in every survey, to track year-on-year trends, a crime victimization survey can contain a special section which varies in topic every year depending on the need of the time. There can also be micro-surveys for specific communities and/or specific crimes conducted separately. For instance, sexual offences against women require dedicated attention and will benefit from targeted surveys. Like in other jurisdictions where crime victimization surveys are carried out regularly, specialized questionnaires along with specially trained teams are needed to assess the extent, and nature of sexual offences against women. Similarly, finding ways to focus on crimes against other vulnerable groups including religious minorities, Scheduled Castes, Scheduled Tribes, and children will provide the insights necessary for developing targeted strategies and responses in these crucial areas.

The utility of crime victimization surveys ultimately depends to a great extent on the accuracy and sensitivity with which they are administered. This presented a big challenge both for a non-governmental organization like CHRI, and for the survey agency. Unfamiliarity with the core areas—crime and policing—created hesitation among the field surveyors, even for those with years of experience in administering survey interviews. We realized the importance of conducting training well before the scheduled survey to allow sufficient time for the team to get familiar with legal terminology. It would be valuable to have volunteers with law backgrounds, either students or young researchers, be part of the teams administering this survey. Aside from legal knowledge, special attention is needed to equip the interviewers with communication skills to deal with people's anxieties over sharing details about their victimization or their experience with the police. A careful balance is necessary to capture details of the crime while at the same time being mindful of any discomfort or pain it may evoke.

Given the required scale, periodicity and their technical nature, crime victimization surveys are a massive undertaking. In India, they are best done at the state level and in partnership between the government, academic institutions, and experts. Committing dedicated funds from the annual state budgets will help institutionalize the surveys and ensure they can be done at regular intervals (preferably annually).

Conducting a regular public crime survey would make vital data on crime and public safety available. For a country as diverse as India, and in which the criminal justice system is not always trusted by the public, a regular survey would not only provide unprecedented data, but over time, and with concerted efforts by government and criminal justice actors like the police, could be a mechanism that strengthens public trust in the police, and the justice system more largely.

Survey Questionnaire (English and Hindi)

Project Vishwas Setu

Crime Victimization and Safety Perception Survey

Commonwealth Human Rights Initiative
New Delhi, India. London, UK. Accra, Ghana
NGO in Special Consultative Status with the Economic & Social Council of the United Nations

Project Vishwas Setu
Crime victimization and safety perception survey

Part A: LISTING SHEET

Listing No.			

Brief Introduction: Commonwealth Human Rights Initiative (CHRI) in collaboration with Indicus Analytics (A Nielson Company)is conducting a crime victimisation survey in Delhi and Mumbai. In this survey we are collecting data on personal and household experience of crime and major public safety concerns across localities, income groups and socio demographics in the these two cities. The survey also seeks to assess personal experience of reporting of crimes to law enforcement agencies and satisfaction levels. The findings will be published in the form of a report and circulated widely to the Central and State governments, police, media and civil society.

संक्षिप्त परिचय:इंडिकस एनालिटिक्स (नेल्सन कंपनी) के सहयोग से कॉमनवेल्थ ह्यूमन राइट्स इनिशिएटिव (सीएचआरआई) दिल्ली और मुंबई में एक अपराध उत्पीड़न सर्वे कर रही है। इस सर्वे में हम इन शहरों की विभिन्न कॉलोनियों में, विभिन्न आय वर्ग एवं सामाजिक जनसंख्या के द्वारा अपराधिक व्यक्तिगत एवं घरेलू अनुभव और प्रमुख जन सुरक्षा से संबंधित डेटा एकत्रित कर रहे हैं। सर्वे कानून प्रवर्तन एजेंसियों और संतुष्टि के स्तर के लिए अपराधों की रिपोर्टिंग के व्यक्तिगत अनुभव का भी आकलन करना चाहता है। निष्कर्ष एक रिपोर्ट के रूप में प्रकाशित किया जाएगा और केन्द्र तथा राज्य सरकारों, पुलिस, मीडिया और नागरिक समाज के लिए व्यापक रूप से परिचालित किया जाएगा।

Thank you for giving your valuable time to answer the questionnaire. We are also grateful for your support.
प्रश्नावली का जवाब देने के लिए अपना बहुमूल्य समय देने के लिए धन्यवाद!हम आपकी सहायता के लिए भी आभारी हैं।

Household ID	City	Zone		Thana	Locality Name
Name of Interviewer:					
Region/Address:					
Date of Interview: DAY/MONTH/YEAR			**Phone No**		
Type of dwelling:	1=Independent house/bungalow		2=Apartment/flat in a building		3=Slum/jhuggi

PART A: Listing

A1. Demographicsजनसांख्यिकी

1. Respondent details (Select an adult member for the survey)
    उत्तरदाता का विवरण (सर्वे के लिए किसी वयस्क सदस्य को चुनें)

Name of the respondent उत्तरदाता का नाम	Gender लिंग		Age (in years) उम्र (वर्ष में)	Whether CWE मुख्य कमाने वाले हैं या नहीं	
	Male पुरुष	Female महिला		Yes हाँ	No नहीं
	1	2		1	2

2. CWE मुख्य कमाने वाले

Age (in years) उम्र (वर्ष में)	Genderलिंग		Education of CWE मुख्य कमाने वाले की शिक्षा (Code)	Occupation of Chief Wage Earner (CWE) मुख्य कमाने वाले का व्यवसाय	Mother tongue of CWE मुख्य कमाने वाले की मातृभाषा	Annual household Income वार्षिक घरेलू आय		
	Male पुरुष	Female महिला				Below 3Lacs 3 लाख से कम	Between 3–10Lacs 3–10 लाख के बीच	Above 10 Lacs 10 लाख से अधिक
	1	2				1	2	3

Education: शिक्षा:	1=Illiterate अशिक्षित	2=Literate but no formal schooling/ School-Upto4 years शिक्षित लेकिन कोई औपचारिक स्कूली शिक्षा नहीं / चौथी कक्षा तक स्कूल	3=School-5 to 9 years, 5वीं से 9वीं कक्षा तक स्कूल	4=SSC/ HSC एसएससी / एचएससी
5= Some College (including a Diploma) but not Graduateकुछ कॉलेज (डिप्लोमा सहित) लेकिन ग्रैजुएट नहीं		6=Graduate/ Post Graduate: General ग्रैजुएट / पोस्ट ग्रैजुएट:जनरल		7= Graduate/ Post Graduate: Professional ग्रैजुएट / पोस्ट ग्रैजुएट: प्रोफेशनल
Occupation (in the last one year): व्यवसाय (पिछले एक वर्ष का):				
1=Unskilled अकुशल	2=Shop Owners दुकान मालिक	3=Businessmen with No employees व्यवसायी बिना कर्मचारी के		4=Businessmen with 1-9 employees व्यवसायी 1–9 कर्मचारी वाले
5=Businessmen with 10+ employees		6=Self Employed professional		7=Clerical/Salesman

Commonwealth Human Rights Initiative
New Delhi, India. London, UK. Accra, Ghana
NGO in Special Consultative Status with the Economic & Social Council of the United Nations

व्यवसायी 10 से अधिक कर्मचारी वाले	स्व नियोजित पेशेवर	क्लेरिकल / सेल्समेन
8=Supervisory Level सुपरवायजर स्तर	9=Officers/Executives-Junior ऑफिसर्स / एग्जीक्यूटिव्स—जुनियर	10=Officers/Executives-Mid/Senior ऑफिसर्स / एग्जीक्यूटिव्स—मिडिल / सीनियर

3.   Household detailsघर का विवरण

Total no. of Male members पुरुष सदस्यों की कुल संख्या	No. of Adults (above 18) वयस्कों की संख्या (18 से ऊपर)	Total no. of female members महिला सदस्यों की कुल संख्या	No. of married members विवाहित सदस्यों की संख्या	No. of working members काम करने वाले सदस्यों की संख्या	Religion धर्म	Caste (if applicable) जाति (यदि लागू हो)
1	2	3	4	5	6	7

Religion: 1=Hindu, 2=Muslim,3=Christian,4=Sikh, 5=Other धर्म: 1=हिन्दु, 2=मुस्लिम. 3=क्रिस्चन / ईसाई. 4=सिख. 5=अन्य		
Caste जाति	1=Generalसामान्य	2=SC/STअनुसूचित जाति / अनुसूचित जनजाति	3=Othersअन्य

4. How long have you lived in Delhi? (in years)आप दिल्ली में कितने समय से रहते हैं? (वर्ष में)	
5. How long have you lived at your current address? (in years) आप अपने वर्तमान पते पर कितने समय से रहते हैं? (वर्ष में)	

6. Which of the following languages you can speak/read/write. इनमें से कौन सी भाषाओं को आप बोल सकते हैं / पढ़ सकते हैं / लिख सकते हैं। **Only Speak=1; Can speak &read, but not write=2; Speak, Read and write=3** केवल बोल सकते हैं=1; बोल सकते हैं और पढ़ सकते हैं लेकिन लिख नहीं सकते हैं=2; बोल, पढ़ और लिख सकते हैं=3	English अंग्रेजी			Hindi हिन्दी			Marathi मराठी		
	1	2	3	1	2	3	1	2	3

7. Is the home you live in your own or rented? जिस घर में आप रहते हैं वह आपका अपना है या किराए का?	Owned without mortgage बिना ऋण के अपना	Owned, but paying off अपना, लेकिन बकाया नहीं है	Rented किराए का
	1	2	3

MULTIPLE RESPONSESALLOWED for Question 8, 9,10
प्रश्न 8, 9, 10 के लिए एक से अधिक जवाब की अनुमति

8. Household assets: Does your house have a……… (Read out)**MULTIPLE RESPONSESALLOWED**
घरेलू संपत्तियां : क्या आपके घर में ……… (पढ़ें) है? **एक से अधिक जवाब की अनुमति**

Ceiling Fan छत का पंखा	LPG Stove एलपीजी स्टोव	Two-Wheeler टू-व्हीलर	Colour TV रंगीन टीवी	Refrigerator रेफ्रिजरेटर / फ्रिज	Washing Machine वाशिंग मशीन
1	2	3	4	5	6
Computer/ Laptop कम्प्यूटर / लैपटॉप	Car कार	Air-onditioner एयर-कंडीशनर	Water-purifier वाटर-प्यूरीफायर	Cellphone सेलफोन	Agri Land at Native place पैतृक स्थान पर खेती की जमीन
7	8	9	10	11	12

9. Do you have the following in your home (read out)?**MULTIPLE RESPONSES ALLOWED**
क्या आपके पास निम्नलिखित में से आपके घर में ………………… (पढ़ें)है?**एक से अधिक जवाब की अनुमति**

Electricity connection बिजली कनेक्शन	Private/ Separate toilet निजी / अलग शौचालय	Tap-water नल का पानी	More than one room (excluding the kitchen) एक से अधिक कमरे (रसोई को छोड़कर)
1	2	3	4

10. Is your home protected by any of the following?**MULTIPLE RESPONSES ALLOWED**
क्या आपका घर इनमें से किसी भी से संरक्षित है?**एक से अधिक जवाब की अनुमति**

Special door/window locks and grills विशेष दरवाजा / विंडो लॉक और ग्रिल	A security guard एक सुरक्षा गार्ड	Neighbourhood Chowkidar पड़ोस में चौकीदार	Not protected संरक्षित नहीं
1	2	3	4

11. Do you have a bank account? क्या आपके पास बैंक खाता है?		1=Yesहाँ	2=Noनहीं
12. Do you have a Voter ID card/Aadhar card क्या आपके पास मतदाता पहचान पत्र (वोटर आईडी) / आधार कार्ड है?		1=Yesहाँ	2=Noनहीं

Commonwealth Human Rights Initiative
New Delhi, India. London, UK. Accra, Ghana
NGO in Special Consultative Status with the Economic & Social Council of the United Nations

A2. Incidence of crimeअपराध की घटना

I am going to give you some examples that will give you an idea of the kinds of crimes this study covers. As I go through them, tell me if any of these happened to you in the last one year from May 2014-June 2015.
मैं आपको कुछ उदाहरण देने जा रहा हूँ जो आपको इस सर्वे में शामिल किये गये अपराधों के प्रकार के बारे में एक आयडिया देगा। जैसे ही मैं उसे बताऊं, आप मुझे बताएं कि इनमें से कोई भी आपके साथ पिछले एक साल मई 2014 – जून 2015 में हुआ।

Did any incidence mentioned below experienced by you or any member of your household in the last one year from May 2014-June 2015 ? पिछले एक साल मई 2014 – जून 2015 में नीचे दिये किसी भी घटना का अनुभव आपके या आपके घर के किसी भी सदस्य द्वारा किया गया था?				Whether the incidence took place inside the city or outside घटना शहर के भीतर हुआ था या बाहर		Did you report to the police? क्या आपने पुलिस को रिपोर्ट किया था?		If you face a similar crime in future, would you report to the police? यदि आप भविष्य में इसी तरह के अपराध का सामना करते हैं तो, क्या आप पुलिस को रिपोर्ट करेंगे?	
	Yes हाँ	No नहीं	If Yes, Ask for section * यदि हाँ तो ... सैक्शन के लिए पूछें	In city शहर में	Outside बाहर	Yes हाँ	No नहीं	Yes हाँ	No नहीं
B1. Theftचोरी	1	2	B1	1	2	1	2	1	2
B2. Assault resulting in injury, including physical injuryशारीरिक चोट सहित चोट के परिणामस्वरूप हमला करना	1	2	B2	1	2	1	2	1	2
B3. House Break-inघर का ताला तोड़ना	1	2	B3	1	2	1	2	1	2
B4 Sexual Harassment (to be asked from adult female member of the household)लैंगिक / यौन उत्पीड़न (केवल घर के वयस्क महिला सदस्य से पूछाजाए)	1	2	B4	1	2	1	2	1	2
B5 Criminal intimidationअपराधिक धमकी	1	2	B5	1	2	1	2	1	2
B6. Un-natural Deathअप्राकृतिक मृत्यु	1	2	B6	1	2	1	2	1	2
B7. Missing personsव्यक्ति गुम होना / खो जाना	1	2	B7	1	2	1	2	1	2

*Circle the relevant sectionउपयुक्त सैक्शन को सर्कल करें

Commonwealth Human Rights Initiative
New Delhi, India. London, UK. Accra, Ghana
NGO in Special Consultative Status with the Economic & Social Council of the United Nations

Project Vishwas Setu
Crime victimization and safety perception survey

PART B, C & D

Listing No.				

Household ID	City	Zone	Thana	Locality Name

Name of Interviewer:				
Region/Address:				
Date of Interview: DAY/MONTH/YEAR			Phone No	
Type of dwelling:	1=Independent house/bungalow	2=Apartment/flat in a building		3=Slum/jhuggi

PART B: Details of crime

B1.Theft (*This includes only where respondent is sure loss of item is due to theft*)(**Multiple options are allowed**)
चोरी (इसमें केवल वही शामिल है जिसके बारे में उत्तरदाता को यकीन है कि सामान चोरी की वजह से गुम हुआ है) (एक से अधिक विकल्पों की अनुमति है)

Code	A	B	C	D	E	F	G	H	I
	Luggage सामान / लगेज	Wallet/ Purse बटुआ / पर्स	Credit/ Debit card क्रेडिट / डेबिट कार्ड	Jewelry ज्वेलरी / आभूषण	Cellphone सेलफोन	TV टीवी	Computer/ Laptop कम्प्यूटर / लैपटॉप	Cash नगद	Car कार
B1.1 In the past 1 Year, have you been a victim of theft in any of the above ways? पिछले 1 साल में, क्या आप उपरोक्त में से किसी भी तरीके से चोरी का शिकार हुए हैं?									
Yes हाँ	1	1	1	1	1	1	1	1	1
No नहीं	2	2	2	2	2	2	2	2	2
B1.2 In the past one year, how many times have the items been stolen? (No.s) पिछले एक साल में, यह चीज कितनी बार चोरी हुआ है? (संख्या)									
B1.3 If stolen, where did this happen?(**Multiple options are allowed**) यदि चोरी हुआ तो यह कहाँ हुआ था?(एक से अधिक विकल्पों की अनुमति है)									
Your home without break-in ताला तोड़े बगैर आपके घर	1	1	1	1	1	1	1	1	1
With House Break-in घर में ताला तोड़कर	2	2	2	2	2	2	2	2	2
Family/ friends home परिवार / दोस्तों के घर	3	3	3	3	3		3	3	3
Your workplace आपके कार्यस्थल	4	4	4	4	4		4	4	4
Commercial place (mall/theatre/ restaurant/ grocery store/market) व्यवसायिक स्थान (मॉल / थिएटर / रेस्तरां / किराना दुकान / बाजार)	5	5	5	5	5		5	5	5
In open areas/on the street खुले जगहों में / गली में	6	6	6	6	6		6	6	6
In public bus सार्वजनिक बस में	7	7	7	7	7		7	7	7
In the metro मेट्रो में	8	8	8	8	8		8	8	8
In an auto/cab ऑटो / कैब में	9	9	9	9	9		9	9	9
B1.4 Please name the locality where the theft happened?(If response in B1.3 is 1 or 2, Don't ask the locality name) कृपया उस स्थान का नाम बताएं जहाँ चोरी हुआ था?(यदि बी1.3 में जवाब 1 या 2 है तो स्थान का नाम न पूछें)									
B1.5 What time did it happen?(**Write the time in completed hours**)यह किस समय हुआ था?(**पूर्ण घंटे में समय लिखें**)									

1

Commonwealth Human Rights Initiative
New Delhi, India. London, UK. Accra, Ghana
NGO in Special Consultative Status with the Economic & Social Council of the United Nations

Time of occurrence घटने का समय (00:01 to 23:59)									

B1.6 In case you were a victim of any of the crimes listed above, did you report to the police?
अगर आप ऊपर दिये अपराधों में से किसी का शिकार हुए थे तो क्या आपने पुलिस को रिपोर्ट किया था?

Yesहाँ	1	1	1	1	1	1	1	1	1
Noनहीं	2	2	2	2	2	2	2	2	2

B2. Assault resulting in injury, including physical injury
शारीरिक चोट सहित, चोट के परिणामस्वरूप हमला करना

Code	A	B	C	D	E
	Grabbed/shoved/slapped/beat पकड़ा / धकेला / थप्पड़ मारा / आघात करना	Attack you by throwing rocks/bottles at you आप पर पत्थर / बोतल फेंककर हमला करना	Attack you with a gun or a knife बंदूक या चाकू से आप पर हमला करना	Attack you with any other dangerous object किसी अन्य खतरनाक वस्तु से आप पर हमला करना	Attack you in any other way किसी अन्य तरीके से आप पर हमला करना

B2.1 Have you over the past one year been physically attacked by someone in any of the above ways: (read out)
क्या आप पर पिछले एक साल में किसी के द्वारा उपरोक्त में से किसी भी तरीके से शारीरिक रूप से हमला किया गयाहै : (पढ़ें)

Yesहाँ	1	1	1	1	1
Noनहीं	2	2	2	2	2

B2.2 If Yes, how many times has this happened past one year?यदि हाँ तो पिछले एक साल में यह कितनी बार हुआ है?

No. of times बार					

B2.3 How many people attacked you?कितने लोगों ने आप पर हमला किया है?

One personएक व्यक्ति	1	1	1	1	1
Two Peopleदो लोग	2	2	2	2	2
More than Two People दो लोग से अधिक	3	3	3	3	3

B2.4 Where did this happen?यह कहाँ हुआ था?

Your home without break-in ताला तोड़े बगैर आपके घर	1	1	1	1	1
With House Break-in घर में ताला तोड़कर	2	2	2	2	2
Family/ friends home परिवार / दोस्तों के घर	3	3	3	3	3
Your workplace आपके कार्यस्थल	4	4	4	4	4
Commercial place (mall/theatre/restaurant/grocery store/market) व्यवसायिक स्थान (मॉल / थिएटर / रेस्तरां / किराना दुकान / बाजार)	5	5	5	5	5
In open areas/on the street खुले जगहों में / गली में	6	6	6	6	6
In public bus सार्वजनिक बस में	7	7	7	7	7
In the metro मेट्रो में	8	8	8	8	8
In an auto/cab ऑटो / कैब में	9	9	9	9	9

B2.5 Name of the locality where it happened?(If response in B2.4 is 1 or 2, Don't ask the locality name)
उस स्थान का नाम बताएं जहाँ यह हुआ था?(यदि बी2.4 में जवाब 1 या 2 है तो स्थान का नाम न पूछें)

Locality Nameस्थान का नाम					

B2.6 What time did it happen?(**Write the time in completed hours**)यह किस समय हुआ था?(**पूर्ण घंटे में समय लिखें**)

Time of occurrence घटने का समय (00:01 to 23:59)					

B2.7 Did you know the offender(s) by name or by sight at the time of the offence?
क्या आप उस अपराधी(अपराधियों) को नाम से या देखने से जानते थे जो अपराध के समय पर था?

Commonwealth Human Rights Initiative
New Delhi, India. London, UK. Accra, Ghana
NGO in Special Consultative Status with the Economic & Social Council of the United Nations

Code	A	B	C	D	E
	Grabbed/shoved/ slapped/beat पकड़ा / धकेला / थप्प ड़ मारा / आघात करना	Attack you by throwing rocks/bottles at you आप पर पत्थर / बोतल फेंककर हमला करना	Attack you with a gun or a knife बंदूक या चाकू से आप पर हमला करना	Attack you with any other dangerous object किसी अन्य खतरनाक वस्तु से आप पर हमला	Attack you in any other way किसी अन्य तरीके से आप पर हमला करना
Did not know offender अपराधी को नहीं जानते थे	1	1	1	1	1
(At least one) known by sight (कम से कम एक को) देखने से जानते थे	2	2	2	2	2
(At least one) known by name (कम से कम एक को) नाम से जानते थे	3	3	3	3	3
Did not see the offender अपराधी को नहीं देखा था	4	4	4	4	4
B2.8 In case you were a victim of any of crime listed above, did you report to the police? अगर आप ऊपर दिये अपराधों में से किसी का शिकार हुए थे तो क्या आपने पुलिस को रिपोर्ट किया था?					
Yesहाँ	1	1	1	1	1
Noनहीं	2	2	2	2	2

B3. House Break-inघर का ताला तोड़ना

Code	A	B	C	D
	Forcing a door or window दरवाजे या खिड़की से जबरदस्ती	Manipulating a lock ताले में हेर–फेर	Entering through an open door or window किसी खुले दरवाजे या खिड़की के माध्यम से प्रवेश	Using force, or threatening to use force, against you or any other person आपके या किसी अन्य व्यक्ति के खिलाफ बल प्रयोग करना, या बल प्रयोग करने की धमकी देना
B3.1 In the last 1 year, has anyone broken in or attempted to break into your home by any of the above ways? पिछले 1 साल में, क्या कोई आपके घर में उपरोक्त में से किसी भी तरीके से ताला तोड़कर घुसा है या घुसने की कोशिश की है?				
Yesहाँ	1	1	1	1
Noनहीं	2	2	2	2
B3.2 In past one year, how many times has the incident happened? पिछले एक साल में यह घटना कितनी बार हुआ है?				
B3.3 Was it accompanied by any theft/assault? क्या यह किसी चोरी / हमला के साथ हुआ था?				
Theft चोरी	1	1	1	1
Assault हमला	2	2	2	2

3

Commonwealth Human Rights Initiative
New Delhi, India. London, UK. Accra, Ghana
NGO in Special Consultative Status with the Economic & Social Council of the United Nations

B4. Sexual Harassment (To be asked from adult female member of the household)
लैंगिक/यौन उत्पीड़न

Code	A	B	C	D	E
	Passed lewd or unwelcome sexual comments अश्लील या अप्रिय यौन टिप्पणियां करना	Continuously stared at in a lewd or threatening manner लगातार अश्लील या डराने के तरीके से घूरना	Followed by men till you were scared or uncomfortable पुरुषों द्वारा तब तक आपका पीछा करना जब तक कि आप डर न जाएं या असहज न हो जाएं	Touched indecently/groped/pinched अशिष्टता से छूना/टटोलना/चिकोटी काटना	Sending unwanted messages through SMS/e-mail/social media/internet/making telephone calls एसएमएस/ईमेल/सोशल मीडिया/इंटरनेट के माध्यम से अवांछित संदेश भेजना/टेलीफोन कॉल करना
B4.1 Over the past one year hasanyone done, or tried to harass you in any of the ways mentioned above? क्या पिछले एक साल में किसी ने ऊपर बताये तरीके में से कोई भी आपको किया है या परेशान करने की कोशिश की है?					
Yesहाँ	1	1	1	1	1
Noनहीं	2	2	2	2	2
B4.2 If Yes, how many times has this happened past one year? यदि हाँ तो, पिछले एक साल में यह कितनी बार हुआ है?					
No. of timesबार					
B4.3 Where did this happen?यह कहाँ हुआ था?					
Your home without break-in ताला तोड़े बगैर आपके घर	1	1	1	1	1
With House Break-in घर में ताला तोड़कर	2	2	2	2	2
Family/ friends home परिवार/दोस्तों के घर	3	3	3	3	3
Your workplace आपके कार्यस्थल	4	4	4	4	4
Commercial place (mall/theatre/ restaurant/grocery store/market) व्यवसायिक स्थान (मॉल/थिएटर/रेस्तरां/किराना दुकान/बाजार)	5	5	5	5	5
In open areas/on the street खुले जगहों में/गली में	6	6	6	6	6
In public bus सार्वजनिक बस में	7	7	7	7	7
In the metro मेट्रो में	8	8	8	8	8
In an auto/cab ऑटो/कैब में	9	9	9	9	9
B4.4 Name of the locality where it happened?(If response in B4.3 is 1 or 2, Don't ask the locality name) उस स्थान का नाम बताएं जहाँ यह हुआ था? (यदि बी4.3 में जवाब 1 या 2 है तो स्थान का नाम न पूछें)					
Locality Name स्थान का नाम					
B4.5 What time did it happen?(Write the time in completed hours)यह किस समय हुआ था?(पूर्ण घंटे में समय लिखें)					
Time of occurrence घटने का समय (00:01 to 23:59)					
B4.6 Did you know the offender(s) by name or by sight at the time of the offence? क्या आप उस अपराधी(अपराधियों) को नाम से या देखने से जानते थे जो अपराध के समय पर था?					

Commonwealth Human Rights Initiative
New Delhi, India. London, UK. Accra, Ghana
NGO in Special Consultative Status with the Economic & Social Council of the United Nations

Code	A	B	C	D	E
	Passed lewd or unwelcome sexual comments अश्लील या अप्रिय यौन टिप्पणियां करना	Continuously stared at in a lewd or threatening manner लगातार अश्लील या डराने के तरीके से घूरना	Followed by men till you were scared or uncomfortable पुरुषों द्वारा तब तक आपका पीछा करना जब तक कि आप डर न जाएं या असहज न हो जाएं	Touched indecently/groped/pinched अशिष्टता से छूना / टटोलना / चिकोटी काटना	Sending unwanted messages through SMS/e-mail/social media/internet/making telephone calls एसएमएस / ईमेल / सोशल मीडिया / इंटरनेट के माध्यम से अवांछित संदेश भेजना / टेलीफोन कॉल करना
Did not know offender अपराधी को नहीं जानते थे	1	1	1	1	1
(At least one) known by sight (कम से कम एक को) देखने से जानते थे	2	2	2	2	2
At least one) known by name (कम से कम एक को) नाम से जानते थे	3	3	3	3	3
Did not see the offender अपराधी को नहीं देखा था	4	4	4	4	4
B4.7 In case you were a victim of any of crime listed above, did you report to the police? अगर आप ऊपर दिये अपराधों में से किसी का शिकार हुए थे तो क्या आपने पुलिस को रिपोर्ट किया था?					
Yes हाँ	1	1	1	1	1
No नहीं	2	2	2	2	2

B5. Criminal intimidation
अपराधिक धमकी

B5.1 In the last one year, did anyone threaten you (or your family) with injury or damaging your property for not following their demands?
पिछले एक साल में क्या किसी ने भी अपनी मांगों का पालन नहीं करने पर आपको (या आपके परिवार को) चोट या आपकी संपत्ति को नुकसान पहुँचाने की धमकी दी है?

1=Yes हाँ	2=No नहीं

B5.2 If Yes, how many times has this happened in past one year? यदि हाँ तो, पिछले एक साल में यह कितनी बार हुआ है?

No. of times बार

B5.3 Name of the locality where it happened? (If incidence happened at home, Don't ask for the locality name)
उस स्थान का नाम बताएं जहाँ यह हुआ था? (यदि घटना घर पर हुआ है तो स्थान का नाम न पूछें)

Locality Name स्थान का नाम

B5.4 Did you know the offender(s) by name or by sight at the time of the offence?
क्या आप उस अपराधी(अपराधियों) को नाम से या देखने से जानते थे जो अपराध के समय पर था?

Did not know offender अपराधी को नहीं जानते थे	1
(At least one) known by sight (कम से कम एक को) देखने से जानते थे	2
At least one) known by name (कम से कम एक को) नाम से जानते थे	3
Did not see the offender अपराधी को नहीं देखा था / देखी थी	4

B5.5   In case you were a victim of any of crime mentioned above, did you report to the police?
अगर आप ऊपर दिये अपराधों में से किसी का शिकार हुए थे तो क्या आपने पुलिस को रिपोर्ट किया था?

1=Yes हाँ	2=No नहीं

B6. Un-natural Death (*This does not include suicides that may have happened in households.*)
अप्राकृतिक मृत्यु

Commonwealth Human Rights Initiative
New Delhi, India. London, UK. Accra, Ghana
NGO in Special Consultative Status with the Economic & Social Council of the United Nations

Code	A	B
	Member of your household was murdered आपके घर के सदस्य की हत्या हुई हो	Member of your household died in aroad/train accident आपके घर का सदस्य सड़क/ट्रेन दुर्घटना में मरा हो
B6.1 Over the past one year, has any of the above mentioned incidents happened to someone in your household? पिछले एक साल में ऊपर बताये घटनाओं में से कोई भी आपके घर में किसी के साथ हुआ है?		
Yesहाँ	1	1
Noनहीं	2	2
B6.2 If Yes, how many times has this happened past one year? यदि हाँ तो, पिछले एक साल में यह कितनी बार हुआ है?		
No. of timesबार		
B6.3 Name of the locality where it happened?उस स्थान का नाम बताएं जहाँ यह हुआ था?		
Locality Nameस्थान का नाम		
B6.4 What time did it happen?(**Write the time in completed hours**)यह किस समय हुआ था?(**पूर्ण घंटे में समय लिखें**)		
Time of occurrence (00:01 to 23:59) घटने का समय		
B6.5 Did you know the offender(s) by name or by sight at the time of the offence? क्या आप उस अपराधी(अपराधियों) को नाम से या देखने से जानते थे जो अपराध के समय पर था?		
Did not know offenderअपराधी को नहीं जानते थे	1	1
(At least one) known by sight (कम से कम एक को) देखने से जानते थे	2	2
At least one) known by name (कम से कम एक को) नाम से जानते थे	3	3
Did not see the offender अपराधी को नहीं देखा था	4	4
B6.6 In case you were a victim of any of crime listed above, did you report to the police? अगर आप ऊपर दिये अपराधों में से किसी का शिकार हुए थे तो क्या आपने पुलिस को रिपोर्ट किया था?		
Yesहाँ	1	1
No नहीं	2	2

B7. Missing Persons व्यक्तिगुम होना

B7.1 Has anyone in your household gone missing and/or disappeared? क्या आपके घर में कोई भी व्यक्ति गुम हुआ है और/या गायब हुआ है?	1=Yesहाँ	2=Noनहीं
If the answer to Question B7.1 is Yes, continue to B7.2 onwards **यदि प्रश्न बी7.1 में जवाब हाँ है तो बी7.2 से आगे जारी रखें**		
B7.2. Is the missing person below 18 years old? क्या गुमशुदा व्यक्ति 18 वर्ष से कम का है?	1=Yesहाँ	2=Noनहीं
B7.3. Please specify the gender of the missing person.कृपया गुमशुदा व्यक्ति का लिंग बताएं।	1=Male पुरुष	2=Female महिला
B7.4 What time did it happen?यह किस समय हुआ था?[**Time of occurrence (00:01 to 23:59)**] **(Write the time in completed hours)**		
B7.5 Name of the place, where it happened?उस स्थान का नाम बताएं जहाँ यह हुआ था?		
B7.6. Did you report to the police?क्या आपने पुलिस को रिपोर्ट किया था?	1=Yesहाँ	2=Noनहीं

6

Commonwealth Human Rights Initiative
New Delhi, India. London, UK. Accra, Ghana
NGO in Special Consultative Status with the Economic & Social Council of the United Nations

PART C: Reporting of crime to police and satisfaction/dis-satisfaction

First, note down the crimes for which the respondent household had approached the police. In case of multiple cases reported within a section, mention each one separately. Then, mark the Section, Crime heading and Codes in the tables.

सबसे पहले, उन अपराधों को टिक करें जिसके लिए उत्तरदाता का घर पुलिस से संपर्क किया था। अगर एक सैक्शन में केस रिपोर्ट किया गया है तो हरेक को अलग–अलग बताएं। उसके बाद सैक्शन, अपराध के शीर्षक पर निशान लगायें और टेबल में कोड करें।

B1. Theft चोरी

Code	A	B	C	D	E	F	G	H	I
	Luggage सामान / लगेज	Wallet/Purse बटुआ / पर्स	Credit/Debit card क्रेडिट / डेबिट कार्ड	Jewelry ज्वेलरी / आभूषण	Cellphone सेलफोन	TV टीवी	Computer/ Laptop कम्प्यूटर / लैपटॉप	Cash नगद	Car कार

B2. Assault resulting in injury, including physical injury शारीरिक चोट सहित चोट के परिणामस्वरूप हमला करना

Code	A	B	C	D	E
	Grabbed/shoved/slapped/beat पकड़ा / धकेला / थप्पड़ मारा / आघात करना	Attack you by throwing rocks/bottles at you आप पर पत्थर / बोतल फेंककर हमला करना	Attack you with a gun or a knife बंदूक या चाकू से आप पर हमला करना	Attack you with any other dangerous object किसी अन्य खतरनाक वस्तु से आप पर हमला करना	Attack you in any other way किसी अन्य तरीके से आप पर हमला करना

B3. House Break-in घर का ताला तोड़ना

Code	A	B	C	D
	Forcing a door or window दरवाजे या खिड़की से जबरदस्ती	Manipulating a lock ताले में हेर–फेर	Entering through an open door or window किसी खुले दरवाजे या खिड़की के माध्यम से प्रवेश	Using force, or threatening to use force, against you or any other person आपके या किसी अन्य व्यक्ति के खिलाफ बल प्रयोग करना, या बल प्रयोग करने की धमकी देना

B4. Sexual Harassment (To be asked from adult female member of the household if respondent is male) यौन उत्पीड़न (केवल घर के वयस्कमहिला सदस्य से पूछाजाए)

Code	A	B	C	D	E
	Passed lewd or unwelcome sexual comments अश्लील या अप्रिय यौन टिप्पणियां करना	Continuously stared at in a lewd or threatening manner लगातार अश्लील या डराने के तरीके से घूरना	Followed by men till you were scared or uncomfortable पुरुषों द्वारा तब तक आपका पीछा करना जब तक कि आप डर न जाएं या असहज न हो जाएं	Touched indecently/groped/pinched अशिष्टता से घूना / टटोलना / चिकोटी काटना	Sending unwanted messages through SMS/e-mail/social media/internet/making telephone calls एसएमएस / ईमेल / सोशल मीडिया / इंटरनेट के माध्यम से अवांछित संदेश भेजना / टेलीफोन कॉल करना

B5. Criminal intimidation आपराधिक धमकी

	Threaten you (or your family or property) with injury for not following their demands उनके मांगों का पालन नहीं करने पर चोट के साथ आपको (या आपके परिवार या संपत्ति को) धमकी

B6. Un-natural Death अप्राकृतिक मृत्यु

Code	A	B
	Member of your household was murdered आपके घर के सदस्य की हत्या हुई हो	Member of your household died in a road/train accident आपके घर का सदस्य सड़क / ट्रेन दुर्घटना में मरा हो

B7.   Missing Persons व्यक्ति गुम होना / खो जाना

Commonwealth Human Rights Initiative
New Delhi, India. London, UK. Accra, Ghana
NGO in Special Consultative Status with the Economic & Social Council of the United Nations

C.1. Reporting and response of police रिपोर्ट करना और पुलिस की प्रतिक्रिया

Sr. No.	Mention relevant section no. (B1-B6) उपयुक्त सैक्शन संख्या लिखें (बी1–बी6) Section heading सैक्शन का शीर्षक Crime code अपराध का कोड							B7. Missing Persons गुमशुदा व्यक्ति
1	**How did you report?** आपने कैसे रिपोर्ट किया था?							
1.1	Called 100 100 पर कॉल किया	1	1	1	1	1	1	1
1.2	Called relevant police helpline like 1091, 1094 1091, 1094 उपयुक्त पुलिस हेल्पलाइन पर कॉल किया	2	2	2	2	2	2	2
1.3	Went to the police station पुलिस स्टेशन / थाना गया	3	3	3	3	3	3	3
1.4	Approached a PCR van पीसीआर वैन से संपर्क किया	4	4	4	4	4	4	4
1.5	Online ऑनलाइन	5	5	5	5	5	5	5
1.6	Other (specify) अन्य (बताएं)	6	6	6	6	6	6	6
1.7	Other (specify) अन्य (बताएं)	7	7	7	7	7	7	7
2	**What did the police do?** (Multiple responses allowed) पुलिस ने क्या किया था?							
2.1	File a complaint शिकायत दर्ज किया	1	1	1	1	1	1	NA
2.2	Register an FIR एफआईआररजिस्टर किया	2	2	2	2	2	2	NA
2.3	Dispatched a PCR van पीसीआर वैन के पास भेजा गया	3	3	3	3	3	3	NA
2.4	Did not take your complaint and asked you to go to another police station आपकी शिकायत को नहीं सुना और आपको दूसरे पुलिस स्टेशन पर जाने के लिए कहा	4	4	4	4	4	4	NA
2.5	Reached the spot where you called from and made inquiries उस स्पॉट पर पहुंचा जहाँ से आपने कॉल किया था और पूछताछ किया था	5	5	5	5	5	5	NA
2.6	Directed you to the police station you should go to आपको निर्देश दिया गया कि आपको पुलिस स्टेशन जाना चाहिए	6	6	6	6	6	6	NA
2.7	Took any injured persons for medical assistance किसी घायल व्यक्ति को चिकित्सा सहायता के लिए ले गये	7	7	7	7	7	7	NA
2.8	Did not do anything कुछ नहीं किया था	8	8	8	8	8	8	NA
2.9	Filed a Missing Persons Report and informed you of the same गुमशुदा व्यक्ति का रिपोर्ट फाइल किया और उसके बारे में आपको सूचित किया था	NA	NA	NA	NA	NA	NA	1
2.10	Registered an FIR in case of a missing child and informed you of the same गुमशुदा बच्चे के मामले में एक एफआईआर रजिस्टर किया और उसके बारे में आपको सूचित किया था	NA	NA	NA	NA	NA	NA	2
2.11	Publicized photograph of the missing person at various public places and through local newspaper and television channel	NA	NA	NA	NA	NA	NA	3

Commonwealth Human Rights Initiative
New Delhi, India. London, UK. Accra, Ghana
NGO in Special Consultative Status with the Economic & Social Council of the United Nations

	गुमशुदा व्यक्ति के फोटो को सार्वजनिक स्थानों और स्थानीय अखबार और टेलीविजन चैनल के माध्यम से प्रचार किया था							
2.12	Made inquiries in the neighborhood including at schools, hospitals and mortuaries स्कूलों, अस्पतालों और शवगृहों सहित पड़ोस में पूछताछ किया था	NA	NA	NA	NA	NA	NA	4
2.13	In case of a minor girl, set up a task force for locating the girl एक नाबालिक लड़की के केस में, लड़की का पता लगाने के लिए एक टास्क फोर्स गठन किया	NA	NA	NA	NA	NA	NA	5
2.14	Did not take your complaint and asked you to go to another police station आपकी शिकायत को नहीं सुना था और आपको दूसरे पुलिस स्टेशन पर जाने के लिए कहा गया था	NA	NA	NA	NA	NA	NA	6
2.15	Did not do anything कुछ नहीं किया था	NA	NA	NA	NA	NA	NA	7

C.2Briefly describe the experience when you contacted the police (please take down steps clearly and in detail in a separate sheet, if required).
पुलिस द्वारा लिए गए कदमों का संक्षेप में वर्णन करें (यदि आवश्यक हो तो कृपया अलग शीट में कदमों को साफ–साफ और विस्तार से लिखें)

Mention relevant section no. (B1-B7)							
Section heading							
Code							

9

Commonwealth Human Rights Initiative
New Delhi, India. London, UK. Accra, Ghana
NGO in Special Consultative Status with the Economic & Social Council of the United Nations

C.3. Whether you are/were satisfied with the action taken by the police?(*This refers only to the first response of the police. It does not cover status and outcome of the case investigation.*)क्या आप पुलिस द्वारा की गई कार्रवाई से आप संतुष्ट हैं/थे? *(यह पुलिस की पहली प्रतिक्रिया को दर्शाता है। इसमें पुलिस की छानबीन की स्थिति और परिणाम सम्मिलित नहीं है।)*

Sr. No.	Mention relevant section no. (B1-B7)							
	Section heading							
	Code							
1	Satisfiedसंतुष्ट	1	1	1	1	1	1	1
2	Not satisfiedसंतुष्ट नहीं	2	2	2	2	2	2	2

If satisfied, Ask for C.4, otherwise C.5

C.4. For what reasons were you satisfied? You can give more than one responseकिन कारणों से आप संतुष्ट थे? आप एक से अधिक जवाब दे सकते हैं।

Sr. No.	Mention relevant section no. (B1-B7)							
	Section heading							
	Code							
1	They listened carefully उन्होंने ध्यान से सुना था	1	1	1	1	1	1	1
2	They registered my complaint correctly उन्होंने सही–सही मेरे शिकायत को रजिस्टर किया था	2	2	2	2	2	2	2
3	They registered my complaint without delay उन्होंने देरी किए बिना मेरी शिकायत रजिस्टर किया था	3	3	3	3	3	3	3
4	They explained the action they will take उन्होंने उस कार्रवाई के बारे में समझाया जो वे करेंगे	4	4	4	4	4	4	4
5	They arrived without delayदेरी किए बिना पहुँच गए	5	5	5	5	5	5	5
6	They acted fastउन्होंने तेज कार्रवाई की	6	6	6	6	6	6	6
7	Any other (please specify)कोई अन्य	7	7	7	7	7	7	7

C.5. For what reasons were you dissatisfied? You can give more thanone response किन कारणों से आप असंतुष्ट थे? आप एक से अधिक जवाब दे सकते हैं।

Sr. No.	Mention relevant section no. (B1-B7)							
	Section heading							
	Code							
1	They were rude and impolite while registering my FIR at the police station पुलिस स्टेशन में मेरे एफआईआर दर्ज करते समय अशिष्ट और असभ्य थे	1	1	1	1	1	1	1
2	They refused to register my FIR and told me to go away from the police station उन्होंने मेरा एफआईआर दर्ज करने से मना कर दिया और मुझे पुलिस स्टेशन से चले जाने के लिए कहा गया	2	2	2	2	2	2	2
3	They put me at fault and tried to persuade me to not register an FIR	3	3	3	3	3	3	3

10

Commonwealth Human Rights Initiative
New Delhi, India. London, UK. Accra, Ghana
NGO in Special Consultative Status with the Economic & Social Council of the United Nations

	उन्होंने गलती मुझ पर डालकर एकआईआर दर्ज नहीं कराने के लिए मुझे मनाने की कोशिश की								
4	They asked for a bribe उन्होंने रिश्वत मांगी	4	4	4	4	4	4	4
5	They made me wait without any reason and took a long time to register my FIR उन्होंने बिना किसी कारण के इंतजार करने के लिए कहा और मेरा एफआईआर दर्ज करने में लंबा समय लिया	5	5	5	5	5	5	5
6	PCR van took more than an hour to arrive at the spot from where I called पीसीआर वैन उस स्पॉट पर पहुँचने में एक घंटे से अधिक लिया जहाँ से मैने कॉल किया था	6	6	6	6	6	6	6
7	They did not assist injured persons उन्होंने घायल हुए व्यक्तियों की सहायता नहीं की थी	7	7	7	7	7	7	7
8	Any other reason कोई अन्य कारण (कृपया बताएं)	8	8	8	8	8	8	8

C.6. If you did not report to the police, why did you not report? यदि आपने पुलिस को रिपोर्ट नहीं किया था तो, क्यों नहीं किया था?

Sr. No.	Mention relevant section no. (B1-B7)							
	Section heading							
	Code							
1	Fear of retaliation जवाबी कार्रवाई का डर	1	1	1	1	1	1	1
2	Lack of evidence साक्ष्यों का अभाव	2	2	2	2	2	2	2
3	Didn't know where to report नहीं मालूम था कि कहां रिपोर्ट करें	3	3	3	3	3	3	3
4	Didn't know any of the helpline numbers किसी भी हेल्पलाइन नंबर के बारे में मालूम नहीं था	4	4	4	4	4	4	4
5	Did not think the police would entertain your complaint नहीं सोचा था कि पुलिस आपकी शिकायत को सुनेगा	5	5	5	5	5	5	5
6	Did not think the police would be able to do anything about the case नहीं सोचा था कि पुलिस मामले के बारे में कुछ भी करने में सक्षम होगा	6	6	6	6	6	6	6
7	Family matters do not need to be reported पारिवारिक मामलों को रिपोर्ट करवाने की जरूरत नहीं है	7	7	7	7	7	7	7
8	Did not want to get stuck in police/court matters पुलिस/अदालत मामले में फंसना नहीं चाहता था	8	8	8	8	8	8	8
9	Scared to go to the police station पुलिस स्टेशन में जाने से डरता था	9	9	9	9	9	9	9
10	Other reasons अन्य कारण	10	10	10	10	10	10	10

Commonwealth Human Rights Initiative
New Delhi, India. London, UK. Accra, Ghana
NGO in Special Consultative Status with the Economic & Social Council of the United Nations

D. Perception of Safety/सुरक्षा का अनुभव

D1 What time would you start worrying about safety of an adult male member of your household who is out alone at night?
अपने घर के एक वयस्क पुरुष सदस्य की सुरक्षा के बारे में रात को किस समय उनके अकेले बाहर रहने पर चिंता करना शुरू कर देंगे?

after 7 pm 7 बजे के बाद	after 8 pm 8 बजे के बाद	after 9 pm 9 बजे के बाद	after 10 pm 10 बजे के बाद	after 11 pm 11 बजे के बाद	After midnight मध्य रात्रि के बाद	Would not worry चिंता नहीं करेंगे
1	2	3	4	5	6	7

D2 What time would you start worrying about safety of an adult female member of your household who is out alone at night?
अपने घर की एक वयस्क महिला सदस्य की सुरक्षा के बारे में रात को किस समय उनके अकेले बाहर रहने पर चिंता करना शुरू कर देंगे?

after 7 pm 7 बजे के बाद	after 8 pm 8 बजे के बाद	after 9 pm 9 बजे के बाद	after 10 pm 10 बजे के बाद	after 11 pm 11 बजे के बाद	After midnight मध्य रात्रि के बाद	Would not worry चिंता नहीं करेंगे
1	2	3	4	5	6	7

D3 Do you feel safe leaving your home locked for many days?
क्या आप अपने घर को कई दिनों तक ताला लगाकर छोड़ देनेपर सुरक्षित महसूस करते हैं?

1=Yes/हाँ	2=No/नहीं	3=Don't know/मालूम नहीं

D4 Do you feel safe traveling using public transport alone during the day? **(1=Yes, 2=No, 3= Don't Know)**
क्या आप दिन के दौरान अकेले सार्वजनिक परिवहन का इस्तेमाल करते हुए यात्रा करनेपर सुरक्षित महसूस करते हैं? **(1=हाँ, 2=नहीं, 3=मालूम नहीं)**

DTC/BEST buses डीटीसी / बीईएसटी बसें			Grameen Sewa ग्रामीण सेवा			Delhi/Mumbai Metro/Local Train दिल्ली / मुम्बई मेट्रो / लोकल ट्रेन			Delhi/ Mumbai metro feeder buses दिल्ली / मुम्बई मेट्रो की फीडर बसें			Auto ऑटो			Shared auto साझा ऑटो			Radio Taxi रेडियो टैक्सी			Other taxi services अन्य टैक्सी सेवाएं		
1	2	3	1	2	3	1	2	3	1	2	3	1	2	3	1	2	3	1	2	3	1	2	3

D5 At what time in the evening would you **stop feeling safe** while traveling using public transport?
सार्वजनिक परिवहन इस्तेमाल करते हुए यात्रा करते समय शाम को किस समय में आप सुरक्षित **महसूस करना बंद** कर देंगे?

after 7 pm 7 बजे के बाद	after 8 pm 8 बजे के बाद	after 9 pm 9 बजे के बाद	after 10 pm 10 बजे के बाद	after 11 pm 11 बजे के बाद	After midnight मध्य रात्रि के बाद	Would not worry चिंता नहीं करेंगे
1	2	3	4	5	6	7

D6 At what time in the evening would you stop feeling safe while traveling in your personal transport (cycle, bike, car)?
अपने निजी वाहन (साइकिल, बाइक, कार) में यात्रा करते समय शाम को किस समय में आप सुरक्षित महसूस करना बंद कर देंगे?

after 7 pm 7 बजे के बाद	after 8 pm 8 बजे के बाद	after 9 pm 9 बजे के बाद	after 10 pm 10 बजे के बाद	after 11 pm 11 बजे के बाद	After midnight मध्य रात्रि के बाद	Always feel safe हमेशा सुरक्षित महसूस करेंगे
1	2	3	4	5	6	7

D7 Do you feel safe walking around in your neighbourhood during the day?
क्या आप दिन के दौरान अपने पड़ोस में चलने पर सुरक्षित महसूस करते हैं?

1=Yes/हाँ	2=No/नहीं	3=Don't know/मालूम नहीं

D8 At what time in the evening would you stop feeling safe walking around alone in your neighborhood?
शाम को किस समय में आप अपने पड़ोस में अकेले टहलने पर सुरक्षित महसूस करना बंद कर देंगे?

after 7 pm 7 बजे के बाद	after 8 pm 8 बजे के बाद	after 9 pm 9 बजे के बाद	after 10 pm 10 बजे के बाद	after 11 pm 11 बजे के बाद	After midnight मध्य रात्रि के बाद	Always feel safe हमेशा सुरक्षित महसूस करेंगे
1	2	3	4	5	6	7

D9 At what time in the evening would you stop feeling safe withdrawing money from your neighborhood ATM?
शाम को किस समय में आप अपने पड़ोस के एटीएम से पैसा निकालने पर सुरक्षित महसूस करना बंद कर देंगे?

after 7 pm 7 बजे के बाद	after 8 pm 8 बजे के बाद	after 9 pm 9 बजे के बाद	after 10 pm 10 बजे के बाद	after 11 pm 11 बजे के बाद	After midnight मध्य रात्रि के बाद	Always feel safe हमेशा सुरक्षित महसूस करेंगे
1	2	3	4	5	6	7

D10 How much of a problem do you think crime is in your local area
आपके स्थानीय क्षेत्र में अपराध आपको कितनी बड़ी समस्या लगती है

Big problem बड़ी समस्या	Somewhat of a problem but not very big कुछ हद तक समस्या लेकिन बड़ी समस्या नहीं	Not much of a problem बहुत समस्या नहीं	Don't know मालूम नहीं
1	2	3	4

12

Commonwealth Human Rights Initiative
New Delhi, India. London, UK. Accra, Ghana
NGO in Special Consultative Status with the Economic & Social Council of the United Nations

D11 What in your opinion is the single most prevalent crime in your residential area? आपकी राय में आपके आवासीय क्षेत्र में एक सबसे प्रचलित अपराध कौन सा है?	(write here In detail) (यहाँ विस्तार से लिखें)

D12   Which of the following crimes do you fear you are likely to be a victim of? **MULTIPLE RESPONSES ALLOWED**
निम्नलिखित अपराधों में से किससे आपके शिकार होने की संभावना का डर आपको होता है? **एक से अधिक जवाब की अनुमति**

Theftचोरी	Assaultहमला	Un-natural death अप्राकृतिक मृत्यु	Sexual crimeयौन अपराध	Criminal intimidation अपराधिक धमकी
1	2	3	4	5

D13 Do you know where your nearest police chowki or police station is? क्या आपको मालूम है कि आपका नजदीकी पुलिस चौकी या पुलिस स्टेशन कहाँ है?	1= Yesहाँ	2=Noनहीं

D14 How would you rate your local police?
अपने स्थानीय पुलिस को आप कैसे आंकलन/रेट करेंगे?

1=Very Positive बहुत सकारात्मक	2=Positive सकारात्मक	3=I don't have an opinion मेरी कोई राय नहीं है	4=Negative नकारात्मक	5=Very Negative बहुत नकारात्मक

D15 How safe do you feel your neighbourhood is?
आपको अपना पड़ोस कितना सुरक्षित लगता है?

1=Very safe बहुत सुरक्षित	2=Safe सुरक्षित	3=Moderate सामान्य	4=Unsafe असुरक्षित	5=Very unsafe बहुत असुरक्षित

13

References

Common Cause and Lokniti – Centre for the Study of Developing Societies. (2018). *Status of policing in India report 2018: A study of performance and oerceptions*. https://commoncause. in/pdf/SPIR2018.pdf

Commonwealth Human Rights Initiative and Association for Advocacy and Legal Initiatives. (2020). *Police registration of sexual offences: A guide on procedures and holding police accountable.* https://www.humanrightsinitiative.org/download/1610003834Police%20 Registration%20of%20Sexual%20Offences%20English.pdf

Operation Shistachar: In 20 days, 370 arrested, 2400 detained for harassing women, The Indian Express: http://indianexpress.com/article/cities/delhi/operation-shishtachar-in-20-days-370-arrested-2400-detained-for-harassing-women. Express News Service, New Delhi, August 31, 2015.

Hoffmeye-Zlotnik, J. H. P. (2003). *New sampling designs and the quality of data*. http://mrvar.fdv. uni-lj.si/pub/mz/mz19/hoff.pdf

Ministry of Statistics and Programme Implementation. (2015). *National sample survey 71st round "key indicators of social consumption: Health"*. http://mospi.nic.in/sites/default/files/national_ data_bank/ndb-rpts-71.htm

Murphy, P. (2008). An overview of primary sampling units (PSUs) in multi stage samples of demographic surveys. *Proceedings of the Survey Research Methods Section, American Statistical Association*.

National Crime Records Bureau, Ministry of Home Affairs. (2014). *Crime in India: 2014*. https:// ncrb.gov.in/en/crime-india-year-2014

National Research Council. (2014). *Estimating the incidence of rape and sexual assault*. The National Academies Press. https://doi.org/10.17226/18605

Turner, A. G., & United Nations Secretariat Statistics Division. (2003). *Sampling strategies*. http:// unstats.un.org/unsd/demographic/meetings/egm/Sampling_1203/docs/no_2.pdf

Chapter 3
Safety Trends and Reporting of Crime (SATARC): A Crime Victimisation Survey

Neha Sinha and Avanti Durani

1 Introduction

IDFC Institute conducted a survey of 20,597 households titled Safety Trends and Reporting of Crime (SATARC). The survey asked respondents whether they, or in certain cases a member of their household, had been a victim of seven crimes—theft, assault, house break-in, harassment, criminal intimidation, unnatural death, and missing person–in the past year (October 2015 to September 2016), their experiences with the police, their perceptions of safety, and about the behavioural changes they may have adopted to avoid victimisation. The survey was conducted between November 2016 and February 2017 across four major cities—Mumbai, Delhi, Bengaluru, and Chennai. This chapter covers the research objective, methodology including sample design, survey instrument, and execution framework, key findings from the survey, and learnings for the way forward.

The SATARC survey was an attempt to marshal evidence about the extent and nature of crime, satisfaction with the police, and perceptions of safety to bridge the gap in public data on crime, law enforcement, and safety. The objective of the survey was to systematically assess households' perception of safety and the police,

Neha Sinha was the former Deputy Director and an Associate Fellow and Avanti Durani was the former Assistant Director and a Junior Fellow at IDFC Institute, a Mumbai based think/do tank. The team which carried out this survey consisted of Avanti Durani, Neha Sinha, Dr. Renuka Sane and Rithika Kumar. The authors also thank Sridhar Ganapathy, former Senior Associate at IDFC Institute, for his able research assistance.

N. Sinha · A. Durani (✉)
Artha Global, Mumbai, Maharashtra, India
e-mail: neha.sinha@artha.global; avanti.durani@artha.global

identify behavioural changes adopted by households to keep themselves safe, evaluate people's opinion of police, and estimate the incidence of certain personal and household crimes.

The SATARC survey serves as an illustration of what can be achieved at the national level. Data from such surveys can potentially complement official crime records by evaluating people's attitude towards the police and courts, assessing the impact of crime on quality of life, and identifying crimes that are not reported to the police. The data can be used for recognising those most vulnerable to crime and devising strategies to build enough safeguards to protect them. In effect, this can be a critical tool to elevate the quality of life and economic participation of those marginalised by crime. The importance of a crime victimisation survey (CVS) cannot be emphasised enough for an emerging economy like India. Plugging this gap in public data is an important step for rule of law.

2 Sampling and Survey Methodology

Sample Design

The survey was conducted in four major metropolitan centres—Mumbai, Delhi, Bengaluru, and Chennai. These urban agglomerations were selected based on the criteria that they are thriving centres of economic activity and livelihood creation, which makes them ideal for assessing the impact of crime and safety on citizens. Each city was divided into its already existing police zones—the police administrative regions within the police Commissionerate boundaries. Assuming a level of confidence at 95% and margin of error at 5%, the sample size for each police zone was estimated as 384. To safeguard against non-response, a buffer of 15% was added which took the minimum sample size to 450 per zone.

Sample size computation:

$$n = \text{Deff} \times \frac{z^2 \times (p) \times (1-p)}{d^2}$$

where:

n: sample size
Deff: Design effect was assumed to be 1 in the absence of many layers of stratification
z: statistic of 1.96 for the level of confidence at 95%
p: Assumed at 50%
d: Margin of error at 5%

In addition, 90 purposive interviews for victims of the surveyed crimes were done in each zone to allow for population-level estimates of crime incidence and victim's experience with police. The total sample size including the purposive

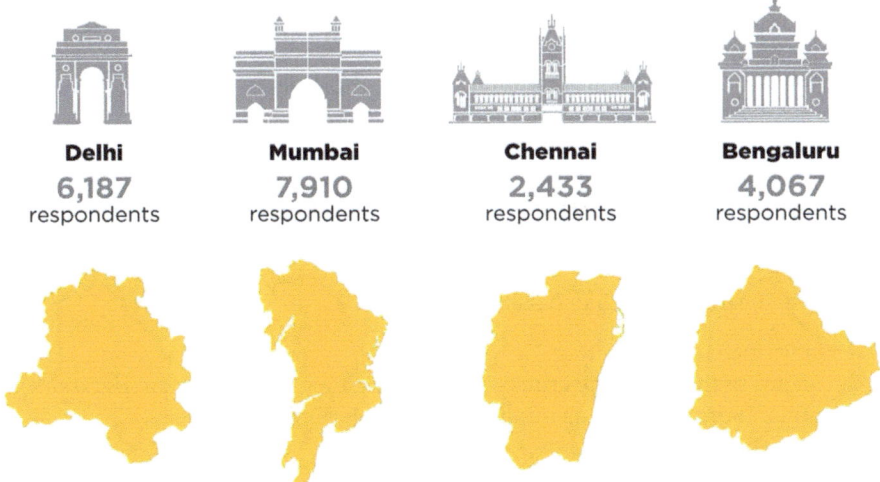

Delhi	Mumbai	Chennai	Bengaluru
6,187	**7,910**	**2,433**	**4,067**
respondents	respondents	respondents	respondents

Note: This includes the total number of randomly and purposively sampled respondents in each city.

Source: SATARC Survey, IDFC Institute, 2017

Fig. 3.1 Sample size of each of the surveyed cities

interviews across the four cities came up to 20,597. The sample size for each city is shown below (Fig. 3.1).

Sample selection was done using stratified random sampling to achieve the age and gender distribution of each city's adult[1] population. Quotas for the age-gender distribution were determined using the population data as per the Government of India's Census Data for 2011. In the absence of population data at the police zone level, it was assumed to be evenly distributed across the zones within each city.

The survey ensured randomisation at two levels: selection of a household and selection of a respondent within the household. Landmarks were chosen within each zone to ensure sufficient geographic spread and a "right-hand rule" was applied to survey 20–25 households near each landmark. At least 3 households were skipped between two surveyed households. The randomly surveyed sample was self-weighted against the age-gender distribution of the adult population. The weights used for estimating results were calculated using the following formula:

$$fw = w1 / w2$$

where:

fw: final weights
*w*1: desired sample per gender for a given age bracket/desired total sample for the city

---

[1] 18 years and above.

*w*2: achieved random sample per gender for a given age bracket/achieved total sample for the city

Population estimations were done for details on crime incidence, opinion about police, and public perception about safety.

Survey Instrument

The survey instrument included the following:

1. Demographic details
2. Incidence of the following crimes—Theft, Assault, House break-in, Harassment, Criminal Intimidation, Unnatural Death and Missing Person
3. Details of crime incidence
4. Reporting of the incident to the police
5. Opinions about police
6. Perceptions of safety

The survey was administered in either English, Hindi, Kannada, or Tamil. The English survey instrument is provided in the Annexure.

Definition of Crimes

The seven surveyed crimes were divided into two categories: Personal crimes, i.e. those committed against the individual (theft, assault, harassment, and criminal intimidation) and Household crimes, i.e. those committed against the entire household (house break-in, unnatural death and missing person). In order to achieve accuracy in responses, questions on personal crimes were asked only if the selected respondent was a victim. The definitions used to describe these crimes were based on the relevant sections of the Indian Penal Code, 1860. Simplified versions of these definitions were conveyed to the respondents with the help of showcards. Descriptions of the surveyed crimes are below:

1. Theft

    (a) Someone dishonestly took any of your movable property without your permission (express or implied).
    (b) Someone stole an item from you.

2. Assault

    (a) Someone used force or made any gesture to use force on you, without your consent, in order to commit an offence or cause injury, fear or annoyance.
    (b) Someone used force or violence against you/attacked you.

3. Harassment

   (a) You were victim of any of the following form of sexual harassment:

      Physical contact and advances involving unwelcome and explicit sexual overtures
      Lewd or unwelcome comments
      A demand or request for sexual favours
      Stalked/followed you
      Indecently exposed themselves to you
      Making sexually coloured remarks

   (b) Someone harassed you in the following ways:

      Physical contact and advances involving unwelcome and explicit sexual overtures,
      Lewd or unwelcome comments,
      A demand or request for sexual favours,
      Stalked/followed you,
      Indecently exposed themselves to you
      Making sexually coloured remarks

4. Criminal intimidation

   (a) You were threatened against injury to your body, reputation or property, or to the body or reputation of anyone in your household, with the intent to cause alarm to you or to cause you to do any act which you are not legally bound to do, or to stop you from doing any act which you are legally entitled to do, as the means of avoiding the execution of such threat.

   (b) Someone threatened to hurt you or a member of your household, or damage your property, to try and make you do something or stop you from doing something, to fulfil their demands.

5. House break-in

   (a) A person entered your property/dwelling with the intent to commit an offence or to intimidate, insult or annoy any person in possession of such property/dwelling, by entering into or remaining or quitting the house or any part of it.

   (b) Someone entered your house without your permission and may have tried to commit a crime.

6. Unnatural Death

   (a) A person in your household passed away due to reasons other than natural causes, including sickness, ill health, disease, etc. The deceased person may have died due to an unnatural reason such as, culpable homicide, murder, or accidental death; however, it does not include suicide.

(b) A person in your household was murdered or died in an accident. Please don't include cases where death occurred due to natural causes like sickness, ill health, disease.

7. Missing Person

(a) The whereabouts of your household member is not known, and is not traceable. No information regarding such person whether dead or alive is available.
(b) You have no knowledge of the whereabouts of a household member.

Outline of the Survey

At the outset, after taking consent from the respondent, the survey captured information on the locality, police zone, nearest police station, and type of dwelling of the respondent. Thereafter, the first section was on *demographic details of the household*. This included information on the age and gender of the household members, based on which a respondent was selected according to the age and gender quota assigned for that day. Detailed information on employment, education, marital status, religion, language, and length of stay in the city and current address was recorded. The demographic details of the sample are elaborated below and continued in the Annexure.

The respondent was then asked if he/she, or in certain cases a household member, has been a victim of any of the seven crimes in the past year. The following section on *details of crime incidence* was administered only if the respondent or household member, as required, was a victim of at least one of the surveyed crimes. The section captured details of the crime such as nature of the crime, place and time of the crime, familiarity with the offender, reporting of the crime to the police, amongst other details. As a follow up, the respondents were asked about their experience of *reporting the crime to the police*, only if the crime was reported. This section was only administered to the victim, or the household member, who approached the police to report the crime in order to ensure the accuracy of information about the experience. The section captured information on how they approached the police, the initial action taken by the police, the experience of reporting the crime, and reasons for satisfaction or dissatisfaction at the stage of reporting the crime. The survey did not ask about the police's response beyond registration of the crime or survey police personnel. Separately, for those who did not report the crime, we asked them the reasons for not approaching the police.

The next section was on *opinions about the police*. All respondents, independent of them having faced a crime, were asked about their views on the police. This included questions on whether police can be relied on, if the police are doing a good job of maintaining safety in their area, and so on. The final section was on *safety perceptions* where we asked the respondents several questions to gauge their views on safety in their area. We asked the respondents if they worried about household members being outside their homes after dark, or were worried about walking alone in the area, took precautions to keep themselves safe, their views on the severity of the crime in their area, amongst several other questions.

Survey Execution

Training

Experienced interviewers, who had worked previously on social surveys and were familiar with the data collection methods, were selected for the training. Intensive and immersive training sessions were conducted for the fieldworkers and supervisors, before the survey was administered in the field. The field workers were apprised of the purpose of the survey, sensitivity of the subject, and trained on data collection and administration of the survey instrument. The final cohort of trainers were selected based on their performance in mock interviews. Nearly half of the selected surveyors were women.

Ethics Review and Consent

Following international best practices, before going into field work, we sought approval from an independent ethics review board/institutional review board (IRB) to ensure that procedures followed during the survey adequately protected the rights of the respondents. Their consent was taken at the time of administering each individual survey and they were made aware of the social and ethical concerns related to the survey, their right of refusal, and confidentiality of their personal data to ensure that they participated willingly.

Administration and Data Collection

The survey was conducted simultaneously across the four cities between November 2016 and February 2017. The respondents were asked questions on each of the seven crimes that they were victims of, for the period of October 2015 to September 2016, and their experience while reporting the crime to the police. The survey administration for data collection, conducted by Kantar Public, happened over three stages: pilots (administering the survey to a select number of households), fieldwork, and audits/backchecks. Robustness and quality of the collected data was ensured through the backchecks and audits.

Prior to rolling out the survey, we conducted pilot interviews in all four cities to test the questionnaire and survey administration process and make any improvements, if necessary. This was an important step since the learnings from this stage were incorporated into the instrument and the final data collection process to make them more robust.

3   Key Findings

Summary Statistics of the Random Sample

This section describes the demographic characteristics of the respondents across cities. The sample was drawn in proportion with the size of the population in each city. The data presented here includes information about the randomly surveyed sample only. Of the sample, 38% were from Mumbai, followed by 30% from Delhi. The remaining 20% and 12% were residents of Bengaluru and Chennai (Table 3.1).

The sample was representative of the adult population by age and gender distribution. In the case of Delhi and Mumbai, males in the sample accounted for 53% and 54% of the population. In Chennai and Bengaluru, males constituted 50% and 52%. The remaining sample included women in each city, making the sample nearly equidistributed between male and female respondents (Table 3.2).

The bulk of the sample in each city was in the age group of 21–40 years. In all the four cities, this band constituted 50–60% of the sample. This was followed by the age band of 41–50 years, with 15–18% of the sample across the four cities. The mean age of the sample lies between 37 and 40 years (Table 3.3).

Table 3.1 Distribution of sample by city (%)

Delhi	Mumbai	Chennai	Bengaluru
30	38	12	20

Source: SATARC Survey, IDFC Institute, 2017

Table 3.2 Gender distribution by city (%)

Gender	Delhi	Mumbai	Chennai	Bengaluru
Male	53	54	50	52
Female	47	46	50	48

Source: SATARC Survey, IDFC Institute, 2017

Table 3.3 Age distribution by city (%)

Age	Delhi	Mumbai	Chennai	Bengaluru
18–20	10	9	7	8
21–30	31	30	27	33
31–40	24	23	24	25
41–50	17	17	18	15
51–60	10	11	12	10
61–70	6	6	7	6
70+	3	4	4	3

Source: SATARC Survey, IDFC Institute, 2017

Crime Incidence

The survey data allowed us to estimate the overall crime incidence for each crime in each city. Theft was the most prevalent of the surveyed crimes across the four cities. In Delhi, 8.26% of people reported being a victim of a theft. The proportions were 4.14% in Mumbai and 2% in both Chennai and Bengaluru. The results and population level estimates are presented below (Table 3.4).

Table 3.4 Crime incidence

Crime	City	Sample size (n)	Victims at sample level (n)	Victimisation (%) at population level	Victims at population level (n)
Theft	Delhi	5164	424	8.26	13,87,428
	Mumbai	6604	273	4.14	5,13,422
	Chennai	2010	40	2.00	94,005
	Bengaluru	3415	69	1.98	1,90,186
Assault	Delhi	5164	54	1.04	1,74,266
	Mumbai	6604	34	0.52	65,075
	Chennai	2010	4	0.21	9,644
	Bengaluru	3415	0	0.00	0
Harassment	Delhi	5164	60	1.15	1,92,377
	Mumbai	6604	27	0.39	48,682
	Chennai	2010	5	0.25	11,623
	Bengaluru	3415	12	0.33	31,354
House break-in	Delhi	5164	53	1.01	1,70,318
	Mumbai	6604	36	0.52	64,331
	Chennai	2010	5	0.27	12,751
	Bengaluru	3415	2	0.04	4,253
Criminal intimidation	Delhi	5164	14	0.27	45,646
	Mumbai	6604	17	0.26	31,657
	Chennai	2010	1	0.04	1,777
	Bengaluru	3415	1	0.03	3,264
Unnatural death	Delhi	5164	8	0.15	25,183
	Mumbai	6604	4	0.06	7,440
	Chennai	2010	0	0.00	0
	Bengaluru	3415	0	0.00	0
Missing person	Delhi	5164	4	0.08	12,986
	Mumbai	6604	0	0.00	0
	Chennai	2010	0	0.00	0
	Bengaluru	3415	0	0.00	0
Other	Delhi	5164	3	0.06	9,862
	Mumbai	6604	0	0.00	0
	Chennai	2010	2	0.09	4,094
	Bengaluru	3415	6	0.19	18,336

Source: SATARC Survey, IDFC Institute, 2017

Underreporting of Crime: Survey Results in Comparison to Official Records

In order to understand the relationship between crime incidence as reported in the survey and official records, we looked at the number of respondents who mentioned that they faced a crime (theft), who subsequently approached the police to report this, and finally managed to file a First Information Report (FIR). The FIRs are what ultimately reflect in official crime statistics published by the National Crime Records Bureau (NCRB, 2016). This analysis helped highlight the level of underreporting that occurs for crimes, particularly theft in this case. The results presented here are at the population level.

According to the survey, 13.9 lakh people were victims of theft in Delhi. Of these, 6.18 lakhs approached the police to report the crime but only 99,239 were successful in registering their case. In terms of proportion of the population, a higher proportion of victims approached the police to report the incident in Mumbai (32%) and Delhi (45%), compared to Bengaluru (18%) and Chennai (20%). However, after approaching the police, a higher proportion managed to file an FIR in Bengaluru (40%) and Chennai (41%), than in Mumbai (18%) and Delhi (16%) (Fig. 3.2).

Below is a comparison of the data from SATARC Survey with theft reported in 2016 as per NCRB's Crime in India report (Table 3.5):

In effect, only 6–8% of victims of theft lodged an FIR with the police in the four cities. It is this fraction of cases that are finally reflected in official records, leaving the remaining 92–94% unreported. As police performance is based primarily on crime statistics, suppressed crime rates are an incomplete measure of the delivery of law and order and safety (Table 3.6).

Based on data from the survey, it is clear that the true rate of crime is high compared to official records. A low official crime rate may not necessarily mean a "lack of crime" instead, it points to a more serious problem, both for the citizens and for the police. A low crime rate masks the extent of the problem at the ground level, which may result in lower resource allocation for the police. This in turn may impact their capacity to deliver sound law and order to the people. Correct diagnosis of the issues, through improved estimation of crime, can better prepare the police as a public institution. A CVS gives the police a better understanding of crime and helps bridge the gap in public data benefitting both the people and the police.

Reporting to and Satisfaction with Police

The results presented in this section pertain to theft only and are at the sample level.

To begin with, respondents who had been a victim of theft were asked to recall which item had been stolen. The most common item across all the cities was mobile phones (44% in Mumbai, 42% in Delhi, 36% in Bengaluru, and 35% in Chennai).

There is massive under-reporting of theft

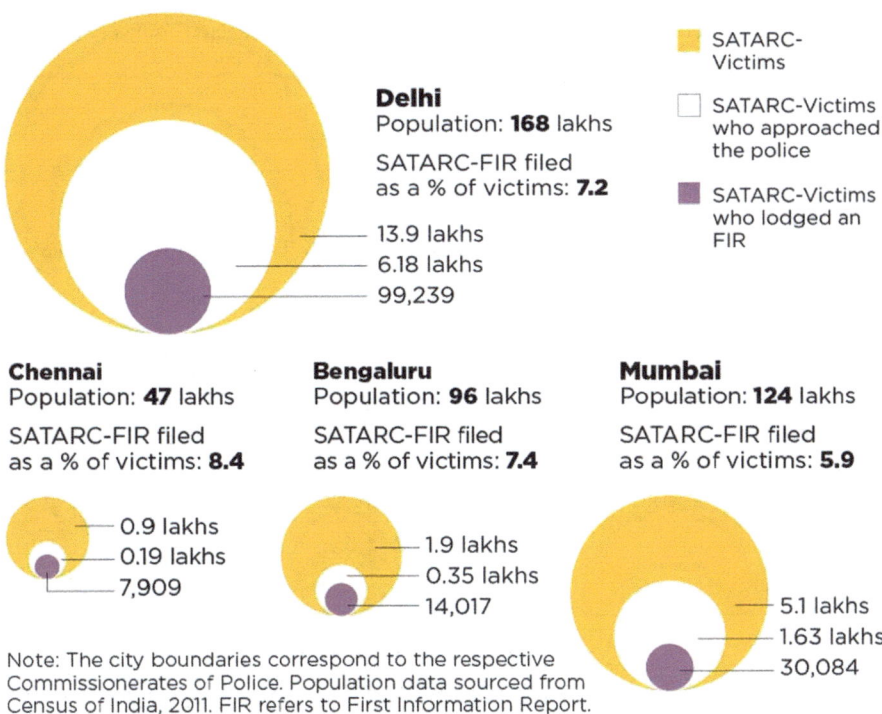

Delhi
Population: **168** lakhs

SATARC-FIR filed
as a % of victims: **7.2**

— 13.9 lakhs
— 6.18 lakhs
— 99,239

■ SATARC-
Victims

□ SATARC-Victims
who approached
the police

■ SATARC-Victims
who lodged an
FIR

Chennai
Population: **47** lakhs

SATARC-FIR filed
as a % of victims: **8.4**

— 0.9 lakhs
— 0.19 lakhs
— 7,909

Bengaluru
Population: **96** lakhs

SATARC-FIR filed
as a % of victims: **7.4**

— 1.9 lakhs
— 0.35 lakhs
— 14,017

Mumbai
Population: **124** lakhs

SATARC-FIR filed
as a % of victims: **5.9**

— 5.1 lakhs
— 1.63 lakhs
— 30,084

Note: The city boundaries correspond to the respective
Commissionerates of Police. Population data sourced from
Census of India, 2011. FIR refers to First Information Report.
The numbers indicate victims who approached/registered an FIR by themselves or
through a household member.

Note: The results are presented at the population level.

Source: SATARC Survey, IDFC Institute, 2017

Fig. 3.2 Magnitude of under-reporting of thefts crimes in the surveyed cities

Table 3.5 Comparison of theft crimes using results from the SATARC Survey (2016–17) and
NCRB Crime in India Report (2016)

City	Theft victims who lodged an FIR (SATARC) (*n*)	Theft cases reported in 2016 (NCRB)[a] (*n*)
Delhi	99,239	1,26,467
Mumbai	30,084	9,839
Chennai	7,909	3,070
Bengaluru	14,017	10,578

Source: SATARC Survey, IDFC Institute, 2017
Note: The results are presented at the population level
[a]https://ncrb.gov.in/sites/default/files/Crime%20in%20India%20-%202016%20Complete%20
PDF%20291117.pdf

Table 3.6 Magnitude of underreporting of theft crimes

City	Theft victims at population level (SATARC) (n)	Theft cases reported in 2016 (NCRB)[a] (n)	Magnitude of underreporting of theft crimes
Delhi	13,87,428	1,26,467	11×
Mumbai	5,13,422	9,839	52×
Chennai	94,005	3,070	31×
Bengaluru	1,90,186	10,578	18×

Source: SATARC Survey, IDFC Institute, 2017
[a]https://ncrb.gov.in/sites/default/files/Crime%20in%20India%20-%202016%20Complete%20PDF%20291117.pdf

Table 3.7 Which items were stolen? (theft) (%)

	Delhi	Mumbai	Chennai	Bengaluru
Luggage	15	10	4	7
Wallet/purse	16	18	16	14
Credit/debit card	2	3	2	4
Jewellery you were wearing/carrying	3	5	8	9
Mobile	42	44	35	36
Laptop	1	1	4	1
Cash	14	12	10	24
Car	3	1	1	1
Other	5	6	21	3

Source: SATARC Survey, IDFC Institute, 2017

This was followed by wallet/purse in Mumbai (18%) and Delhi (16%), and cash in Bengaluru (24%) (Table 3.7).

Subsequently, they were asked where the incident occurred. The most common response from the victims was in a public bus in Bengaluru (33%), Delhi (25%), and Chennai (24%). In Mumbai the most common response was in their home with break-in (23%). This was followed by in open areas/on the street/train station in Bengaluru (23%) and Mumbai (19%), in their home without break-in Chennai (22%), and in their home with break-in in Delhi (21%) (Table 3.8).

When asked what time of day the incident occurred, unfortunately, a large portion of the respondents could not recall the time across all four cities (69–82%). From those who were able to, their responses were 12 pm–12 am in Delhi (7%), 12 pm–6 pm in Mumbai (8%) and Chennai (12%), and 6 pm–12 am in Bengaluru (14%) (Table 3.9).

Of those who did approach the police to report the theft incident, we asked them which mode of communication they used to initially contact the police. The top response from the respondents across all four cities was by going to the police station (78% in Mumbai, 74% in Chennai, 73% in Delhi, and 72% in Bengaluru). The next most common response was also the same across all the four cities—called 100 or any other relevant police helpline (16% in Delhi, 12% in Chennai and Bengaluru, and 8% in Mumbai) (Table 3.10).

Table 3.8 In which place did the incident occur? (theft) (%)

Place	Delhi	Mumbai	Chennai	Bengaluru
In open areas/on the street/train station	20	19	14	23
In a public bus	25	6	24	33
Your home with break-in	21	23	9	2
Your home without break-in	8	13	22	7
Commercial place (mall/theatre/restaurant/grocery store/ market)	7	8	7	18
In the metro/local train	7	17	4	4
Your workplace	8	5	8	6
Family/friend's home	0	2	9	2
In an auto/cab	1	2	1	1
Other	2	6	2	5

Source: SATARC Survey, IDFC Institute, 2017

Table 3.9 What time of the day did the incident occur? (theft) (%)

Time	Delhi	Mumbai	Chennai	Bengaluru
6 am–12 pm	2	4	2	4
12 pm–6 pm	7	8	12	9
6 pm–12 am	7	4	6	14
12 am–6 am	2	3	2	5
Don't know	82	81	78	69

Source: SATARC Survey, IDFC Institute, 2017

Table 3.10 What mode of communication did you use to report the incident to the police? (theft) (%)

Mode	Delhi	Mumbai	Chennai	Bengaluru
Went to the police station	73	78	74	72
Called 100 or any other relevant police helpline	16	8	12	12
Online complaint reporting	5	7	7	6
Approached a police control room (PCR) van	4	5	6	5
Other	2	3	1	5

Source: SATARC Survey, IDFC Institute, 2017

The respondents were then asked to recall the initial action taken by the police when the incident was reported to them. The most common answer across the four cities was that the police filed a complaint—63% in Delhi, 60% in Mumbai, 46% in Bengaluru, and 41% in Chennai. In Bengaluru and Chennai, 25% and 21% of the respondents, respectively, managed to register an FIR[2] while in Mumbai and Delhi, the proportions were lower at 13% and 12%, respectively (Table 3.11).

---

[2] Section 378 of the IPC defines "theft" and section 379 of the IPC provides for punishment for theft. As per the latter, the offence is "cognisable" meaning a police officer can arrest without warrant. It is also non-bailable.

Table 3.11 What was the initial action taken by the police when the incident was reported to them? (theft) (%)

Action	Delhi	Mumbai	Chennai	Bengaluru
Filed a complaint	63	60	41	46
Registered a first information report (FIR)	12	13	21	25
Dispatched a PCR van	6	5	6	2
Did not entertain your complaint because the case was not under that police stations jurisdiction	3	4	6	4
Took the wounded persons, if any, for medical assistance	2	4	2	3
Directed you to the police station you should go to	3	7	7	6
Reached the spot where you called from and made inquiries	4	4	13	7
Did not do anything	6	1	4	5
Other	0	1	0	2

Source: SATARC Survey, IDFC Institute, 2017

Table 3.12 Reasons for satisfaction for theft victims (%)

Reason	Delhi	Mumbai	Chennai	Bengaluru
They registered my complaint with accuracy	41	50	45	83
They listened attentively	75	55	79	89
They explained their future course of action	21	23	44	33
They registered my complaint promptly	35	41	58	32
They took action quickly	14	17	39	18
They arrived in time	10	17	38	29
Other	2	3	0	8

Source: SATARC Survey, IDFC Institute, 2017

The survey then asked victims who approached the police if they were satisfied with their experience of reporting to the police. More than half of them were satisfied with the police's response at the time of reporting the crime in Delhi (52%) and Mumbai (55%). The proportions were higher in Chennai (82%) and Bengaluru (70%). The respondents had to then select from a predetermined list of responses the reasons for satisfaction and dissatisfaction with the police response. This was a multiple-choice question.

The main reason for satisfaction was the police's attentiveness in dealing with the victim. This was followed by accuracy in registering the complaint, promptness in attending to the victim, and quick and timely action (Table 3.12).

Dissatisfaction was primarily due to the long wait in registering the FIR, refusal in registering the FIR, or the police dissuading the victim from registering an FIR (Table 3.13).

Soft skills emerge as the key to satisfaction. Given that the police are the first interface with the criminal justice system, data on the reasons for satisfaction and dissatisfaction can be useful inputs in developing training and sensitisation programmes for the police.

Table 3.13 Reasons for dissatisfaction for theft victims (%)

Reason	Delhi	Mumbai	Chennai	Bengaluru
They were arrogant and ill-mannered	12	14	6	19
They pinned the blame on me and tried to dissuade me from registering an FIR	9	16	31	16
I required external influence to register the FIR	8	5	19	19
They asked us/me to pay an amount	10	6	25	13
The PCR van took over an hour to arrive at the spot from where I called	15	8	13	22
They refused to register my FIR and asked me to leave	8	16	25	38
They made me wait without any reason and took a long time to register my FIR	33	49	31	41
They did not assist the wounded persons	11	3	19	25
Other	36	19	0	6

Source: SATARC Survey, IDFC Institute, 2017

Table 3.14 Reasons for not approaching the police for theft victims (%)

Reason	Delhi	Mumbai	Chennai	Bengaluru
Afraid to go to the police station	8	12	28	21
Took help from another agency/person to resolve issue	1	5	2	8
Didn't know the helpline number	2	4	12	10
Lack of evidence	19	21	51	31
Did not want to report family matters	6	10	13	20
Felt that the police will not entertain the complaint	30	21	19	18
Didn't think it was serious	21	35	16	33
Did not think the police will be able to do anything about the case	19	19	18	15
Other reasons	4	14	2	8
Didn't know where to go	21	10	19	17
Fear of retaliation	4	6	6	16
Did not want to get stuck in police/court matters	19	20	14	35

Source: SATARC Survey, IDFC Institute, 2017

Notably, a large number of victims did not approach the police. According to the survey, 55% of victims in Delhi, 68% in Mumbai, almost 80% and 82% in Chennai and Bengaluru did not approach the police to register the crime. The respondents had to then select from a predetermined list of reasons for not approaching the police. Some of the top reasons why people refrain from approaching the police ranged from the belief that the police will not entertain the complaint or lack of evidence, no expectation of response from the police or fear of getting stuck in police and court matters.

This was a multiple-choice question. The results presented here pertain to theft only and are presented at the sample level (Table 3.14).

Opinion on Police

As with any public service, it is important to gauge public opinion about the police. Opinion about the police is an important parameter towards building a people's police. Public opinion gauged through a systematic survey can be used as input towards confidence building measures. It can be used to build mutual trust such that the police machinery is able to derive legitimacy from its own people—a principle strongly recommended for modern policing globally. Respondents were asked to express how much they agree or disagree with a statement about police on a Likert Scale. Overall, people agreed most with the statement that the police can be relied upon when needed (75–91% across all four cities) and agreed least with the statement that the police are underpaid and overworked (28–53% across all four cities). The results presented here indicate the proportion that agreed with the statement, estimated at the population level (Table 3.15).

When these questions are looked at through the lens of age, gender, and victim of the surveyed crimes versus non-victim, there were interesting observations. The results for age and gender are estimated at the population level. The results for victim versus non-victim are presented at the sample level.

Statement: The police can be relied on when needed

When asked whether the police can be relied on when needed, in Delhi, the proportion that agreed with this statement the most were between 18 and 20 years (79%). In Mumbai, those between 41–50 years and 70+ years agreed with this the most (88%). In Chennai (96%) and Bengaluru (100%), those above the age of 70 years, agreed with this statement the most (Table 3.16).

In Delhi (77%) and Bengaluru (84%), men agreed with this statement more than women. The reverse was seen in Chennai (92%). In Mumbai the proportions were the same (85%) (Table 3.17).

In all four cities, the non-victim respondents agreed with this statement more than respondents who had been a victim of any of the surveyed crimes (Delhi 75%, Mumbai 86%, Chennai 91%, and Bengaluru 81%). This seems to indicate that the opinion about whether the police can be relied on when needed may decrease once they interact with them (Table 3.18).

Table 3.15 Opinion on police (%)

Statement	Delhi	Mumbai	Chennai	Bengaluru
Police presence in a secluded area makes you feel safe	63	80	76	64
Police can be relied on when needed	75	85	91	81
Police will treat you respectfully when you reach out to them	59	71	77	47
Police are doing a good job at maintaining a safe environment in the city	59	76	80	64
Police are underpaid and overworked	28	53	46	46
The police in your locality understand the issues that impact the community	57	69	80	58

Source: SATARC Survey, IDFC Institute, 2017

Table 3.16 Opinion by age (%)

Age (years)	Delhi				Chennai				Bengaluru				Mumbai			
	Agree	Disagree	Neither agree nor disagree	Don't know	Agree	Disagree	Neither agree nor disagree	Don't know	Agree	Disagree	Neither agree nor disagree	Don't know	Agree	Disagree	Neither agree nor disagree	Don't know
18–20	79	10	10	1	94	2	2	3	85	11	3	1	86	6	6	2
21–30	74	12	13	1	93	3	2	2	81	15	3	2	84	7	7	2
31–40	75	12	11	2	89	4	4	4	81	14	3	2	84	9	5	2
41–50	75	10	13	2	88	3	3	6	78	16	5	2	88	7	4	1
51–60	74	12	12	2	91	4	3	2	77	15	4	4	87	7	5	2
61–70	70	13	15	2	91	4	2	2	83	15	1	1	85	8	5	2
70+	74	10	15	1	96	4	–	–	100	–	–	–	88	4	4	4

Source: SATARC Survey, IDFC Institute, 2017

Table 3.17 Opinion by gender (%)

	Delhi		Chennai		Bengaluru		Mumbai	
Gender	Male	Female	Male	Female	Male	Female	Male	Female
Agree	77	72	90	92	84	79	85	85
Disagree	11	12	4	3	13	15	8	7
Neither agree nor disagree	11	14	2	3	3	4	6	5
Don't know	1	2	4	2	1	3	2	2

Source: SATARC Survey, IDFC Institute, 2017

Table 3.18 Opinion by victim versus non-victim (%) (sample level)

	Delhi		Chennai		Bengaluru		Mumbai	
	Victim	Non-victim	Victim	Non-victim	Victim	Non-victim	Victim	Non-victim
Agree	70	75	71	91	65	81	75	86
Disagree	17	10	15	3	29	14	15	7
Neither agree nor disagree	13	12	8	3	4	3	8	5
Don't know	1	2	6	3	2	2	2	2

Source: SATARC Survey, IDFC Institute, 2017

Statement: The police are underpaid and overworked

When asked whether they thought the police are underpaid and overworked, those that agreed with this statement the most were 70+ years in Delhi (38%) and Mumbai (57%), 21–30 years in Chennai (53%), and 61–70 years in Bengaluru (56%) (Table 3.19).

In Mumbai (54%), Bengaluru (48%), and Chennai (47%), men agreed with this statement more than women. In Delhi, the proportions were the same (28%) (Table 3.20).

In Bengaluru (50%), Chennai (44%), and Delhi (29%), the victim respondents agreed with this statement more than respondents who had not been a victim of any of the surveyed crimes. In Mumbai, non-victim respondents (54%) agreed with this statement more than the surveyed victims. This may indicate that those who interact with the police to report their crime may be able to witness the workload and working conditions of the police during their interaction, which may lead them to have a more favourable opinion of the police in this regard (Table 3.21).

Statement: The police in your locality understand the issues that impact the community

When asked whether they thought the police in their locality understand the issues that impact the community, those that agreed with this statement the most were 70+ years in Delhi (62%), Mumbai (76%), and Bengaluru (71%), and 21–30 years in Chennai (87%) (Table 3.22).

In Mumbai (69%), Bengaluru (62%), and Delhi (60%), men agreed with this statement more than women. In Chennai, women (82%) agreed more with this statement than men (Table 3.23).

Table 3.19 Opinion by age (%)

Age (years)	Delhi				Chennai				Bengaluru				Mumbai			
	Agree	Disagree	Neither agree nor disagree	Don't know	Agree	Disagree	Neither agree nor disagree	Don't know	Agree	Disagree	Neither agree nor disagree	Don't know	Agree	Disagree	Neither agree nor disagree	Don't know
18–20	33	40	16	11	46	16	15	23	42	32	18	8	55	27	10	8
21–30	28	41	16	15	53	15	12	20	46	30	16	7	51	30	9	9
31–40	27	41	17	15	43	21	16	20	47	31	14	7	52	31	10	8
41–50	26	41	18	15	43	22	14	21	46	30	17	7	56	30	8	6
51–60	26	40	20	15	42	25	15	18	45	28	19	7	53	28	10	9
61–70	32	34	16	18	40	19	16	25	56	21	14	9	56	26	9	10
70+	38	30	23	9	49	11	21	19	35	18	10	37	57	23	8	12

Source: SATARC Survey, IDFC Institute, 2017

Table 3.20 Opinion by gender (%)

Gender	Delhi		Chennai		Bengaluru		Mumbai	
	Male	Female	Male	Female	Male	Female	Male	Female
Agree	28	28	47	45	48	44	54	52
Disagree	39	41	20	18	30	29	30	28
Neither agree nor disagree	18	16	13	17	15	17	9	10
Don't know	15	14	21	21	8	9	7	10

Source: SATARC Survey, IDFC Institute, 2017

Table 3.21 Opinion by victim versus non-victim (%) (sample level)

	Delhi		Chennai		Bengaluru		Mumbai	
	Victim	Non-victim	Victim	Non-victim	Victim	Non-victim	Victim	Non-victim
Agree	29	28	44	45	50	46	40	54
Disagree	45	40	21	19	21	30	31	29
Neither agree nor disagree	17	17	15	15	22	16	17	9
Don't know	9	15	19	21	7	8	12	8

Source: SATARC Survey, IDFC Institute, 2017

In all four cities, the non-victim respondents agreed with this statement more than respondents who had been a victim of any of the surveyed crimes (Delhi 58%, Mumbai 70%, Chennai 80%, and Bengaluru 58%). This seems to indicate that the opinion about whether the police in their locality understand the issues that impact the community may decrease once they interact with them (Table 3.24).

Statement: The police will treat you respectfully when you reach out to them
When asked whether the police will treat you respectfully when you reach out to them, in Delhi, those between 51 and 70 years (62%) agreed with the statement the most. And those above 61 years in Mumbai (75%), and 70+ years in Chennai (86%) and Bengaluru (62%) agreed with the statement the most. This indicates that senior and elderly citizens have an amicable relationship with the police (Table 3.25).

In Delhi (61%) and Bengaluru (47%), men agreed with this statement more than women. In Chennai, women (78%) agreed with this statement more than men. In Mumbai the proportions were the same (71%) (Table 3.26).

In all four cities, the non-victim respondents agreed with this statement more than respondents who had been a victim of any of the surveyed crimes (Delhi 59%, Mumbai 72%, Chennai 77%, and Bengaluru 46%). This seems to indicate that the opinion about whether the police will treat you respectfully when they reach out to them may decrease once they interact with them (Table 3.27).

Statement: The police are doing a good job at maintaining a safe environment in the city
When asked whether the police are doing a good job at maintaining a safe environment in the city, those who were above the age of 70 years in Delhi (63%), Mumbai

Table 3.22 Opinion by age (%)

Age (years)	Delhi				Chennai				Bengaluru				Mumbai			
	Agree	Disagree	Neither agree nor disagree	Don't know	Agree	Disagree	Neither agree nor disagree	Don't know	Agree	Disagree	Neither agree nor disagree	Don't know	Agree	Disagree	Neither agree nor disagree	Don't know
18–20	61	21	12	7	81	5	10	3	58	21	14	7	70	16	10	4
21–30	57	20	13	9	87	6	4	2	58	24	12	6	67	17	11	5
31–40	58	20	15	7	78	9	9	4	59	23	11	6	67	18	11	4
41–50	55	23	14	8	74	10	8	8	55	25	13	7	70	16	10	4
51–60	57	22	14	8	77	9	10	5	56	22	11	11	69	17	9	5
61–70	60	22	11	7	77	9	10	4	59	21	9	11	71	15	9	5
70+	62	21	13	5	85	6	8	2	71	13	2	13	76	8	9	7

Source: SATARC Survey, IDFC Institute, 2017

Table 3.23 Opinion by gender (%)

	Delhi		Chennai		Bengaluru		Mumbai	
Gender	Male	Female	Male	Female	Male	Female	Male	Female
Agree	60	55	79	82	62	54	69	68
Disagree	20	22	9	7	22	24	17	15
Neither agree nor disagree	14	13	7	9	10	13	10	11
Don't know	6	10	5	3	6	9	4	6

Source: SATARC Survey, IDFC Institute, 2017

Table 3.24 Opinion by victim versus non-victim (%) (sample level)

	Delhi		Chennai		Bengaluru		Mumbai	
	Victim	Non-victim	Victim	Non-victim	Victim	Non-victim	Victim	Non-victim
Agree	55	58	71	80	52	58	51	70
Disagree	24	21	17	8	32	23	24	16
Neither agree nor disagree	16	13	6	8	11	12	19	10
Don't know	4	9	6	4	5	7	6	5

Source: SATARC Survey, IDFC Institute, 2017

(85%), and Chennai (89%) agreed with this statement the most. In Bengaluru, those between 61 and 70 years (73%) agreed with this statement the most. Once again, senior and elderly citizens seem to have a higher degree of trust in the police's ability to maintain a safe environment in the city (Table 3.28).

In Delhi (61%) and Bengaluru (68%), the proportion of men that agreed with this statement was higher than the proportion of women. In Mumbai (77%) and Chennai (82%), women agreed with this statement more than men (Table 3.29).

In all four cities, the non-victim respondents agreed with this statement more than the respondents who had been a victim of any of the surveyed crimes (Delhi 59%, Mumbai 78%, Chennai 80%, and Bengaluru 63%). This seems to indicate that the opinion about whether the police are doing a good job at maintaining a safe environment in the city may decrease once they face a crime or interact with the police (Table 3.30).

Statement: Police presence in a secluded area makes you feel safe
When asked whether police presence in a secluded area makes them feel safe, in Mumbai (87%) and Chennai (89%), those above the age of 70 years agreed with this statement the most. In Bengaluru, those between 61 and 70 years agreed with this statement the most (75%). In Delhi, those that agreed with this statement the most were between 51 and 70 years (65%). This seems to indicate that elderly people and senior citizens welcome the presence of police in secluded areas to give them a sense of security (Table 3.31).

In Delhi (66%) and Bengaluru (65%), the proportion of men who agreed with this statement was higher than the proportion of women. In Mumbai (82%) and Chennai (77%), women agreed with this statement more than men (Table 3.32).

Table 3.25 Opinion by age (%)

Age (years)	Delhi				Chennai				Bengaluru				Mumbai			
	Agree	Disagree	Neither agree nor disagree	Don't know	Agree	Disagree	Neither agree nor disagree	Don't know	Agree	Disagree	Neither agree nor disagree	Don't know	Agree	Disagree	Neither agree nor disagree	Don't know
18-20	61	26	9	4	75	5	11	8	43	30	17	10	70	14	12	4
21-30	57	23	14	6	84	6	7	3	47	29	14	10	70	14	12	4
31-40	58	26	11	5	73	9	12	5	45	28	16	11	69	15	12	4
41-50	60	23	11	6	74	8	11	8	47	26	17	10	73	13	9	4
51-60	62	22	10	6	71	7	19	4	43	27	15	14	69	13	11	6
61-70	62	17	14	7	73	8	18	1	55	20	14	11	75	11	10	4
70+	60	18	12	10	86	6	9	–	62	15	2	21	75	6	11	8

Source: SATARC Survey, IDFC Institute, 2017

Table 3.26 Opinion by gender (%)

	Delhi		Chennai		Bengaluru		Mumbai	
Gender	Male	Female	Male	Female	Male	Female	Male	Female
Agree	61	57	75	78	47	46	71	71
Disagree	22	25	9	5	28	26	15	11
Neither agree nor disagree	12	11	11	13	15	15	11	11
Don't know	5	7	5	4	9	13	3	6

Source: SATARC Survey, IDFC Institute, 2017

Table 3.27 Opinion by victim versus non-victim (%) (sample level)

	Delhi		Chennai		Bengaluru		Mumbai	
	Victim	Non-victim	Victim	Non-victim	Victim	Non-victim	Victim	Non-victim
Agree	55	59	67	77	46	46	49	72
Disagree	31	23	10	7	23	28	20	13
Neither agree nor disagree	10	12	17	12	21	15	25	20
Don't know	4	6	6	4	10	11	6	5

Source: SATARC Survey, IDFC Institute, 2017

In all four cities, the non-victim respondents agreed with this statement more than the respondents who had been a victim of any of the surveyed crimes (63% in Delhi, 82% in Mumbai, 76% in Chennai, and 64% in Bengaluru). This seems to indicate that the opinion about whether presence in a secluded area makes you feel safe may decrease once they interact with them or face a crime (Table 3.33).

The survey also asked respondents about their comfort in approaching a male or female officer to report an issue. In Delhi, the proportion of people who were more comfortable approaching a male officer (36%), female officer (30%) or indifferent (34%), were approximately evenly divided. In Mumbai (69%) and Chennai (55%), most people were indifferent towards the gender of the officer. In Bengaluru, most felt comfortable approaching a male officer (51%) as compared to a female officer (8%) (Table 3.34).

When analysed by age, similar results are seen in Delhi with the proportions almost evenly split across all age ranges. In Mumbai, those between 21-30 years and 51–60 years feel most comfortable approaching a male officer (21% each), those between 18 and 20 years feel most comfortable approaching a female officer (15%), and those above 70 years are most indifferent (83%). In Chennai, those above 70 years (45%) feel most comfortable approaching a male officer, those between 18 and 20 years (17%) feel more comfortable approaching a female officer, and those between 61 and 70 years are most indifferent (62%). In Bengaluru, the youngest (18–30 years) and oldest (70+ years) are most comfortable approaching a male officer (53%) as compared to the others, those between 51 and 60 years are most comfortable approaching a female officer (10%) and those between 61 and 70 years are most indifferent (48%) (Table 3.35).

Table 3.28 Opinion by age (%)

Age (years)	Delhi				Chennai				Bengaluru				Mumbai			
	Agree	Disagree	Neither agree nor disagree	Don't know	Agree	Disagree	Neither agree nor disagree	Don't know	Agree	Disagree	Neither agree nor disagree	Don't know	Agree	Disagree	Neither agree nor disagree	Don't know
18–20	62	24	10	4	86	3	8	3	60	21	10	9	77	12	8	2
21–30	58	22	15	5	86	6	5	3	63	23	9	5	76	12	9	3
31–40	59	23	13	6	77	9	10	4	64	20	10	6	75	13	9	3
41–50	58	23	14	5	72	10	12	6	62	23	9	5	78	13	7	2
51–60	60	23	13	5	74	10	13	4	63	18	11	8	73	16	9	3
61–70	61	23	14	3	79	7	10	4	73	18	5	3	79	11	7	4
70+	63	20	15	2	89	4	8	–	66	–	13	21	85	7	6	2

Source: SATARC Survey, IDFC Institute, 2017

Table 3.29 Opinion by gender (%)

	Delhi		Chennai		Bengaluru		Mumbai	
Gender	Male	Female	Male	Female	Male	Female	Male	Female
Agree	61	57	77	82	68	59	76	77
Disagree	22	23	9	6	20	22	13	12
Neither agree nor disagree	14	12	8	10	8	11	8	8
Don't know	3	7	5	3	5	8	2	3

Source: SATARC Survey, IDFC Institute, 2017

Table 3.30 Opinion by victim versus non-victim (%) (sample level)

	Delhi		Chennai		Bengaluru		Mumbai	
	Victim	Non-victim	Victim	Non-victim	Victim	Non-victim	Victim	Non-victim
Agree	55	59	65	80	62	63	49	78
Disagree	30	22	13	7	22	21	23	12
Neither agree nor disagree	11	14	17	9	13	10	22	7
Don't know	4	5	4	4	2	6	6	3

Source: SATARC Survey, IDFC Institute, 2017

In Delhi, the majority of men (58%) are more comfortable approaching a male officer and the majority of women are comfortable approaching a female officer (59%). In Mumbai, while the majority are indifferent, there is a preference for men (26%) and women (21%) to approach officers of their same gender. In Bengaluru and Chennai, men (54% and 45%, respectively) and women (48% and 24%, respectively) feel more comfortable approaching male officers (Table 3.36).

At the sample level, when analysed by victims versus non-victims of the surveyed crimes, the proportions were once again almost evenly divided in Delhi and most respondents were indifferent in Mumbai and Chennai. In Bengaluru, while 50% of the respondent victims were indifferent, 43% felt more comfortable approaching a male officer. Among the non-victim respondents, the majority (51%) felt more comfortable approaching a male officer (Table 3.37).

There is often a preference among people for approaching a male officer as they feel he may be better suited for solving their problems as policing is perceived to be a more physical profession.[3] Going forward, if such questions are disaggregated by type of crime, police task, or some other criteria, public perceptions of female officers can also be tracked over time, along with any shifting trends therein. Such results can be useful inputs to build confidence in the public towards women officers.

---

[3] CSDS (2018).

Table 3.31 Opinion by age (%)

Age (years)	Delhi				Chennai				Bengaluru				Mumbai			
	Agree	Disagree	Neither agree nor disagree	Don't know	Agree	Disagree	Neither agree nor disagree	Don't know	Agree	Disagree	Neither agree nor disagree	Don't know	Agree	Disagree	Neither agree nor disagree	Don't know
18–20	63	23	12	2	83	5	7	5	58	23	11	7	81	10	6	2
21–30	61	22	15	3	83	7	6	3	62	21	12	4	81	10	6	2
31–40	63	23	11	2	70	11	12	7	67	20	10	3	79	12	6	3
41–50	63	21	13	3	70	9	12	9	64	20	11	4	80	13	5	2
51–60	65	20	12	3	69	8	13	9	62	22	9	7	77	13	8	2
61–70	65	22	10	2	78	7	8	7	75	16	4	4	79	11	7	4
70+	64	23	12	1	89	2	9	–	67	10	10	13	87	5	6	3

Source: SATARC Survey, IDFC Institute, 2017

Table 3.32 Opinion by gender (%)

	Delhi		Chennai		Bengaluru		Mumbai	
Gender	Male	Female	Male	Female	Male	Female	Male	Female
Agree	66	60	75	77	65	63	79	82
Disagree	20	24	9	7	21	19	13	9
Neither agree nor disagree	12	13	10	10	11	11	6	7
Don't know	2	3	7	6	3	7	2	3

Source: SATARC Survey, IDFC Institute, 2017

Table 3.33 Opinion by victim versus non-victim (%) (sample level)

	Delhi		Chennai		Bengaluru		Mumbai	
	Victim	Non-victim	Victim	Non-victim	Victim	Non-victim	Victim	Non-victim
Agree	62	63	67	76	63	64	55	82
Disagree	27	21	12	8	16	21	21	11
Neither agree nor disagree	9	13	17	10	20	11	19	6
Don't know	3	2	4	6	1	5	5	2

Source: SATARC Survey, IDFC Institute, 2017

Table 3.34 When reporting a complaint/crime, would you be more comfortable approaching a male or female officer? (%)

	Delhi	Mumbai	Chennai	Bengaluru
Male officer	36	20	35	51
Female officer	30	12	10	8
Indifferent	34	69	55	41

Source: SATARC Survey, IDFC Institute, 2017

Safety Perceptions and Adaptive Behaviours

Our understanding of safety perceptions is limited since it is primarily informed by anecdotal evidence rather than data. These are important parameters not captured by any official records. The survey asked respondents about their perceptions of safety and behavioural adaptations as a result of these perceptions. The idea behind assessing perceptions and attitudinal data is to see how abstract concepts can be quantified for policy analysis and track how societies adapt and shift behaviours with improvement or deterioration in their sense of security.

We used three ways to gauge a person's perception of safety. First, we directly asked respondents whether they felt crime is a serious problem in their area, whether they thought that the crime levels in their local area had gone up, down, or stayed the same over the last few years, and the sources for their impression about crime in their city. We present the data on perceptions by city, age, and gender for these questions.

Table 3.35 Opinion by age (%)

Age	Delhi			Mumbai			Chennai			Bengaluru		
	Male officer	Female officer	Indifferent	Male officer	Female officer	Indifferent	Male officer	Female officer	Indifferent	Male officer	Female officer	Indifferent
18–20	38	31	31	19	15	66	33	17	50	53	7	40
21–30	37	29	35	21	11	68	30	13	57	53	7	40
31–40	36	32	33	20	11	69	38	10	52	51	7	42
41–50	35	30	35	20	13	67	33	10	57	52	9	39
51–60	38	28	35	21	10	69	39	6	55	45	10	45
61–70	36	31	33	15	11	74	36	2	62	45	7	48
70+	35	28	37	8	8	83	45	6	49	53	2	45

Source: SATARC Survey, IDFC Institute, 2017

Table 3.36 Opinion by gender (%)

	Delhi		Mumbai		Chennai		Bengaluru	
Gender	Male	Female	Male	Female	Male	Female	Male	Female
Male officer	58	11	26	12	45	24	54	48
Female officer	5	59	4	21	3	17	4	12
Indifferent	37	30	70	67	52	58	43	40

Source: SATARC Survey, IDFC Institute, 2017

Table 3.37 Opinion by victim versus non-victim (%) (sample level)

	Delhi		Mumbai		Chennai		Bengaluru	
	Victim	Non-victim	Victim	Non-victim	Victim	Non-victim	Victim	Non-victim
Male officer	33	36	18	19	25	33	43	51
Female officer	30	30	8	13	13	11	7	8
Indifferent	37	33	74	68	62	55	50	41

Source: SATARC Survey, IDFC Institute, 2017

Table 3.38 Perception by city (%)

Perception	Delhi	Mumbai	Chennai	Bengaluru
Serious problem	51	16	5	21
Somewhat of a problem but not very big	24	26	8	29
Not much of a problem	20	46	76	41
Don't know	5	13	11	8

Source: SATARC Survey, IDFC Institute, 2017

Question: How serious is the problem of crime in your area?
About half the population in Delhi (51%) perceived crime to be a serious problem. A much smaller percentage of the population in Bengaluru (21%) and Mumbai (16%) viewed crime to be a serious problem. As per the survey, a small percentage of the population (6%) viewed crime to be a serious problem in Chennai. In fact, about 76% of the population perceived crime as not much of a problem in Chennai (Table 3.38; Fig. 3.3).

Amongst the age groups, the population in the youngest age group of 18–20 years felt crime was a serious problem in Delhi. In Chennai, Mumbai, and Bengaluru, those in the same group felt it was not much of a problem (Table 3.39).

Almost half of males and females felt that crime was a serious problem in Delhi. In the case of Chennai, almost three fourths of males and females felt that it was not much of a problem. In Bengaluru and Mumbai, large proportions of males and females were of the same opinion and did not feel crime was much of a problem (Table 3.40).

Question: Do you think that crime levels in your local area have gone up, down, or stayed the same over the last few years?
We then asked people if they thought that crime levels in their local area had gone up, down, or stayed the same over the last few years. In Delhi, 46% thought that crime had gone up in the last few years, whereas 42% in Chennai and 39% in

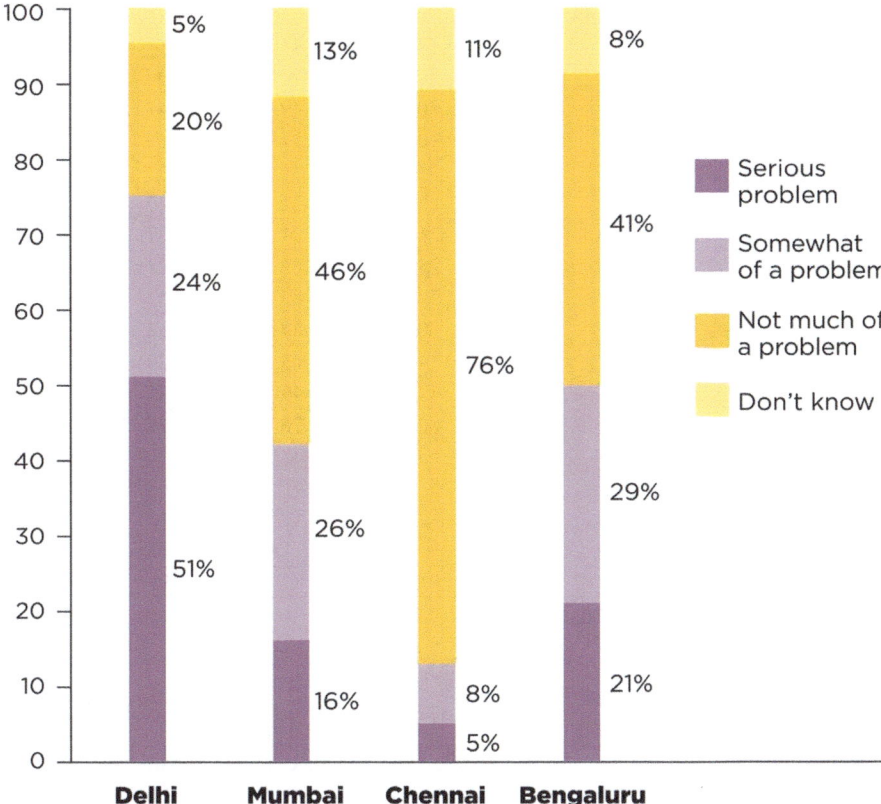

Note: The results are presented at the population level. Perceptions are presented by city as a percentage

Source: SATARC Survey, IDFC Institute, 2017

Fig. 3.3 How serious is the problem of crime in your area?

Mumbai thought it had gone down. 42% in Bengaluru thought that crime levels had stayed the same (Table 3.41).

Over half of those in the youngest age group in Delhi felt that crime had gone up in their area. Data from Chennai showed the opposite. 62% in the age group of 18–20 years in Chennai felt that crime had come down in their area. In Mumbai, 43% of people in the age group of 41–50 years felt that crime levels had come down. In Bengaluru, almost half in the age group of 61–70 years felt that crime levels had stayed the same (Table 3.42). Men and women shared similar perceptions about crime levels, across all the surveyed cities (Table 3.43).

Question: What are sources for your impression about crime in your city?

Following this, we tried to assess the sources from which people form an impression about crime in their city. This was a multiple-choice question. In Delhi (74%), Chennai (86%), and Bengaluru (75%), television programmes were the top sources from where people formed their impression about crime in their city. In Mumbai,

Table 3.39 Perception by age (%)

	City	18–20	21–30	31–40	41–50	51–60	61–70	70+
Serious problem	Delhi	60	51	49	49	47	48	52
	Mumbai	16	15	17	16	16	17	17
	Chennai	5	3	4	4	3	7	12
	Bengaluru	18	21	21	24	20	16	30
Somewhat of a problem but not very big	Delhi	21	24	24	26	27	26	14
	Mumbai	25	27	25	26	27	28	20
	Chennai	7	10	8	8	5	8	2
	Bengaluru	30	28	29	28	32	30	41
Not much of a problem	Delhi	14	19	23	20	20	21	29
	Mumbai	47	46	46	47	45	42	45
	Chennai	80	80	76	74	77	69	71
	Bengaluru	43	41	42	43	40	48	20
Don't know	Delhi	5	7	4	4	6	5	5
	Mumbai	12	13	12	12	13	13	18
	Chennai	8	7	12	14	15	15	15
	Bengaluru	8	10	7	6	9	6	10

Source: SATARC Survey, IDFC Institute, 2017

Table 3.40 Perception by gender (%)

	Delhi		Chennai		Bengaluru		Mumbai	
Gender	Male	Female	Male	Female	Male	Female	Male	Female
Serious problem	50	51	4	5	20	22	16	15
Somewhat of a problem but not very big	25	23	7	9	30	29	27	24
Not much of a problem	20	20	76	76	43	39	45	47
Don't know	5	6	12	10	7	10	12	14

Source: SATARC Survey, IDFC Institute, 2017

Table 3.41 Perceptions by city (%)

Perception	Delhi	Mumbai	Chennai	Bengaluru
Up	46	14	5	20
Down	17	39	42	27
Stayed the same	29	30	38	42
Don't know	8	18	14	11

Source: SATARC Survey, IDFC Institute, 2017

Table 3.42 Perceptions by age (%)

	City	18–20	21–30	31–40	41–50	51–60	61–70	70+
Up	Delhi	54	45	45	45	46	47	48
	Mumbai	14	13	14	13	13	15	14
	Chennai	7	3	5	6	5	10	8
	Bengaluru	23	20	18	21	21	18	16
Down	Delhi	13	16	17	19	20	14	16
	Mumbai	37	37	39	43	37	39	43
	Chennai	62	40	43	42	40	40	32
	Bengaluru	33	28	26	27	22	25	30
Stayed the same	Delhi	26	29	31	30	25	31	29
	Mumbai	31	30	30	27	32	29	23
	Chennai	25	45	36	33	38	36	47
	Bengaluru	34	39	45	43	44	50	41
Don't know	Delhi	8	10	7	6	9	8	8
	Mumbai	18	20	17	16	18	17	21
	Chennai	7	11	16	19	17	14	13
	Bengaluru	10	13	11	9	13	7	13

Source: SATARC Survey, IDFC Institute, 2017

Table 3.43 Perceptions by gender (%)

	Delhi		Chennai		Bengaluru		Mumbai	
Gender	Male	Female	Male	Female	Male	Female	Male	Female
Up	46	46	5	6	19	20	14	13
Down	18	15	44	41	28	27	40	38
Stayed the same	29	29	35	41	43	41	30	30
Don't know	7	9	16	12	10	12	16	20

Source: SATARC Survey, IDFC Institute, 2017

most people formed their impression from word of mouth (71%). The second most cited source of information was word of mouth in Delhi (72%), newspaper in Chennai (80%) and Bengaluru (66%), and newspaper and television programmes in Mumbai (both at 64%) (Table 3.44).

Television programmes, newspapers, word of mouth and relatives'/friends' experiences were the top sources of information on crime across age groups in the four cities. Personal experience was amongst the top sources of information across age groups in Delhi (Table 3.45).

Television programmes and word of mouth were the top sources of information about crime for males and females across the four cities (Table 3.46).

Second, we asked about people's worries about taking certain actions.

Table 3.44 Perception by city (%)

Source	Delhi	Mumbai	Chennai	Bengaluru
Personal experience	58	36	37	35
Relatives'/friends' experience	61	47	63	63
Newspaper	51	64	80	66
Television programmes	74	64	86	75
Radio	14	13	20	30
Internet	19	17	13	17
Information from police	10	27	27	25
Information from resident associations	35	32	34	15
Word of mouth	72	71	59	65
Other	5	5	0	5

Source: SATARC Survey, IDFC Institute, 2017

Question: After what time do you start worrying about the safety of a female member of your household who may be outside home unaccompanied?

The survey found that post 9 pm, 87% of people in Delhi started worrying about a female household member who was outside the home unaccompanied. The percentages were lower in Bengaluru (54%), Chennai (48%), and Mumbai (30%). By 11 pm, about 97% of the population in Delhi, 89% in Bengaluru, 90% in Chennai, and 76% in Mumbai were worried if a female household member was outside home alone (Table 3.47; Fig. 3.4).

Breaking it further down, we found that all age groups were equally concerned about a female member being outside the home unaccompanied after 8 pm in Delhi, after 10 pm in Mumbai and Chennai (Table 3.48).

Both men and women seemed equally worried about the female household member being outside home unaccompanied after evening (Table 3.49).

Question: After what time do you start worrying about the safety of a male member of your household who may be outside home unaccompanied?

Concerns about safety extended to men as well. By 11 pm, 95% of people in Delhi started worrying about a male household member who was outside home unaccompanied, followed by Bengaluru (83%), Chennai (84%), and Mumbai (60%) (Table 3.50; Fig. 3.5).

Breaking the time bands further, in Delhi, Bengaluru, and Chennai, people across age groups were most concerned about a male member being outside home unaccompanied after 10 pm. In Mumbai, most people across age groups were worried about safety after 11 pm (Table 3.51).

Almost 51% of females in Chennai were worried about a male member being outside home unaccompanied after 10 pm. There was an appreciable increase in worry across cities and gender after 10 pm vis-a-vis 9 pm (Table 3.52).

We asked respondents whether they felt safe walking in their own neighbourhood during the day or night, in their own homes during the same time frame.

Table 3.45 Perception by age (%)

	City	18–20	21–30	31–40	41–50	51–60	61–70	70+
Personal experience	Delhi	61	57	55	58	58	60	67
	Mumbai	34	37	38	36	37	34	28
	Chennai	33	37	39	40	31	43	21
	Bengaluru	29	32	36	38	36	42	57
Relatives'/friends' experience	Delhi	56	59	61	64	64	65	63
	Mumbai	44	50	47	47	49	43	38
	Chennai	64	59	64	68	64	65	61
	Bengaluru	65	61	62	63	66	62	70
Newspaper	Delhi	54	52	51	49	51	44	45
	Mumbai	67	65	66	65	63	57	54
	Chennai	82	77	84	84	83	75	67
	Bengaluru	69	67	67	68	59	59	74
Television programmes	Delhi	74	74	74	74	75	71	72
	Mumbai	68	65	63	64	62	59	64
	Chennai	92	85	86	87	86	85	81
	Bengaluru	78	74	74	76	74	79	80
Radio	Delhi	12	15	14	14	15	12	14
	Mumbai	14	13	14	11	11	9	10
	Chennai	17	14	25	25	17	23	11
	Bengaluru	28	27	28	31	33	37	52
Internet	Delhi	28	24	18	15	13	10	11
	Mumbai	30	23	17	12	8	8	8
	Chennai	21	10	15	14	11	12	8
	Bengaluru	19	17	16	18	16	23	15
Information from police	Delhi	11	10	12	11	8	10	10
	Mumbai	26	27	28	28	26	25	22
	Chennai	29	23	29	28	25	39	18
	Bengaluru	25	23	26	26	28	23	22
Information from resident associations	Delhi	36	34	34	36	38	36	35
	Mumbai	33	31	33	31	31	31	29
	Chennai	28	28	35	37	37	51	32
	Bengaluru	16	12	15	19	17	16	15
Word of mouth	Delhi	71	73	71	73	74	74	69
	Mumbai	72	69	71	71	72	73	73
	Chennai	59	57	59	63	56	67	40
	Bengaluru	68	63	65	62	70	73	62
Other	Delhi	5	5	5	3	5	3	5
	Mumbai	4	5	5	4	6	5	5
	Chennai	–	0	1	0	–	–	2
	Bengaluru	7	5	5	6	5	6	7

Source: SATARC Survey, IDFC Institute, 2017

Table 3.46 Perception by gender (%)

Gender	Delhi		Chennai		Bengaluru		Mumbai	
	Male	Female	Male	Female	Male	Female	Male	Female
Personal experience	59	56	36	38	33	38	38	34
Relatives'/friends' experience	62	59	60	67	62	64	48	47
Newspaper	54	47	80	80	67	65	66	62
Television programmes	74	74	85	86	74	77	62	66
Radio	15	13	22	17	27	33	12	13
Internet	22	16	15	11	14	21	20	14
Information from police	12	9	25	28	25	25	27	27
Information from resident associations	36	34	34	35	14	16	32	31
Word of mouth	74	71	53	64	66	64	71	71
Other	4	5	1	0	6	5	5	4

Source: SATARC Survey, IDFC Institute, 2017

Table 3.47 Perception by city (%)

Time	Delhi	Mumbai	Chennai	Bengaluru
By 7 pm	23	4	6	16
By 9 pm	87	30	48	54
By 11 pm	97	76	90	89
Always safe	1	13	8	8

Source: SATARC Survey, IDFC Institute, 2017

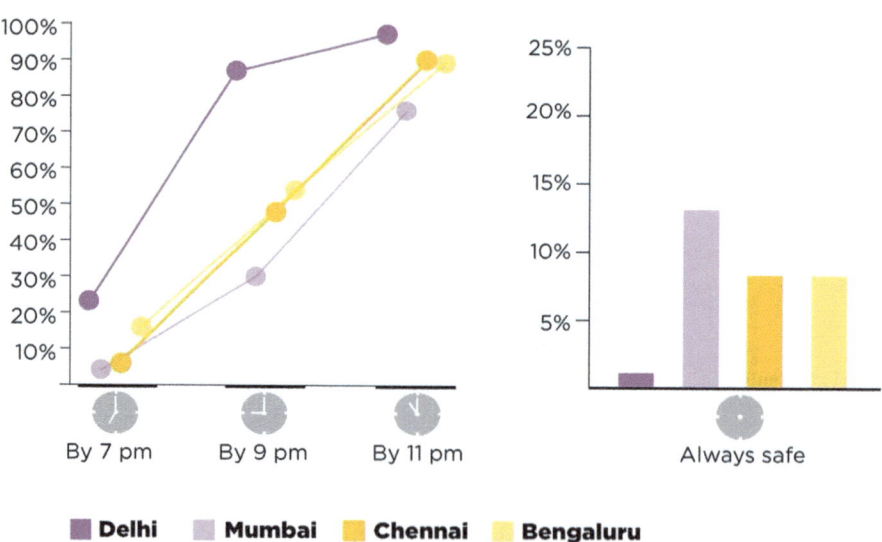

Note: *The results are presented at the population level. Perceptions are presented by city as a percentage.*

Source: SATARC Survey, IDFC Institute, 2017

Fig. 3.4 After what time do you start worrying about the safety of a female member of your household who may be outside home unaccompanied?

Table 3.48 Perception by age (%)

	City	18–20	21–30	31–40	41–50	51–60	61–70	70+
After 7 pm	Delhi	23	22	23	25	24	24	19
	Mumbai	2	3	3	3	5	6	3
	Chennai	3	7	5	7	6	2	4
	Bengaluru	19	18	17	15	15	10	2
After 8 pm	Delhi	34	38	37	35	33	34	46
	Mumbai	12	11	11	10	8	8	9
	Chennai	12	12	14	17	17	20	9
	Bengaluru	22	20	19	18	16	20	29
After 9 pm	Delhi	31	29	25	26	29	30	23
	Mumbai	18	17	16	13	15	14	18
	Chennai	31	27	28	28	27	25	28
	Bengaluru	17	20	20	19	18	18	8
After 10 pm	Delhi	7	7	9	7	8	5	6
	Mumbai	24	23	24	24	25	24	20
	Chennai	37	37	38	33	33	44	49
	Bengaluru	16	18	17	18	24	24	19
After 11 pm	Delhi	2	2	2	2	3	3	4
	Mumbai	21	23	21	25	22	21	24
	Chennai	4	5	6	6	5	3	4
	Bengaluru	16	15	17	15	18	21	27
After midnight	Delhi	1	1	2	3	2	2	2
	Mumbai	14	13	11	11	12	10	7
	Chennai	1	2	2	1	2	–	–
	Bengaluru	4	3	3	4	2	1	6
Always feel safe	Delhi	1	1	1	1	1	2	–
	Mumbai	9	10	13	14	14	17	19
	Chennai	11	10	7	8	10	6	6
	Bengaluru	5	7	9	11	6	6	10

Source: SATARC Survey, IDFC Institute, 2017

Table 3.49 Perception by gender (%)

	Delhi		Chennai		Bengaluru		Mumbai	
Gender	Male	Female	Male	Female	Male	Female	Male	Female
After 7 pm	23	23	5	6	17	15	4	4
After 8 pm	34	39	14	15	20	18	11	9
After 9 pm	29	26	29	27	19	19	16	16
After 10 pm	7	8	35	39	18	19	22	25
After 11 pm	3	2	6	4	15	18	21	24
After midnight	2	2	1	2	3	4	12	12
Always feel safe	1	1	9	8	8	7	14	10

Source: SATARC Survey, IDFC Institute, 2017

Table 3.50 Perception by city (%)

Time	Delhi	Mumbai	Chennai	Bengaluru
By 7 pm	2	1	0.4	5
By 9 pm	40	11	22	31
By 11 pm	95	60	84	83
Always safe	1	20	12	13

Source: SATARC Survey, IDFC Institute, 2017

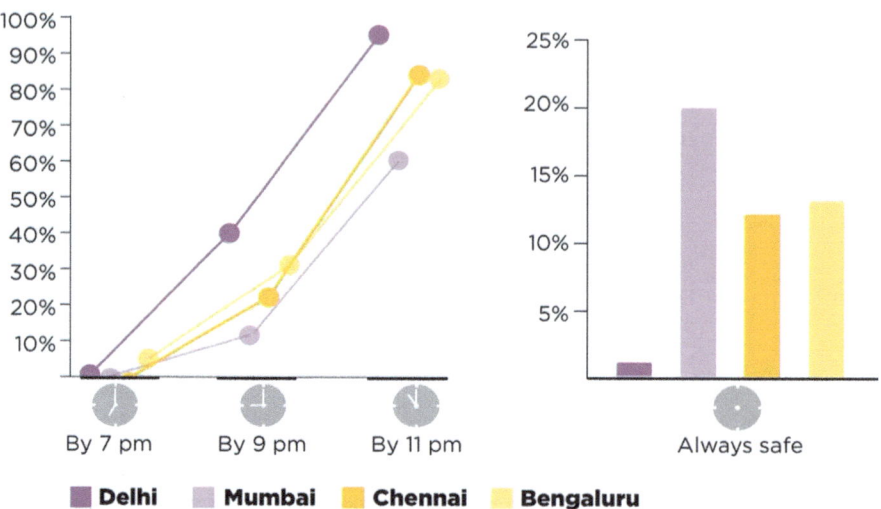

Note: The results are presented at the population level. Perceptions are presented by city as a percentage.

Source: SATARC Survey, IDFC Institute, 2017

Fig. 3.5 After what time do you start worrying about the safety of a male member of your household who may be outside home unaccompanied?

Question: After what time in the evening would you worry about safety while walking alone in your neighbourhood?

In Delhi, by 9 pm, 63% of people mentioned that they started worrying about their safety while walking alone in their own neighbourhood. The corresponding numbers were 41% in Bengaluru, 23% in Chennai, and 14% in Mumbai. By 11 pm, 94% in Delhi were worried about their safety while walking alone in their neighbourhood, followed by 84% in Bengaluru, 81% in Chennai, and 60% in Mumbai. When asked whether they always felt safe, i.e. did not worry at any point of time, the figures were 23% in Mumbai, 16% in Chennai, 12% in Bengaluru, and only 3% in Delhi (Table 3.53).

Looking at the data by age group for each city, we found that people across age groups were worried about walking alone in the neighbourhood from 8 pm onwards

Table 3.51 Perception by age (%)

	City	18–20	21–30	31–40	41–50	51–60	61–70	70+
After 7 pm	Delhi	2	3	1	2	2	1	1
	Mumbai	2	1	2	1	1	2	2
	Chennai	–	0	1	–	1	–	–
	Bengaluru	3	6	6	4	8	2	–
After 8 pm	Delhi	14	15	12	13	12	14	13
	Mumbai	4	4	4	4	3	3	4
	Chennai	3	5	3	3	3	3	4
	Bengaluru	9	9	8	9	9	6	8
After 9 pm	Delhi	26	24	23	24	26	25	26
	Mumbai	7	6	7	6	7	6	6
	Chennai	19	17	18	21	15	18	11
	Bengaluru	22	19	18	17	11	15	15
After 10 pm	Delhi	35	33	38	35	34	34	31
	Mumbai	19	17	19	20	19	18	20
	Chennai	42	46	49	43	48	51	56
	Bengaluru	31	33	30	29	26	25	13
After 11 pm	Delhi	20	20	21	20	19	20	25
	Mumbai	29	32	30	28	30	25	28
	Chennai	16	14	15	18	16	14	14
	Bengaluru	19	20	22	21	25	28	33
After midnight	Delhi	3	3	3	4	4	3	3
	Mumbai	22	22	20	18	19	20	13
	Chennai	2	4	4	4	4	3	4
	Bengaluru	3	4	5	5	6	5	–
Always feel safe	Delhi	1	2	2	1	2	2	–
	Mumbai	17	18	19	22	21	26	29
	Chennai	18	14	10	12	13	12	11
	Bengaluru	13	10	12	15	15	19	31

Source: SATARC Survey, IDFC Institute, 2017

Table 3.52 Perception by gender (%)

	Delhi		Chennai		Bengaluru		Mumbai	
Gender	Male	Female	Male	Female	Male	Female	Male	Female
After 7 pm	2	2	0	1	5	5	2	1
After 8 pm	12	16	3	4	9	9	4	3
After 9 pm	23	26	19	16	18	17	6	6
After 10 pm	34	36	43	51	32	27	18	19
After 11 pm	23	17	16	15	22	22	27	33
After midnight	4	3	4	3	4	4	20	20
Always feel safe	2	1	14	10	10	16	23	17

Source: SATARC Survey, IDFC Institute, 2017

Table 3.53 Perceptions by city (%)

Time	Delhi	Mumbai	Chennai	Bengaluru
By 7 pm	9	2	1	6
By 9 pm	63	14	23	41
By 11 pm	94	60	81	84
Always feel safe	3	23	16	12

Source: SATARC Survey, IDFC Institute, 2017

Table 3.54 Perceptions by age (%)

	City	18–20	21–30	31–40	41–50	51–60	61–70	70+
After 7 pm	Delhi	9	10	8	8	8	9	7
	Mumbai	1	2	1	1	1	3	4
	Chennai	2	0	–	1	2	1	–
	Bengaluru	6	8	5	5	10	4	–
After 8 pm	Delhi	28	26	27	27	23	27	23
	Mumbai	5	4	4	3	4	4	4
	Chennai	3	5	4	5	5	3	–
	Bengaluru	17	15	16	13	10	9	18
After 9 pm	Delhi	29	28	27	25	28	28	26
	Mumbai	9	8	9	8	7	7	10
	Chennai	17	16	20	20	16	22	22
	Bengaluru	25	25	20	18	15	15	6
After 10 pm	Delhi	18	16	18	17	18	17	20
	Mumbai	19	18	19	19	20	18	9
	Chennai	45	46	45	37	40	41	42
	Bengaluru	23	25	26	26	26	28	29
After 11 pm	Delhi	13	14	14	15	14	15	21
	Mumbai	29	28	27	27	29	26	29
	Chennai	16	12	15	18	12	18	8
	Bengaluru	14	14	17	19	23	21	31
After midnight	Delhi	2	4	4	4	4	2	1
	Mumbai	19	18	18	17	15	16	11
	Chennai	3	5	5	4	3	2	2
	Bengaluru	4	3	4	4	4	8	6
Always feel safe	Delhi	1	3	3	2	3	3	1
	Mumbai	19	21	22	24	24	26	32
	Chennai	14	16	12	16	22	13	26
	Bengaluru	11	10	12	15	12	14	12

Source: SATARC Survey, IDFC Institute, 2017

in Delhi. There is a substantial jump in people being worried after 10 pm vis-a-vis 9 pm in Chennai (Table 3.54).

There was no appreciable difference in perception between male and females when asked if they worried about walking alone in their neighbourhood after evening (Table 3.55).

Table 3.55 Perceptions by gender (%)

	Delhi		Chennai		Bengaluru		Mumbai	
Gender	Male	Female	Male	Female	Male	Female	Male	Female
After 7 pm	8	10	1	0	5	7	1	2
After 8 pm	23	30	3	5	14	15	3	5
After 9 pm	26	29	18	18	22	19	8	9
After 10 pm	18	16	36	49	26	24	17	20
After 11 pm	17	11	16	13	17	17	26	30
After midnight	4	2	5	3	4	4	17	17
Always feel safe	3	2	20	11	11	14	28	17

Source: SATARC Survey, IDFC Institute, 2017

Table 3.56 Perception by city (%)

	Delhi	Mumbai	Chennai	Bengaluru
Yes	73	85	83	73
No	26	14	15	25
I don't know	1	1	2	1

Source: SATARC Survey, IDFC Institute, 2017

Table 3.57 Perception by age (%)

	City	18–20	21–30	31–40	41–50	51–60	61–70	70+
Yes	Delhi	71	72	73	77	72	74	75
	Mumbai	84	85	84	85	85	88	93
	Chennai	85	86	79	82	82	87	91
	Bengaluru	70	73	73	73	71	75	88
No	Delhi	28	27	25	21	27	25	24
	Mumbai	15	15	16	14	15	12	7
	Chennai	15	12	18	16	16	12	9
	Bengaluru	29	26	24	26	28	24	12
Don't know	Delhi	1	1	2	2	1	1	1
	Mumbai	1	0	0	1	1	–	–
	Chennai	–	1	3	3	2	1	–
	Bengaluru	2	1	2	1	1	1	–

Source: SATARC Survey, IDFC Institute, 2017

Question: Do you feel safe when you are alone at home during the day?
In Mumbai 85% and in Chennai 83% of people felt safe when they were alone at home during the day. Just under three fourths of people in Delhi and Bengaluru (both at 73%) felt safe when they were home alone during the day (Table 3.56).

No particular age group or gender felt vulnerable at home during the day in any city (Tables 3.57 and 3.58).

Table 3.58 Perception by gender (%)

	Delhi		Chennai		Bengaluru		Mumbai	
Gender	Male	Female	Male	Female	Male	Female	Male	Female
Yes	75	71	78	89	75	71	87	83
No	24	28	19	10	23	28	13	16
Don't know	1	2	3	1	2	1	0	1

Source: SATARC Survey, IDFC Institute, 2017

Table 3.59 Perception by city (%)

	Delhi	Mumbai	Chennai	Bengaluru
Yes	56	78	81	68
No	43	20	17	27
I don't know	2	1	2	4

Source: SATARC Survey, IDFC Institute, 2017

Table 3.60 Perception by age (%)

	City	18–20	21–30	31–40	41–50	51–60	61–70	70+
Yes	Delhi	55	52	57	57	56	61	62
	Mumbai	75	77	77	79	80	83	90
	Chennai	82	82	77	78	79	85	91
	Bengaluru	70	67	64	70	73	75	78
No	Delhi	44	46	41	41	43	37	38
	Mumbai	23	22	22	20	19	17	10
	Chennai	18	16	20	19	19	14	9
	Bengaluru	22	27	30	28	26	24	22
Don't know	Delhi	1	2	2	2	1	2	–
	Mumbai	2	2	1	1	1	–	–
	Chennai	–	2	3	3	2	1	–
	Bengaluru	8	6	6	2	1	1	–

Source: SATARC Survey, IDFC Institute, 2017

Question: Do you feel safe when you are alone at home at night?

We then asked whether they felt safe at home alone at night. In Chennai (81%) and Mumbai (78%), more than three fourths of people felt safe while home alone at night. In Bengaluru, only 68% felt safe alone at home at night and the number was lower in Delhi at 56% (Table 3.59).

In Delhi, more than half the population across all age groups felt safe being alone at home at night. In the case of Chennai, around 80% across age groups felt safe alone at home at night. Encouragingly, over 90% of those in the age group of 70+ years felt safe in Chennai. In Bengaluru, those in the age group of 21–30 years and 31–40 years were most worried about their safety when alone at home at night. The sense of safety was higher amongst those in the age brackets of 50+ years in Mumbai (Table 3.60).

Table 3.61 Perception by gender (%)

Gender	Delhi		Chennai		Bengaluru		Mumbai	
	Male	Female	Male	Female	Male	Female	Male	Female
Yes	61	49	77	84	71	66	82	75
No	37	49	20	15	24	31	18	24
Don't know	2	2	3	1	6	3	1	2

Source: SATARC Survey, IDFC Institute, 2017

Table 3.62 Perception by city (%)

Time	Delhi	Mumbai	Chennai	Bengaluru
By 7 pm	13	2	2	9
By 9 pm	55	14	28	48
By 11 pm	83	55	79	83
Always feel safe	2	17	13	8

Source: SATARC Survey, IDFC Institute, 2017

In Delhi, 61% male and 49% female felt safe alone at home at night. In Bengaluru, 66% women felt safe at home at night. The proportions of those who felt safe were higher in Chennai and Mumbai (Table 3.61).

We also asked questions about the time after which people worry about withdrawing money from an ATM and using public transport.

Question: After what time in the evening would you worry about safety while withdrawing money alone from your neighbourhood ATM?

In Delhi, by 9 pm, 55% of people mentioned that they would worry about their safety while withdrawing money from their neighbourhood ATM. The corresponding numbers were 48% in Bengaluru, 28% in Chennai, and 14% in Mumbai. By 11 pm, 83% in Delhi and Bengaluru would worry about their safety while withdrawing money from their neighbourhood ATM, followed by 79% in Chennai and 55% in Mumbai. When asked whether they always felt safe, i.e. did not worry at any point of time, the figures were 17% in Mumbai, 13% in Chennai, 8% in Bengaluru, and only 2% in Delhi (Table 3.62; Fig. 3.6).

No distinct trend could be seen by age groups in any city (Table 3.63).

Looking at the issue from a gender lens, around 43% of women compared to 36% of men in Chennai were worried about withdrawing cash from an ATM after 10 pm. In Delhi, 20% of men and 24% of women were worried after 8 pm. In Bengaluru, 23% of men were worried about withdrawing cash from an ATM after 9 pm compared to 20% of women. In Mumbai, a much lower percentage of men and women were worried before 10 pm (Table 3.64).

Question: After what time in the evening would you worry about safety when travelling alone by public transport?

By 9 pm, 55% of people in Delhi mentioned that they would worry about their safety while travelling alone by public transport. The corresponding numbers were

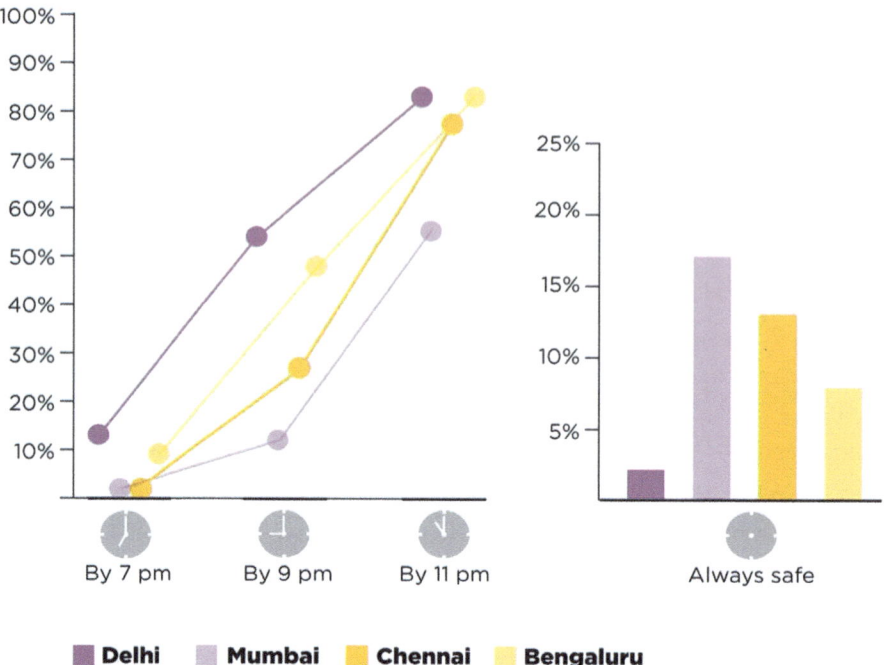

Note: The results are presented at the population level. Perceptions are presented by city as a percentage.

Source: SATARC Survey, IDFC Institute, 2017

Fig. 3.6 After what time in the evening would you worry about safety while withdrawing money alone from your neighbourhood ATM?

40% in Bengaluru, 23% in Chennai, and 12% in Mumbai. By 11 pm, 96% in Delhi worry about their safety while travelling alone by public transport, followed by 84% in Bengaluru, 81% in Chennai and 60% in Mumbai. When asked whether they always felt safe, i.e. did not worry at any point of time, the figures were 22% in Mumbai, 14% in Chennai, 12% in Bengaluru, and only 2% in Delhi (Table 3.65).

In Chennai, people got worried across all age groups after 10 pm. The youngest and the oldest were most concerned about using public transport after evening. Between 44% and 48% were worried in the age groups 18–20 years, 21–30 years, and 31–40 years. Similarly, between 45% and 47% of those above the age of 61 years were worried about using public transport after evening in Chennai. A large segment of population (18–26%) across all age groups always felt safe while using public transport in the evening in Mumbai (Table 3.66).

The difference in perception about safety while using public transport after evening grew after 10 pm. This could be seen in Delhi and Chennai. In Mumbai, the difference grew after 11 pm (Table 3.67).

We also asked which type of public transport people felt safe using during the day. This was a multiple-choice question. In Delhi, the most preferred mode of transport was metro/local train (80%), in Mumbai (95%) and Bengaluru (97%) it

Table 3.63 Perception by age (%)

	City	18–20	21–30	31–40	41–50	51–60	61–70	70+
After 7 pm	Delhi	11	13	13	13	14	11	9
	Mumbai	2	2	1	1	2	2	2
	Chennai	3	1	1	3	3	2	2
	Bengaluru	6	10	8	9	12	6	6
After 8 pm	Delhi	25	23	20	23	18	20	16
	Mumbai	6	4	4	4	4	6	8
	Chennai	7	8	4	5	5	5	4
	Bengaluru	19	18	17	16	15	15	20
After 9 pm	Delhi	19	22	21	17	20	18	13
	Mumbai	9	8	8	7	8	7	4
	Chennai	20	18	22	23	17	21	13
	Bengaluru	25	23	23	19	21	23	8
After 10 pm	Delhi	25	21	22	22	22	21	32
	Mumbai	19	17	19	17	18	14	10
	Chennai	39	39	43	36	39	45	34
	Bengaluru	18	22	21	22	16	17	4
After 11 pm	Delhi	6	6	6	6	6	7	9
	Mumbai	22	26	24	25	24	22	16
	Chennai	11	10	11	16	9	6	4
	Bengaluru	16	12	15	14	18	15	29
After midnight	Delhi	2	2	2	3	3	2	2
	Mumbai	18	17	15	17	12	11	6
	Chennai	–	4	3	2	1	1	2
	Bengaluru	6	4	4	5	4	6	8
Always feel safe	Delhi	1	2	2	2	3	1	–
	Mumbai	15	17	18	18	17	17	20
	Chennai	15	14	11	12	18	8	8
	Bengaluru	7	8	9	10	8	6	12
Not applicable	Delhi	11	12	13	13	13	20	20
	Mumbai	10	10	10	11	17	21	34
	Chennai	5	7	4	4	8	12	34
	Bengaluru	4	3	3	4	7	13	14

Source: SATARC Survey, IDFC Institute, 2017

was local bus, and in Chennai it was shared auto (96%). This was followed by auto in Delhi (77%) and Bengaluru (91%), metro/local train in Mumbai (90%), and local bus in Chennai (95%). The least preferred mode of transport was non-radio (or other) taxi services in Delhi (22%), Bengaluru (38%), and Chennai (61%), and radio taxi services in Mumbai (46%) (Table 3.68).

In a perfectly safe environment, the answers to these questions would be that people are not worried at all.

Third, we attempted to assess the precautions that people take to stay safe. As a result of poor perceptions of safety, people tend to adopt behavioural changes to

Table 3.64 Perception by gender (%)

| | Delhi | | Chennai | | Bengaluru | | Mumbai | |
Gender	Male	Female	Male	Female	Male	Female	Male	Female
After 7 pm	13	13	1	2	7	10	1	2
After 8 pm	20	24	5	6	17	18	4	5
After 9 pm	21	19	20	19	23	20	7	8
After 10 pm	23	21	36	43	23	18	18	17
After 11 pm	7	5	13	8	15	14	24	25
After midnight	2	2	3	2	3	6	16	14
Always feel safe	3	1	16	10	7	9	21	13
Not applicable	11	16	6	9	4	6	9	17

Source: SATARC Survey, IDFC Institute, 2017

Table 3.65 Perception by city (%)

Time	Delhi	Mumbai	Chennai	Bengaluru
By 7 pm	3	1	1	4
By 9 pm	55	12	23	40
By 11 pm	96	60	81	84
Always feel safe	2	22	14	12

Source: SATARC Survey, IDFC Institute, 2017

keep themselves safe, such as not leaving the house past a certain time. Poor perceptions of safety lead households to adopt precautionary measures to overcome the feeling of insecurity, which in turn impose costs on households and workplaces. It is critical to acknowledge and address the detrimental impact of such perceptions to both full and equal participation in civic life or the workforce. Accordingly, we asked respondents to select the various types of behaviours they adopt to avoid victimisation from a predetermined list. This was a multiple-choice question. The results are presented at the population level (Tables 3.69, 3.70, and 3.71).

These behavioural changes are symptomatic of a lack of rule of law and must be addressed to allow citizens freedom of choice and action. A poor perception of safety has implications for a person's participation in society. In minor cases, people may avoid certain areas at certain times of the day, but in extreme cases, they might withdraw from civic life and the workforce altogether. In the absence of direct data on safety, crime rate is often viewed as a proxy to gauge safety standards. However, a low rate of crime does not necessarily imply a high sense of safety.

4   Learning and Way Forward

Evidence-based policymaking has gained momentum globally in the last few decades. Data collected through surveys such as the National Family Health Surveys and the Assessment of School Education Report have been instrumental to

Table 3.66 Perception by age (%)

	City	18–20	21–30	31–40	41–50	51–60	61–70	70+
After 7 pm	Delhi	2	4	2	3	3	4	4
	Mumbai	1	1	1	1	1	2	2
	Chennai	1	0	–	1	1	2	2
	Bengaluru	3	4	4	4	7	3	–
After 8 pm	Delhi	28	22	18	18	18	22	15
	Mumbai	5	3	3	2	3	6	5
	Chennai	4	4	3	3	4	3	4
	Bengaluru	16	15	12	15	12	8	12
After 9 pm	Delhi	32	32	30	31	31	30	28
	Mumbai	8	8	7	7	8	7	11
	Chennai	18	17	21	19	19	18	15
	Bengaluru	29	25	24	20	17	21	7
After 10 pm	Delhi	27	30	35	32	33	29	43
	Mumbai	20	18	21	21	21	21	16
	Chennai	47	48	44	38	32	45	47
	Bengaluru	20	27	25	24	24	22	23
After 11 pm	Delhi	7	9	10	10	10	9	8
	Mumbai	29	30	28	28	26	23	29
	Chennai	14	12	16	20	19	17	6
	Bengaluru	18	16	21	19	23	25	31
After midnight	Delhi	2	2	3	4	3	3	1
	Mumbai	19	19	18	16	19	18	11
	Chennai	3	5	5	6	6	4	4
	Bengaluru	3	4	3	4	2	2	3
Always feel safe	Delhi	2	2	2	2	1	3	–
	Mumbai	18	21	21	24	22	24	26
	Chennai	13	14	11	13	19	12	21
	Bengaluru	11	9	12	14	15	20	25

Source: SATARC Survey, IDFC Institute, 2017

Table 3.67 Perception by gender (%)

	Delhi		Chennai		Bengaluru		Mumbai	
Gender	Male	Female	Male	Female	Male	Female	Male	Female
After 7 pm	2	3	1	1	4	4	1	1
After 8 pm	14	28	3	4	13	14	3	4
After 9 pm	30	33	18	19	23	22	6	10
After 10 pm	36	27	37	49	27	22	19	21
After 11 pm	12	5	18	13	21	18	24	33
After midnight	3	2	6	5	3	3	20	16
Always feel safe	2	1	17	10	9	16	27	15

Source: SATARC Survey, IDFC Institute, 2017

Table 3.68 Do you feel safe using public transport during the day?

Transport	Delhi	Mumbai	Chennai	Bengaluru
Local bus	71	95	95	97
Metro/local train	80	90	94	70
Auto	77	84	94	91
Shared auto	51	69	96	43
Radio taxi (e.g. Tab cab, Uber, etc.)	32	46	64	39
Other taxi services	22	51	61	38

Source: SATARC Survey, IDFC Institute, 2017

Table 3.69 Adaptive behaviours by city (%)

Behaviour	Delhi	Mumbai	Chennai	Bengaluru
Avoid walking alone	51	33	60	51
Be aware of surroundings	49	34	44	49
Keep personal belongings out of sight	47	40	39	36
Only travel in crowded train/bus	36	42	46	38
Avoid walking in certain areas at certain times	36	26	37	28
Take self-defence classes	21	29	6	25
Only use licensed cabs	18	24	17	30
Dress within accepted social boundaries	17	15	8	26
Other	5	5	0	6
No precautions	9	17	30	11

Source: SATARC Survey, IDFC Institute, 2017

policymaking in the health and education sectors. The discourse on law and order has been limited to official records on crime and media reports of incidences. However, neither of the two provide a complete picture of ground realities. Official crime records capture only a portion of the crimes faced by the citizens (See Table 3.6). CVS can complement official crime records, systematically diagnose problems in law and order, and help develop solutions for better service delivery in policing.

The availability of data on crime, safety perceptions, experience with the police, and opinions on the police at the city and police zone level render itself useful to evaluate and customise strategies for each problem and location. To illustrate, we present the map of victims[4] distribution of theft across police zones in Delhi as per data from SATARC survey. Data showed that the north, north west, and outer regions had the maximum number of victims of theft (Table 3.72; Fig. 3.7).

Data from a CVS can provide the state and police leadership with a management tool for various functions, including targeted resource and budgetary allocations,

---

[4] Data presented at sample level.

Table 3.70 Adaptive behaviours by age (%)

	City	18–20	21–30	31–40	41–50	51–60	61–70	70+
Try to avoid walking alone	Delhi	53	49	53	55	46	51	43
	Mumbai	32	32	34	34	32	31	35
	Chennai	63	57	62	63	59	69	42
	Bengaluru	53	46	50	52	56	60	79
Only use licensed cabs	Delhi	18	16	17	19	18	20	22
	Mumbai	23	23	25	25	23	21	22
	Chennai	16	15	17	21	15	14	15
	Bengaluru	31	30	27	28	32	31	33
Travel only in a crowded train or bus	Delhi	34	38	37	37	33	36	38
	Mumbai	43	42	43	43	38	39	37
	Chennai	42	44	47	48	46	54	32
	Bengaluru	37	36	37	42	36	46	35
Keep personal belongings (e.g. phone/ jewellery) out of sight of others	Delhi	45	49	46	48	46	39	43
	Mumbai	45	41	38	41	39	35	41
	Chennai	46	34	40	40	41	52	26
	Bengaluru	35	36	37	32	38	45	23
Avoid walking through certain areas and at certain times of the day	Delhi	39	36	36	38	36	32	29
	Mumbai	29	27	28	25	25	24	23
	Chennai	40	35	36	41	37	44	22
	Bengaluru	26	25	27	31	31	37	20
Take self-defence classes	Delhi	23	21	23	21	20	22	13
	Mumbai	32	31	28	28	26	26	32
	Chennai	8	7	6	7	6	4	–
	Bengaluru	23	24	24	24	29	28	29
Be generally aware of the surroundings	Delhi	47	48	52	49	48	52	49
	Mumbai	34	34	33	33	34	33	34
	Chennai	45	44	44	46	38	48	32
	Bengaluru	50	47	51	49	46	55	54
Dress within generally accepted social boundaries	Delhi	19	16	18	18	16	14	14
	Mumbai	18	15	16	15	15	13	12
	Chennai	9	9	7	11	6	6	2
	Bengaluru	23	26	26	25	27	29	27
Other	Delhi	5	5	6	6	5	3	3
	Mumbai	3	4	5	6	5	7	10
	Chennai	–	0	–	1	–	1	–
	Bengaluru	5	6	6	7	7	8	10
Don't take any precautions	Delhi	8	9	9	8	14	12	11
	Mumbai	15	17	18	17	19	18	20
	Chennai	30	32	26	27	34	25	51
	Bengaluru	9	12	13	12	9	9	–

Source: SATARC Survey, IDFC Institute, 2017

Table 3.71 Adaptive behaviours by gender (%)

	Delhi		Chennai		Bengaluru		Mumbai	
Gender	Male	Female	Male	Female	Male	Female	Male	Female
Try to avoid walking alone	47	55	57	63	50	53	28	39
Only use licensed cabs	19	17	16	18	31	29	26	21
Travel only in a crowded train or bus	35	38	43	49	36	39	40	43
Keep personal belongings (e.g. phone/jewellery) out of sight of others	44	50	36	42	35	36	39	42
Avoid walking through certain areas and at certain times of the day	36	36	33	41	27	28	26	27
Take self-defence classes	24	19	9	4	25	25	30	27
Be generally aware of the surroundings	50	49	39	48	51	46	32	36
Dress within generally accepted social boundaries	14	21	9	7	25	27	15	16
Other	4	6	0	0	7	6	5	4
Don't take any precautions	12	7	32	29	11	12	20	14

Source: SATARC Survey, IDFC Institute, 2017

Table 3.72 Distribution of victims of theft across police zones in Delhi (%)

District	Victims of theft
Central	7
North	15
North East	9
North West	15
Outer	13
West	8
South West	5
East	9
South East	7
New Delhi	7
South	5

Source: SATARC Survey, IDFC Institute, 2017
Note: The results are presented at the sample level

informed decision making for deployment, personnel training, and public record of performance measurement. Such data, across crimes, can be a useful tool to determine strategies around location of police stations, and form a basis for staffing, designing targeted interventions and operational requirements. Bridging this gap in public data on law and order is an important step for good governance, improved quality of life, and inclusive, market-based economic growth.

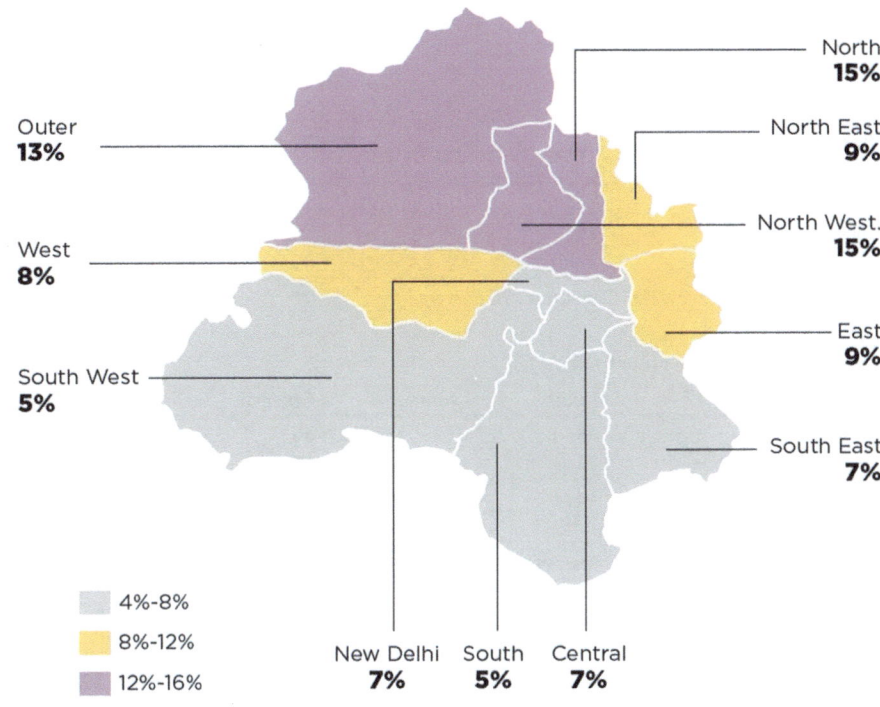

Note: Results presented for the sample

Note: The results are presented at the sample level.

Source: SATARC Survey, IDFC Institute, 2017

Fig. 3.7 Distribution of victims of theft across police zones in Delhi (%)

Table 3.73 Mean age of the respondents

Age (years)	Delhi	Mumbai	Chennai	Bengaluru
Mean	37.4	38.6	39.2	36.5

Source: SATARC Survey, IDFC Institute, 2017

Annexure

Summary Statistics of the Random Sample

In Delhi, the sample included 90% Hindus, followed by 9% Muslims. The sample in Chennai and Bengaluru had 87% Hindus each. Mumbai's sample included 78% Hindus. Of the remaining sample, Muslims constituted 5% in Chennai, 10% in Bengaluru, and 18% in Mumbai. The sample in Chennai had 6% Christians, maximum amongst the four cities and also included 3% respondents who did not disclose their religion (Table 3.74).

Table 3.74 Religion distribution by city (%)

Religion	Delhi	Mumbai	Chennai	Bengaluru
Hindu	90	78	87	87
Muslim	9	18	5	10
Christian	0	1	6	3
Sikh	1	1	–	0
Atheist	0	0	–	0
Other	1	2	0	0
Do not wish to disclose	–	1	3	0

Source: SATARC Survey, IDFC Institute, 2017

Table 3.75 Caste distribution by city (%)

Caste	Delhi	Mumbai	Chennai	Bengaluru
General	58	61	56	56
SC/ST	23	15	17	16
OBC	18	20	10	15
Do not wish to disclose	1	4	17	12

Source: SATARC Survey, IDFC Institute, 2017

Table 3.76 Education distribution by city (%)

Education	Delhi	Mumbai	Chennai	Bengaluru
Illiterate	9	6	1	3
Literate but no formal schooling/schooling up to 4 years	4	5	2	5
Schooling from 5 to 9 years	23	23	23	18
SSC/HSC	38	44	51	47
Attended college (including diploma course), but not graduate	6	8	6	9
Graduate/post graduate: General	17	13	14	16
Graduate/post graduate: Professional	4	2	3	2

Source: SATARC Survey, IDFC Institute, 2017

Across the four cities, between 56% and 61% of the respondents were in the general caste category. Around 15–17% were scheduled caste or scheduled tribes (SC/ST) in Mumbai, Chennai, and Bengaluru. The SC/ST constituted 23% of the respondents in Delhi. The Other backward categories (OBC) constituted 18%, 20%, 10%, and 15% in Delhi, Mumbai, Chennai, and Bengaluru. In Chennai and Bengaluru, around 17% and 12% of the sample did not disclose their caste category. The numbers were much smaller in Delhi and Mumbai at 1% and 4% (Table 3.75).

Almost half of the sample had completed secondary or higher secondary school certification (SSC/HSC) in Chennai and Bengaluru. In Mumbai and Delhi, those with SSC/HSC level of education were 38% and 44%. The next large category was those with 5–9 years of school education. This was around 23% in Delhi, Mumbai, and Chennai and 18% in Bengaluru. About 13–17% of the sample had Graduates and Post Graduates (general) degrees across the four cities (Table 3.76).

Table 3.77 Marital status distribution by city (%)

Marital status	Delhi	Mumbai	Chennai	Bengaluru
Married	73	70	80	78
Unmarried	21	23	15	16
Divorced	0	0	0	0
Widowed	5	6	5	5
Abandoned	0	0	0	0
Other	0	0	0	0

Source: SATARC Survey, IDFC Institute, 2017

Table 3.78 Occupation distribution by city (%)

Occupation	Delhi	Mumbai	Chennai	Bengaluru
Unskilled	9	16	7	17
Shop owner	6	6	9	6
Businessman with no employees	5	4	5	10
Businessman with 1–9 employees	2	2	4	4
Businessman with 10+ employees	1	1	1	1
Clerk/salesman	7	10	10	6
Junior level executive/officer	4	2	2	4
Mid-level executive/officer	3	2	2	4
Senior level executive/officer	2	2	1	2
Self employed	7	6	7	3
Student	9	8	6	6
Not working	36	34	34	27
Other	8	7	13	9

Source: SATARC Survey, IDFC Institute, 2017

Bulk of the sample included married respondents. About 80% of the sample was married in Delhi and Bengaluru and around 70% were married respondents in Mumbai and Chennai. The unmarried constituted 21% and 23% in Delhi and Mumbai, while 15% and 16% were unmarried in Chennai and Bengaluru (Table 3.77).

The largest percentage of the sample were not working across the four cities. Almost 27% of respondents in Bengaluru were not working, while in the remaining three cities those not working included 34–36% of the respondents. The other important occupations were clerks/salesperson, self-employed, student, unskilled and other (Table 3.78).

The sample in Delhi, Bengaluru, and Chennai included 71–76% who had been residing in the city for more than 10 years. In Mumbai, this number was as high as 89%. The next big category included those who had resided in the city for 5–10 years (Table 3.79).

Similarly, those staying in their current place of residence for more than 10 years constituted 45%, 57%, 62%, and 79% in Bengaluru, Chennai, Delhi, and Mumbai. Those living in the same residence for 5–10 years were 23% of the sample in Delhi,

Table 3.79 Number of years of stay in the city (%)

Years	Delhi	Mumbai	Chennai	Bengaluru
<1 year (0.5)	1	0	1	–
1–2 years (1.5)	1	1	2	1
2–5 years (3.5)	5	3	9	5
5–10 years (7.5)	17	7	15	24
>10 years (10)	76	89	74	71

Source: SATARC Survey, IDFC Institute, 2017

Table 3.80 Number of years of stay in the current residence (%)

Years	Delhi	Mumbai	Chennai	Bengaluru
<1 year (0.5)	2	1	2	0
1–2 years (1.5)	4	2	5	2
2–5 years (3.5)	10	7	16	19
5–10 years (7.5)	23	12	20	33
>10 years (10)	62	79	57	45

Source: SATARC Survey, IDFC Institute, 2017

Table 3.81 Familiarity with the local language by city (%)

Familiarity level	Delhi	Mumbai	Chennai	Bengaluru
Read	87	73	97	82
Write	86	69	95	78
Speak	99	78	99	99
None of the above	1	17	0	1

Source: SATARC Survey, IDFC Institute, 2017

12% in Mumbai, 20% in Chennai, and 33% in Bengaluru. This suggests that most respondents weren't new to the city and their neighbourhood—an important factor when analysing victim experience and perceptions of safety (Table 3.80).

Another important factor when studying crime incidence, experiences with police and perceptions with safety is familiarity with language. Almost the entire sample could speak in the native languages—Hindi, Tamil, and Kannada in Delhi, Chennai, and Bengaluru, respectively. In Mumbai, 78% of the respondents could speak Marathi. The reading and writing abilities were slightly lower at 87% and 86% for Hindi in Delhi, 73% and 69% for Marathi in Mumbai, 82% and 78% for Kannada in Bengaluru. Chennai again stood out with 97% and 95% respondents reporting reading and writing ability for Tamil (Table 3.81).

Survey Questionnaire (English)
Safety Trends and Reporting of Crime (SATARC) Survey (2016)

INTERVIEWER TO SAY: Good morning / afternoon / evening. My name is _____ (name of the Interviewer) from IMRB International. We are currently undertaking a survey among the residents of this city about the state of law and order and safety of the people.

Please note that your answers are completely _confidential_. The information taken from you would be collated at the city level and your name would not appear anywhere in context of this study.

Also, you do not have to answer any question, if you do not wish to. However, we seek your cooperation in providing complete information. This can help improve policing in your city over time.

The interview will take about 25–30 minutes. We value your cooperation for this exercise.

GEO TAG THE HOUSEHOLD

Name of Interviewer	
Name of Supervisor	
Date (dd/mm/yyyy)	
Household Serial Number	
Random / Purposive for victim	
City	
Police Zone (DROP DOWN LIST)	
Police Zone	Inside the zone / border area
Thana (TO BE FILLED FROM MAP)	
Locality	
Type of Dwelling (Household) (Code)	
Code: Type of Dwelling	1 = Independent House 2 = Apartment/Flat 3 = Chawl 4 = Slum 5 = Other

Part A: Demographic Details of the Household

A1a. Including you, how many people reside in this household? Please include children, but do not include guests or part time servants.

A1b. Starting from the youngest member of the household, could you please tell me their age and gender one by one?

CAPI: Need number of rows as per response from A1a. Columns of Relationship with Respondent, gender, age are to be kept. Additional Column (single code) of "selected respondent" to be kept too. CAPI should be able to re-arrange the order of members by age, it should not stop if the order is incorrect. (CAPI—Relationship to the respondent is used for identifying the person. This replaces the person's name and serial number from previous versions of the questionnaire)

INTERVIEWER: ONCE THE AGE AND GENDER OF ALL RESPONDENTS ARE CAPTURED, SELECT THE RESPONDENT REQUIRED AS PER QUOTA, ASK IF HE/SHE CAN GIVE THE INTERVIEW AND CONTINUE THE INTERVIEW WITH HIM / HER.
ASK HIM / HER THE RELATIONSHIP OF EACH HOUSEHOLD MEMBER WITH HIM / HER.

Relationship with respondent—Drop down list	Age	Gender
Husband		Male / Other (CAPI: Option)
Wife		Female / Other (CAPI: Option)
Son		Male / Other (CAPI: Option)
Daughter		Female / Other (CAPI: Option)
Father		Male / Other (CAPI: Option)
Mother		Female / Other (CAPI: Option)
Father-in-law		Male / Other (CAPI: Option)
Mother-in-law		Female / Other (CAPI: Option)
Brother		Male / Other (CAPI: Option)
Sister		Female / Other (CAPI: Option)
Brother-in-law		Male / Other (CAPI: Option)
Sister-in-law		Female / Other (CAPI: Option)
Grand father		Male / Other (CAPI: Option)
Grand mother		Female / Other (CAPI: Option)
Grand son		Male / Other (CAPI: Option)
Grand daughter		Female / Other (CAPI: Option)
Uncle		Male / Other (CAPI: Option)
Aunt		Female / Other (CAPI: Option)
Nephew		Male / Other (CAPI: Option)
Niece		Female / Other (CAPI: Option)
Friend		Male / Female / Other (CAPI: Option)
Servant		Male / Female / Other (CAPI: Option)
Others		Male / Female / Other (CAPI: Option)

INTERVIEWER: SELECT RESPONDENT AS PER QUOTA.
Ask the Respondent:

Contact Number of Respondent:				
Address of Household				

A2. Details of the Respondent

A2a. Whether Chief Wage Earner (CWE) (Code)

Code: Whether CWE	1=Yes	2=No		

A2.b More Details of the Respondent

Age (in Years)	
Gender (Code)	
Religion (Code)	
Caste (Code)	
Education (Code)	
Occupation (in the last one year) (Code)	

Code: Education	1=Illiterate	2=Literate but no formal schooling/Schooling upto 4 years	3=Schooling from 5 to 9 years	
	4=SSC/HSC	5=Attended College (including Diploma Course), but not Graduate	6=Graduate/Post Graduate: General	7=Graduate/Post Graduate: Professional

Code: Occupation	1=Unskilled	2=Shop Owner	3=Businessman with No employees	4=Businessman with 1–9 employees	5=Businessman with 10+ employees
	6=Clerk/Salesman	7=Junior level Executive/Officer	8=Mid level Executive/Officer	9=Senior level executive/Officer	10=Self Employed
	11 = Student	12. Not Working	13= Other		

Code: Religion	1=Hindu	2=Muslim	3=Christian	4=Sikh	5= Atheist	6=Other	7= Do not wish to disclose

Code: Caste	1=General	2=SC/ST	3=OBC	4 = Do not wish to disclose	

Marital Status	1= Married	2= Unmarried	3= Divorce	4= Widowed	5=Abandoned	6=Other

| A3a. **How long have you resided in the current city?** (in Years/ months) | |
| A3b. **How long have you resided at the current address?** (in Years/months) | |

A4. Do you know (Marathi for Mumbai; Hindi for Delhi; Kannada for Bangalore, and Tamil for Chennai)? Multiple Responses allowed		
1 = Read	2 = Write	3 = Speak
4 = None of the above (Single code if this option selected)		

Part B: Incidence of Crime

Please let us know if you personally (not another member of your household) have been a victim of any of the following crimes listed below in the past 1 year (October 2015–September 2016) in your city:

SHOWCARD B1

Crime	Yes	No	CAPI
B1. Theft	1	2	Cover C1
B2. Assault resulting in injury	1	2	Cover C2
B4. Harassment	1	2	Cover C4
B5. Criminal intimidation	1	2	Cover C5

Please let us know if your household has been a victim of any of the following crimes listed below in the past 1 year (October 2015–September 2016) in your city:

SHOWCARD B2

Crime	Yes	No	CAPI
B3. House Break-in	1	2	Cover C3
B6. Unnatural Death	1	2	Cover C6
B7. Missing persons	1	2	Cover C7

B8. Have you been the victim of any other crime in the last year, excluding the ones mentioned above?

1=Yes	2=No

IF YES, what crime(s) have you been the victim of? (WRITE IN)

CAPI: Ask B8 irrespective of answers given in B1 to B7. From B1 to B7, wherever the respondent has said "Yes", the respective section from Part C should appear. If not coded "Yes" in any of B1 to B7, move directly to Section E.

Part C: Details of Crime

CAPI: Ask section C1 if coded "1" in B1

C1: Theft (*Includes only theft, not loss of items due to other reasons*)

C1.1 How many times have you been the victim of theft in the last 1 year?

Number of times	

INSTRUCTION TO THE INTERVIEWER: IN CASE OF MORE THAN ONE INCIDENT, ASK THE RESPONDENT TO ANSWER THE FOLLOWING QUESTIONS FOR THE MOST RECENT INCIDENT. IF TWO OR MORE INCIDENTS HAPPEN TOGETHER, ASK THE RESPONDENT TO ANSWER THE FOLLOWING QUESTIONS FOR THE INCIDENT THE RESPONDENT CONSIDERS MORE HEINOUS.

C1.3 Please let us know, which of the following items were stolen. MULTIPLE CODING POSSIBLE

SHOWCARD C1.3

Luggage	Wallet/Purse	Credit/Debit card	Jewelry you were wearing/ carrying	Mobile
1	2	3	4	5
Laptop		Cash	Car	Other
6		7	8	9

C1.3a Was the incident accompanied by any other crime?

1=Yes	2=No

CAPI: If Code Yes in C1.3a, go to C1.3b else C1.4

C1.3b Which were the crimes?

CAPI: Please show the list of crimes mentioned in Part B, Others and None of the Above. It should not display the crime under which this qn is being asked, e.g. In C1, theft will not be an option etc.

2= Assault	3=House Break-in	4= Harassment	5= Criminal Intimidation
6= Unnatural Death	7=Missing person		0= None of the above

C1.4 Where did the incident occur? SINGLE ANSWER

SHOWCARD C1.4

Your home without break-in	Your home with break-in	Family /friends' home	Your workplace	Commercial place (mall / theatre / restaurant / grocery store /market)
1	2	3	4	5
In open areas/on the street/train station	In a public bus	In the metro/local train	In an auto/cab	Other
6	7	8	9	10

C1.5 Name the locality where the incident occurred. (CAPI: Don't ask the locality if response for C1.4 is 1 or 2)

1 =Name of locality (record name)	2= Don't remember

C1.7 When did the incident occur? (Mention the month and the week when it happened)

CAPI: Drop down list of months—Oct'15 to Sept'16 to appear

Drop down list of week (1st / not sure)

C1.8 What time did the incident occur? (Write the time in completed hours)

Time of occurrence – CAPI: Record as 12h clock, i.e. am/pm (Code: 1= Time, 2= Don't know)

C1.9 Did you have insurance for the item that was stolen?

1=Yes	2=No

CAPI: IF C1.9 is YES, go to C1.9a else C1.10

C1.9a Did you need an FIR to claim insurance, if any?

1=Yes	2=No

C1.10 Did you or anyone else from your household approach the police?

1=Yes	2=No

C1.11 Did you approach any person/agency, other than the police, to address the issue?

1=Yes	2=No

C1.12 Whom did you approach? (Don't ask if response for C1.11 is 2)

SHOWCARD

1=MLA/MP	2=Local corporator	3=Citizens group/NGO	4=Others (Please Specify)

C1.13 Did this agency/person help address the issue? (Don't ask if response for C1.11 is 2)

1=Yes	2=No

C1.14 If you face a similar incident in the future, would you approach the police?

1=Yes	2=No

CAPI: Ask section C2 if coded "1" in B2

		C2: Assault resulting in injury			
Code	**A**	**B**	**C**	**D**	**E**
	Grabbed/shoved/sla pped/beaten	Attacked by rocks/bottles	Attacked with a gun/knife	Attacked with any other dangerous object	Attacked in any other way

C2.1 Have you been physically attacked by someone in any of these ways in the last 1 year?

SHOWCARD C2.1

	A	B	C	D	E
Yes	1	1	1	1	1
No	2	2	2	2	2

C2.2a In the last 1 year, how many times did the incident occur?

Number of times					

ASK ONLY IF MORE THAN ONE OPTIONS CODED AS "YES" IN C2.1. ELSE SKIP TO C2.2c

C2.2b. Which of these was the most recent incident? SINGLE ANSWER

CAPI: only the options where "1" has been coded in C2.1, should appear.

Most recent incident	A	B	C	D	E

INTERVIEWER TO SAY: The following questions are only about the most recent incident of assault resulting in injury. IF TWO OR MORE INCIDENTS HAPPEN TOGETHER, ASK THE RESPONDENT TO ANSWER THE FOLLOWING QUESTIONS FOR THE INCIDENT THE RESPONDENT CONSIDERS MORE HEINOUS.

CAPI: The title of most recent crime should appear while asking all the following questions of Section C2

C2.2c Was the incident accompanied by any other crime?

1=Yes		2=No	

If Yes, go to C2.2d else C2.3b

C2.2d Which were the crimes?

CAPI: Please show the list of crimes mentioned in Part B, Others and None of the Above. It should not display the crime under which this qn is being asked, e.g. In C1, theft will not be an option etc.

1= Theft		3=House Break-in		4= Harassment		5= Criminal Intimidation
6= Unnatural Death		7=Missing person				0= None of the above

C2.3b How many people attacked you?

One person	1	1	1	1	1	1
Two people	2	2	2	2	2	2
More than two people	3	3	3	3	3	3

C2.4 Where did the incident occur?
SHOWCARD C2.4

Your home without break-in	1	1	1	1	1	
Your home with break-in	2	2	2	2	2	
Family/friends' home	3	3	3	3	3	
Your workplace	4	4	4	4	4	
Commercial place (mall / theatre / restaurant / grocery store / market)	5	5	5	5	5	
In open areas/on the street/train station	6	6	6	6	6	
In a public bus	7	7	7	7	7	
In the metro/local train	8	8	8	8	8	
In an auto/cab	9	9	9	9	9	

C2.5 Name of the locality where the incident occurred (Don't ask the locality name if response for C2.4 is 1 or 2)

(Code: 1 =Name of the locality, 2=Don't know)

C2.6 When did the incident occur? (Mention the month and the week when it happened)

CAPI: Drop down list of months – Oct'15 to Sept'16 to appear

Drop down list of week (1st / not sure)

C2.7 What time did the incident occur? (Write the time in completed hours)

Time of occurrence

CAPI: Record as 12 h clock, i.e. am/pm (Code: 1= Time, 2= Don't know)

C2.8 Did you have insurance?

1= Yes   2= No

If Yes, then go to C2.8a else C2.9.

C2.8a Did you need an FIR to claim insurance, if any?

Yes	1	1	1	1	1
No	2	2	2	2	2

C2.9 Did you know the offender(s) by name or by sight at the time of the incident?

Did not know the offender(s)	1	1	1	1	1
Knew (atleast one offender) by sight	2	2	2	2	2
Knew (atleast one offender) by name	3	3	3	3	3
Did not see the offender(s)	4	4	4	4	4
None of the above	5				

C2.10 Did you or anyone else from your household approach the police?

Yes	1	1	1	1	1
No	2	2	2	2	2

C2.11 Did you approach any person/agency, other than police, to address the issue?

Yes	1	1	1	1	1
No	2	2	2	2	2

C2.12 Whom did you approach? (Don't ask if response for C2.11 is 2)
SHOWCARD

1=MLA/MP   2=Local corporator   3=Citizens group/NGOs   4=Others (Please Specify)

C2.13 Did this agency/person help address the issue? (Don't ask if response for C2.11 is 2)

Yes	1	1	1	1	1
No	2	2	2	2	2

C2.14 If you face a similar incident in the future, would you approach the police?

Yes	1	1	1	1	1
No	2	2	2	2	2

CAPI: Ask section C3 if coded "1" in B3

Code	A	B	C	D	E
	Forced open a door or window	Manipulated a lock	Entered through an open door or window	Used force, or threatened to use force, against you or any other household member	Other CAPI: Add this for all questions in Section C3
C3.1 Has anyone broken in or attempted to break into your house in any of these ways in the last 1 year? **SHOWCARD C3.1**					
Yes	1	1	1	1	1
No	2	2	2	2	2
C3.2a How many times has the incident occurred in the last 1 year?					
Number of times					

ASK ONLY IF MORE THAN ONE OPTIONS CODED AS "YES" IN C3.1. ELSE SKIP TO C3.2c

C3.2b. Which of these was the most recent incident? SINGLE ANSWER

CAPI: only the options where "1" has been coded in C3.1, should appear.

	A	B	C	D
Most recent incident	A	B	C	D

INTERVIEWER TO SAY: The following questions are only about the most recent incident of house break-in. **IF TWO OR MORE INCIDENTS HAPPEN TOGETHER, ASK THE RESPONDENT TO ANSWER THE FOLLOWING QUESTIONS FOR THE INCIDENT THE RESPONDENT CONSIDERS MORE HEINOUS.**

CAPI: The title of most recent crime should appear while asking all the following questions of Section C3

C3.2c Was the incident accompanied by any other crime?

1= Yes	2= No

If yes, go to C3.2d, else C3.3

C3.2d Which were the crimes?

CAPI: Please show the list of crimes mentioned in Part B, Others and None of the Above. It should not display the crime under which this qn is being asked, e.g. In C1, theft will not be an option etc.

1= Theft	2= Assault	4= Harassment	5= Criminal Intimidation
6= Unnatural Death	7=Missing person		0= None of the above

C3.3. When did the incident occur. Mention the week and month when it happened

CAPI: Drop down list of months – Oct'15 to Sept'16 to appear

Drop down list of week (1st / not sure)

C3.a Did you have insurance? 1=Yes, 2=No (If Yes, then go to C3.4b else C3.5)

C3.4b Did you need an FIR to claim insurance, if any?

Yes	1	1	1	1	1
No	2	2	2	2	2

C3.5 Did you or anyone else from your household approach the police?

Yes	1	1	1	1	1
No	2	2	2	2	2

C3.6 Did you approach any person/agency, other than police, to address the issue?

Yes	1	1	1	1	1
No	2	2	2	2	2

C3.7 Whom did you approach? (Don't ask if response in C3.6 is 2)

SHOWCARD

1=MLA/MP	2=Local corporator	3=Citizens group/NGOs	4=Others (Please Specify)

C3.8 Did this agency/person help address the issue? (Don't ask if response for C3.6 is 2)

Yes	1	1	1	1	1
No	2	2	2	2	2

C3.9 If you face a similar incident in the future, would you approach the police?

Yes	1	1	1	1	1
No	2	2	2	2	2

CAPI: Ask section C4 only if coded "1" in B4

C4: Harassment

(to be asked irrespective of gender of the respondent)

Code	A	B	C	D	E	F
	Followed till you were scared or uncomfortable	Sent unwanted messages through SMS/e-mail/social media/internet/telephone calls	Passed or made lewd or unwelcome comments, gestures or actions	Continuously stared at you in a lewd or threatening manner	Touched indecently/groped/pinched	Indecently exposed themselves to you
C4.1 Has anyone harassed/or tried to harass you in any of these ways in the last 1 year?						
SHOWCARD C4.1						
Yes	1	1	1	1	1	1
No	2	2	2	2	2	2
C4.2a How many times has the incident occurred in the last 1 year?						
SHOWCARD						
Almost everyday	1	1	1	1	1	1
More than once a week	2	2	2	2	2	2
About once a week	3	3	3	3	3	3
Two-three times a month	4	4	4	4	4	4
About once a month	5	5	5	5	5	5
5–10 times in last one year	6	6	6	6	6	6
2–4 times in last one year	7	7	7	7	7	7
Once in last one year	8	8	8	8	8	8

ASK ONLY IF MORE THAN ONE OPTIONS CODED AS "YES" IN C4.1. ELSE SKIP TO C4.2c

C4.2b. Which of these was the most recent incident? SINGLE ANSWER

CAPI: only the options where "1" has been coded in C4.1, should appear.

Most recent incident	A	B	C	D	E	F
INTERVIEWER TO SAY: The following questions are only about the most recent incident of harassment. **IF TWO OR MORE INCIDENTS HAPPEN TOGETHER, ASK THE RESPONDENT TO ANSWER THE FOLLOWING QUESTIONS FOR THE INCIDENT THE RESPONDENT CONSIDERS MORE HEINOUS.**						
CAPI: The title of most recent crime should appear while asking all the following questions of Section C4						
C4.2c Was the incident accompanied by any other crime?						
1=Yes			2= No			
If yes go to C4.2d, else C4.3						
C4.2d Which were the crimes? **CAPI: Please show the list of crimes mentioned in Part B, Others and None of the Above. It should not display the crime under which this qn is being asked, e.g. In C1, theft will not be an option etc.**						
1= Theft	2= Assault		3= House Break-in		5= Criminal Intimidation	
6= Unnatural Death	7=Missing person			0= None of the above		
C4.3 Where did the incident occur? (Do not ask if crime selected is "D") SHOWCARD C4.3						
Your home without break-in		1	1	1	1	1
Your home with break-in		2	2	2	2	2
Family/friends' home		3	3	3	3	3
Your workplace		4	4	4	4	4
Commercial place (mall/ theatre / restaurant / grocery store /market)		5	5	5	5	5
In open areas/on the street/train station		6	6	6	6	6
In a public bus		7	7	7	7	7
In the metro/local train		8	8	8	8	8
In an auto/cab		9	9	9	9	9
C4.4 Name of the locality where the incident occurred. (Don't ask the locality name if response for C4.3 is 1 or 2. Do not as if the crime selected is "D")						

(Code: 1 = Name of the locality, 2 = Don't know)

C4.5 When did the incident occur? (Mention the week and the month when it happened)

CAPI: Drop down list of months — Oct'15 to Sept'16 to appear
Drop down list of week (1st / not sure)

C4.6 What time did the incident occur? (Write the time in completed hours)

Time of occurrence – Record as 12 h clock, i.e. am/pm (1= Time, 2= Don't know)

C4.7 Did you know the offender(s) by name or by sight at the time of the incident?
SHOWCARD C4-7

Did not know the offender(s)	1	1	1	1	1	1
Knew (atleast one offender) by sight	2	2	2	2	2	2
Knew (atleast one offender) by name	3	3	3	3	3	3
Did not see the offender(s)	4	4	4	4	4	4
None of the above	5					

C4.8 Did you or anyone else from your household approach the police?

Yes	1	1	1	1	1	1
No	2	2	2	2	2	2

C4.9 Did you approach any person/agency, other than police, to address the issue?

Yes	1	1	1	1	1	1
No	2	2	2	2	2	2

C4.10 Whom did you approach? (Don't ask if response for C4.9 is 2) SHOWCARD

1=MLA/MP   2=Local corporator   3=Citizens group/NGO   4=Others (Please Specify)

C4.11 Did this agency/person help address the issue? (Don't ask if response for C4.9 is 2)

Yes	1	1	1	1	1	1
No	2	2	2	2	2	2

C4.12 If you face a similar incident in future, would you approach the police?

Yes	1	1	1	1	1	1
No	2	2	2	2	2	2

CAPI: Ask section C5 if coded "1" in B5

C5. Criminal Intimidation

C5.1 Has anyone threatened you in any of the following ways for not fulfilling their demands in the last 1 year? SHOWCARD C5.1

(A) Harm to you	1=Yes / 2=No
(B) Harm to your family member	1=Yes / 2=No
(C) Damage to and/or seizure of property	1=Yes / 2=No
(D) Other	1=Yes / 2=No

C5.2 How many times has the incident occurred in the last 1 year? (Ask for each option mentioned above, if coded as "1=Yes" in C5.1)

SHOWCARD

Almost everyday	1
More than once a week	2
About once a week	3
Two-three times a month	4
About once a month	5
5–10 times in last one year	6
2–4 times in last one year	7
Once in last one year	8

ASK ONLY IF MORE THAN ONE OPTIONS CODED AS 'YES' IN C5.1. ELSE SKIP TO C5.2b

C5.2a. Which of these was the most recent incident? SINGLE ANSWER

CAPI: only the options where "1" has been coded in C5.1, should appear.

INSTRUCTIONS TO THE INTERVIEWER: IN CASE OF MORE THAN ONE INCIDENT, ASK THE RESPONDENT TO ANSWER THE FOLLOWING QUESTIONS FOR THE MOST RECENT INCIDENT. IF TWO OR MORE INCIDENTS HAPPEN TOGETHER, ASK THE RESPONDENT TO ANSWER THE FOLLOWING QUESTIONS FOR THE INCIDENT THE RESPONDENT CONSIDERS MORE HEINOUS

C5.2b Was the incident accompanied by any other crime?

1= Yes	2= No

If yes, C5.2c, else C5.3

C5.2c Which were the crimes?

CAPI: Please show the list of crimes mentioned in Part B, Others and None of the Above. It should not display the crime under which this qn is being asked, e.g. In C1, theft will not be an option etc.

1= Theft	2= Assault	3= House Break-in	4= Harassment
6= Unnatural Death	7=Missing person		0= None of the above

C5.3 Name of the locality where the incident occurred.

(Code: 1 =Name of the locality, 2=Don't know)

C5.4 When did the incident occur? (Mention the week and the month when it happened)

CAPI: Drop down list of months — Oct'15 to Sept'16 to appear

Drop down list of week (1st / not sure)

C5.5 Did you know the offender(s) by name or by sight at the time of the incident?

SHOWCARD C5.5

Did not know the offender(s)	1
Knew (atleast one offender) by sight	2
Knew (atleast one offender) by name	3
Did not see the offender(s)	4
None of the above	5

C5.6 Did you or anyone else from your household approach the police?

1=Yes	2=No

C5.7 Did you approach any person/agency, other than police, to address the issue?

1=Yes	2=No

C5.8 Whom did you approach? (Don't ask if response for C5.7 is 2) SHOWCARD

1=MLA/MP	2=Local corporator	3=Citizens group/NGOs	4=Others (Please Specify)

C5.9 Did this agency/person help address the issue? (Don't ask if response for C5.7 is 2)

1=Yes	2=No

C5.10 If you face a similar incident in future, would you approach the police?

1=Yes	2=No

CAPI: Ask section C6 if coded "1" in B6

C6: Unnatural Death (*This does not include suicide*)

	Member of your household was murdered	Member of your household died in an accident
C6.1 Has any of the above mentioned incident(s) happened to someone in your household in the last 1 year? SHOWCARD C6.1		
Yes	1	1
No	2	2
C6.2a How many times has the incident occurred in the last 1 year?		
No. of times		
ASK ONLY IF MORE THAN ONE OPTIONS CODED AS "YES" IN C6.1. ELSE SKIP TO C6.2c		
C6.2b. Which of these was the most recent incident? SINGLE ANSWER		
CAPI: only the options where "1" has been coded in C6.1, should appear.		
Most recent incident	A	B
INTERVIEWER TO SAY: The following questions are only about the most recent incident of unnatural death		
CAPI: The title of most recent crime should appear while asking all the following questions of Section C6		
C6.2c Was the incident accompanied by any other crime?		
1= Yes	2= No	
If yes, C6.2d, else C6.3		
C6.2d Which were the crimes?		
CAPI: Please show the list of crimes mentioned in Part B, Others and None of the Above. It should not display the crime under which this qn is being asked, e.g. In C1, theft will not be an option etc.		

1= Theft	2= Assault	3= House Break-in	4= Harassment
5= Criminal Intimidation	7=Missing person		0= None of the above

C6.3 Name of the locality where the incident occurred.	
(Code: 1 =Name of the locality, 2=Don't know)	
C6.4 When did the incident occur? (Mention the week and the month when it happened)	
CAPI: Drop down list of months — Oct'15 to Sept'16 to appear	
Drop down list of week (1st / 2nd / 3rd / 4th / 5th / not sure)	
C6.5 What time did the incident occur? (Write the time in completed hours)	
Time of occurrence — Record as 12 h clock, i.e. am/pm (Code: 1= Time, 2= Don't know)	
C6.6 Did you need an FIR to claim insurance, if any?	
Yes	1
No	2
C6.7 Did you know the offender(s) by name or by sight at the time of the incident?	
SHOWCARD C6.7	
Did not know the offender(s)	1
Knew (atleast one offender) by sight	2
Knew (atleast one offender) by name	3
Did not see the offender(s)	4
None of the above	5
C6.8 Did you or anyone else from your household approach the police?	
Yes	1
No	2
C6.9 Did you approach any person/agency, other than police, to address the issue?	
Yes	1

	No	2		2

C6.10 Whom did you approach? (Don't ask if response for C6.9 is 2)

SHOWCARD

1=MLA/MP	2= Local corporator	3=Citizens group/NGOs	4=Others (Please Specify)

C6.11 Did this agency/person help address the issue? (Don't ask if response for C6.9 is 2)

Yes	1	1
No	2	2

C6.12 If you face a similar incident in future, would you approach the police?

Yes	1
No	2

CAPI: Ask section C7 only if coded "1" in B7

C7: Missing Persons

C7.1 Has anyone in your household gone missing and/or disappeared in the last 1 year?	1=Yes	2=No
C7.2 Is the missing person an adult (more than 18 years of age)?	1=Yes	2=No
C7.3 Please specify the gender of the missing person.	1=Male	2=Female; 3=Other
C7.3a Was the incident accompanied by any other crime?	1 = Yes	2 = No

If yes, C7.3b, else C7.4

C7.3b Which were the crimes?

CAPI: Please show the list of crimes mentioned in Part B, Others and None of the Above. It should not display the crime under which this qn is being asked, e.g. In C1, theft will not be an option etc.

1= Theft	2= Assault	3= House Break-in	4= Harassment

5= Criminal Intimidation	6=Unnatural Death	0= None of the above
C7.4 When did the incident occur? (Mention the month and the week when it happened)		
CAPI: Drop down list of months — Oct'15 to Sept'16 to appear		
Drop down list of week (1st / not sure)		
C7.5 What time did the incident occur? (Write the time in completed hours)	1= TIme	2=Don't know
[Time of occurrence (Record as 12 h clock, i.e. am/pm) (Code: 1= Time, 2= Don't know)		
C7.6 Name of the locality where the incident occurred.	1 =Name of the locality	**2 =Don't know**
C7.7 Did you or anyone else from your household approach the police?	1=Yes	2=No
C7.8 Did you approach any person/agency, other than police, to address the issue?	1=Yes	2=No
C7.9 Whom did you approach? (Don't ask if response in C7,8 is 2)	1=MLA/MP	2=Local corporator
SHOWCARD	3=Citizens group/NGOs	4=Others, specify
C7.10 Did this agency/person help address the issue? (Don't ask if response in C7,8 is 2)	1=Yes	2=No
C7.11 If you face a similar incident in future, would you approach the police?	1=Yes	2=No

CAPI INSTRUCTIONS FOR PART D

Part D (exluding D.6) is to be asked only if:	Coded "1" in any of B1 to B7 AND
	Coded "1" in C1.10 OR C2.10 OR C3.5 OR C4.8 OR C5.6 OR C6.8 OR C7.7
D.6 is to be asked only if:	Coded "1" in any of B1 to B7 AND
	Coded "2" in C1.10 OR C2.10 OR C3.5 OR C4.8 OR C5.6 OR C6.8 OR C7.7
ELSE MOVE TO SECTION E	(IF NOT CODED "1" in any of B1 to B7, move to Section E)

Part D: Reporting of Crime to the Police — Interviewer may prompt if necessary

SHOW LIST OF CRIMES WHEN THE POLICE HAS BEEN APPROACHED (List from Showcard B1 / B2 for all the crimes coded "Yes" for Approaching Police — in C1.10, C2.10, C3.5, C4.8, C5.6, C6.8, C7.7)

ASK Doa ONLY IF MORE THAN ONE INCIDENTS OF APPROACHING POLICE ARE THERE. THIS SHOULD BE DYNAMIC SUCH THAT EVEN IF POLICE IS APPROACHED FOR ONE CRIME, THE QUES WILL STILL COME ASKING ABOUT WHO WENT TO POLICE.

Doa. Recalling the crime incidences you talked about some time back, can you please tell me, who from your household approached the police? MULTIPLE ANSWERS POSSIBLE

CAPI to have list of crimes reported to police on the side and list of household members (relationship with the respondent) as the options for each of them

"Crime 1"	Self	Member 1	Member 2	Member 3	Member 4	Member 5	...
"Crime 2"	Self	Member 1	Member 2	Member 3	Member 4	Member 5	...
"Crime 3"	Self	Member 1	Member 2	Member 3	Member 4	Member 5	...

CAPI to ensure that the entire list of crime reported appears on the left and the entire list of household members (relationship with the respondent) appears as options of reportees for each crime.

The above codes should go beyond 4 to incorporate if household was victim of more than 3 crimes.

Doc. Check the availability

CAPI to show a list of crime and person (relationship with respondent) who approached the police and allow to mark if the person is available or not.

Scenario 1 : "Self" is the only option selected for all the crimes in Doa

• Ask Part D for each crime one by one to the same respondent and then go to Part E, F, and A2

Scenario 2 : "Self" is selected for some crimes and "Others" for the remaining crimes.

• Ask part D to the respondent for all the crimes where police was approached by 'Self' followed by Part E, F, and A2
• For the remaining crimes, check availability of the person who approached the police
  ○ If the person(s) is (are) available, take their interview of Part D once interview with the main respondent is over
  ○ If the person(s) is (are) not available, take appointment when they are available and come back for their interview. All those who approached police, will answer the section for their respective crimes

Scenario 3 : "Self" is not an option for any crime

• Skip part D for the main respondent and continue to administer Part E, F, and A2
• For Part D, check availability of the person(s) who approached the police

o   If the person(s) is (are) available, take their interview of Part D once interview with the main respondent is over
o   If the person(s) is (are) not available, take appointment when they are available and come back for their interview. All those who approached police, will answer the section for their respective crimes

CAPI: following questions need to be asked for the most recent incidence of all the crimes which are reported to the police — one by one

CAPI: In case the interviewer is unable to get data on Part D even after repeated visits to the household, we will discard the interview. The survey will be marked incomplete / non-response and the interviewer will have to replace this survey with another.

D1. Reporting and response of police

	Mention relevant crime where police was approached	C1	C2	C3	C4	C5	C6	C7
1	How did you approach the police? Multiple responses allowed SHOWCARD D1							
1.1	Called 100 or any other relevant police helpline	1	1	1	1	1	1	1
1.2	Went to the police station	2	2	2	2	2	2	2
1.3	Online Complaint reporting	3	3	3	3	3	3	3
1.4	Approached a Police Control Room (PCR) van	4	4	4	4	4	4	4
1.5	Other	5	5	5	5	5	5	5
D2	What did the police do? Multiple responses allowed (Show options 1–7 for C1–C6, Show options 9–17 for C7) SHOWCARD D2a / D2b							
2.1	Filed a complaint	1	1	1	1	1	1	NA
2.2	Registered a First Information Report (FIR)	2	2	2	2	2	2	NA
2.3	Dispatched a PCR van	3	3	3	3	3	3	NA
2.4	Did not entertain your complaint because the case was not under that police station's jurisdiction	4	4	4	4	4	4	NA
2.4	Took the wounded persons, if any, for medical assistance	4	4	4	4	4	4	NA
2.5	Directed you to the police station you should go to	5	5	5	5	5	5	NA
2.6	Reached the spot where you called from and made inquiries	6	6	6	6	6	6	NA

2.7	Did not do anything	7	7	7	7	7	7	7	NA
2.8	Other	8	8	8	8	8	8	8	NA
2.9	Informed you after they filed a Missing Persons Report (MPR)	NA	NA	NA	NA	NA	NA	NA	1
2.10	Registered an FIR in case of a missing child and informed you of the same	NA	NA	NA	NA	NA	NA	NA	2
2.11	Displayed photographs of the missing person at various places including public spaces, local newspapers, television	NA	NA	NA	NA	NA	NA	NA	3
2.12	Initiated inquires in the neighborhood including at educational institutions, hospitals and mortuaries for any possible information on that person	NA	NA	NA	NA	NA	NA	NA	4
2.13	In case of a minor, set up a task force for locating the child	NA	NA	NA	NA	NA	NA	NA	5
2.14	Did not entertain your complaint because the case was not under that police station's jurisdiction	NA	NA	NA	NA	NA	NA	NA	6
2.15	Directed you to the police station you should go to	NA	NA	NA	NA	NA	NA	NA	6
2.16	Did not do anything	NA	NA	NA	NA	NA	NA	NA	7
2.17	Other	Na	NA	NA	NA	NA	NA	NA	8

D3. Did you feel satisfied with the police response after you approached the police? *(This refers only to the first response of the police. It does not cover status and outcome of the case investigations)*

Sr. No.	Mention relevant crime code (C1–C7)							
1	Yes	1	1	1	1	1	1	1
2	No	2	2	2	2	2	2	2

D4. Which of the following was the reason you felt satisfied with the police response to the incident? Multiple Response Allowed

(Ask only if response to D3 is 1)

SHOWCARD D4

Sr. No.	Mention relevant crime code (C1–C7)							
1	They listened attentively	1	1	1	1	1	1	1
2	They registered my complaint with accuracy	2	2	2	2	2	2	2
3	They registered my complaint promptly	3	3	3	3	3	3	3
4	They explained their future course of action	4	4	4	4	4	4	4
5	They arrived in time	5	5	5	5	5	5	5
6	They took action quickly	6	6	6	6	6	6	6
7	Other reason	7	7	7	7	7	7	7

D5. Why were you not satisfied with the police response to the incident? Multiple Responses Allowed (Ask only if response to D3 is 2)

SHOWCARD D5

Sr. No.	Mention relevant crime code (C1–C7)							
1	They were arrogant and ill-mannered	1	1	1	1	1	1	1
2	They refused to register my FIR and asked me to leave	2	2	2	2	2	2	2
3	They pinned the blame on me and tried to dissuade me from registering an FIR	3	3	3	3	3	3	3
4	They made me wait without any reason and took a long time to register my FIR	4	4	4	4	4	4	4
5	I required external influence to register the FIR	5	5	5	5	5	5	5
6	The PCR van took over an hour to arrive at the spot from where I called	6	6	6	6	6	6	6
7	They did not assist the wounded persons	7	7	7	7	7	7	7
8	They asked us/me to pay an amount	8	8	8	8	8	8	8
9	Other	9	9	9	9	9	9	9

D7. Were you satisfied with the action taken by the police? (This refers only to status and outcome of the case investigations)

Sr. No.	Mention relevant crimde code (C1–C7)							
1	Yes	1	1	1	1	1	1	1
2	No	2	2	2	2	2	2	2

D8. What is the status of the case?

Sr. No.	Mention relevant crime code (C1–C7)							
1	Investigation in progress	1	1	1	1	1	1	1
2	Case Closed/Resolved	2	2	2	2	2	2	2
3	Don't Know the status	3	3	3	3	3	3	3

D6. If you did not approach the police, what was the reason for not approaching?

SHOWCARD D6

Sr. No.	Mention relevant crime code (C1–C7)							
1	Didn't know where to go	1	1	1	1	1	1	1
2	Didn't know any of the helpline numbers	2	2	2	2	2	2	2
3	Felt that the police will not entertain the complaint	3	3	3	3	3	3	3
4	Did not think the police will be able to do anything about the case	4	4	4	4	4	4	4
5	Afraid to go to the police station	5	5	5	5	5	5	5
6	Did not want to get stuck in police/court matters	6	6	6	6	6	6	6
7	Did not want to report family matters	7	7	7	7	7	7	7
8	Lack of evidence	8	8	8	8	8	8	8
9	Fear of retaliation /Scared of the repurcussions	9	9	9	9	9	9	9
10	Took help from another agency/person for addressing the issue	10	10	10	10	10	10	10
11	Didn't think it was serious	11	11	11	11	11	11	11
12	Other reasons	12	12	12	12	12	12	12

CAPI: ASK SELECTED RESPONDENT

Part E: Opinion on the Police – Interviewer may prompt if necessary

INTERVIEWER: ASK THIS TO THE SELECTED RESPONDENT

E1. What are your personal opinions on the following? (Code)

1. The Police can be relied on when needed	
2. The Police is underpaid and overworked	
3. The Police in your locality understands the issues that impact the community	
4. The Police will treat you respectfully when you reach out to them	
5. The police are doing a good job at maininting a safe environment in the city	
6. Police presence in a secluded area makes you feel safe	

Codes: 1 = Agree, 2 = Disagree, 3 = Neither agree nor disagree 4 = Don't Know

E3. Do you know where your nearest police chowki/station is?

1 = Yes	2 = No

E4. When reporting a complaint/crime, whom would you be more comfortable approaching?

1 = Male officer	2 = Female officer	3 = Indifferent

Part F: Perception of Safety – Interviewer may prompt if necessary

F1. After what time in the evening, would you worry about an adult male member of your household who may be outside home unaccompanied?

after 7 pm	after 8 pm	after 9 pm	after 10 pm	after 11 pm	after midnight	always feel safe
1	2	3	4	5	6	7

F2. After what time in the evening, would you worry about an adult female member of your household who may be outside home unaccompanied?

after 7 pm	after 8 pm	after 9 pm	after 10 pm	after 11 pm	after midnight	always feel safe
1	2	3	4	5	6	7

F3. Do you worry about safety of your house while leaving it locked for many days?

1 = Yes	2 = No	3 = Don't know	

F4. Do you feel safe when you are alone at home during the day?

1 = Yes	2 = No	3 = Don't know	

F5. Do you feel safe when you are alone at home at night?

1 = Yes	2 = No	3 = Don't know	

F6a. Do you use public transport? Yes/No

F6. Do you feel safe using public transport during the day? Code: 1 = Yes, 2 = No, 3 = Don't Know

Local buses			Metro/Local Train			Auto			Shared auto			Radio Taxi (e.g. Tab cab, Uber etc.)			Other taxi services		
1	2	3	1	2	3	1	2	3	1	2	3	1	2	3	1	2	3

F7. After what time in the evening, would you worry about safety while traveling alone on public transport?

CAPI: Not to be asked if coded "Don't use public transport" in F6a

after 7 pm	after 8 pm	after 9 pm	after 10 pm	after 11 pm	After midnight	Always feel safe
1	2	3	4	5	6	7

F8. After what time in the evening, would you worry about safety while traveling alone in your personal vehicle?

Not Applicable (No personal vehicle)	after 7 pm	after 8 pm	after 9 pm	after 10 pm	after 11 pm	After midnight	Always feel safe
1	2	3	4	5	6	7	8

F9. Do you feel safe walking alone in your neighbourhood during the day?

1 = Yes	2 = No	3 = Don't know

F10. After what time in the evening, would you worry about safety while walking around alone in your neighborhood?

after 7 pm	after 8 pm	after 9 pm	after 10 pm	after 11 pm	After midnight	Always feel safe
1	2	3	4	5	6	7

F11. After what time in the evening, would you worry about safety while withdrawing money alone from your neighborhood ATM?

after 7 pm	after 8 pm	after 9 pm	after 10 pm	after 11 pm	After midnight	Always feel safe	Not Applicable
1	2	3	4	5	6	7	8

F12. According to you, how serious is the problem of crime is in your local area?

Serious problem	Somewhat of a problem but not very big	Not much of a problem	Don't know
1	2	3	4

F13. Do you think that crime levels in your local area have gone up, down or stayed the same over the last few years?

1 = Up	2 = Down	3 = Stayed the same	4 = Don't know

F15. Do you take any of these precautions to avoid becoming a victim of crime while away from home? Multiple Responses Allowed

SHOWCARD F15

Try to avoid walking alone	Only use licensed cabs	Travel only in a crowded train or bus	Keep personal belongings (e.g., phone / jewelry) out of sight of others	Avoid walking through certain areas and at certain times of the day
1	2	3	4	5
Take Self Defence Classses	Be generally aware of the surroundings	Dress within generally accepted social boundaries	Other	Don't take any precautions
6	7	8	9	10

F16. What, in your opinion, is the single most prevalent crime in your neighbourhood?

(write here in detail) — Include standard words — to be explained during training

F17. Do you worry about becoming a victim of any of the crimes in the next year? Multiple Responses Allowed

	Yes	No	Don't Know
Theft			
Assault			
House Break-in			
Harassment			
Criminal intimidation			

F18. Which of the following sources have helped you form an impression about crime in your city? Multiple Responses Allowed

Personal Experience	Relatives'/Friends' Experience	Newspaper	Television Programmes	Radio
1	2	3	4	5
Internet	Information from Police	Information from Resident Associations	Word of Mouth	Other
6	7	8	9	10

Continuation from Part A.

A5. Please share more details **of your Household Members**

A5. **Details of the CWE**

Age (in Years/ months) – Autofill from A2b if coded 1 in A2a	
Gender (Code) – Autofill from A2b if coded 1 in A2a	
Religion (Code) – Autofill from A2b if coded 1 in A2a	
Caste (Code) – Autofill from A2b if coded 1 in A2a	
Education (Code) – Autofill from A2b if coded 1 in A2a	
Occupation (in the last one year) (Code) – Autofill from A2b if coded 1 in A2a	

Code: Education	1=Illiterate	2=Literate but no formal schooling/Schooling upto 4 years	3=Schooling from 5 to 9 years
4=SSC/HSC	5=Attended College (including Diploma Course), but not Graduate	6=Graduate/Post Graduate: General	7=Graduate/Post Graduate: Professional

Code: Occupation	1=Unskilled	2=Shop Owner	3=Businessman with No employees	4=Businessman with 1–9 employees	5=Businessman with 10+ employees
	6= Salaried Person	7=Clerk/Salesman	8=Junior level Executive/Officer	9=Mid level Executive/Officer	10=Senior level executive/Officer
	11=Self Employed	12 = Student	13. Not Working		

Code: Religion	1=Hindu	2=Muslim	3=Christian	4=Sikh	5= Atheist	6=Other	7= Do not wish to disclose

Code: Caste	1=General	2=SC/ST	3=OBC

Marital Status	1= Married	2= Unmarried	3= Divorce	4= Widowed	5=Abandoned	6=Other

A7. **Annual Household Income**

Below 1 Lacs	Between 1 and 3 Lacs	Between 3 and 7 Lacs	Between 7 and 10 Lacs	Above 10 Lacs	Do not want to disclose
1	2	3	4	5	6

A8. Type of Accommodation

Own property	Rented	Rent Free (e.g. relative's place)	Official Accommodation
1	2	3	4

A9. **Household Assets: Do you have the following in your house?** (Read out) Multiple Responses Allowed

Ceiling fan	Gas connection	Refrigerator	TV	Microwave oven	Water-purifier
1	2	3	4	5	6
Washing machine	Air-conditioner	Computer/Laptop	Cell phone	Two wheeler	Car
7	8	9	10	11	12

A10. **Household utilities: Do you have the following in your house?** (Read out) Multiple Responses Allowed

SHOWCARD A10

Electricity connection	Telephone (landline) connection	Internet connection
1	2	3
Tap-water	Private toilet (inside the house)	More than one room (excluding the kitchen)
4	5	6

A11. Household security: **Is your house protected by any of the following?** (Read out) Multiple Responses Allowed

SHOWCARD A11

Double door at entry or door with sophisticated locks or peephole	Security guard	Neighbourhood chowkidar
1	2	3
Window bars and grills	CCTV	No Protection
4	5	6

A12. **Does anyone in your household have a bank account?**	1=Yes	2=No
A13. **Do you have a Government issued identity card such as Voter card/Aadhar card?**	1=Yes	2=No
A14. Do you give permission to IMRB to share your contact details with IDFC Institute for purpose of audit?	1 = Yes	2 = No

References

Common Cause and the Lokniti – Programme for Comparative Democracy at the Centre for the Study of Developing Societies (CSDS). (2018). *Status of policing in India report 2018: A study of performance and perceptions*. Centre for the Study of Developing Societies.

National Crime Records Bureau, Ministry of Home Affairs. (2016). *Crime in India 2016*. https://ncrb.gov.in/sites/default/files/Crime%20in%20India%20-%202016%20Complete%20PDF%20291117.pdf

Chapter 4
Status of Policing in India Reports: 2018 and 2019

Radhika Jha and Vipul Mudgal

1   Introduction

The Status of Policing in India Report (SPIR) is a series of baseline documents prepared to assess the impact of policing on the ground. The reports are designed to evaluate the performance of the police in major Indian states along with the perceptions of relevant stakeholders—citizens as well as police personnel.

SPIR 2018- *A Study of Police Performance and Perceptions* includes a measurement of performance on parameters such as disposal of cases, prison composition, police infrastructure, police diversity, and disposal of cases of crimes against vulnerable communities, using official data. Building upon this foundation of official statistics, the study further explores common people's experiences with crime and routine policing matters, their levels of trust and satisfaction with the police, fear of the police, and both perceptions and experiences of the use of violence and excessive force by the police.

The Status of Policing in India Report 2019- *Police Adequacy and Working Conditions* focuses on the working conditions of police; the availability of resources, infrastructure, and capacity of the police structures across States through an analysis of official data and a survey of police personnel. This chapter presents a summary of the SPIR reports of 2018 and 2019, methodologies used, and major findings.

As distinct from a traditional crime victimization survey, the SPIR series attempt to get a perspective on policing in the Indian states by using a multipronged approach – studying the perceptions of the people as well as the police personnel on the prevalence of crime, their experiences in crime registration, overall perception of crime disposal, attitudes to maintaining peace and harmony, police adequacy and

R. Jha (✉)
Lead Researcher, Status of Policing in India Report (SPIR), New Delhi, India

V. Mudgal
Director and CEO, Common Cause, New Delhi, India

working conditions, etc. The survey findings are juxtaposed with an analysis of the official time-series data from the National Crime Records Bureau (NCRB) and the Bureau of Police Research and Development (BPR&D) on crime rates, disposal rates by the police and the courts, infrastructure, budget, training, etc.

SPIR 2018 and 2019 go beyond just a statistical analysis of crime victimization in the states, and delve into more complex areas of the *how* and *why* behind crime. The reports cover areas such as people's experiences of contacting the police, fear of the police as reported both by the people and the police themselves, and the differences in experiences and perceptions of different sections of the society, along with the prejudices within the police. The study looks at how these perceptions and experiences translate into a "disconnect" between the people and the police.

The SPIR series treat the police as not just the most visible face of the State but also a lynchpin of its apparatus of legitimacy and the authority of law. Hence, the attempt is to address the macro as well as micro perspectives of policing in India. The SPIR 2018 is a birds' eye view of policing in the major Indian states whereas the SPIR 2019 is a worm's eye view where the average police station is the unit of data collection.

The SPIR series of research and survey-based studies are designed to measure the impact of policing on the ground with an objective of aiding a decisive policy change. The idea is to provide a snapshot of policing in different states of India in a comparable matrix and to highlight the most glaring need-gaps. The surveys examine differences in the perceptions of multiple publics based on their caste, class or religious backgrounds. The findings give us a clue as to where we stand and the direction in which we could be headed.

The first two reports, i.e., SPIR 2018 and 2019, are meant to be baseline documents which will work as building blocks for more rigorous and actionable research in the future. They will also work as primary reference points for time-series data to be generated over time.

This chapter examines the relevant findings of the two reports across the following thematic areas: crime and safety; crime registration and police investigation; human rights violation by the police and corruption within the police; prejudice against vulnerable communities; and political interference in crime investigation. Under each thematic head, the relevant findings from both the Status of Policing in India Report 2018 (public survey) as well as from the SPIR 2019 (police personnel survey) have been analyzed and presented.

While the main content relies heavily upon the original reports, some of the analysis and cross tabulations of the survey data have been done specifically for this chapter and are not mentioned in the original reports. Before investigating the main findings of the report, the survey design, questionnaire design, and the survey executing have been detailed in the section below on "research methods". Toward the end, the chapter discusses the learnings from these findings, future scope for research, and the way forward.

2   Sampling and Survey Methodology

Survey Design

Status of Policing in India Report 2018: A Study of Performance and Perceptions is based on a sample survey of 15,563 respondents across 188 assembly constituencies in 22 states of India. The surveyed states were Andhra Pradesh, Assam, Bihar, Gujarat, Haryana, Himachal Pradesh, Karnataka, Kerala, Madhya Pradesh, Maharashtra, Nagaland, Odisha, Punjab, Rajasthan, Tamil Nadu, Uttar Pradesh, West Bengal, Delhi, Jharkhand, Chhattisgarh, Uttarakhand, and Telangana. The surveys were conducted by the Lokniti Program for Comparative Democracy, Center for the Study of Developing Societies (CSDS), in the months of June and July, 2017.

The sampling for this study was done in three stages. One of the key objectives of the study was to provide state-wise analyses of performance and perception of policing. Therefore, the sample size for all 22 states was determined on their size. In big states such as Uttar Pradesh and Tamil Nadu, 880 interviews each were to be targeted. In midsized states such as Odisha and Karnataka, 720 interviews and in small states such as Delhi and Nagaland, 480 interviews each were to be targeted.

In the first stage, the sampling of Assembly Constituencies (ACs) was done, and with a target of about 80 interviews per seat, the number of ACs to be sampled per state were arrived at. A total of 188 assembly constituencies were randomly selected using the Probability Proportionate to Size method. In the second stage, four polling stations (PS) within each sampled AC were selected using the Systematic Random Sampling Method. In all, 752 polling stations were selected by listing all the PSs within the sampled ACs in the serial order followed by the Election Commission. The third and final stage of sampling was selection of the respondents. In every polling station, 35 respondents were selected from the latest electoral rolls using the Systematic Random Sampling Method. This procedure ensured that the selected sample was fully representative of the cross-section of voters in the country. In each sampled polling station, a list of sampled respondents was prepared by listing their name, age, gender, and address.

"Status of Policing in India Report 2019: A Study of Police Adequacy and Working Conditions" is based on a sample survey of 11,834 police personnel and 10,535 interviews of family members of police personnel across 105 locations in 21 states of India. The surveyed states were: Andhra Pradesh, Assam, Bihar, Chhattisgarh, Gujarat, Haryana, Himachal Pradesh, Jharkhand, Karnataka, Kerala, Madhya Pradesh, Maharashtra, Nagaland, Odisha, Punjab, Rajasthan, Telangana, Uttar Pradesh, Uttarakhand, West Bengal, and Delhi. The surveys were conducted by the Lokniti-Program for Comparative Democracy, CSDS, between February and April 2019. The states surveyed were common in both studies except Tamil Nadu which had to be excluded in SPIR 2019 as permission was denied at many places.

Prior to the data collection, letters were sent to the Superintendents of the Police (SP) of the selected locations, informing them about the research objectives and requesting permission for data collection. Further, a letter of endorsement of the research was provided by the President, Mr N. Ramachandran and the Chairman, Mr Prakash Singh (both former police officers), of the Indian Police Foundation. This letter was also sent to the SPs of the selected locations, and a copy was carried by field investigators at the time of data collection. At most locations, the police personnel were forthcoming about participating in the survey.

In this study, the locations in the states were chosen using purposive heterogeneous sampling method to capture the social diversity, geographical spread, and the administration of the police. Five locations were chosen from each state in such a way that two locations would capture the policing of population in rural areas, two locations would capture the policing of population in the urban areas, and one would preferably capture the policing of population in capital or metropolitan cities. The locations were also chosen keeping in mind the geographical spread of the states (to capture the coastal policing, etc.). The locations with comparatively higher SC and ST populations were also given higher preference.

The second and final stage of sampling was the selection of the respondents. In every location, 120 respondents were to be selected using quota sampling method. Through this procedure, it was ensured that in the selected sample, every fifth respondent was a woman and that out of every five respondents interviewed, at least four were of the ranks of constables or head constables. The interviews of the police were typically carried out at the police housing quarters or the police stations in a given location.

Questionnaire Design

The questionnaires for all the surveys were designed after a series of discussions and brainstorming meetings with domain experts. Most questions in the questionnaire were structured, i.e., close-ended. However, a few selected questions were kept open-ended in order to find out the respondent's spontaneous feelings about an issue without giving options. To check the accuracy and credibility of the questions set in the questionnaire, it was necessary to administer it in the field. A pilot fieldwork and pretesting of questionnaires were conducted after which many questions were reframed and some were added or omitted. This process also allowed us to shorten the questionnaire and improve the instructions for field investigators. Translation was done for each state by the regional team which was familiar with the local languages before administering the questionnaire in the field.

The questionnaires for both the surveys, for SPIR 2018 and 2019, were designed after brainstorming sessions with field experts. The themes of each of these questionnaires were focused around the research objectives of the two studies. The broad themes covered in the SPIR 2018 questionnaire were: people's experience with the police, trust in police, people's perception of discrimination by the police, fear of police, and the overall perception on different aspects of policing. The themes of the SPIR 2019 questionnaire, conducted with the police personnel, were: working conditions of the police, availability of resources and infrastructure, investigation of crime by the police, conditions of vulnerable groups such as women, minorities, SCs, STs, and OBCs within the police, perception of the personnel toward these vulnerable groups, and police use of force and human rights violations by the police. While the two surveys were on widely different themes, there were some points of similarity, such as on questions related to the crime, its investigation, level of sympathy of police use of violence (*vis-à-vis* police's willing to use violence), fear of police (*vis-à-vis* police perception about human rights violations), etc. Some of the findings on these themes from the two studies have been presented here. While the findings may be compared and contrasted, since the questionnaire design and data collection process for the two studies were quite different, the findings cannot be analyzed together.

Survey Execution

A two-day training workshop was organized in each state before the survey fieldwork began in order to train the field investigators (FIs) and supervisors to carry out the fieldwork operations. The trainers conducted an intensive and interactive workshop wherein investigators attended an orientation program and were trained in interviewing techniques and communication with the respondents. A comprehensive and detailed interviewing guide, designed on the basis of the questionnaire and survey methodology, was prepared for the interviewers. For a better understanding of the questionnaire, mock interviews were also conducted by the interviewers. Field investigators, who were mainly students of social sciences belonging to colleges and universities in different parts of the country, were selected to carry out the field work. They conducted face to face interviews with the respondents in local languages using a standardized questionnaire.

All questionnaires were manually screened for consistency and quality check. The questionnaire had codes (of precoded questions) that were used for data punching. A team was constituted for checking the codes and making corrections if required. The analyses presented in the reports have been done using the Statistical Package for the Social Sciences (SPSS). In order to be representative at the state level, the achieved sample of every state was weighted by locality, religion, caste group, and gender based on Census 2011 figures for SPIR 2018.

3   Key Findings

In the following section, findings from both SPIR 2018 and SPIR 2019 have been presented. The findings pertaining to the common people's opinions and experiences are from SPIR 2018, while those pertaining to the police personnel's opinions, attitudes, and experiences are from SPIR 2019. The two surveys were carried out separately and in different years. Findings from the analysis of official data of the NCRB and BPR&D have also been noted where relevant.

1. *Crime and Safety*

SPIR 2018: Findings from People's Survey

Perception and experience of crime by the people is a more reliable indicator of the status of law and order in a region than the registered crime rates, owing to the vast under-reporting of crime in the country. Therefore, in the survey with the common people, questions regarding both—perceptions and experiences of crime and reporting were asked.

Results from SPIR 2018 show that 37 percent of the respondents felt that criminal activities such as burglary, murder, physical assault, and chain snatching occur in their locality frequently (very often and sometimes clubbed together), indicating that more than one out of three respondents felt that such incidents are common in their locality (Table 4.1). When seen across states, this perception was highest in states such as Jharkhand (72%), Uttar Pradesh (67%), Delhi (64%), Karnataka (61%), and Madhya Pradesh (57%), where the cumulative percentage of respondents who said that such incidents take place "often" and "sometimes" was higher than 50 percent.

In order to understand people's perception of the incidence of crime across locations, state-wise responses to the question on frequency of crime in one's locality were derived into a unique score for each state. This score indicates the overall degree of incidence of crime in a single figure. Arranging the states in descending order of their scores- highest score first, representing least amount of perceived incidence of crime, we arrived at the following distribution, which displays the relative position of each state regarding this question. We see that Kerala fares best among all the states, meaning that the occurrence of murder, physical assault, burglary, and related crimes as perceived by the people is lowest there, while Jharkhand comes last, signaling that incidence of crime as perceived by the people is greatest there.

Starting from Madhya Pradesh and up till Jharkhand (states with a negative score), people are more likely to report a high frequency of crimes, whereas other states with a score higher than zero are more likely to report that crimes 'never' or 'rarely' occur in their locality.

Table 4.1 "How often do incidents such as burglary, murder, physical assault, chain snatching occur in your locality-very often, sometimes, rarely or never?"

Very often	9
Sometimes	28
Rarely	24
Never	33
No response	6

Source: SPIR 2018, Common Cause
Note: Figures are in percentages. Figures are rounded off

As is evident from Table 4.2, people's perceptions of crime differs greatly from the actual number of reported crimes in the same region. For example, the *Crime in India* Report 2018 by the National Crime Records Bureau (NCRB) provides actual incidents as well as rates of *reported* crimes that were registered by the police. A bare reading of this data indicates that Kerala has the highest rate of total cognizable crimes under the Indian Penal Code (IPC) and the Special and Local Laws (SLL). Yet, in our survey we find that in the above table Kerala scores the highest, meaning that it has the lowest frequency of crime as perceived by the people. This contrast in the two numbers could be a result of two factors: one, that the reporting of crime in a region may be indicative of a better police-public relationship where better reporting is possible and therefore people in general feel safer. Secondly, the difference could be attributed to the fact that people's perceptions are relative and in a locality

Table 4.2 State-wise ranking on people's perception of incidence of crime

Rank	State	Perceived frequency of crime				Score
		Very often	Sometimes	Rarely	Never	
1	Kerala	3.6	14.5	26.1	52.9	11.0
2	Assam	0.4	19.1	39.7	38.6	9.7
3	Odisha	4.3	23.2	12.7	55.8	9.3
4	West Bengal	3.1	19.1	35.1	38.5	8.7
5	Nagaland	2.2	16.6	36.8	33.7	8.3
6	Uttarakhand	5.9	23.0	16.7	49.2	8.0
7	Andhra Pradesh	10.2	12.3	34.8	36.4	7.5
8	Himachal Pradesh	4.8	28.3	16.6	47.6	7.4
9	Telangana	9.0	16.5	15.4	42.6	6.6
10	Gujarat	6.5	26.5	21.9	39.8	6.2
11	Chhattisgarh	1.3	27.3	16.4	37.2	6.1
12	Tamil Nadu	9.0	26.9	30.7	31.8	4.9
13	Punjab	5.5	31.7	32.1	22.3	3.4
14	Bihar	5.4	31.9	39.6	18.0	3.3
15	Maharashtra	6.8	39.1	22.7	27.9	2.6
16	Haryana	23.6	27.6	7.3	39.3	1.1
17	Madhya Pradesh	9.1	47.7	19.6	14.7	−1.7
18	Karnataka	18.0	42.9	14.9	20.7	−2.3
19	Rajasthan	15.7	35.9	14.8	12.7	−2.7
20	Uttar Pradesh	18.4	48.0	11.7	16.2	−4.1
21	Delhi	27.1	37.1	16.7	14.5	−4.6
22	Jharkhand	13.2	59.0	20.2	5.6	−5.4

Source: SPIR 2018, Common Cause
Note: The state rankings for Incidence of crime are based on summated scores that were arrived after weighing each Index category. The category of Crime Occurs includes incidence of crime as very often and sometimes and the category of Crime does not Occur includes incidence of crime as rarely and never. The "very often" category was weighed as −0.2, the "sometimes" category was weighed as −0.1, the "rarely" category was weighed as 0.1, the "never" category was weighed as 0.2. A higher summated score here indicates positive assessment, i.e., less incidence of crime.

which sees lower incidence of crime, even a slight spike in the incidence could lead to a general public perception of such incidents occurring "very often", whereas in another region where such incidents are much more in number and are common-place, the perceived level of crime could be low. Statistician JeffErey S. Rosenthal suggests that public fear of crime does not coincide with actual crime statistics. Using the term "headline bias", Rosenthal explains, that when something makes the news, the public believes it happens often. However, he states that the reason why "something makes the headlines is because it doesn't happen a lot".[1]

People's perception of the prevalence of criminality in the locality differs signifi-cantly from their contact with the police. While the survey did not have a direct question on whether the respondent, or someone from their family, had faced any crime in the recent years, the respondents were asked if they had had any contact with the police—i.e., whether they or someone in their family had contacted the police, or the police had contacted them in the last 4–5 years, and the reasons behind the same. The findings reveal that 14 percent respondents have had some form of contact with the police in the last 4–5 years, while the majority, 82 percent, did not have any such contact.

Of those who had any police contact in the last 4–5 years, while most respon-dents had contacted the police themselves (69%), in about 16 percent cases, the police had contacted the respondents. An interesting finding was that when seen across the economic profile of people who had been contacted by the police, the poorest were nearly twice as likely to have been contacted by the police as the rich (Fig. 4.1). However, it is important to note that since only about 14 percent of the survey sample, or 2202 people, had had any kind of contact with the police in the last 4–5 years, the above analysis being done using a much smaller sample.

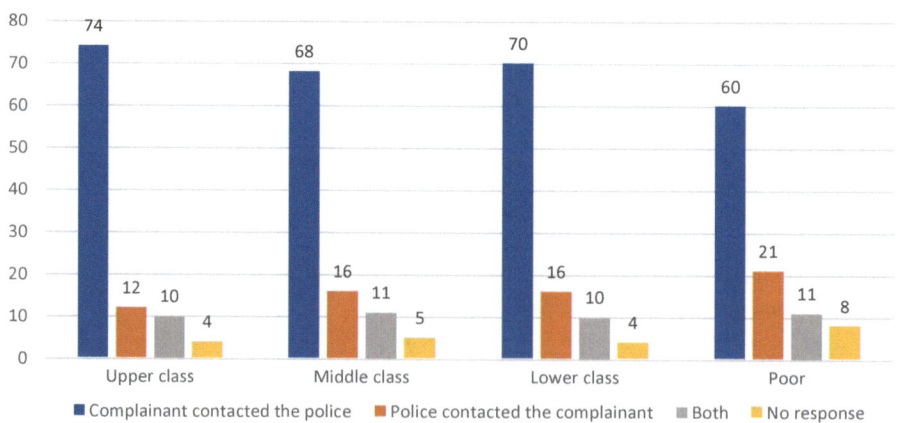

Note: *Figures are percentages. Figures are rounded off. N=2202.*

Source: SPIR 2018, Common Cause

Fig. 4.1 "Did you or someone from your family contact the police or the police contacted you?"

---

[1] Lorrigio, P (January 19, 2008). "You're Safer Than You Think: Statistics Expert". *Toronto Star.* Retrieved December 14, 2020 from https://www.thestar.com/news/crime/2008/01/19/youre_safer_than_you_think_statistics_expert.html.

Question (If the respondent had had contact with the police in the last 4–5 years)
What was the reason for contacting the police or the police contacting you?

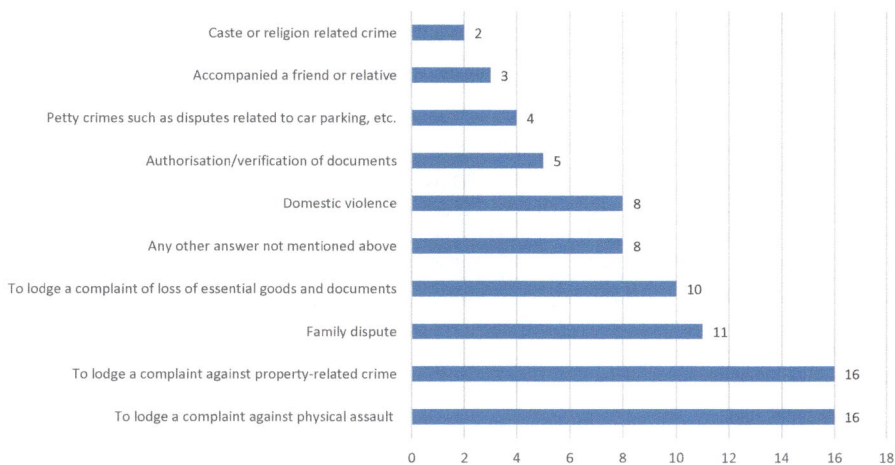

Note: Figures are in percentages. Rest of the respondents did not respond. Figures are rounded off.

Source: SPIR 2018, Common Cause

Fig. 4.2   Reason for police contact

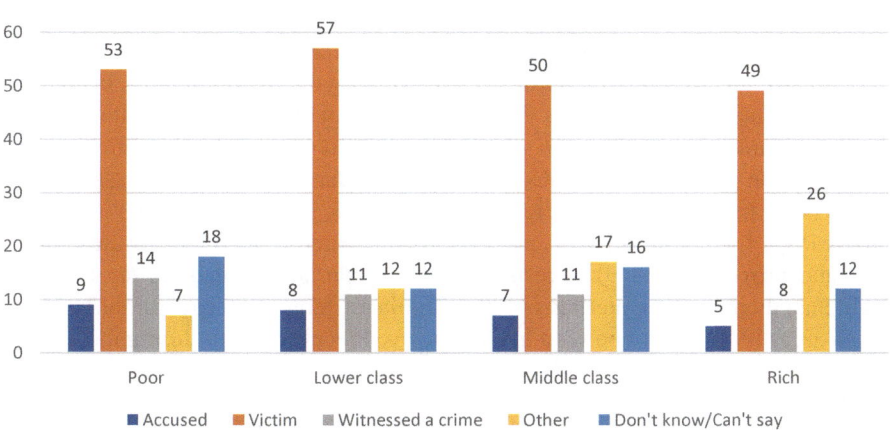

Note: Figures are percentages. Figures are rounded off.

Source: SPIR 2018, Common Cause

Fig. 4.3   "Were you an accused, victim or witnessed a crime?"

The most common reason for people to contact the police[2], as reported by them, was to lodge a complaint against physical assault and to lodge a complaint against property-related crimes (16% cases each), followed by family dispute (11%), and to lodge a complaint of loss of essential goods and services (10%) (Fig. 4.2).

Again, with regards to the contact with the police, the poorest are nearly twice as likely to be the accused (9%) than the rich (5%) (Fig. 4.3).

Table 4.3 Sense of safety among people during different times of the day

	Those who feel very unsafe	Those who feel somewhat unsafe	Those who feel not very unsafe	Those who feel not at all unsafe	Overall those who feel unsafe	Overall those who feel safe
Perception of safety early morning	13	18	19	47	**31**	**66**
Perception of safety during the day	12	18	20	47	**30**	**67**
Perception of safety at night	23	21	16	36	**44**	**52**

Source: SPIR 2018, Common Cause
Note: Figures are percentages. Rest of the respondents did not respond. Figures are rounded off

Question asked: How unsafe do you feel in your village/neighborhood during different times of the day—very, somewhat, not very or not at all?

In order to assess people's overall feeling of safety in their locality, respondents were asked whether or not they feel safe in their village or neighborhood at night, during the day, and early morning. Nearly an equal proportion of one-third persons (31%) stated feeling unsafe in the morning and during the day (Table 4.3). In contrast, a high percentage of respondents (44%) indicated that they do not feel safe at night.

To get a more comprehensive sense of perception of safety at different intervals of the day, an Index was computed. This revealed that 34 percent expressed feeling highly safe in their village/ neighborhood and 28 percent stated feeling highly unsafe (Fig. 4.4). While an equal proportion of men and women feel unsafe at night, a greater proportion (51%) of respondents in urban areas stated feeling unsafe at night than their rural counterparts (40%). Similar differences across rural (28%) and urban areas (34%) could be seen in the perceived level of safety during the day.

---

[2] People were asked to report on the causes of contact with the police for up to two instances. Because of very few responses regarding a second instance of contact with the police (*n = 747*, excluding those who said "don't know/can't say"), only the first responses of people's contact with the police have been analyzed here. The trends mentioned here, however, are consistent across both the responses regarding incidents of contact with the police.

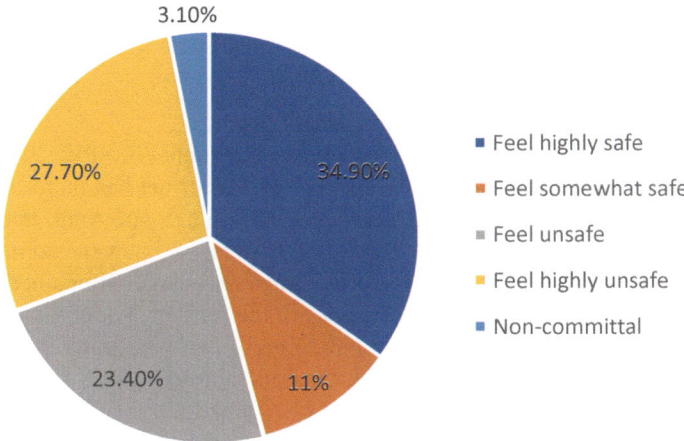

Source: SPIR 2018, Common Cause

Fig. 4.4 Index of safety

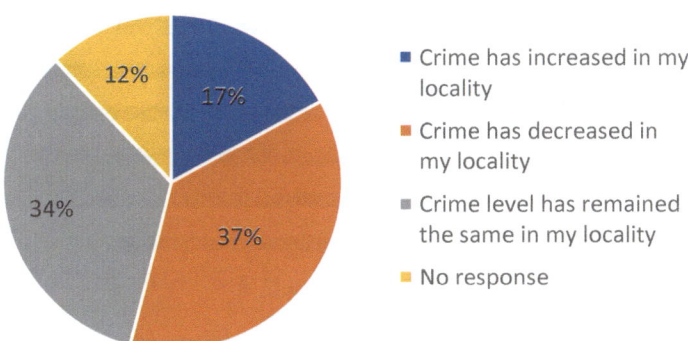

Note: Figures are rounded off.

Source: SPIR 2018, Common Cause

Fig. 4.5 Over one-third believes that crime in their locality has reduced

Question asked: In the last 2–3 years, has crime in your locality increased, decreased or remained the same?

An important aspect of understanding citizens' sense of security entails understanding their perceptions of crime and security in their locality. Fewer people expressed that crime had increased (17%) in their locality compared to 37 percent of those who considered a reduction in the incidence of crime (Fig. 4.5). A little over one-third (34%) stated that there was no change in the occurrence of crime. As the locality increases in size and urbanity, the perception of increase in crime also grows, i.e., respondents in cities were most likely to report an increase in crime in their locality than those in towns. Twenty-seven percent of those in cities reported an increase in crime in the last 2–3 years, in towns, the percentage of those respondents who reported so dropped to nearly 12 percent, while 15 percent said so in villages. On the other hand, though, nearly similar proportions of respondents from these localities said that crime had decreased in the last 2–3 years—38 percent in villages and towns each and 35 percent in cities.

SPIR 2019: Findings from Police Personnel's Survey

When a similar question was asked to the police personnel in SPIR 2019, the percentage of civil police personnel who responded that crime has increased in their jurisdiction was the same as the percentage of personnel who think that crime in their jurisdiction has decreased in the past 2–3 years—36 percent each. Roughly, one-fifth of the police reported that the crime rates have largely remained the same. The police personnel were probed further as to the reasons behind the increase or decrease in crime. Interestingly, while police personnel who think that crime has increased are most likely to attribute the phenomenon to societal reasons such as unemployment and lack of education, those who think that crime has decreased are most likely to offer improved policing (police becoming more active, stricter, etc.) as a primary reason for crime reduction.

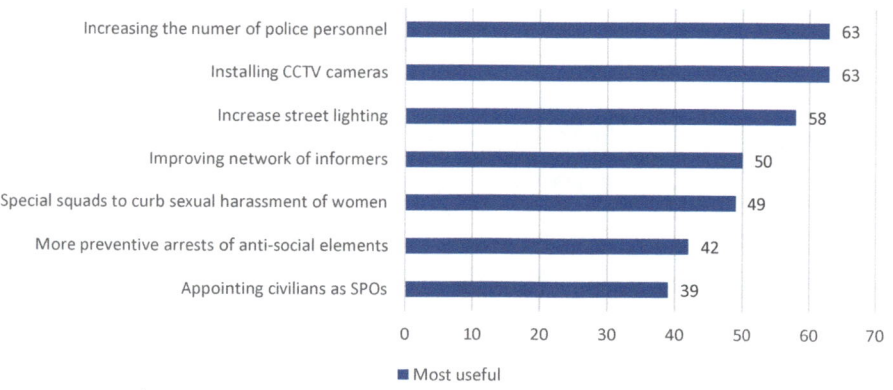

All figures are in percentages and rounded off. Only responses to "most useful" (rating of 10 on a scale of 10) have been given here. Rest of the respondents rated below 10 or did not answer.

Source: SPIR 2019, Common Cause

Fig. 4.6 Police's opinion on measures to curb crime

Question: On a scale of one to ten, please tell me how useful is this for reducing crime in your area? All those who rated between 01 and 06 have been clubbed as "less useful", those who have rated between 07 and 09 have been marked as "more useful" and those who have rated it 10 have been denoted as "most useful"

Please note that these are seven different independently asked questions.

When we asked police personnel to rate the importance of some of the mentioned measures to curb crime, about three out of five civil police personnel (63%) considered installing CCTVs in all areas and said that increasing manpower was most important (Fig. 4.6). Police personnel also felt that appointing civilians as special police officers is least helpful in curbing crime, compared to other measures.

Table 4.4 "What is the most important step that the police should take to control crime?"

Spread education/awareness	13
There should be more patrolling	10
Increase the staff in police	10
Police should be stricter	8
Laws/rules should be stricter	8
Police should work honestly and with more dedication	7

Source: SPIR 2019, Common Cause
All figures are in percentages and are rounded off

Question asked: In your opinion, what is the most important step that the police should take to control crime? _____

On being asked an open-ended question about the most important steps that the police can take to control crime, "spreading education/awareness" had the highest proportion of responses among civil police personnel, with about 13 percent police reporting it as the most important step to control crime (Table 4.4).

2. Crime Registration and Police Investigation

SPIR 2018: Findings from People's Survey

In the same manner as the increasing crime rates do not necessarily indicate a deterioration in police performance, people's experience with crime and their perception of safety does not necessarily indicate their experience with the police and their satisfaction with the police. Therefore, in order to assess people's satisfaction with the police work and their experience with crime registration, separate questions were asked in the survey.

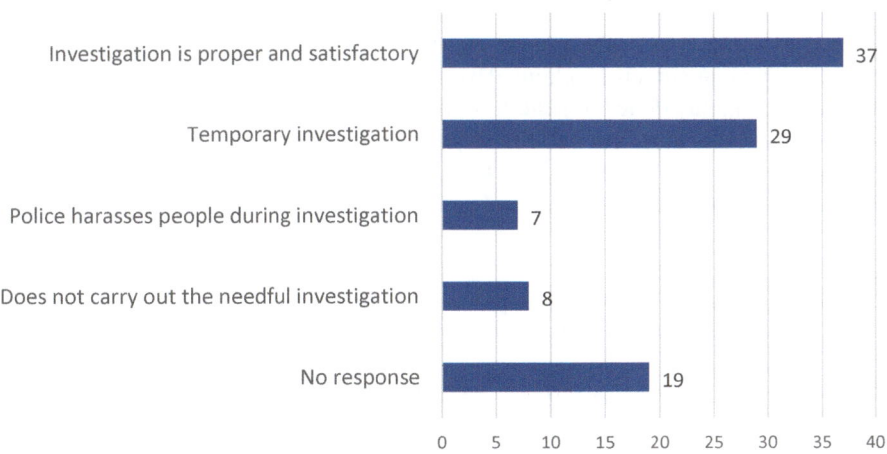

Note: Figures are percentages and are rounded off.

Source: SPIR 2018, Common Cause

Fig. 4.7 People's opinion on police's investigation

Question asked: In your opinion, is the police's investigation of such incidents (of crime) proper and satisfactory or is it temporary investigation?

On being asked about the overall level of satisfaction with police's investigation of crimes such as murder, assault, robbery, etc., the people elicited a mixed response. On one hand, more than one in three citizens felt that their investigation is satisfactory and proper (37%). On the other hand, about 29 percent expressed that the investigation is not up to the mark and often faulty in nature. Nearly seven percent reported that the police harass people during investigation and eight percent believed that the police do not carry out the needful inspection (Fig. 4.7). Satisfaction with police's investigation is highest in towns, among upper castes and those who belong to upper class. Further, experience of harassment by police during investigation is mostly reported by Scheduled Tribes, Scheduled Castes, Muslims, and those residing in small cities.

Some questions were asked specifically to the 14 percent of people who had had contact with the police in the last 4–5 years, to assess the patterns of reporting and the experiences of the people with the police, as opposed to general perceptions.

The survey revealed that the most common mode of contacting the police remains visiting the police station in person, with nearly 70 percent respondents having contacted the police by visiting the police station and only about 14 percent reached out to the police over the phone. Further, the respondents in most cases were accompanied by either a family member (38%), neighbor or friend (17%) or an influential person (14%) while visiting the police station, with just about one of five persons visiting the police station alone.

In India, while the registration of cognizable complaints[3] is mandated under law, many complaints are not registered. Preventing, refusing, and delaying the process of First Information Report (FIR) and complaint registration impede access to justice at the very beginning. This is also one of the central reasons why crime rates cannot be used as a marker of police performance, because of the common practice of non-registration of crime.[4] In a study done by the Uttar Pradesh Police Commission in 1970–71, it was unanimously admitted by the officers that concealment and minimization were commonly done by them. It was noted, contrastingly, that increase in crime rates in some cases may be a result of improving registration of crimes in that state.[5]

Findings from our survey suggest that among those who had any kind of contact with the police in the last 4–5 years, 61 percent respondents were able to successfully

---

[3] Cognizable offences are those in which a police officer can arrest without warrant (First Schedule, Criminal Procedure Code, 1973). It includes serious and violent offences such as rape, murder, kidnapping, etc.

[4] Rao, U. N., Dr., & Tiwari, Arvind. "A Study on Non-Registration of Crimes: Problems & Solutions" (Rep.). Bureau of Police Research and Development, Ministry of Home Affairs, Government of India. http://www.bprd.nic.in/WriteReadData/userfiles/file/201612200235022990797Report-Non-Registrationof CrimesProblems&Solutions.pdf (accessed November 24, 2017).

[5] Chandra, P. "NCRB Data Names Kerala as India's 'Crime Capital', But Here's Why It's a Good Thing". India Times, September 27, 2016. https://www.indiatimes.com/news/ india/ncrb-data-names-kerala-as-india-s-crime-capitalbut-here-s-why-it-s-a-good-thing-262492.html (accessed November 24, 2017).

register their FIR/ complaint[6] and about 24 percent were unable to do so. Those in rural areas were relatively more likely to report success in filing complaint/ FIR.

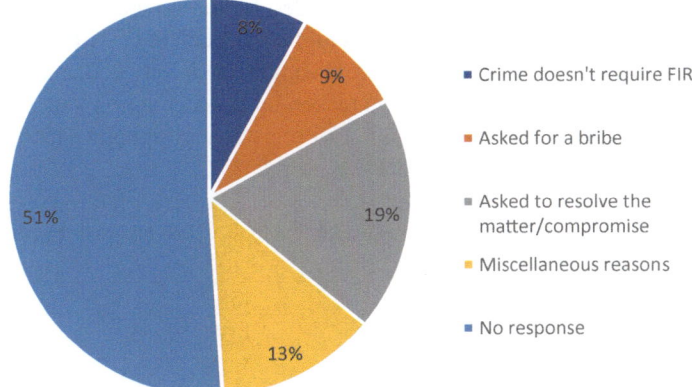

Note: Only among those who reported non-registration of FIR; n= 518. Figures are rounded off.

Source: SPIR 2018, Common Cause

Fig. 4.8 Reasons for non-registration of complaint/FIR

Question asked: Why did the police not file your complaint/ FIR?
One-fifth of the respondents (19%) whose complaint or FIR was not registered were asked to resolve the matter or arrive at a compromise (Fig. 4.8). This was the most commonly cited reason for non-registration of complaint/ FIR. Nearly one in ten (9%) said the non-registration was because they were asked to pay a bribe by the police. A disproportionately high number of one in two respondents (51%) did not reveal the reason for non-registration of complaint/ FIR.

There is a difference of ten percentage points in the complaints/FIR that were read out[7] (52%) and those that were written (42%). However, when looked at in terms of locality, a divergent trend emerges. The FIR/complaint was far more likely to be read out in rural areas than urban areas (57% as opposed to 40%). On the other hand, urban areas accounted for a greater percentage of complaints that were formally written and recorded (52%). Sixty percent of those whose complaint/FIR was

---

[6] In the survey, the terms complaint and FIR were used interchangeably because many respondents would not be familiar with the difference. Therefore, it needs to be noted that even if the complaint of the respondent was noted by the police, it does not indicate registration of FIR necessarily.

[7] A First Information Report (FIR) is an official registration by the police of a cognizable offence. It is a written document and Section 154(1) of the Code of Criminal Procedure (CrPC), 1973 provides that every information relating to the commission of a cognizable offence, if given orally to an Officer-in-Charge of a Police Station shall be reduced to writing by him or under his direction, be read over to the informant. Every such information whether given in writing or reduced to writing, shall be signed by the person giving it, substance thereof shall be entered in a book in a prescribed manner.

registered, received a copy of their complaint[8] whereas 30 percent did not. Men and those in urban areas were more likely to receive a copy of their complaint/FIR.

Respondents who reported contact with the police in the last 4–5 years were asked whether they were satisfied with the help provided by the police. Around a quarter (24%) stated that they were very satisfied, a higher proportion of 41 percent were somewhat satisfied, nearly one in ten (9%) were somewhat dissatisfied, and 14 percent were fully dissatisfied. The most common reason for dissatisfaction with the police help was the outright refusal by the police to register a complaint (19%), demand a bribe (13%) or abusive behavior (12%).

Table 4.5 Reasons for people to be hesitant to approach the police (as reported by the common people)

Fear of police	15
Police extracts money/ is corrupt	15
Problem could be resolved by community elders	8
It is not good for the family name and prestige to be involved with the police	4
Police is not fair to everyone	4
Lawyers/ friends/ associates suggested not to go to police	2
Did not feel the need to/no such opportunity arose	2
Previous experience with police was bad	2
Fear of dominant caste / religious group	1
Other reasons	7
Do not know	41

Source: SPIR 2018, Common Cause
Note: Figures are in percentages and are rounded off

Question: Very often, even in times of need, people are hesitant to visit the police or seek help. What is the single most important reason for this?

People, when asked why they hesitated in approaching the police, were most likely to say fear of police (15%), followed by demands for bribes (14.5%) (Table 4.5). Studies globally have pointed toward the fear of police being a major reason for failure of the people to report crime, particularly amongst vulnerable communities such as women, people of color, etc.

SPIR 2019: Findings from Police Personnel's Survey

The unwillingness of the police to register FIRs is glaringly visible even in the responses of the police personnel in SPIR 2019. Despite the landmark case of *Lalita Kumari versus Government of Uttar Pradesh*, 2013 (in which the Indian Supreme Court held that if a victim's statement discloses information about a cognizable offence, the registration of the FIR is mandatory), it is common for police personnel to refuse filing FIRs even in serious, cognizable cases. This is apparent even from the findings of our survey with police personnel. When asked to choose between directly registering FIRs or conducting preliminary investigations for serious

---

[8] Section 154(2) of the CrPC provides that a copy of the information as recorded under sub-section (1) shall be given forthwith, free of cost, to the informant.

complaints, about 61 percent of the civil police reported that they agreed more with the statement that— "*No matter how serious a complaint, there must be a preliminary investigation before registering an FIR*". Only 37 percent of the civil police personnel reported that they agreed more with this statement— "*For all serious complaints, FIR must be directly registered*".

Further, there is a tendency amongst the police personnel to link crime *registration* with the actual *prevalence of crime* in an area, which can then reflect poorly on their performance as custodians of law and order. A 2016 BPR&D study notes that management of crime statistics by police functionaries has linkages with performance appraisal, and this is one of the most important reasons for non-registration of crimes in India.[9] In order to assess if this is indeed the case, the police personnel in the 2019 survey were asked to choose between the following statements: (1) "*An increase in the number of FIRs indicates an increase in crime in the given jurisdiction*"; or (2) "*An increase in the number of FIRs does not indicate an increase in crime, rather, it indicates that there is only increase in registration of complaints by police*". Fifty-four percent of the civil police personnel are of the opinion that it indicates a surge in crime in the given jurisdiction. About 43 percent reported that it indicates an increase in "registration" of the complaints by the police. More experienced personnel are also more likely to believe that an increase in FIRs denotes a hike in complaints registration by police. However, counter-intuitively, police personnel with higher levels of education are more likely to hold both the problematic opinions, that a preliminary investigation is necessary before registration of FIR even in serious cases and that an increase in crime rates indicates an increase in crime in the given jurisdiction.

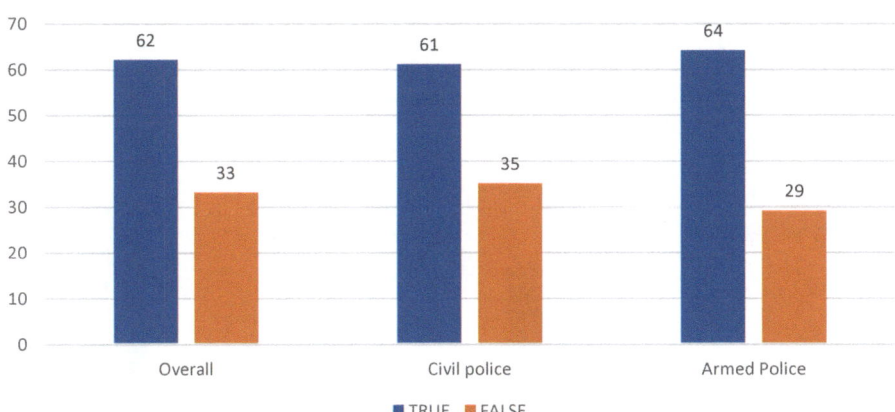

Note: All figures are in percentages and are rounded off. Rest of the respondents did not answer.

Source: SPIR 2019, Common Cause

Fig. 4.9 "The number of crimes reported are lesser than the number of crimes committed in the society"

---

[9] Rao, U.N.B., 2016, "A Study on Non-Registration of Crimes: Problems and Solutions." Mumbai: Tata Institute of Social Sciences. Available at http://www.bprd.nic.in/WriteReadData/userfiles/file/201612200235022990797Report-Non-RegistrationofCrimesProblems&Solutions.pdf [Accessed 26 July 2019].

Question asked: There is a perception among common people that the numbers of crime reported are lesser as compared to the number of crimes committed in reality. To what extent do you think this is true—completely true, somewhat true, somewhat false, completely false?

Answer categories of completely true and somewhat true have been clubbed as "true to some extent", whereas the answer categories of "completely false and somewhat false" have been clubbed as "false to some extent".

Police personnel also agree to a significant extent, somewhat paradoxically, that the number of crimes reported are lesser than the number of crimes committed in the society. Sixty-two percent police personnel agreed with the statement that "*the number of crimes reported are lesser than the number of crimes committed in the society*" (Fig. 4.9).

When we asked the police their opinion on how hesitant a common person is to contact them even when there is a need, about 43 percent of the police personnel reported that the common person is hesitant (very hesitant and somewhat hesitant combined). Nearly 52 percent reported that the common person is barely hesitant to contact the police (Fig. 4.10). The most commonly cited reason for people being hesitant to approach the police was that people are fearful of the police.

3. Human Rights Violation and Corruption

SPIR 2018: Findings from People's Survey

The fact that a large number of people believe that a major reason for people to be hesitant of going to the police is because it is corrupt, as mentioned above, indicates that police contact and corruption are intrinsically linked in the perception of the people. Similarly, findings suggest that fear is a major indicator hindering people-police contact. In this sub-section, therefore, we look at the survey findings pertaining to corruption in and human rights violations by the police.

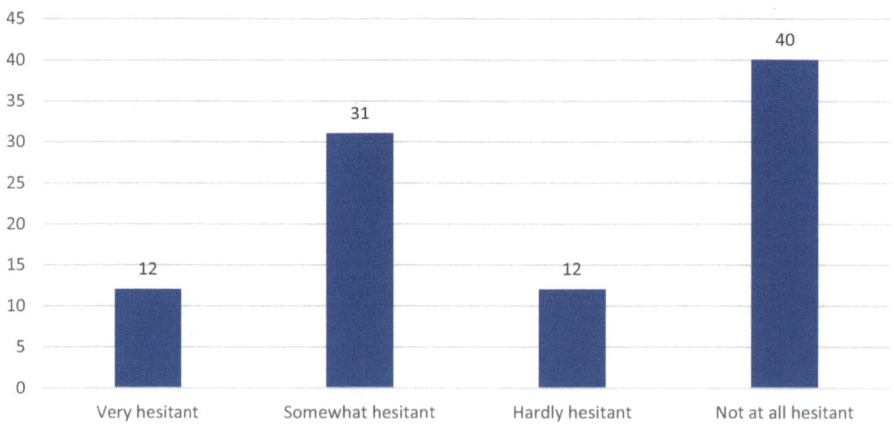

Note: All figures are in percentages and are rounded off. Rest of the respondents did not answer.

Source: SPIR 2019, Common Cause

Fig. 4.10 "To what extent is a common person hesitant to contact the police even when there is a need?"

Table 4.6 Paying a bribe to get work done by the police

	Those who had to pay a bribe to get work done	Those who did not have to pay a bribe to get work done
Overall	**34**	**50**
Upper caste	34	51
OBC	37	47
Scheduled caste	34	50
Scheduled tribe	22	55
Muslims	38	48

Source: SPIR 2018, Common Cause
Note: Figures are percentages. Rest of the respondents did not respond

Question: "(If during the last 4–5 years whenever you contacted a police officer or visited the police station) did you have to pay bribe to get your work done?"

Among those people who had had contact with the police in the last 4–5 years, 34 percent had to pay a bribe to get their work done, while one out of two (50%) said they did not have to pay a bribe to get their work done. While men and women were nearly equally likely to be affected by corruption in the police, across class categories, the poor were most likely to be compelled to pay bribe. Similarly, Muslims, OBCs, socio economically poor respondents were also most likely to have paid money to the police (Table 4.6).

When we look at the people's overall perception of corruption within the police, including the perceptions of those who did not have any contact with the police in the last 4–5 years, the proportion of people who believe that police is corrupt goes up significantly. Over 50 percent people agree with the statement (fully agree and somewhat agree combined) that the "*police is corrupt- it does not do its job without a bribe*", while 31 percent disagree. Within the different categories of police, senior police officers are thought to be least corrupt, while local and traffic police are considered more corrupt. It needs to be noted here, however, that while corruption is seen to be high amongst the police, but that is not a major deterrent for the people to approach the police. As mentioned in the above section under Table 4.4, while both corruption and fear of police are the most cited reasons for people to be hesitant of approaching the police, just 15 percent of the people overall say that they are hesitant to go to the police because it is corrupt or because they extract money.

In terms of the fear of police, an index was created using the citizens' survey questions. It was found that 14 percent of the respondents are highly fearful of the police and 30 percent are somewhat fearful of it. Twenty-four percent were found to be not much fearful and 27 percent turned out to be not at all fearful. People are most fearful of being beaten up by the police (about two in five). Across religions, Sikhs are the most fearful of the police (Fig. 4.11).

A possible explanation of the Hindus being more fearful of the police (14% highly fearful as against 10% Muslims and 11% Christians) is that the poor and vulnerable communities, who tend to be more distrustful of the police, are not evenly distributed. For instance, the category "Hindus" includes a large number of

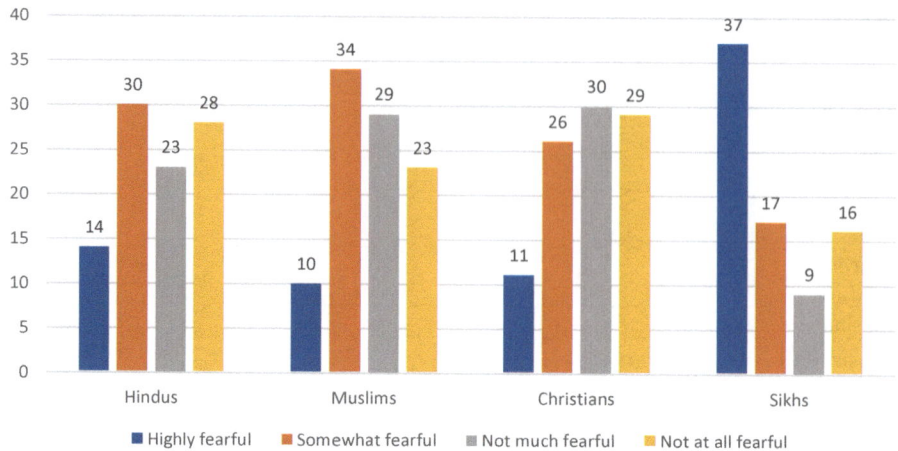

Source: SPIR 2018, Common Cause

Fig. 4.11 Religion-wise distribution of police fear

the SC/ST/OBC respondents and the category "Christians" includes tribal respondents in the insurgency-affected areas of the Central and North-Eastern India. We also know from the responses of SPIR 2018 that the poor are also more likely to be contacted by the police than the rich (see Fig. 4.1). The higher levels of fear of the police among the Sikhs could be attributed to widespread accusations of extrajudicial killings by the police during more than two decades of militancy and separatist violence in Punjab where the Sikhs are mainly concentrated.

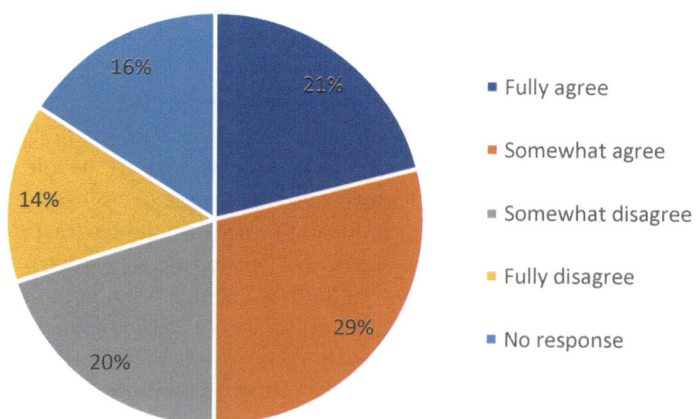

Source: SPIR 2018, Common Cause

Fig. 4.12 "There is nothing wrong in the police being violent toward criminals"

Question asked: There is nothing wrong in the police being violent toward criminals. Do you agree or disagree? (Probe further whether fully or somewhat)

Despite the high levels of fear, people also, to a significant extent, condone violence by the police. One in two respondents from the citizens' survey agreed with the statement that *"there is nothing wrong with the police being violent toward criminals"* (Fig. 4.12).

SPIR 2019: Findings from Police Personnel's Survey

The police personnel, in the survey, were also asked to rate their own force in terms of the level of corruption vis-à-vis other institutions. When asked if the police institution is more, less or as corrupt as other government institutions, most police personnel (43%) respond that it is less corrupt than other government institutions. Only about six percent of personnel feel that the police is more corrupt, while nearly 15 percent of personnel are of the opinion that it is as corrupt as other institutions.

On questions to measure the inclination to use violence, it was found that the police personnel themselves expressed willingness to use violence. Nearly one out of five police personnel (19%) feels that killing dangerous criminals is better than a legal trial. Further, three out of four (75%) personnel feel that it is justified for the police to be violent toward criminals. As many as 83 percent police personnel believe that there is nothing wrong in the police beating up criminals to extract confessions. Again, disturbingly, police personnel with higher levels of education are more likely to hold such opinions. An index was created on the inclination of the police to use or justify violence based on these questions. Overall, 35 percent police personnel have a high inclination to use or justify violence, while 43 percent police personnel have a medium inclination to do so. Police personnel in states like Karnataka, Chhattisgarh, and Nagaland have the highest inclination to use/justify violence, while those in the states of Odisha, West Bengal, and Punjab have the lowest inclination to do so. Almost paradoxically, in Punjab, the fear of the police amongst common people, as reported in the citizens' survey of 2018, is the highest across all states. In contrast, for Karnataka, the fear of police amongst the people is also amongst the highest (after Punjab), as is the inclination amongst the police personnel to use/justify violence.

4. Crime and Prejudice

SPIR 2018: Findings from People's Survey

Evidence from secondary data and several studies have shown that the criminal justice system in India leans against vulnerable communities such as SCs, STs, OBCs, Muslims, women, and poor people. Analysis of NCRB and BPR&D data in SPIR 2018 and 2019 shows that Dalits, Tribals, Muslims, and women are under-represented in the police, while all these groups, barring women, are over-represented in the prisons. The disposal of cases of crimes against women, children, SCs, and STs, both by the police and by the courts, is much poorer than the disposal of overall cognizable crime cases. These trends point toward a systemic bias against the vulnerable sections of the society within the criminal justice system in general, including the institution of police.

In the Status of Policing in India Report 2018, state-wise indices were created on several thematic areas so as to compare states' performances using official data by the BPRD as well as the NCRB. This included time-series analysis of the data over a period of five years across the selected states. The thematic pillars used for this analysis were:

(a) Crime rates, including rates of total cognizable crimes, violent crimes, crimes against women, SCs, STs, and children
(b) Disposal of cases by police and courts
(c) Police diversity, including the representation of women, SCs, STs, OBCs, and Muslims in the police forces
(d) Police infrastructure
(e) Prison data including the percentage of SCs, STs, and Muslims in prisons in proportion to their population in the state
(f) Disposal of cases of crimes against SCs, STs, women, and children

Analysis of crime data shows that at the all-India level, while the rate of total cognizable crime has more or less remained constant, with a slight decrease in the year 2016, but the rate of crimes against women, children, SCs, and STs have been increasing. The rate of crimes against children have had an almost three times increase, from 8.9 to 24, between 2012 and 2016. The introduction of new laws such as Protection of Children from Sexual Offences Act (POCSO), 2012 may have created an enabling structure for increase in registration of these crimes.

In terms of diversity, when looking at the five year average of 2012 to 2016, only two out of the 22 selected states for this study have been able to meet the reserved quota for SCs (Punjab and Uttarakhand); six states have been able to fulfill the reserved quota for STs (Bihar, HP, Karnataka, Nagaland, Telangana, Uttarakhand); and a slightly higher number of nine states have been able to achieve the reservation benchmark for OBCs (Andhra Pradesh, Assam, Jharkhand, Karnataka, Maharashtra, Odisha, Punjab, Telangana, and Uttarakhand). While this number might seem high at first glance, but it needs to be understood in the context of the fact that not even half the number of selected states (22) have been able to meet the reservation criteria for OBCs, and much lesser for STs and SCs. Popular myths pertaining to reservations "eating up" on the general seats are largely unfounded, particularly since reservations criteria are set mostly in proportion to the percentage of the community in question in that state. Even as of 2016, UP Police has met less than 40 percent of the reserved quota for OBCs, and the percentage of reserved seats filled has indeed fallen drastically in UP from 61 percent in 2013 to 39.6 percent in 2016. Similarly, in Tamil Nadu, as in many other states, the percentage share of seats reserved for SCs filled has fallen from 91.1 percent in 2012 to 63 percent in 2016. There is reason to believe, therefore, that things are in fact deteriorating instead of improving when it comes to representation of SCs, STs, and OBCs in the police force.

Analysis of official data from SPIR 2019 further indicates that STs, OBCs, and women in police are less likely to be at the officer-level rank (Assistant

Sub-Inspector to Deputy Superintendent of Police)[10] than the general police personnel. Among the selected states, the proportion of SC, ST, OBC, and women officers is lower than the overall proportion of officers. As against 13.4 percent general officers, there are 11.5 percent SC officers, 11.6 percent ST officers, 11.1 percent OBC officers, and 10.1 percent women officers. As per 2020 official data[11], women comprise about 10 percent of the total police force.

On the other hand, several studies in different states have been conducted on the disproportionate representation of minorities and vulnerable communities in the prisons. This has been found to be true particularly in the case of Muslims. When coupled with poor conviction rates and incidents of false implication, as recognized by courts, this points to a deeper problem of biases within the structure leading to hyper-incarceration of a particular section of the society. As we see in the survey findings, there is also a significant public agreement that often Dalits, Adivasis, and Muslims are falsely implicated. For the analysis of this Index, the percentage of SC, ST, and Muslim prisoners has been taken in proportion to their respective populations in the state as a five-year average, and it was found that in case of SCs, only four states (West Bengal, Uttarakhand, Punjab, and Karnataka) out of the selected 22 have SC prisoners in proportion to or less than their population in the State; in case of STs, this number is three (Himachal Pradesh, Madhya Pradesh, and Nagaland), and in case of Muslims, all of the 22 states have a higher proportion of Muslim prisoners than the Muslim population in the State. The differences are as glaring as more than seven times the Muslim population in Nagaland in 2014, almost six times the population of STs in Uttar Pradesh in 2015, and more than double the percentage of SC population in three states in 2015 (Kerala, Gujarat, and Assam). At the all-India level as well, this ratio continues to be skewed adversely against SCs, STs, and Muslims through all five years.

Further, the data on disposal of cases of crimes against SCs, STs, women, and children show that the charge sheeting rate, disposal of cases by police and courts, and the conviction rates are consistently lower for crimes against SCs, STs, women, and children, as compared to the overall crimes. Only a few states stand out in terms of the disposal rate of crimes against these groups being the same as or better than the overall disposal rate of IPC and SLL crimes in that state.

Thus, the official data analysis points to an institutional bias within the criminal justice system against vulnerable groups such as SCs, STs, OBCs, women, and Muslims. On the one hand, the representation of these groups in the police is poor, on the other hand they are over-represented in the prisons (except women). Further, the disposal of cases of crimes against SCs, STs, women, and children is much poorer than the overall disposal rates in the country.

---

[10] The data for SCs, STs, and OBCs are only available till the rank of DySP. Therefore, the percentage of officers amongst women in police and the overall police force has also been taken as the proportion of ASI to DySP to enable comparison across categories. It must be noted, further, that the reservation for SCs, STs is applicable even during the first promotion.

[11] Data on Police Organizations 2021, Bureau of Police Research and Development, Ministry of Home Affairs.

This systemic bias is also reflected in the survey findings of both the general public as well as the police personnel.

Table 4.7 Opinion on false implication of marginalized communities by the police

	Those who agree that there is false implication	Those who disagree that there is false implication
View of all respondents on false implication of SCs in petty crimes by the police	38	39
Views of only SCs on false implication of SCs by the police	35	43
View of all respondents on false implication of STs on Maoist charges by the police	28	42
View of only STs on false implication of STs on Maoist charges by the police	27	42
View of all respondents on the false implication of Muslims in terrorism-related cases	27	43
View of only Muslims on the false implication of Muslims in terrorism-related cases	47	31

Source: SPIR 2018, Common Cause
Note: Figures are percentages. Rest of respondents did not respond

Question asked: Now I will read out three statements. Please tell me whether you agree or disagree with each? (Probe further whether "fully" or "somewhat" agrees or disagrees). (a) Often members of backward castes such as Dalits are falsely implicated in petty crimes such as theft, robbery, dacoity by the police. (b) Often Tribals are falsely implicated on Maoist charges by the police. (c) Often Muslims are falsely implicated in terrorism-related cases by the police.

The survey data support this argument, with a notable section of the general population believing that police discriminates on the basis of caste (25%), religion (19%), gender (30%), and class (51%). People also feel that police is likely to falsely implicate persons from vulnerable communities. Thirty-eight percent people are of the opinion that SCs are falsely implicated in petty crimes by the police, 28 percent feel that STs are falsely implicated on charges of being Maoists, and 27 percent believe that Muslims are falsely implicated on terrorism-related charges. While the views of SC and ST respondents do not differ significantly on these questions from the views of the overall respondents, but a much higher (47%) of only Muslim respondents believe that the Muslims are falsely implicated in terrorism-related charges (Table 4.7).

SPIR 2019: Findings from Police Personnel's Survey

One in four (24%) police personnel believes that migrants are very much naturally prone to committing crimes, 13 percent each believe that slum dwellers and

Table 4.8 "Are the following communities naturally prone to committing crimes?"

	Very much	Somewhat	Rarely	Not at all
Muslims	14	36	25	17
Dalits	7	28	30	24
Tribals	5	26	31	27
People from poor households	7	27	29	29
Street vendors/hawkers	10	35	29	19
Slum dwellers	13	32	24	21
Industrialists	13	31	26	21
Migrants from other states	24	36	20	14
Nonliterate people	13	33	27	19
Nat/Saperas/NTs/ DNTs	9	25	27	24
Transgenders and Hijras	8	27	32	25

Source: SPIR 2019, Common Cause
Note: All figures are in percentages and rounded off. Rest of the respondents did not answer

industrialists are very much naturally prone to committing crimes. One out of two (very much and somewhat combined) police personnel believes that Muslims are naturally prone to committing crimes (Table 4.8).

One of the frequent complaints of women, SCs, and STs is that police refuse to register cases of crimes against them because they do not believe the victim. Not only do such prejudices hinder crime investigation, but are likely to negatively impact the quality of investigation, trial, and the outcome. While such a bias is evident from the analysis of official data on disposal of cases, it is also reflected in the survey findings on views of police personnel regarding cases of crimes against women, SCs, and STs.

On gender-based violence, more than a quarter of the police personnel believe that cases of domestic violence and dowry are very much false and motivated, while 18 and 16 percent respectively believe that cases of sexual harassment and rape are very much false and motivated (Table 4.9).

Similarly, 21 percent police personnel hold the opinion that cases under the SC/ST (Prevention of Atrocities) Act, 1989 are very much false and motivated, while 32 percent are of the opinion that they are somewhat false and motivated. While in cases of gender-based violence, there is not much difference in the responses of male and female personnel, in the question regarding cases of crimes against SCs and STs, upper caste police personnel are much more likely to believe that these cases are false and motivated.

As is evident from recent news reports, the fear of "misuse of law" by women, SCs, and STs has been raised as an issue by the government as well as the courts. The Supreme Court judgement in the case of *Dr Subhash Kashinath Mahajan versus State of Maharashtra, 2018* issued guidelines to prevent "misuse" of the Scheduled Castes and the Scheduled Tribes (Prevention of Atrocities) Act 1989 (SC/ST Act) and made it mandatory to seek prior sanction in writing from the appointing authority if the accused is a public servant, and from the senior

Table 4.9 "To what extent are the following cases false and motivated?"

	Very much	Somewhat	Very rare	Not at all
Domestic violence	26	40	20	10
Dowry	25	34	24	12
Sexual harassment	18	34	25	18
Rape	16	27	28	24
Cases under the SC/ST (Prevention of Atrocities) Act	21	32	26	15

Source: SPIR 2019, Common Cause
Note: Figures are in percentages. Rest of the respondents did not respond

superintendent of police of the district if the accused is not a public servant. Apart from various judgments, the court relied extensively on the 2002 Law Commission report and National Crime Records Bureau (NCRB) data.

Again, On July 27, the Supreme Court laid down directions in *Rajesh Sharma and Ors. versus State of UP* "to prevent the misuse of Section 498A [on a husband or his relative subjecting a woman to cruelty] of the Indian Penal Code (IPC) as acknowledged in certain studies and decisions".

However, the skewed reading of the crime figures and the conviction rates by the courts to use as evidence to point toward the misuse of these laws was criticized by activists, academicians, and legal experts alike. In a later case of *Social Action Forum for Manav Adhikar (SAFMA) versus Union of India, 2018,* the *Rajesh Sharma* judgement was modified, while the *Dr Subhash Kashinath Mahajan* case was effectively undone by the government through its 2019 amendment to the SC/ST Act.

However, the persistent fear of misuse prevails amongst all pillars of the criminal justice system, even after the judgements were overturned, creating further hurdles in the registration, investigation, and trial of the case. As is evident from the analysis of the official data, the low conviction rates are only a symptom of the overall bias against these groups within the justice system, and cannot be used to evince any kind of misuse of the law.

5. Crime Investigation and Political Interference

SPIR 2019: Findings from Police Personnel's Survey
While findings from the previous sections suggest that there is poor registration of crimes and less than satisfactory investigation of the crimes by the police, it is also important to understand the problems faced by the police personnel in the course of crime investigation. In order to assess this, questions were posed to the police personnel regarding the obstacles encountered by them during crime investigation.

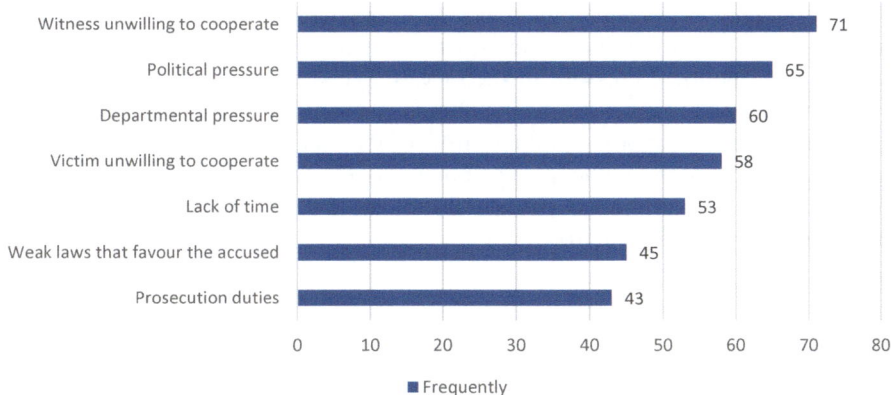

Note: All figures are in percentages and are rounded off. Rest of the respondents did not answer.
Source: SPIR 2019, Common Cause

Fig. 4.13 "How often have you encountered the following during investigation of a crime?"

Question asked: Considering the past 2–3 years of your work experience, how often have you encountered the following during investigation of a crime–many times, sometimes, rarely or never?

When we asked civil police personnel an open-ended question about the biggest obstacle they faced during crime investigation, around 28 percent reported pressure from politicians as the biggest hindrance. This is almost three times higher than "lack of witnesses", the second most cited hurdle in police investigation. When asked about the frequency of political pressure impeding their investigation, 33 percent of the civil police personnel reported that they have faced political pressure "many times" during an investigation in the past 2–3 years. As seen in Fig. 4.13 below, nearly two-thirds (65%) of the police personnel report having faced political pressure in the course of crime investigation frequently (many times and sometimes clubbed together).

Table 4.10 What is the most common consequence of not complying with such pressures?

Transfer/ posting to a different area	63
Suspension/ Dismissal	12
Threat to personal safety	5
Harsh public criticism	5
Others	3
No response	13

Source: SPIR 2019, Common Cause
Note: All figures are in percentages. Figures are rounded off and might not add up to 100

Question asked: What is the most common consequence of not complying with such pressures–transfer, suspension, threat to physical safety, harsh public criticism or others?

Further, about 38 percent of the police personnel report "always" facing political pressure in cases involving influential persons, while 34 percent reported "sometimes" facing political pressure in such cases. When the police personnel fail to comply with such pressure, the most common consequence is posting or transfer to a different area–with more than three-fifths of the civil police reporting the same. About 12 percent reported the most common consequence to be suspension or dismissal from service, while five percent also reported threat to their personal safety or physical assault (Table 4.10).

4 Learning and Way Forward

Researchers working on police must bear in mind that the idea of police reforms is to be seen as a consistent process and not as a one-time event. It is also connected to wider political and administrative reforms. The task ahead is not only to work toward an efficient police force but, more importantly, for an accountable police force. In some ways, the issues of efficiency and accountability are intertwined. For instance, both efficient and accountable policing require better training and capacity building, improved forensic or legal infrastructure, continuous monitoring and procedures for the redress of citizens' complaints. Many international agencies including the United Nations have issued guidelines in this regard after wide consultations with subject experts, practicing police officers, experts of the criminal justice system, academics, and other stakeholders.[12]

The SPIR series attempts to study, among other things, the functioning, perceptions, police-community relations, and the problem areas of policing. By filling the gap between official data and lived experiences and perceptions of the stakeholders, the SPIR series is an endeavor to provide a dashboard of indicators for policymakers, think-tanks, and advocacy groups to push for a more people-centric police force. So, the task at hand includes shedding light on both police adequacy, measured in terms of facilities, equipment or diversity, etc. and on the system of checks and balances through the citizens' perspective to ensure that the police personnel are held responsible when they fail to perform their legally mandated duties.

It is in this light that the objective of the SPIR series is to understand the perception of the people about the police, as well as the perception of the police personnel themselves about its functioning, problems, and actual ground conditions. The two studies intended to provide a snapshot on policing in the country through multiple matrices and through several sociodemographic lenses such as caste, religion, gender, class, and geographic location. The studies focused on several crucial aspects of policing and the functioning of the criminal justice system in India such as the

---

[12] Handbook on Police Accountability, Oversight and Integrity (2011) UN Office on Drug and Crime, Criminal Justice Handbook Series. UN Publications.

satisfaction of people with the police, crime investigation, corruption and human rights violations, discrimination by the police, working conditions of the police, and pressures on them.

1. *What did We Learn?*

An overarching learning from the SPIR series is that the police performance is differential for disparate groups of society. It is often the case that the same force could work in civilized, responsible and sensitive ways to one section while being just the opposite for some others, particularly for the poorest and the most vulnerable communities. We have also learnt that the poor are often at the receiving end of arbitrary treatment and brutality. That is why it is imperative to look at efficiency and accountability through the perspectives of the weak. The reports also bring out for the benefit of researchers, policymakers, and advocacy groups the lack of diversity in the system which is essential for improving caste, class or gender sensitivities through better awareness, training, and capacity-building.

Findings of the two studies suggest that while it is true that an average Indian reports overall satisfaction with the police, which is consistent with the global trend, but the same person also complains of corruption and abuse of authority. The findings from the two studies show that the citizens' overall satisfaction does not diminish the fear or the police. While people continue to feel unsafe because of crime, their hesitance to approach the police contributes to the lack of accountability of the police. Fear of the police is high amongst the people, as is also recognized by the police personnel themselves, but there is very little willingness to change the factors that contribute to this fear, with the use of violence by the police being condoned to a great extent by their own bosses, as well as by civilians.

Reporting and registration of crime are further hindered by the police assuming a discretionary role in matters of registration, going against the law of the land. Amongst those people who approached the police but their complaint was not registered, the biggest reason for the non-registration, as reported by the people, was that the police asked the complainants to resolve the matter or arrive at a compromise. A significant proportion of the police personnel themselves responded that no matter how serious a crime, there should be a preliminary investigation by the police before registering an FIR. Such opinions, which are clearly in violation of legal statutes and precedents, need to be countered in the form of training and setting down mandatory guidelines.

The SPIR series shows that the unwillingness to register cases becomes worse when it comes to crimes against vulnerable communities. People report discrimination by the police on the basis of caste, class, religion, and gender, and the police personnel report low levels of trust in female, SC and ST victims. This bias shows up not just at the time of reporting and registration, but also in the form of false implications, as perceived by the people themselves. Nearly one out of two Muslim respondents feels that Muslims are falsely implicated in cases of terrorism, while nearly one out of two police personnel is of the opinion that Muslims are naturally inclined to commit crimes. Such prejudices play out in the form of disproportionately higher rates of incarceration of vulnerable communities, reinforcing a systemic bias.

One of the major factors negatively impacting police investigation is political pressure, particularly in crimes involving influential persons. Not surprisingly, therefore, one of the foremost demands of the advocates of police reforms has been "operational autonomy" in police functioning. The Supreme Court recognized that the police are under pressure to serve the interests of the political parties in power. In response, it gave directions for fixed tenures of officers at key operational posts, in its landmark judgment of 2006 in the *Prakash Singh versus Union of India* case. It ruled that the law and order and investigation functions of the police should be separated. The separation of crime investigation duties of the police was also highlighted in the Second Administrative Reforms Commission report. It recommended insulating "crime investigation, ... both from political interference and from the day-to-day law and order functions that the police are saddled with." Unfortunately, these directives have not been complied with, and in fact have been severely diluted by the State governments. So much so that punishment postings and political interference continue to be a common feature of police work.

2. *What We Still have to Learn and Next Steps*

We still have to learn the range of requirements for building accountability of institutions like the police which have a direct and unequal power equation with the general public. The requirements of systemic access and transparency are as important as issues of personal integrity and abuse. Future research in the area will have to evolve qualitative and quantitative methods of review and evaluation of police actions, operations, statutory duties, and safeguards against the misuse of special rights and privileges of the police. A similar study of the systemic checks and balances in the entire criminal justice apparatus, including the judiciary, prisons, and legal aid will also be very useful.

While the two SPIR reports provide an overall picture of the manner in which policing works and provide a snapshot of people's response as well as expectations from it, a more focused study on specific aspects of policing is required. For instance, the functioning of the police in states which are "conflict zones" or states impacted by either some kind of internal disturbance or external aggression, would presumably be very different from other states. It was with that consideration that states such as Jammu and Kashmir (now the Union Territories of Jammu and Kashmir and Ladakh) were kept out of the sample of the above studies. However, the next study in the series, SPIR 2020-21 (Volume I)- Policing in Conflict- Affected Regions, captures the working of the police in the conflict states.

These findings from SPIR 2018 and 2019 suggest that the nature of crime, reporting, and investigation is not simply law and order failure, but has several layers of sociocultural moorings which need to be studied in detail. The Status of Policing in India Reports series is an attempt to do that, and the forthcoming reports will address other seminal issues in detached, rigorous, and policy-oriented ways.

Survey Questionnaire (English)

State ID	Official No. of A.C.	Official No. of P.S.	Respondent No.
			As in voter list

POLICE STUDY - 2017
LOKNITI, CSDS-COMMON CAUSE STUDY

F1. State Name:

F2. A.C. Name: _____

F3. P.S. Name: _____

F4. Name of the Respondent: _____

F5. Address of the respondent *(Give landmark)*: _____

F6. Date of interview *(dd/mm/yyyy)*: _____

F7. Name of the Investigator *(Code Roll No.)*: _____

INVESTIGATOR'S INTRODUCTION AND STATEMENT OF INFORMED CONSENT

My name is_____and I have come on behalf of Centre for the Study of Developing Societies (also give your university's reference), a social science research organization and Common Cause, an NGO in Delhi. We are conducting a survey on people's perception and experience of dealing with the police. Every person over the age of 18 has an equal chance of being included in this study. You have been selected by chance. There is no risk and also no benefit in participating in this survey and your participation is voluntary. This survey is an independent study and is not linked to any political party or government agency. Your identity and the information you provide will be kept strictly confidential. Participation in this survey is voluntary. We hope that you will take part in this survey since your participation is important. It usually takes 30 to 35 minutes to complete this interview. Please spare some time for the interview and help me in sucessfully completing the survey.

F8. May I begin the interview now?
       1. Respondent agrees to be interviewed
       2. Respondent does not agree to be interviewed

INTERVIEW BEGINS:

Z1. Let us begin by talking about this village/ town you live in. How long have you lived here? *(Number of years)* _____ 97. Entire life   98. Don't know

Z1a. Which state do your ancestors belong to? *(Record state name & consult Codebook for coding)*
Name of State: _____ 98. Don't know

Z2. What is your age? *(in completed years)*_____98. No Response *(Code 95 for 95 yrs & above)*

Z3. Gender: 1. Male   2. Female   3. Other

Z4. Up to what level have you studied? *(Record exactly and consult code book)*
    _____ 9. No response

Q1. How often do incidents such as burglary, murder, physical assault, chain snatching occur in your locality-very often, sometimes, rarely or never? 1. Very often   2. SomeTimes   3. Rarely
       4. Never   8. DK

Q1a. In your opinion, is the police's investigation of such incidents proper and satisfactory or is it temporary investigation?   1. Investigation is proper and satisfactory   2. Temporary investigation
       3. Police harasses people during investigation
       4. Does not carry out the needful investigation   8. DK

Q2. What kind of police presence would you like to see in your village/area- greater, less or no change?
       1. Greater   2. Less   3. No change, same as before   8. DK

Q3. From time to time, for different purposes, people have some kind of contact with the police. In the last 4-5 years, have you or your family member had any kind of contact with the police?

2. Yes   1. No   8. DK

(If in Q3 the respodent's answer is NO or DK, then please do no ask questions Q3a to Q8a and move to Q9)

Q3a. *(If in Q3, answer is yes)* So did you or someone from your family contact the police or the police contacted you?

1. I contacted the police   2. Police contacted me   3. Both   8. DK   9. NA

Q3b. *(If in Q3, answer is yes)* What was the reason for contacting the police or the police contacting you? *(Investigator can write down upto two reasons for police contact and alongside each reason, kindly ask the respondent whether she or he was an accused, victim or witnessed a crime.)*

Q3ba.   **Reason for police contact**

a._____ 98. DK/CS   99.NA

1. Accused   2. Victim   3. Witnessed a crime   4. Other_____   8. DK   9. NA

Q3bb.   b._____ 98. DK/CS   99.NA

1. Accused   2. Victim   3. Witnessed a crime   4. Other_____   8. DK   9. NA

Q4. How did you first contact the police- over the phone, visited the police station, via internet/online or police visited residence or workplace?

1. Over the phone   2. Visited the police station   3. Via internet/ Online

4. Police visited the residence/workplace of the respondent   5. Other_____ 8. DK 9.NA

Q5. Who assisted you in contacting the police or visiting the police station?

1. Family member   2. Influential person   3. Neighbour / friend

4. Any other person_____   5. Nobody, went alone   8.DK   9.NA

Q6. On contacting the police, was your complaint/ FIR registered?   2.Yes   1. No

8. Can't say   9. N.A.

Q6a. *(If no in Q6)* So in that case, why did the police not file your complaint/ FIR? *(Record answer and consult codebook)* _____ 98.DK 99.NA

Q6b. *(If yes in Q6)* How was the FIR registered-was it read out, written or via mail?

1. Oral/ read out   2. Written   3. Email/via internet

4. Other_____   8. DK   9. N.A.

Q6c. *(If yes in Q6)* Did you get a copy of the FIR?   2.Yes   1. No   8. DK   9. N.A.

Q7. During the last 4-5 years, whenever you contacted a police officer or visited the police station, did you have to pay a bribe to get your work done?   2.Yes   1. No   8. DK   9.NA

Q8. How satisfied or dissatisfied were you with the help provided at the police station? *(If satisfied or dissatisfied, probe further whether fully or somewhat)* 1. Very satisfied   2. Somewhat satisfied   3. Somewhat dissatisfied

4. Very dissatisfied 8. DK   9. NA

Q8a. *(If somewhat or fully dissatisfied in Q8),* What was the main reason for your dissatisfaction? *(Record answer and consult codebook)*_____ 98.DK   99.NA

Q9. In the future, if you have a problem that requires police help, would you go to the police?

2.Yes   1. No   3. Probably   4. Have no other option   8.DK

Q10. How unsafe do you feel in your village/ neighbourhood- very, somewhat, not very or not at all?

	Very unsafe	Somewhat	Not very unsafe	Not at all unsafe	DK
a. Early morning	1	2	3	4	8
b. During the day	1	2	3	4	8
c. At night	1	2	3	4	8

Q11. Usually both men and women work in the police force. In your opinion who is more:

		Police woman	Police man	Both	Neither	DK
a	**a.** Honest	1	2	3	4	8
b	**b.** Hardworking	1	2	3	4	8
	And........					
c.	**c.** Whom would you approach for help	1	2	3	4	8

Q12. Listed below are a number of institutions. Please tell me how much trust do you have in each of th m- a lot, somewhat, not much or not at all?

		A lot	Somewhat	Not much	Not at all	DK
a.	**a.** Local police like police inspector, Sub inspector, SHO	1	2	3	4	8
b.	**b.** Senior police officer like SP, DCP	1	2	3	4	8
c.	**c.** Traffic police	1	2	3	4	8
d.	**d.** Army/Paramilitary	1	2	3	4	8
e.	**e.** Court	1	2	3	4	8
f.	**f.** Government official	1	2	3	4	8

Q13. Often women and young girls are scared to seek help from the police or visit the police station. In your opinion, what is the main reason for this? *(Record answer and consult the codebook for coding).*
_____ 98. DK

Q14. On a scale of 10 points where the 1st point at left stands for extremely ineffective and the 10th point at the right stands for extremely effective. In your opinion, where would you place the following in terms of effectiveness to get work done from the police? ***SHOW THE SCALE AND EXPLAIN (If no answer is given, then code 98)*** **Extremely ineffective**   **Effectiveness**

a.	**a.** Political connection	01	02	03	04	05	06	07	08	09	10
b.	**b.** Money	01	02	03	04	05	06	07	08	09	10
c.	**c.** Personal connections in the police	01	02	03	04	05	06	07	08	09	10
d.	**d.** Seeking help from local goon	01	02	03	04	05	06	07	08	09	10

Q15. In the last 2-3 years, has crime in your locality increased or decreased?
1. Increased   2. Decreased   3. Remained the same   8. DK

Q16. Now I will read out two statements. Please tell me which statement would you agree the most with?
Statement 1: Police is not able to function properly due to lack of training and other resources.
Statement 2: It is not that the police lacks resources, they are in fact lazy and not motivated to serve people.
1. Agree with statement 1   2. Agree with statement 2   8. DK

Q17. Do you think the police intentionally implicates people under false charges?
2. Yes   1. No   3. May be   8. Can't say

Q18. In an area, whenever there is an instance of fight between people from two religious communities, do you think the police sides with any particular religious community or remains impartial?
1. Sides with a particular religious community   2. Remains impartial   8. DK

Q18a. *(If answer in Q18 is police sides with a particular religious community)*, In your opinion, which religious community does the police take sides with? *(Record answer and consult codebook)*
_____98. DK   99. NA

Q19. How satisfied are you with police performance and their work in your area? *(If satisfied or dissatisfied, probe further whether fully or somewhat.)* 1. Fully satisfied   2. Somewhat satisfied
3. Somewhat dissatisfied 4. Fully dissatisfied   8. DK

Q20. Do you know of anyone who....?

	Yes	No	DK/CS
a. Died in mysterious circumstances under police custody	2	1	8
b. Been taken into unlawful detention by police/army	2	1	8
c. A woman who is a victim of sexual harassment or eve teasing by the police.	2	1	8
d. A victim of fake encounter	2	1	8
e. A victim of police firing, lathi charge.	2	1	8
f. A victim of police torture.	2	1	8

Q21. Very often , even in times of need, people are hesitant to visit the police or seek help. What is the single most important reason for this? _____ 98. DK

Q22. Now I will read out some statements. Please tell me whether you would agree or disagree with the following? *(Probe further whether 'fully' or 'somewhat' agree or disagree)*

	Agree Fully	Somewhat	Disagree Somewhat	Fully	NR
a. Police is blamed unnecessarily even when it does its job well	1	2	3	4	8
b. There is nothing wrong in politicians interfering in the transfer and posting of police officers.	1	2	3	4	8
c. There is nothing wrong in the police being violent towards criminals.	1	2	3	4	8

Q23. Looking at the present number of these communities in the police force, are there adequate numbers of the following groups in the police ?

	Adequate	Less than adequate	More than adequate	DK
a. Scheduled Caste such as Dalits	1	2	3	8
b. OBC	1	2	3	8
c. Scheduled Tribes such as Adivasis	1	2	3	8
And what about the following?				
d. Muslims	1	2	3	8
e. Women	1	2	3	8

Q24. On a scale of 10 points where the 1st point at left stands for extremely corrupt and the 10th point at the right stands for not at all corrupt. In your opinion, where would you place the following institutions in terms of corruption? *SHOW THE SCALE AND EXPLAIN* (If no answer is given, then code 98)

	Extremely corrupt							Not at all corrupt		
a. Local police- police inspector, Sub inspector, SHO, Beat constable	01	02	03	04	05	06	07	08	09	10
b. Senior police officer- SP, DCP	01	02	03	04	05	06	07	08	09	10
c. Traffic police	01	02	03	04	05	06	07	08	09	10
d. Army/Paramilitary	01	02	03	04	05	06	07	08	09	10
e. Court	01	02	03	04	05	06	07	08	09	10
f. Government official	01	02	03	04	05	06	07	08	09	10

Q25. Now I will read out a few statements. Please tell me whether you agree or disagree with these statements?
(Probe further whether strongly or somewhat agree or disagree)

	Agree		Disagree		NR
	Fully	Somewhat	Somewhat	Fully	
a. Police as a profession is better than other occupations because of easy access to power and security.	1	2	3	4	8
b. Compared to other professions, it is difficult to work in the police force because of high stress levels and long working hours.	1	2	3	4	8
c. Police is corrupt- it does not do its job without a bribe.	1	2	3	4	8

Q26. Often people are scared of police due to different reasons. What about you- how scared are you of the following- a lot, somewhat, not much or not at all?

	Very	Somewhat	Not much	Not at all	DK
a. Fear of being beaten up by the police	1	2	3	4	8
b. Fear of being arrested by the police for no reason	1	2	3	4	8
c. Fear of the police coming to your house	1	2	3	4	8
d. Fear of being falsely implicated in police cases.	1	2	3	4	8
e. Fear of sexual harassment or eve teasing by the police.	1	2	3	4	8

Q27. Have you ever seen a police officer violating the law?   2.Yes   1.No   8.DK

Q27a *(If answer is yes in Q27)* Then did you file a complaint?   2.Yes   1.No   8.DK   9.NA

Q27b Do you think there should be a separate body for filing complaint against police officers who violate the law?
2.Yes   1.No   8.DK

Q28. Often the police says that it is not allowed to work independently and free from political interference. Please tell me how much interference do these groups have in the functioning of the police in your locality- a lot, somewhat, not much or not at all?

	A lot	Somewhat	Not much	Not at all	DK
a. Political party & politicans	1	2	3	4	8
b. Local goons / *gundas*	1	2	3	4	8
c. Senior police officers	1	2	3	4	8
d. Economically powerful groups	1	2	3	4	8
e. Influential and dominant caste of your area	1	2	3	4	8

Q29. Do you know of someone or have heard of a case of domestic violence in your village/ locality?
2.Yes   1.No   8.DK

Q29a *(If answer is yes in Q29)* Do you know if the victim of domestic violence filed a complaint or not?
2.Yes   1.No   8.DK   9.NA

Q29b In cases of domestic violence, is the police helpful to the victim?   2.Yes   1.No   8.DK

Q30. It is often argued that police harasses certain groups of people. Have you seen the police harassing the following communities? Q30a. Is the police right or wrong in taking action against these communities?

	Yes	No	DK	Q30a. Right	Wrong	DK
a. Rickshaw pullers	2	1	8	2	1	8
b. street vendors	2	1	8	2	1	8
c. Nat dancers/street performers/*Madaris/Saperas* (specify Denotified and Nomadic Tribes in every state)	2	1	8	2	1	8
d. Beggars	2	1	8	2	1	8
e. Hijras/ Kinnars/ Kothi	2	1	8	2	1	8

Q31. According to you, in the police force of your village/ locality? *(Record answer and consult codebook for coding)*

a. Which religious community's members are more in number?_____98. DK

b. b. Which caste's members are more in number?_____998. DK

Q32. It is widely believed that police discriminates between people on the basis of different things. In your opinion, does the police discriminate?

	Yes	No	DK/CS
a. On the basis of caste.	2	1	8
b. On the basis of religion.	2	1	8
And does it also discriminate between			
c. Rich and poor.	2	1	8
d. Women and men.	2	1	8
e. People from another state.	2	1	8

Q33. Many people argue that working in the police is not appropriate for women. Now I am going to read out some such arguments. Please tell me whether these arguments are justified or not? *(Probe further whether very or somewhat justified or unjustified).*

	Justified Very	Justified Somewhat	Unjustified Somewhat	Unjustified Very	DK
a. Being in the police requires physical strength and aggressive behavior which women lack.	1	2	3	4	8
b. A woman should prioritise managing home instead of joining the police force.	1	2	3	4	8
c. Women police are incapable of handling high intensity crimes and cases.	1	2	3	4	8
d. Because of inflexible working hours, it is difficult for women to work in the police force.	1	2	3	4	8

Q34. Please tell me whether the following measures in your locality/ area have been introduced or not?

	Introduced	Not introduced	CS
a. All women police station.	1	2	8
b. PCR van patrolling in your locality.	1	2	8
c. Senior citizen helpline.	1	2	8
d. Child helpline number.	1	2	8
e. Helpline for people from North Eastern part of India *(To be asked only in cities)*	1	2	8
f. Help desk for SC & ST in police station.	1	2	8

Q35. If your daughter/son was to be the victim of any crime, would you allow her/him to visit the police station alone to file a complain? *(To be asked to everyone including unmarried respondents)*

       2.Yes   1. No   8.DK

Q35: . *(If yes in Q35)* Would you allow your daughter to visit the police station as much as you would allow your son?

       2. Yes   1. No   8. DK   9. NA

Q36. In your locality, members from which caste/community are more in number? *(Record answer and consult codebook)* _____ 998. DK

Q37. In an area, whenever there is an instance of fight between people from two caste groups, do you think the police sides with any particular caste group or remains impartial?

1. Sides with a particular caste group   2. Remains impartial   8. DK

Q37a. *(If answer in Q37 is police sides with a particular caste group).* In your opinion, which caste group does the police take sides with? *(Record answer and consult codebook)*

_____998. DK   999. NA

Q38. Now I will read out three statements. Please tell me which of these would you agree with? *(Probe further whether 'fully' or 'somewhat' agrees or disagrees).*

	Agree		Disagree		NR
	Fully	Somewhat	Somewhat	Fully	
a. Often members of backward castes such as Dalits are falsely implicated in petty crimes such as theft, robbery, dacoity by the police.	1	2	3	4	8
b. Often tribals are falsely implicated on Maoist charges by the police.	1	2	3	4	8
c. Often Muslims are falsely implicated in terrorism related cases by the police.	1	2	3	4	8

Q39. In any of the above cases, if the person is absolved of charges by the court, should action be initiated against policemen who implicated them?   2. Yes   1. No   8. DK

Q40. In the last 2-3 years, have you tried calling police (100 number) on phone in an emergency situation?

2. Yes   1. No   8. DK

Q40a. *(Only for women)* Have you ever called on the women's helpline number?

2. Yes   1. No   8. DK   9. NA

Q40b. *(If yes in Q40)* Then on calling police did you receive any help?

2. Yes   1. No   3. No one took the call

4. Number was not in use   5. Other_____   8. DK   9.NA

Q40c. *(If yes in Q40)* In your experience, to what extent has access to 100 number improved in the last 2-3 years- a lot, somewhat, not much or not at all? 1. A lot   2. Somewhat   3. Not much

4. Not at all   8.DK   9.NA

Q41. In comparison to other jobs, are the working hours of the police greater or less?

1. Greater   2. Less   3. Same as other jobs   8.DK

Q42. We know that the process of justice often gets delayed and numerous cases remain pending for several years. According to you, which institution is responsible for this delay?

1. Police   2. Court   3. Both   4. Neither

5. Other_____   8. DK

Q43. Often, police harasses those girls and boys who hang out and roam around in public places. In your opinion is this right, somewhat right or wrong?

1. Right   2. Somewhat Right   3. Wrong   8.DK

Q44. In your locality, have you seen the police preventing girls and boys from meeting and hanging out in public area?

2. Yes   1. No   8. DK

BACKGROUND DATA

Personal Information

Z4a, Z4b.

Z4a. Up to what level have your father and your mother studied?

Z4a.Father:_____ Z4b.Mother:_____   9. No response

Z5. What is your main occupation? *(Record exactly and consult codebook & if retired, try to ascer tain his/her previous occupation. If student or housewife, then note down that as well)*

_____ 98. No response

Z5a. Are you the main earner of your household?   2. Yes   1. No

Z5b. *(If No in Z5a)* What is the occupation of the main earner of your household? *(Record exactly and consult codebook)* _____ 99. NA

Z6. How far is the nearest police station/chowki from your village/locality? *(Record answer in kilometer. If answer is more than 100 kilometer then code 96)* _____ 98. Can't say

Z7. Are you married?   1. Married   2. Married (Gauna not performed, not started living together)
3. Widowed   4. Divorced   5. Separated   6. Deserted
7. Unmarried/Single 8. Live with partner but not married   9. NR

Z7a. *(If married)* Do you have a boy or a girl?
1. Boy   2.Girl   3. Both   4. None   8. NR   9. NA

Z8. What is your Caste/Jati-biradari/Tribe name?*(Consult code book for code)*

_____

Z8a. And what is your caste group? *(Double check and consult code book)*
1. Scheduled Caste (SC)   2. Scheduled Tribe (ST)   3. Other Backward Classes (OBC) 4. Other

Z9. What is your religion?   1. Hindu   2. Muslim   3. Christian   4. Sikh 5. Buddhist/Neo Buddhist
6. Jain   7. Parsi   8. No religion   9. Others *(Specify)* _____

Z10. Generally, which language is spoken in your house?*(Consult code book for coding)*

_____ 98. No response

Z11. What kind of mobile phone do you have – a normal phone or a smart phone with a touch screen?
1. Normal phone   2. Smart phone   3. Don't have a phone   8. No answer

Z11a. *(If respondent has a mobile phone)* Does your phone have an internet connection?
2.   Yes   1. No   8. No Answer   9. Not
Applicable

Z12. Do you have an Aadhaar Card?   2.Yes   1. No

Z13. Locality: 1. Village   2. Town *(50,000 to 1 lakh population)*
3. Small City *(1-5 lakh)* 4. Big City *(5-10 lakh)*   5. Metropolitan City *(Above 10 lakh)*

Z13a. *(If Town/Small City/Big City/Metropolitan City)* Type of house where the respondent lives
1. House/Flat/Bunglow   2. House/Flat with 5 or more rooms
3. House/Flat with 4 rooms   4. Houses/Flat with 3 rooms   5. Houses/Flat with 2 rooms
6. House with 1 room   7. Mainly Kutcha house   8. Slum/Jhuggi Jhopri   9. NA.

Z13b. *(If Village)* Type of house where the respondent lives
1. Pucca (both wall and roof made of pucca material)
2. Pucca-Kutcha (Either wall or roof is made of pucca material and other of kutcha material)
3. Kutcha/Mud houses (both wall and roof are made of kutcha material)

4. Hut (both wall and roof made of grass, leaves, un-burnt brick or bamboo)   9. NA.

Household Information

Z14. Total No. of family members living in the household:

Above 18 years:_____   Below 18 years :____ *(If more than 9, Code 9)*

Z15. Total agricultural land including orchard and plantation owned by your household *(as on date of survey):*

_____ *(Ask in local units, but record in standard acres. If more than 99, Code 99)*

Z16. In normal circumstances, what is your monthly household expenditure? *(Record in Rupees, if respondent*

*gives no answer, fill 000000 in the box)*_____

Z17. Do you or members of your household have the following: Yes   No

a. Car/Jeep/Van   1   2

b. Scooter/Motorcycle/Moped   1   2

c. Airconditioner   1   2

(d1. If resp. has computer/laptop)

d. Computer/laptop/Ipad   1   2 1.With Internet 2.Without Net   9. NA

e. Fan/Cooler   1   2

f. Washing machine/Microwave   1   2

g. Fridge   1   2

h. TV   1   2

i. Bank/Post office account   1   2

j. ATM/Debit/Credit card   1   2

k. LPG gas   1   2

l. Toilet inside the house   1   2

m. Motorised pumping set   1   2

n. Tractor   1   2

o. Handpump inside the house   1   2

Z18. Livestock: **Total Number**

a. Goat /sheep/pig: _____

b. Cow/Oxen /buffalo/Camel: _____

c. Any other: _____

Z19. Total monthly household income - putting together the income of all members of the household?

_____

(Record exact amount in Rupees. If respondent does not give any amount then record 000000)

Z20. Mobile/Telephone number of the respondent   _____

FILL AFTER COMPLETING INTERVIEW

E1. Were there any other people immediately present who might be listening during the interview?

1. No one   2. Husband   3. Other adult male family members   4. Adult female family members

5. Any male from neighborhood   6. Any Female from neighborhood 7. Small crowd   8. Any Other_____

E2. In how many questions did the respondent check with others for information to answer for questions?

1. None   2. One or two   3. Three to five   4. Six to ten   5. More than 10

E3. At some stage did you notice something that made you feel that the respondent was answering under some fear or pressure?   1. Yes   2. No   3. Not sure

E4. Which caste community was more in number in the locality you visited? *(Record answer and consult codebook)* _____

E5. Which religious community was more in number in the locality you visited? *(Record answer and for coding refer to Z9 Codes.)* _____

E6. Overall was the respondent cooperative?   1. Yes, very much   2. Somewhat   3. Not at all

E7. Investigator's signature *(Sign in box):*

E8. Name of the Supervisor: _____

E9. Checked by the Supervisor: 1. Yes   2. No

E10. Supervisor's signature *(Sign in box):*

Any additional notes/Cocomments

_____

_____

_____

Q1a. *(If government house in Q1)* Some people are dissatisfied with the conditions of government provided housing quarters, while some people are satisfied with it. Are you satisfied or dissatisfied with the provided housing quarters? *(If satisfied, check 'very' or 'somewhat', If dissatisfied, check 'very' or 'somewhat')*

1. Very satisfied	2. Somewhat satisfied	3. Somewhat dissatisfied
4. Very dissatisfied	8. No response	9. Not applicable

Q1b. *(If somewhat or very dissatisfied in Q1a)* What is the single most important reason for dissatisfaction with the staff quarters? *(Note down answer. Coding will be done at CSDS)*

_____ 98. can't say/no answer   99. Not applicable

Q2. *(If government house in Q1)* On a scale of 1 to 10 where 1 is the smallest issue and 10 is the biggest issue, Please rate these issue for your housing quarters:

	Smallest issue									Biggest issue	Can't say	NA
a. Water supply issues	01	02	03	04	05	06	07	08	09	10	98	99
b. Garbage Disposal issues	01	02	03	04	05	06	07	08	09	10	98	99
c. Drainage system issues	01	02	03	04	05	06	07	08	09	10	98	99
d. Electricity issues	01	02	03	04	05	06	07	08	09	10	98	99

e. Any other issue *(Note answer. Coding will be done at CSDS)*_____

Q3. *(If government house in Q1)* After submitting the application how much time did it take for your housing quarter's allocation? *(If somebody answers in 'year/s', convert it into 'months')*

(Number of months)_____98. Can't say/No answer   99. Not applicable

Q4. On an average, how many hours a day do you actually work?

(Number of hours)_____98. Can't say/No answer

Q5. On an average, how many weekly off-days do you actually get?

(Number of days)_____ 98. Can't say/No answer

Q6. With regards to your duty hours, how many times in a week are you asked to stay back at the police station even after duty hours?   1. Many times   2. Sometimes   3. Rarely
                                                                      4. Never   8. Can't say

Q6a. *(If stays back in Q6.)* What is generally the most important reason for staying back at police station after duty hours? *(Note down answer. Coding will be done at CSDS)*

_____98. CS. 99. NA

Q6b. *(If stays back in Q6.)* Do you get paid for the overtime work?

                          2. Yes   1. No   8. Can't say   9. N.A.

Q7. Given a chance will you be willing to give up this profession and go for another job if the salary and perks remain the same?   2. Yes   1. No   8. Can't say

Q8. How many times are the following facilities provided at your police station or jurisdiction–always, sometimes or never?

	Always	Sometimes	Never	No-response
a. Functional computer	1	2	3	8
b. Storage unit for the documents	1	2	3	8
c. Functional CCTNS software	1	2	3	8
d. Forensic Technology	1	2	3	8

Q8b. And are these facilities available at your police station/jurisdiction?

	Yes	No	No-response
a. Clean Toilets	2	1	8
b. Separate toilet for women	2	1	8
c. Sitting area for people	2	1	8
d. Drinking water	2	1	8
e. Facility for food for prisoners in police custody	2	1	8
f. Committee against sexual harassment	2	1	8

Q9. In the last 2-3 years, how much has the overall cleanliness in the police station increased? – A lot, somewhat, very little, or as it is? 1. A lot 2. Somewhat 3. Very little 4. As it is 8. Can't say/No response

Q10. Considering the past 2–3 years of your work experience, How often have you ever been in the following situations - many times, few times, rarely or never?

	Many times	Few times	Rarely	Never	No-response
a. ou needed a vehicle but the government vehicle/fuel was unavailable.	1	2	3	4	8
b. You had to spend money from your pocket for expenses such as stationary, carbon paper etc.	1	2	3	4	8
c. You were unable to reach the crime scene on time because of shortage of staff at the police station.	1	2	3	4	8
d. You were unable to escort an accused to the court because of shortage of staff at the police station.	1	2	3	4	8
e. You could not investigate cybercrime because of lack of technology/experts.	1	2	3	4	8

Q11. When was the last time you received training on the following issues?

	Last 2-3 years	Before that	Time of joining	Never	No-response
a. About new technology	1	2	3	4	8
b. To solve cyber crimes	1	2	3	4	8
c. About forensic technology	1	2	3	4	8
d. About human rights	1	2	3	4	8
e. About crowd Control	1	2	3	4	8
f. About caste sensitization	1	2	3	4	8
g. About physical training	1	2	3	4	8
h. About weapons training	1	2	3	4	8
i. About new rules/orders	1	2	3	4	8
j. About sensitization towards women	1	2	3	4	8

Q12. In your jurisdiction, do you think the overall crime in your area has increased or decreased in the last 2-3 years?

(If increased, check 'increased a lot' or 'increased a little'; If decreased, check 'decreased a lot' or 'decreased a little')

| 1. It has increased a lot | 2. It has increased a little | 3. It has remained the same |
| 4. It has decreased a little | 5. It has decreased a lot | 8. Don't know/Can't say |

Q12a. *(If crime has increased 'a lot' or 'little' in Q12)* In your opinion what is the most important reason behind this rise in crime? *(Note down answer. Coding will be done at CSDS)_____*

_____ 98. can't say   99. Not applicable

Q12b. *(If crime has decreased 'a lot' or 'little' in Q12)* In your opinion what is the most important reason behind this decline in crime? *(Note down answer. Coding will be done at CSDS)_____*

_____ 98. can't say   99. Not applicable

Q13. Now I will read out two statements. Please tell me which statements you agree with the most? *(Read both the statements)*

Statement 1.   Increase in number of FIRs indicates an increase in the crimes in the given jurisdiction.

Statement 2.   Increase in number of FIRs does not indicate an increase in the crime rather it indicates that their is only increase in registration of the complaints by police.

1. Agree with first statement   2. Agree with second statement   8. No answer/can't say

Q14. Now I will read out two statements. Please tell me which statements you agree with the most? *(Read both the statements)*

Statement 1.   No matter how serious a complaint, there must be a preliminary investigation before registering a FIR.

Statement 2.   For all the serious complaints, FIR must be directly registered without any preliminary investigation.

1. Agree with first statement   2. Agree with second statement   8. No answer/can't say

Q15. Considering your own work experience in police, to what extent are these following complaints false and motivated - A lot, somewhat, very rare or none at all?

	A lot	Somewhat	Very rare	Not at all	No response
a. Domestic Violence	1	2	3	4	8
b. Murder	1	2	3	4	8
c. Theft and Robbery	1	2	3	4	8
d. Crimes under SC/ST act	1	2	3	4	8
e. Dowry	1	2	3	4	8
f. Sexual Harassment	1	2	3	4	8
g. Rape	1	2	3	4	8

Q16. In your opinion, what is the most important step that the police should take to control crime? *(Note down answer. Coding will be done at CSDS)* _____

_____ 98. can't say

Q17. On a scale of one to ten, please tell me how useful the following are the following measures for reducing crime in your area-10 being most useful and 1 being not useful at all: *(If no answer, please code 98. can't say/no answer)*

	Not useful									Most useful
a. Increase street lighting in high crime area.	01	02	03	04	05	06	07	08	09	10
b. Increasing the number of police personnel.	01	02	03	04	05	06	07	08	09	10
c. Installation of CCTV cameras in all areas.	01	02	03	04	05	06	07	08	09	10
d. More preventive arrests of anti-social elements.	01	02	03	04	05	06	07	08	09	10
e. Improving the network of informers/mukhbirs.	01	02	03	04	05	06	07	08	09	10
f. Form special squads for curbing eve teasing.	01	02	03	04	05	06	07	08	09	10
g. Appointing civilians as Special Police Officers.	01	02	03	04	05	06	07	08	09	10

Q18. Considering the past 2-3 years of your work experience, how often have you encountered the following problems during investigation of a crime - many times, sometimes, rarely or never?

	Many times	Sometimes	Rarely	Never	No-response
a. Witnesses unwilling to cooperate	1	2	3	4	8
b. Victims unwilling to cooperate	1	2	3	4	8
c. Lack of time to investigate	1	2	3	4	8
d. Departmental pressure	1	2	3	4	8
e. Political pressure	1	2	3	4	8
f. Weak laws that favor accused	1	2	3	4	8
g. Prosecution duties	1	2	3	4	8

Q19. Of the various things which hinder an investigation, which is the one that hinders it the most? *(Note down answer. Coding will be done at CSDS)*_____

_____98. can't say

Q20. In your opinion, to what extent is a common person hesitant to contact the police even when there is a need - very hesitant, somewhat hesitant, hardly hesitant or not hesitant at all?

1. Very hesitant   2. Somewhat hesitant   3. Hardly hesitant   4. Not at all hesitant   8. No response

Q20a. *(If hesitant)* In your opinion, what is the main reason behind this hesitance? *(Record exactly, consult code book and code later)* _____

_____98. can't say 99. Not applicable

Q21. Imagine your daughter is in another city/village, beyond your zone of influence and she witnesses a crime. Would you advise her to go to the police station alone to report the crime?

2. Yes   1. No   8. Can't say

Q22. There is a perception among common people that the numbers of crime reported are lesser as compared to the number of crimes committed in reality. To what extent do you think this is true? *(If true, check 'completely true' or 'somewhat true'; if false check 'completely false' or 'somewhat false')*

1. Completely true   2. Somewhat true   3. Somewhat false 4. Completely false 8. No response

Q23. Do you agree or disagree with the following statements? *(If agree, check 'fully agree' or 'somewhat agree'; if disagree, check 'fully disagree' or 'somewhat disagree')*

	Agree Fully	Somewhat	Disagree Somewhat	Fully	No response
a. The workload makes it difficult for me to do my job well.	1	2	3	4	8
b. I am not able to devote enough time to my family due to policing duties.	1	2	3	4	8
c. I am permitted to do only those tasks that are asked by my seniors.	1	2	3	4	8
d. My workload is affecting my physical and mental health conditions.	1	2	3	4	8
e. My salary is at par with the kind of work I do.	1	2	3	4	8
f. My work is evaluated in a neutral way.	1	2	3	4	8

Q24. How often do the following instances happen in the police-workplaces - very often, somewhat often, somewhat rare or never?
'Senior officers talk with their juniors in a bad language.'

1. Very often   2. Somewhat often   3.Somewhat rare   4. Never   8.No response

Q25. When dealing with cases involving influential persons, how often does the police feel pressure from the following people - Always, sometimes, rarely or never?

	Always	Sometimes	Rarely	Never	No-response
a. Pressure from seniors in the police force.	1	2	3	4	8
b. Pressure from politicians.	1	2	3	4	8
c. Pressure from common public.	1	2	3	4	8
d. Pressure from media.	1	2	3	4	8
e. Pressure from human rights organization &NGO.	1	2	3	4	8
f. Pressure from Judiciary.	1	2	3	4	8

Q26. *(If they feel pressure in Q25)* What is the most common consequences of not complying with such pressures?

1. Punishment posting/ transfer to another area   2. Suspension/dismissal from service

3. Threat to personal safety, physical assault   4. Harsh public criticism

5. Any other *(record exactly)* -_____   8. No response   9. Not applicable

Q27. According to you, do the following instances happen in the police?

'Senior officers ask their juniors to do household jobs/private-personal jobs even though they're not meant to do it'

2. Yes   1. No   8. Can't say

Q28. Now, I will read out two statements. Please tell which one you agree the most with. *(Read both the statements)*

Statement 1. For small/minor offenses, small/minor punishments by the police is better than legal trial.

Statement 2. For small/minor offenses also, there should be a complete legal trial.

1. Agree with first statement 2. Agree with second statement 8. No answer/can't say

Q29. Sometimes there are instances, when the mob tries to punish the culprits. In your opinion, to what extent is it natural for the mob to punish the culprits on the following issues - to a large extent, somewhat, rarely or not at all?

	To a large extent	Somewhat	Rarely	Not at all	No-response
a. When there is a case of cow-slaughter.	1	2	3	4	8
b. When there is a case of child kidnapping.	1	2	3	4	8
c. When there is a case of rape.	1	2	3	4	8
d. When there is a case of road accident due to driver's negligence.	1	2	3	4	8

Q30. Do you agree or disagree with the following statement? For the greater good of the society, It is alright for the police to be violent towards criminals (*If agree, check 'fully agree' or 'somewhat agree'; if disagree, check 'fully disagree' or 'somewhat disagree')*

1. Fully agree   2. Somewhat agree

3. Somewhat disagree   4. Fully disagree   8.DK

Q31. In your opinion, to what extent are the following people naturally prone towards committing crimes - very much, somewhat, somewhat less or not at all?

	Very much	Somewhat	Somewhat less	Not at all	No-response
a. Migrant people	1	2	3	4	8
b. Hijras/trangender people	1	2	3	4	8
c. Street vendors/hawkers	1	2	3	4	8
d. Muslim people	1	2	3	4	8
e. OBC people	1	2	3	4	8
f. Upper caste Hindu people	1	2	3	4	8

	Very much	Somewhat	Somewhat less	Not at all	No-response
g. People from poor households	1	2	3	4	8
h. Nat/saperas/NTs/DNTs people	1	2	3	4	8
i. Tribal people	1	2	3	4	8
j. Dalit people	1	2	3	4	8
k. Illiterate people	1	2	3	4	8
l. Industrialists	1	2	3	4	8
m. Slum-dwellers	1	2	3	4	8

Q32. There are various societal groups in police. According to you, to what extent are the following groups given equal treatment - completely, somewhat, somewhat less or not at all?

	Very much	Somewhat	Somewhat less	Not at all	No response
a. Tribal police person & non tribal police person personnel	1	2	3	4	8
b. Minority religion police & Other religion Police personnel	1	2	3	4	8
c. Women police person & men police person personnel	1	2	3	4	8
d. Dalit police person & non dalit police person personnel	1	2	3	4	8
e. Junior police personnel and the senior police personnel	1	2	3	4	8

Q33. Many people argue that working in the police is not appropriate for women. Now I am going to read out some such arguments. Please tell me whether you agree or disagree with these arguments? *(If agree, check 'fully agree' or 'somewhat agree'; if disagree, check 'fully disagree' or 'somewhat disagree')*

	Agree Fully	Somewhat	Disagree Somewhat	Fully	No response
a. Being in the police requires physical strength and aggressive behavior which women lack.	1	2	3	4	8
b. Women police are incapable of handling high intensity crimes and cases.	1	2	3	4	8
c. Because of inflexible working hours, it is not alright for women to work in the police force as they cannot attend to homely duties..	1	2	3	4	8

Q34. Now I will read out one statement. Do you agree or disagree with this statement? *(If agree, check 'fully agree' or 'somewhat agree'; if disagree, check 'fully disagree' or 'somewhat disagree')*
'Sometimes, while investigating serious cases, there is nothing wrong in the police beating up criminals to extract confessions'   1. Fully agree   2. Somewhat agree
                                                   3. Somewhat disagree   4. Fully disagree   8.DK

Q35. In the criminal cases of children of following age groups, do you think they should be treated as children/ juveniles the same way as adult criminals?

	Like children /juveniles	Like adult criminals	Like adult criminals in extreme cases *(Silent option)*	No response
a. Children between 16-18 years of age	1	2	3	8
b. Children between 7 to 16 years of age	1	2	3	8

Q36. Now I will read out two statements. Please tell me which statements you agree with the most? *(Read both the statements)*

Statement 1. For the greater good of the society, Killing dangerous criminals is better than a legal trial.

Statement 2. No matter how dangerous a criminal, police should try to catch the criminals and give them a legal trial.

1. Agree with first statement   2. Agree with second statement   8. No answer/can't say

Q37. In 2006, the Supreme Court passed a landmark judgment on police reforms in the case of Prakash Singh vs Union of India. Are you aware of this judgment?

2. Yes   1. No   8. Can't say

Q37a. *(If yes)* Can you name one of the directives given by the Court in this case? *(Note down answer. Coding will be done at CSDS)*_____98. can't say 99. Not applicable

Q38. According to you, how important is it for the police to receive training on the following issues - very important, somewhat important, less important, and not important at all?

	Very important	Somewhat	Less important	Not at all Important	No response
a. About new technology	1	2	3	4	8
b. To solve cyber crimes	1	2	3	4	8
c. About forensic technology	1	2	3	4	8
d. About human rights	1	2	3	4	8
e. About crowd Control	1	2	3	4	8
f. About caste sensitization	1	2	3	4	8
g. About physical training	1	2	3	4	8
h. About weapons training	1	2	3	4	8
i. About new rules/orders	1	2	3	4	8
j. About sensitization towards women	1	2	3	4	8

Q39. If police officers are posted in their home district, would they be more efficient or less efficient?

1. More efficient   2. Less efficient   3. Doesn't make any difference   4. DK

Q40. As compared to other institutions of the government, are the police more corrupt or less corrupt?

1. More corrupt   2. Less corrupt   3. As corrupt as others.   4. Not corrupt at all   8. No response

Q41. In your opinion, what are the two steps that the government must take to ensure that police can do its job in a better way?*(Note down answer. Coding will be done at CSDS)*

a._____98. can't say

b._____98. can't say

BACKGROUND DATA

Personal Information

B5. What is your age? *(in completed years)*_____98. No Response *(Code 95 for 95 yrs & above)*

B6. Gender: 1. Male   2. Female   3. Other

B7. Up to what level have you studied? *(Record exactly and consult code book)*

9. No response

Father Mother **B7a.** Up to what level have your father and mother studied? *(Record exactly and consult code book)*

Father:_____   **Mother:**_____ 9. No response

B8a. And what is your caste group?   1. Scheduled Caste (SC)   2. Scheduled Tribe (ST)
                                            3. Other Backward Classes (OBC)   4. Other

B8b.   **B8b.** What is your Caste/Jati-biradari/Tribe name? *(Consult code book for code)*_____

B9. What is your religion?   1. Hindu   2. Muslim   3. Christian   4. Sikh   5. Buddhist/Neo Buddhist

                                   6. Jain   7. Parsi   8. No religion   9.Others *(Specify)* _____

B10. Are you married?   1. Married   2. Married (No Gauna/not started living together)
                              3. Widowed   4. Divorced   5. Separated   6. Deserted
                              7. Unmarried/Single 8. Live with partner but not married   9. NR

B11. What kind of mobile phone do you have- a simple phone or a smart phone with a touch screen?
          1. Simple phone   2. Smart phone   3. Do not have a phone   8.NR

B11a. *(If respondent has a mobile phone)* Does you phone have an internet connection?
          2. Yes   1. No   8.NR   9. NA

B12. At your home, what language do you speak in the most while conversing with your family members?

          *(Note down answer and consult codebook for codes)*_____98. No response

B13. Type of house in which respondent lives?
          1. House/Flat with 5 or more rooms   2. House/ Flat with 4 rooms   3. House/ Flat with 3 rooms
          4. House with 2rooms   5. House with 1 room   6. kuccha house

Adults Children
B14. Total no. of family members living in the household? **Adults**_____ **Children**_____ *(If more than 9, code 9)*

B15. In normal circumstances, what is your monthly household expenditure? *(Record in rupees and in case
          of no answer fill 000000 in the box)* _____

B16. Do you or members of your household have the following things?
                                                        Yes   No

a.   **a.** Car/Jeep/Van   2   1

b.   **b.** Scooter/Motorcycle/Moped   2   1

c.   **c.** Airconditioner   2   1

d.   **d.** Computer/laptop/i-Pad   2   1

e.   **e.** Washing machine   2   1

f.   **f.** Fridge   2   1

g.   **g.** Television   2   1

h.   **h.** Bank/Post office account   2   1

i.   **i.** ATM/Debit/Credit card   2   1

j.   **j.** LPG gas   2   1

k.   **k.** Toilet inside the house   2   1

B17. Total monthly household income - putting together the income of all members of the household?

          _____*(Record exact amount in Rs. If no amount given then record 000000)*

State ID

0 **1**

POLICE STUDY (Family Member) – 2019
Lokniti, CSDS-Common Cause Study

Respondent No.

Y1. State Name: **ANDHRA PRADESH**

Y2. District HQ/City Name:_____

Y3. Police residence address: _____

Y4. Closest Police Station: _____

Y5. Location: 1. Capital City   2. City   3. District Head Quarter

Y6. Date of Interview: *(dd/mm/yyyy)*: _____

Y7. Name of Investigator: (Roll no. code in box):_____

INVESTIGATOR'S INTRODUCTION AND STATEMENT OF INFORMED CONSENT
My Name is _____ and I am from Lokniti–CSDS: Centre for the Study of the Developing Societies (Please mention your university's name here), a research institute based in Delhi. We are doing a survey of police across the country, to gather their perspective towards the police system and criminal justice system. It covers aspects such as conditions of housing quarters, duty hours, work-stress, obstacles in investigation, etc.
We are interviewing thousands of police personnel and their family, across the country. Based on this study, a report on the status of policing in India will be produced.
This survey is an independent study and it is not linked to any political party or government agency. Whatever information you provide will be kept strictly confidential. The findings of the survey will be used for research work.
Participation in this survey is voluntary and it is entirely up to you answer or not to answer any question that I ask. We hope that you will take part in this survey since your participation is important. It usually takes 30–40 minutes to complete this interview. Please spare some time for the interview and help me in completing this survey.

Y8. May I begin the interview now?   1. Respondent agrees to be interviewed.

2. Respondent does not agree to be interviewed.

B1. What is the rank of the person who works in police? _____
1. Constable   2. Head constable   3. Assistance sub-inspector 4. Sub-inspector   5. Inspector
6. Circle Inspector 7. ASP/Dy. Supretendent of Police   8. Others_____   9. Can't say

F1. What is your relation to the respondent/person who works in police?
1. Partner 2. Their children 3. Their parents 4. Siblings 5. Their Parent in law 6. Others_____8. NR

F2. What is your age? *(in completed years)*_____98. No Response *(Code 95 for 95 yrs & above)*

F3. What is your main occupation? *(Record & consult codebook. If retired, find out previous job. If student/ housewife, then note that down)*_____98. NR

F4. Are you satisfied or dissatisfied with the provided staff quarters? *(If satisfied, check 'very' or 'some what', If dissatisfied, check 'whether' or 'somewhat')*
1. Very satisfied 2. Somewhat satisfied   3. Somewhat dissatisfied 4. Very dissatisfied 8. No response

F4a. *(If dissatisfied)*, what is the single most important reason for dissatisfaction with the staff quarters?*(Note down answer. Coding will be done at CSDS)*
_____ 98. can't say   99. Not applicable

F5. It is often said that policing is a very stressful job. Do you agree or disagree with the statement? *(If agree, check 'fully agree' or 'somewhat agree'; if disagree, check 'fully disagree' or 'somewhat disagree')*
1. Fully agree   2. Somewhat agree   3. Somewhat disagree   4. Fully disagree   8.DK

F5a. *(If agrees)* What do you think is the main reason for such a high level of stress? *(Record exactly, consult code book and code later)*
_____ 98. can't say   99. Not applicable

F6. In your opinion, does your spouse/parent/child *(Use the relation depending upon respondent's relationship with the police officer)* spend enough time with the family?
1. Sufficient time   2. Less than sufficient   3. Far less than sufficient   8. No response

F7. During the last 2-3 years, has your entire family *(entire family means including the police officer):*

	Yes	No	No-response
a. Been outside on a leisure holiday?	2	1	8
b. Visited relatives out of town/village?	2	1	8
c. Gone for a religious pilgrimage?	2	1	8

F8. Is your spouse/parent/child *(Use the relation depending upon respondent's relationship with the police officer)* at home during the following festivals—Always, sometimes, rarely or never?

	Always	Sometimes	Rarely	Never	No-response
a. Diwali	1	2	3	4	8
b. Holi	1	2	3	4	8
c. Eid	1	2	3	4	8
d. State's important festival	1	2	3	4	8

F9. Please tell me whether you would agree or disagree with the following statements? *(If agree, check 'fully agree' or 'somewhat agree'; if disagree, check 'fully disagree' or somewhat disagree')*

	Agree Fully	Agree Somewhat	Disagree Somewhat	Disagree Fully	No response
a. As compared to others, police officers are more prone to getting angry and irritable more easily.	1	2	3	4	8
b. As compared to others, Police officers behave more badly with their subordinate staff.	1	2	3	4	8
c. As compared to others, Police officers behave more badly with their family.	1	2	3	4	8
d. As compared to others, Police officers are more prone to alcoholism.	1	2	3	4	8
e. As compared to others, Police officers suffer more from mental health issue.	1	2	3	4	8
f. As compared to others, Police system is more unfair towards those at the lower rank.	1	2	3	4	8

F10a. If given an option, would you like your son to join the police profession in the future?

    2. Yes   1. No   8. Can't say

F10b. If given an option, would you like your daughter to join the police profession in the future?

    2. Yes   1. No   8. Can't say

F11. In your opinion, is crime higher in police locality than in other neighborhoods?

    2. Yes   1. No, it is less   3. Equally   8. Can't say

F11a. *(If yes in Q11)* What do you think is the main reason behind higher rate of crime? *(Note down answer. Coding will be done at CSDS)*_____98. can't say   99. N.A.

F12. In your opinion, are the following problems found more among police families compared to non police families?

	Much more in police families	Same	Lesser in police	No response
a. Children involved in criminal activities.	1	2	3	8
b. Domestic violence.	1	2	3	8
c. Alcoholism	1	2	3	8

F13. Which one among these four sentences truly describes your economic condition?

(Read out statements 1-4)

1. With our total household income we are able to fulfill all our needs and save some money.
2. With our total household income we are able to fulfill all our needs without any difficulty.
3. With our total household income we are not able to fulfill all our needs and face some difficulty.
4. With our total household income we are not able to fulfill our needs and face a lot of difficulty.   8. NR

References

Bureau of Police Research and Development, Ministry of Home Affairs. (2019). *Data on Police Organisations 2019*: https://knoema.com/atlas/sources/BPRD?regionId=IN https://www.the-star.com/news/crime/2008/01/19/youre_safer_than_you_think_statistics_expert.html

Lorrigio, P. (2008). *You're safer than you think: Statistics expert.* Toronto Star.

Rao, U. N. B., & Tiwari, A. (2016). *"A study on non-registration of crimes: Problems & solutions"* (Rep.). Bureau of Police Research and Development, Ministry of Home Affairs, Government of India: http://www.bprd.nic.in/WriteReadData/userfiles/file/201612200235022990797Report-Non-Registrationof CrimesProblems&Solutions.pdf

United Nations Office on Drug and Crime, Criminal Justice. (2011). *Handbook on police accountability, oversight and integrity.* UN Office on Drug and Crime, Criminal Justice Handbook Series. UN Publications: https://www.unodc.org/pdf/criminal_justice/Handbook_on_police_Accountability_Oversight_and_Integrity.pdf

Chapter 5
The Karnataka Crime Victimization Survey 2018–2019: A Primer for a National Crime Victim Survey

Sudhir Krishnaswamy and Varsha Aithala

1 Introduction

There have been more crime victim surveys (hereafter "CVS") in the last five years than in the last six decades since India became an independent republic. Given the enormous scale and expense of a national CVS, civil society groups have focused on a single or a few major cities. Significantly, no previous survey has generated data on the nature of rural crime victimization. Azim Premji University carried out the Karnataka Crime Victimization Survey 2018–2019 (hereafter "KCVS") in 2018–2019 to fill these gaps through a survey of crime victimization in a region of India. The methods and results of KCVS are critical for the formulation of a national CVS which is currently underway.[1]

KCVS is the most recently conducted CVS in India and is the first State-wide survey that allows for a fuller understanding of crime victimization across urban and rural locations. This survey builds on valuable work carried out earlier. The CHRI Survey (2015)[2] and SATARC (2017)[3] surveyed incidents of crime victimization in the urban populations of Delhi, Mumbai, Chennai, and Bangalore. The KCVS included several major and minor urban centers like Bengaluru, Mangaluru,

---

[1] Ministry of Home Affairs, Government of India "All India Citizens Survey of Police Services" (February 21, 2019) https://www.mha.gov.in/sites/default/files/PRESSRELEASE_21022019.pdf.

[2] Abhijit Sarkar, Dripto Mukhopadhyay, Cheryl Blake and Devika Prasad (2015) "Crime Victimization and Safety Perception: A Public Survey of Delhi and Mumbai", New Delhi: Commonwealth Human Rights Initiative.

[3] Avanti Durani, Rithika Kumar, Renuka Sane and Neha Sinha (2017) "Safety trends and reporting of crime" Mumbai: IDFC Institute.

S. Krishnaswamy · V. Aithala (✉)
National Law School of India University, Bengaluru, Karnataka, India

© The Author(s), under exclusive license to Springer Nature
Switzerland AG 2022
S. Krishnaswamy et al. (eds.), *Crime Victimisation in India*, Springer Series on
Asian Criminology and Criminal Justice Research,
https://doi.org/10.1007/978-3-031-12251-4_5

Mysuru, and Dharwad as well as the rural population of Karnataka State. The survey is wider in scope, to track crime incidence, reporting, and perceptions of safety and security and thereby allows us to study primary victimization (victims' experiences of crimes) and secondary victimization (arising from the treatment of victims by criminal justice agencies - the police, prosecution, and courts).[4] It circumscribes secondary victimization to focus only on the police.

KCVS is designed to allow for the analysis of crime victimization for several diverse variables - across geographies (police administrative ranges and residential location), crime types, gender, caste, religion, and economic class of respondents. Such analyses illuminate the institutional and social character of crime, the lived experience of crime-before, during, and after crimes occur, and the relationship between offenders and victims. The socioeconomic background, age, and gender of the victims as well as the nature and severity of the offenses influence people's willingness to report crime and its registration by police authorities (Broadhurst et al., 2011). This is borne out by recent Indian studies too. The SPIR (2018)[5] found that people's socioeconomic class had an evident influence on their tendency to approach the police. The rich and better educated population were twice as likely to seek police assistance on issues than the poor. Our analysis therefore increases the usefulness of this crime victimization survey as a tool for policymakers to understand the trends of crime, reporting of crime, and recording practices.

KCVS, like other recent surveys, covered personal crimes (murder, homicide, kidnapping and abduction, grievous hurt, assault and death through negligence and extortion) and household property crimes (robbery, trespass, breach of trust, motor vehicle theft, cheating, and forgery). However, it went further to include law and order offenses (riots, arson, unlawful assembly, bribery, and assault) and offenses by government officials (bribery and assault). By including all these major offenses, KCVS presents a fuller picture of crime victimization than any other crime victim survey in India so far.

Crimes of a sensitive nature such as sexual harassment, assault, dowry crimes, and crimes against children were not included, as these require stringent survey protocols to be followed, particularly with respect to security and privacy of respondents. As other surveys like the NFHS already cover gender-based crime, this gap in the KCVS may be plugged by integrating this data set.

KCVS did not survey some serious crimes such as the sale of illegal arms, narcotics, information technology/intellectual property violations, financial offenses and cybercrime, smuggling, crimes by foreigners, bonded labor, and crimes covered by special and local laws. As these crimes are very rare, the small sample size of KCVS is unlikely to register enough occurrences to allow for meaningful statistical analysis.

---

[4] Lorraine Wolhuter, Neil Olley and David Denham (2009) "Victimology: Victimization and Victims' Rights" London and New York: Routledge-Cavendish, p.33.

[5] Common Cause & Lokniti - Center for the Study of Developing Societies (2018) "Status of Policing in India Report, 2018: A Study of Performance and Perceptions" New Delhi: Common Cause.

In this chapter, we describe, analyze, and visualize the key findings that shape our understanding of the experiences of crime victimization in Karnataka. The chapter begins by clarifying the critical methodological choices made to ensure that the survey is comparable with available official crime statistics and allows for administrative insights into police organization in Karnataka. This sets the stage for a more rigorous social scientific causal analysis on questions of crime victimization. We explain the experience of crime by various demographic groups to understand the social and economic determinants of crime victimization, the likelihood of reporting, and perceptions of safety and security of people in the State. We conclude with a few useful lessons for India's first national crime victimization survey.

2   Sampling and Survey Methodology

Sampling Strategy

Using police divisions for crime surveys is an internationally recognized, standard sampling procedure. Karnataka has 30 administrative districts, organized into seven Police Ranges - Central, Northern, North-Eastern, Bellary, Eastern, Southern, and Western - each consisting of three to six districts and headed by an Inspector General of Police. Table 5.1 lists the Police Ranges in Karnataka and the districts covered by them. Within these Police Ranges, major cities - Bengaluru, Mysuru, Hubbali – Dharwad, Mangaluru, Belagavi, and Kalaburgi have Police Commissionerates.

KCVS collected data from the six Police Ranges that existed during the survey period. The Ballari Police Range was created after the completion of our survey. The Ballari Police Range which includes the districts of Ballari, Koppala, and Raichur was carved out of the North-Eastern Police Range described in Table 5.2. Table 5.2 lists and Fig. 5.1 shows the Police Ranges in Karnataka as they existed at the time of the survey and the districts covered by our survey.

Sampling Method

KCVS was administered as a household survey with a structured survey instrument that fits diverse experiences into predetermined response categories. KCVS used the multistage stratified random sampling method. The sample consisted of 2002 households (urban to rural proportion of 700:1300) across six Police Ranges which were representative at household and individual level. The sample was weighted along: urban-rural areas, class, religion, caste, gender, and geographical zones, based on Karnataka's population taken from the Census of India, 2011, and a booster to Muslim and Dalit populations to account for their underrepresentation.

The method of stratification and sample size allocation is shown in Table 5.3.

Table 5.1 Districts and Police Ranges in Karnataka

Sl. No.	Range	Districts	Sl. No.	Range	Districts
1.	Central Range, Bengaluru	Bengaluru	5.	Southern Range, Mysuru	Chamarajanagar
		Chikkaballapura			Hassan
		Tumakuru			Kodagu
		Kolar			Mandya
		KGF			Mysore
		Ramanagara			
2.	Northern Range, Belagavi	Vijayapura (Bijapur)	6.	Western Range, Mangaluru	Chikkmagaluru
		Belagavi			Dakshina Kannada
		Bagalkot			Udupi
		Dharwad			Uttara Kannada
		Gadag			
3.	Eastern Range, Davangere	Chitradurga	7.	North Eastern Range, Kalaburagi	Bidar
		Davangere			Kalaburagi (Gulbarga)
		Haveri			Yadgir
		Shivmogga			
4.	Ballari Range, Ballari	Ballari			
		Koppala			
		Raichur			

Source: Official website, Karnataka State Police (https://ksp.karnataka.gov.in/page/About+Us/Organization/en)

Table 5.2 Districts and Police Ranges in KCVS

Sl. No.	Range	Districts	Sl. No.	Range	Districts
1.	Central	Bangalore Urban	4.	North-Eastern	Ballari
		Bangalore Rural			Bidar
		Chikballapur			Kalaburagi (Gulbarga)
		Kolar			Koppala
		Ramanagara			Raichur
		Tumakuru			Yadgir
2.	Northern	Vijayapura (Bijapur)	5.	Southern	Chamarajanagar
		Belagavi			Hassan
		Bagalkot			Kodagu
		Dharwad			Mandya
		Gadag			Mysore
3.	Eastern	Chitradurga	6.	Western	Chikkamagaluru
		Davanagere			Dakshina Kannada
		Haveri			Udupi
		Shivamogga			Uttara Kannada

Source: KCVS 2018–2019, Azim Premji University

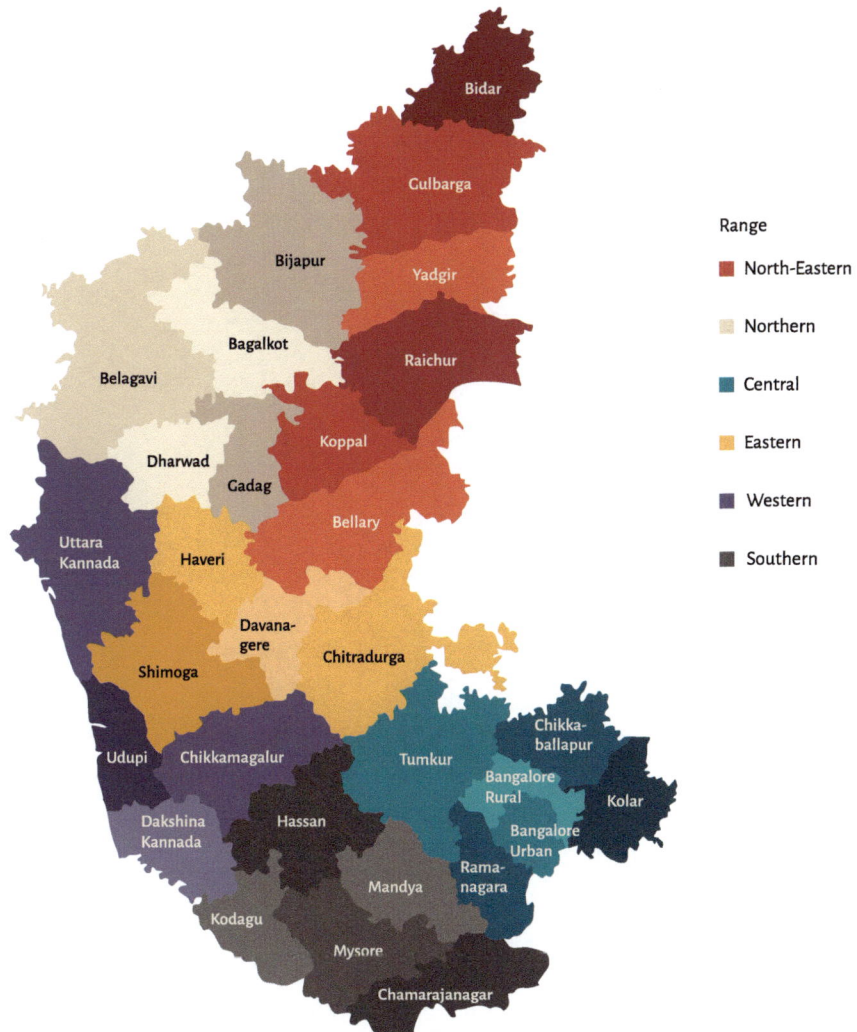

Source: KCVS 2018-19, Azim Premji University

Fig. 5.1 Districts and police ranges in KCVS

The sample size was calculated based on the number of respondents to representatively cover an entire state. As data were collected at the household level, a sample of 20 households was selected within each Police Range. The villages and wards within every range were organized in ascending order of population and the required number of villages and wards were selected through the Probability Proportional to Size method. The selected wards and villages in every range were divided into four geographical segments of equal population. Five households were selected from each of the four segments using the left hand rule of field movement starting from the center of the segment for a total of 20 households in each segment. Survey

Table 5.3 Stratification and sample size allocation

Police range	Population 2011 census	% Population	Total sample size allocated	% Rural pop.	Rural sample size	% Urban population	Urban sample size	No. of villages to select	No. of wards to select
1	2	3	4	5	6	7	8	9	10
Central	16,174,743	26.9	538	36	193	64	345	10	17
Northern	11,758,337	19.6	391	68	267	32	124	13	6
Eastern	6,955,374	11.6	231	72	167	28	64	8	3
North Eastern	11,215,224	18.7	373	72	269	28	104	13	5
Southern	8,158,627	13.6	271	73	199	27	73	10	4
Western	5,842,140	9.7	194	66	128	34	66	6	3
Karnataka	**60,104,445**	**100**	**1998**		**1223**		**777**	**61**	**39**

Source: KCVS 2018–19, Azim Premji University

questions were directed at the head of the household. Where the male head of household was unavailable to answer the survey questions (on account of work), the female members of the household answered the questions.

Questionnaire Scope and Design

The survey questionnaire consisted of three parts to collect detailed information about crimes – Part A: General Questions, Part B: Incident Report, and Part C: Socio Demographic Details. Respondents were asked if they had been a victim of a crime in the year previous to the survey. If the respondent said "yes", an incident report was completed with the details of the crime experienced, such as the victim-offender relationship, time and place of occurrence, use of weapons, and nature of injury. Then social and demographic information of the respondent including age, sex, caste, marital status, education level, and income was recorded. We also collected information on respondent's primary spoken language and occupation, length of residence in their locality and in Karnataka, and the number of times respondents moved residence in five years. However, KCVS did not specifically explore victimization of recent migrants and non-natives by recording their length of stay and based on whether they spoke the primary language of the region.

The KCVS questionnaire was methodically revised and edited to ensure simplicity of language and translated into conversational Kannada by Sigma Research and Consulting Pvt Ltd and then reviewed by an in-house translator at Azim Premji University. Respondents were not expected to describe or classify the crimes they had experienced. Interviewers drew conclusions based on the victim's description as to the nature of the crime. The individual responses and incident reports were read together and matched to the corresponding category of crime as described under the criminal statutes after the survey was completed. For crimes committed by government officials however, incident reports were not created. This was owing to the highly sensitive nature of the information provided and to protect the respondents from any unfavorable actions based purely on the victims' narratives and not corroborated independently.

Survey Administration

Sigma Research and Consulting Pvt Ltd administered the survey and conducted interviews from April 24, 2017 to May 13, 2017 covering 2002 respondents across the State. Standard interview protocols were strictly followed in the conduct of the interviews and in recording the information collected in the field. All field officers were trained on the techniques of conducting interviews and procedures to be followed. All Police Ranges in the State were intimated about the interviews via letters in advance of fieldwork. In particular, the Southern Range police acknowledged receipt of this intimation and offered assistance, if any was required, with the survey. Despite these precautions however, owing to the sensitive nature of the topic, in one instance, interviewers experienced intimidation and harassment from a local political group in an urban area where interviews were conducted. A group of local political workers raised an issue with the interviews being conducted in their neighborhood and took the surveyors to the local police station. The survey team discussed the matter with the police and were asked to return to their homes. The survey organization then changed the team and sent in a different team of surveyors to that location to continue with the interviews. Once the data were collected, it was checked for errors, and standard data confirmation and validations checks were carried out by our team at Azim Premji University. After confirmation, the data were analyzed using the STATA software program.

3   Key Findings

We examined three main aspects of crime victimization: victimization from specific incidents of crimes, reporting behavior, and people's perception of neighborhood safety.

1. *Crime Victimization*

Crime-related data for each calendar year (January 1 to December 31) that is entered by the police at the district/police station level are validated at the police station level. This is consolidated by police agencies at the level of the individual state/union territory, revalidated and provided to the National Crime Records Bureau (NCRB). The NCRB further validates this information collated from all states and union territories and metropolitan cities of India. Discrepancies or errors in the data are communicated to the respective state/union territory for rectification. The final data received from the states/union territories are analyzed and consolidated to generate the national level crime data for the country. This is presented through the annual "Crime in India" reports released by the NCRB.

Official crime statistics released by the NCRB cannot provide the required information to assess the true extent of underreporting of crimes. These data are most often fragmented, incomplete, nonstandard, and duplicated at various levels, making it difficult to get a comprehensive picture of the nature of crime.

Therefore, independent of these official numbers, in our survey, we first calculated the actual crime rate in Karnataka, using incident reports that detailed all incidents of crimes (time and location of crime; description and value of property) as self-reported by our survey respondents. This showed that the actual rate of crimes was much higher than the official crime rate (calculated as the number of incidents of crime in a region per 1,00,000 of the population) for Karnataka. For instance, the rate for crimes against the body as recorded by the police was 96 per 1,00,000

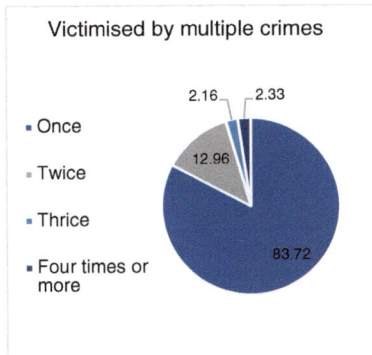

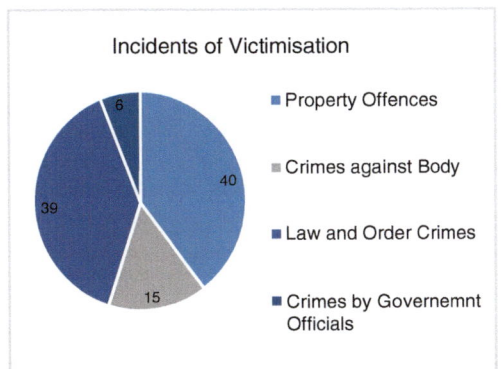

Note: All figures are in percentages   *Note: All figures are in percentages*

Source: KCVS 2018-19, Azim Premji University

Fig. 5.2 Victimization

citizens.[6] The crime rate we calculated for the same offense is 4066 per 1,00,000 citizens (roughly 42 times the official figure!).

This also convinced us to move away from the official records of crime and use a new baseline measure of crime, the "KCVS Victimization Rate", calculated as the number of victims of at least one category of crime, per 100 of the population. This covers crimes not reported to the police by the victims or even if reported, not recorded by the police. Applying the victimization rate as a measure of crime is very useful as this is derived from people's actual experiences of crime and so, forms a better means to understand the true nature of crime. This also has a strong influence on people's perceptions of safety and security in a geographical area.

The KCVS Victimization Rate is around 30%, three times higher than that reported by other surveys like the World Value Survey ("WVS 6 (2010–2014)") and nearly double the rate reported by the CHRI Survey. This translates to 725 separate incidents of victimization experienced by 602 survey respondents over the observation period, meaning that our respondents were victims of more than one crime over this period (Fig. 5.2).

When we review the KCVS results across the four main types of crime - property offenses, crimes against body, law and order crimes, and crimes by government officials (including their sub categories as described earlier), we observe that across the variables of interest we listed earlier, victimization rates from crimes vary greatly across gender, geographies, and caste; and not as much on the other variables we examined, namely, residential locations, religion, and economic class of respondents.

---

[6] According to the National Crime Records Bureau 'Crime in India: 2018', in 2018, India's official crime rate per lakh population was 383.5, for offences affecting the human body, the crime rate was 78.6. Karnataka recorded the rate of total cognizable crimes per 1,00,000 population at 249.7, of which, the crime rate for offences affecting the human body was 66.2

http://ncrb.gov.in/StatPublications/CII/CII2018/pdfs/CII%202018%20SNAPSHOTS%20STATES.pdf, accessed February 4, 2020.

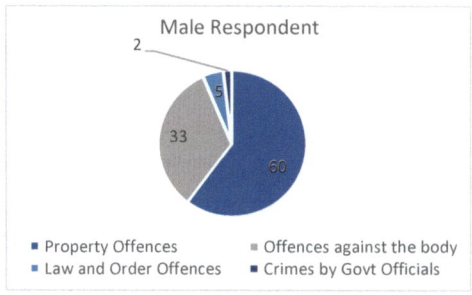
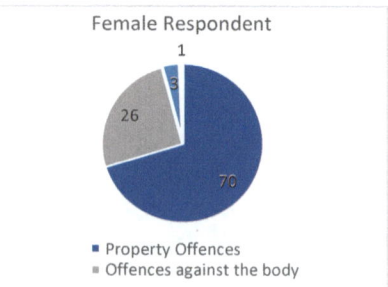

Note: All figures are in percentages

Source: KCVS 2018-19, Azim Premji University

Fig. 5.3 Prevalence of crime by male and female respondents

KCVS results show that 9% more males report being victims of crime than females. Men have a 26% higher probability of being victimized when compared to women. We observe this for all categories of crime reported - property crimes, crimes against the body, and law and order offenses (Fig. 5.3). The gender difference in victimization from crimes against the body is pronounced in urban areas than in rural areas, where 6% more men report being victims of crime than women. These results are interesting when compared with the conclusions of contemporary international surveys like the VOCS (South Africa) (2017), which notes that female-headed householders are victimized at twice the rate of male-headed households in South Africa.

Across Police Ranges in Karnataka, the Northern Range (at 38%) and North-Eastern Range have the highest rates of victimization from crimes while less than a quarter of the respondents in the Central and Western Ranges experienced victimization.

Respondents belonging to the Dalit and Adivasi castes suffered higher rates of victimization from crimes, followed by the OBCs and then the Upper Caste. Dalits are particularly vulnerable to victimization from crime, more than 48% more likely than members of the Upper Caste.

Based on these observations, we can conclude that in Karnataka, crime victimization reduces with an increase in social and economic status and privilege. This is consistent with criminological research around the world which finds a strong relationship between racial and ethnic identity and victimization. Socially and economically disadvantaged people have been subject to higher instances of victimization from crimes.[7] This also ties in with contemporary Indian victimization surveys like the CHRI Survey (2015) which record that high-income households are less affected by crime compared to low-income households.

---

[7] Rajiv Sethi and Glenn C Loury, "Crime and Punishment in Divided Societies" in *Difference without Domination: Pursuing Justice in Diverse Democracies*, Eds. Danielle Allen and Rohini Somanathan, University of Chicago Press, (forthcoming). The authors refer to earlier studies, including by Harcourt (2006) and Alexander (2012), to explain the relationship between race and crime in the US.

As we note in our survey report, the Dalit and Adivasi communities in the State experienced most number of property crimes - theft and house break-ins (with or without use of force), Adivasi and OBCs faced almost twice the rate of victimization from crimes against the body (murder, kidnapping, assault, intimidation, outrage of modesty).

Law and order offenses cover a wide range of disruptions to public peace. We classify those into three broad categories: (i) riots and public disturbances; (ii) exclusionary practices; and (iii) abuse and humiliation. Public disturbances cover bandhs, hartals, agrarian protests, student unrest, labor unrest, incidents of communal or caste or language-targeted violence and gang violence. Exclusionary social actions which amount to restriction or denial of access to public space and resources include denial of access to: public water resources, public transport, places of worship, government buildings, gram sabhas or ward committees, schools or hospitals. Abuse covers verbal abuse and physical assault, the practices of untouchability, public humiliation, and social exclusion of people.

Under the law and order offenses, Dalits, Adivasis, and OBCs were subjected to a much higher percentage of agrarian/farmer revolts, and faced inhuman practices like denial of access to public spaces to worship, verbal and physical abuse, and untouchability offenses, than other caste groups. The range of survey questions asked was broad in scope and intended to capture the true experience of social exclusion that these communities face. For instance, *"Were you affected by the incident in any of the following ways? - deprivation of essential services such as rations, water, medicines; forced not to go to work; forced to participate in the bandh/hartal/agitation/unrest/violence; suffered physical harm; suffered damage to property; and other problems"*. *"Why do you think you were denied access to these [public spaces]? - feud with influential persons in the community; caste, religion, gender, mother tongue, native state, sexual orientation, skin color, disability, other reasons?"*. The official response of the police authorities to these incidents was also recorded in the survey through questions like *"Did the police take any action to restore normalcy in the area?" "How long did it take before the situation to become normal?"*.

The design of the survey questions examining these practices was also determined by their classification under criminal statutes. For instance, protests are categorized as public disturbance and controlled using the powers of the police under the Criminal Procedure Code, denial of access to public spaces is a form of atrocity committed against the scheduled castes and scheduled tribes proscribed under a special law, the Scheduled Castes and the Scheduled Tribes (Prevention of Atrocities) Act, 1989, and the practice of untouchability under the Protection of Civil Rights Act, 1955.

KCVS victimization results also point to some interesting facts – factors such as urbanization are not prime movers driving the experience of crime by the population. Respondents from rural and urban areas of the state faced different nature of crimes - urban respondents experienced economic offenses like cheating and breach of trust and offenses against the body at a higher rate, while rural Karnataka experienced property crimes like vandalism and mischief, as understood under section

Table 5.4 Victimization by law and order offenses by caste

Law and order offenses	General	Dalit	Adivasi	OBC
Victim	13	14	11	16
Not Victim	87	86	89	84
Total	100	100	100	100

Source: KCVS 2018–19, Azim Premji University
Note: All figures are in percentages

425 of the Indian Penal Code. Economic class, determined based on the type of dwelling people inhabit, also played no significant role in the levels of victimization by crimes, particularly, on repeat victimization. Similar to location, class may have some effect only on the category of offenses that people experienced – for property offenses, while the upper and middle class complained of higher levels of theft and criminal breach of trust, respondents of the lower class complained of more house break-ins. Lower-class respondents experienced nearly two times more victimization from law and order offenses in comparison with upper and middle classes. But this could be the effect of overexposure of the lower class populations to collective violence or the result of under-policing of their neighborhoods.

We also note that levels of victimization reflect in people's perceptions of the seriousness of an offense. In our survey for instance, as Tables 5.4, 5.5, and 5.6 show, Dalits and Adivasis are the most victimized by law and order offenses, and more than 78% Adivasis and 73% Dalits also categorized these offenses as being "very serious" or "somewhat serious" in nature.

2. *Reporting Behavior*

The willingness of people to report crime serves as a measure of confidence of people in the police. As we mentioned earlier, crime victim surveys around the world have found differences in reporting behavior based on the nature and gravity of the offense, age and gender of victims, harm or injury to victims, and the extent to which victims/their families feel that the matter is private and should not be reported.

We use the KCVS Victimization Rate as a measure of the experience of crime by victims. To measure incidence of crime, we use two other standards – the rate at which victims report crimes to the police (reporting rate) and the rate at which the police register crimes reported by victims.

Our experience of understanding the reporting behavior of victims of crimes in Karnataka is broadly similar to earlier crime victim surveys - that people do not report crimes to the police. In our survey, only one in four instances of victimization is reported (Table 5.7).

Interestingly, KCVS found that people's perceptions of the seriousness of offenses do not influence their crime reporting behavior. KCVS respondents viewed 80% of incidents involving property and economic offenses and body crimes as "very serious" or "somewhat serious". They viewed 41% of law and order incidents like riots and group violence as "somewhat serious".

Despite this perception, 64% of respondents who felt that property and economic offenses were "very serious" did not report these offenses to the police. Of the

Table 5.5 Victimization by types of law and order offenses by caste

	General	Dalit	Adivasi	OBC
Riots and public disturbances				
Bandhs and Hartals	32	23	8	39
Agrarian unrest	25	31	31	31
Student unrest/Labor unrest	8	10	8	5
Communal/Caste violence	2	6	0	2
Gang violence	3	0	8	3
Linguistic violence	0	0	0	2
Restricting or Denying access				
Denying access to public water resource	10	0	0	5
Denying access to public transport	4	0	0	0
Deny access to place of worship	0	6	8	0
Denying access to government buildings, gram sabha or ward committee	2	4	0	0
Denying access to schools or hospitals	2	0	0	0
Abuse and humiliation				
Verbal abuse	8	8	31	10
Physical assault	3	2	8	3
Untouchability	0	8	0	0
Public humiliation	1	0	0	0
Social exclusion	1	0	0	0
Total	100	100	100	100

Source: KCVS 2018–19, Azim Premji University
Note: All figures are in percentages

Table 5.6 Seriousness of law and order offenses by caste

Law and order offenses: How serious was the event for you?				
	General	Dalit	Adivasi	OBC
Very serious	27	16	21	17
Somewhat serious	33	57	57	41
Not very serious	18	16	14	29
Not serious at all	23	10	7	14
Total	100	100	100	100

Source: KCVS 2018–19, Azim Premji University
Note: All figures are in percentages

Table 5.7 Percentage of instances of victimization reported to the police

Did you report the crime?	Percentage
Yes	24
No	76
Total	100

Source: KCVS 2018–19, Azim Premji University
Note: All figures are in percentages

respondents who viewed crimes against the body to be "very serious", 57% did not report these crimes to the police, while 93% of those who felt these crimes are "somewhat serious", chose not to report. Significantly, almost all respondents who thought that crimes against the body were "not serious at all" did not report these crimes to the police. So, only in case of crimes against the body, the seriousness of the offense may serve as a filter to identify those incidents which are *more likely* to find their way into the formal police reports of crime. Despite the public nature of the offenses and the large number of affected victims, only 20% of the instances of law and order offenses were reported to the police.

Other Indian CVS makes similar observations. For instance, the CHRI Survey (2015) found that more than 53% of crimes in Delhi and 58% of crimes in Mumbai were not reported. When asked to explain the reasons, people's responses related to their fear of being caught in complex and bureaucratic police and court processes, feeling that there was little evidence of the crime, belief that the police would not or could not do anything, and fear of retaliation by the offender. For urban respondents, the police practice of making the complainant wait for an unreasonable time and delays in registering the FIR were the main causes for dissatisfaction with the police as SATARC (2017) reports.

What explains this behavior? We asked respondents several questions to understand their rationale for reporting certain crimes only and conversely, failing to report other crimes they experienced. Survey respondents were asked *"How many times has the incident occurred in the last one year?"*; *"What time did the most recent incident occur?" "What was the location of the incident?" "Did you/your family see the perpetrator?" "Do you know who the perpetrator is?" "Why do you think the incident occurred?"*.

Respondents who were victimized by common crimes were asked if they reported the crime, and if they did, to provide reasons for reporting. For each question, respondents were required to provide their own reasons for reporting and the surveyors did not prompt responses. Once responses were received, the surveyors then matched the responses with the various categories of reasons marked out in the questionnaire, which are detailed in the Annexure.

As Table 5.8 suggests, victims report crimes mainly to recover the stolen items (in case of theft offenses) or to locate missing persons (for offenses against the body). A general obligation to report crime for the welfare of the community comes a distant fourth in the list of reasons that people provided for reporting crimes to the police. This can be explained by looking at the factors that dissuade people from approaching the authorities to report crimes. While reporting behavior varies greatly depending on the category of crime, Table 5.9 highlights some of the main reasons why victims fail to report even serious crimes.

Overall, looking at the nature of crimes, theft records the highest level of reporting in the property and economic offenses category. Other Indian surveys such as those by CHRI and Common Cause (SPIR, 2018) also recorded similar results. The CHRI Survey (2015) noted that while less than 50% of incidents of cell phone and luggage theft were reported to the police in Mumbai and Delhi, theft of high-value items like jewelry, computers or laptops, and cars was the most reported property

Table 5.8 Rationale for reporting the crime to the police

Why report the crime to police?	Percentage
To recover property/person	36
To stop it from happening again	22
Wanted offender to be caught and punish	15
Crime should be reported	12
It was a serious event	8
For insurance reasons	5
Other reasons	2
Total	*100*

Source: KCVS 2018–19, Azim Premji University
Note: All figures are in percentages

Table 5.9 Rationale for not reporting the crime to the police

Reasons for not reporting crimes	Percentage
Did not want to get stuck in police/court system	20
Did not think the police would be able to do anything	17
Lack of evidence	15
Uncomfortable to go to police station	15
Family matters need not be reported	9
Did not think police would entertain the case	7
This is better settled outside the police station	5
Fear of retaliation	4
Did not know where to report	3
Other reasons	2
Police is unfair	2
Did not know helpline number	1
Total	*100*

Source: KCVS 2018–19, Azim Premji University
Note: All figures are in percentages

offense. SPIR (2018) found that victims are more likely to report property-related crimes to the police. Consistent with international trends, this could be owing to the requirement of producing FIRs to insurance companies to process claims on third party insurance of the stolen items. However, we cannot impute a correlation between reporting behavior and insurance policies, since we did not ask survey respondents whether they availed insurance on the stolen property.

We also evaluated the probabilities of victims reporting crimes to the police based on their gender, caste, religion, income groups, and geographic location. This produced certain important results. Male respondents were 23% more likely to report than females. Among income groups, the middle class shows a 12% higher probability of reporting to the police while the upper income group has a 10% lower probability of formal reporting. Urban residents are 16% less likely to report crime incidents than the rural population.

Our analysis on caste and religious lines shows a disturbing result. Of the caste groups, Adivasis showed 34% lower chance of reporting and religious minorities, particularly, Muslims had a 29% lower chance of reporting incidents of crime to the police. Further research is required to unravel the reasons for this variance in reporting among these socioeconomic groups.

We also examined reporting trends based on respondents' formal education and levels of awareness about policing. Our analysis found that with any level of formal education and basic awareness, the likelihood of reporting to the police increases substantially. People who knew the location of the nearest police station in their locality showed a nearly 40% higher chance of reporting crimes than those who did not.

The victims were asked the method they used to report incidents – whether they called the 100 helpline or another police helpline, went to the police station or approached a police officer to report, and also the police response to their report. This is important to examine since crime reporting trends are also strongly influenced by policing behavior. This forms another measure of crime incidence, namely, recording of crimes by the police. KCVS results on this paint an equally dismal picture. Of the reported incidents of property and economic offenses, KCVS data show that complaints were registered by the police in only 50% of the incidents reported and FIRs lodged in only 22% of the reported cases. Similarly, for those incidents of crimes against the body reported to the police, complaints were registered by the police for less than 50% and FIRs lodged for only 20% of the reported incidents of crime. Of the law and order offenses reported to the police, complaints were registered in 34% and FIRs lodged in only 10% of reported cases.

As we note above, only around 13% of the respondents who approached the police in our study could register their complaint with the police. While we cannot establish any systematic class bias by the police in registering complaints, we note a tendency among the police which favored upper class and middle class complainants in registering FIRs. Lower class complainants were encouraged to settle the matter and not file official complaints with the police. Studies like SPIR (2018) have pointed to procedural lapses committed by the police when people approached them to register their case. In rural areas, FIRs were read out in 57% of the cases when compared to urban areas, where 52% of the complaints were written and recorded. Male complainants were more likely to receive written complaints than females.

Our survey exposed certain peculiarities in police response to crimes – for example, based on the types of complaints that was brought before them, police behavior varied. The police readily registered complaints of property offenses but not offenses against the body and law and order offenses. As we describe earlier, FIRs were filed at about 20% for offenses against property and for crimes against the body, complaints were registered by the police for less than 50% of the reported incidents and FIRs lodged for only 20% of these incidents. For law and order offenses, these figures are 50% lower. Instead of recording crimes reported by victims, the police encouraged parties not to file an FIR and instead settle the matter informally. This is despite a legal mandate on the police to file an FIR particularly in cognizable offenses, and if the police refuse, they can be penalized. As the CHRI Survey shows, this points to a huge institutional failure, since a refusal to register an FIR imposes a formidable barrier in the initial stages of the criminal justice process itself, denying access to justice to victims of crime.

It is logical to assume that these factors should negatively influence people's satisfaction with police action to incidents of crime. Our survey results however show a counterintuitive response by people to the police. In about 59% of the cases, victims were satisfied with the response from the police to their complaint. This satisfaction varied based on the type of crime reported: eight out of ten victims of law and order offenses, seven out of ten victims of crimes against the body, and four out of ten victims of property offenses expressed satisfaction with the police action. As discussed in the earlier chapter, the CHRI Survey (2015) also found similar results – 40% of the surveyed group in Delhi and nearly 45% in Mumbai viewed the police in positive light and this result was consistent across income groups in these cities.

We asked respondents to provide reasons for their satisfaction with police response. These related to the police listening to their complaint, registering the complaint accurately or quickly, explaining the action that they would take on the complaint, and finally solving the problem. Our findings suggest that considerate and humane treatment of people by the police generates a better perception of the police in the eyes of the public than solving the crime or resolving their complaint. In fact, as SPIR (2018) points that this may also reflect favorably on the inclination of people to continue to approach the police for their problems in the future too (Fig. 5.4).

Our survey findings suggest that complainants' satisfaction level related to their social and demographic background was not necessarily influenced by the promptness of police action: in our survey, women reported greater satisfaction based on their interactions with the police than men; across religions – Muslims were most dissatisfied with the police (more than 60%) than Hindus and Christians. While these results are aligned to the broader exercise of social power, we observed

Fig. 5.4 Satisfaction with police action

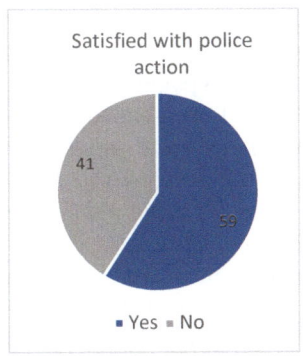

Satisfied with police action

41

59

■ Yes ■ No

Source: KCVS 2018-19, Azim Premji University

Table 5.10 Reason for satisfaction with the police

Reasons for satisfaction with the police	Percentage
They registered the complaint quickly	27
They explained the action that they will take	21
They registered the complaint accurately	20
They solved the problem	19
They listened to the complaint	13
Total	100

Source: KCVS 2018–19, Azim Premji University
Note: All figures are in percentages

different results across the other variables of interest – class, caste, and geographic location. A high 88% of Adivasis and OBCs and 66% Dalits reported being satisfied with the police. Similarly, on class grounds, about 73% of lower-class victims expressed satisfaction. Rural respondents were satisfied with the police action at roughly double the rates that urban respondents reported (Table 5.10).

Given our observations made earlier on the high rates of crime victimization that these groups experience, low rates of crime reporting and even lower rates of recording of crimes by the police, these results are very puzzling. A detailed examination of these factors will be required to unravel the underlying reasons that determine people's responses to crime and policing behavior.

3. *Perceptions of Safety*

Criminological research on the fear of crime has examined whether people's actual risk of victimization and crime rates in their neighborhood are accurate predictors of their level of fear (Lewis & Salem, 1986; Ferraro, 1995; Taylor, 2002; Hinkle, 2015). The topic remains highly contested because many studies have reported little relation between these. One reason that was attributed to this finding was that "fear of crime is not a concrete concept that has been consistently measured with similar survey items across studies" (Yang & Hinkle, 2012) since it is a "visceral, emotional reaction to crime and has not often been measured in such terms" (Farrall & Maruna, 2004). Literature on factors related to the fear of crime can be divided into three main types: (i) environmental cues; (ii) demographic factors; and (iii) neighborhood structure (Ogneva-Himmelberger et al., 2019). In our survey, we questioned people about perceived safety using all three categories with a mix of closed- and open-ended questions like *"What time would you start worrying about safety of an adult [male/female] member of your household who is out alone at night?" "Do you feel safe leaving your home locked for many days?" "Do you feel safe traveling using public transport alone during the day/night?" "How much of a problem do you think crime is in your area?"*. On this theme, we found that public perceptions of fear, safety, and security depend on their spatial and temporal conditions such as their neighborhood, urban/rural location, and the time of the day/night they commute in their locality or use public transport to travel outside it (Table 5.11).

Table 5.11 Traveling on public transport at night

What time would you stop feeling safe while traveling on public transport?	
After 7 p.m.	13
After 8 p.m.	46
After 10 p.m.	77
After 11 p.m.	93
After midnight	100

Source: KCVS 2018–19, Azim Premji University
Note: All figures are in percentages

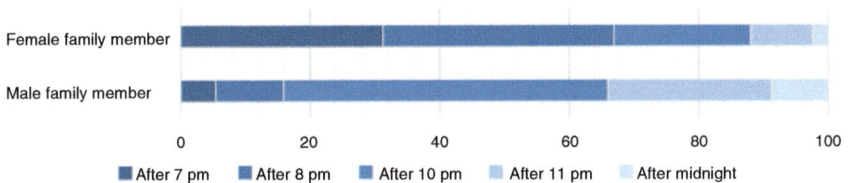

Concern about male/female adult members

Note: All figures are in percentages

Source: KCVS 2018-19, Azim Premji University

Fig. 5.5 Concern about adult family members

An astounding 96% of survey respondents found their neighborhood to be safe, albeit to varying degrees. Not much variation was observed on this among respondents in urban and rural centers, and across religious denominations. Interestingly, more women found their neighborhoods to be safe, in comparison with the men. Around 95% of women felt safe walking in the neighborhood during the day. In a marked difference from urban crime victimization surveys like the CHRI Survey, we found that more people worry about the male members of the family and a much higher number worry about the female members of the family being out of the house alone after 8 p.m. (Fig. 5.5). People's responses could therefore vary based on the demography of the surveyed population, for instance, as Hinkle (2015) points out, the participant's gender could be important – there may be differences across male and female respondents "in their willingness to admit feeling afraid of a crime during a survey or interview" (p. 148) (Fig. 5.6).

Across caste groups, despite experiencing similar victimization from crime as the Dalits, a higher number of Adivasis perceive that crime is a big problem in their neighborhood.

These feelings of safety and security determined people's usage of public transport (Fig. 5.7). Almost all respondents (99%) felt safe using the state road transport buses (KSRTC), followed by trains (83%). Private buses, autos, and taxis were considered safe by 80%, 73%, and 43% of the respondents, respectively (Fig. 5.8).

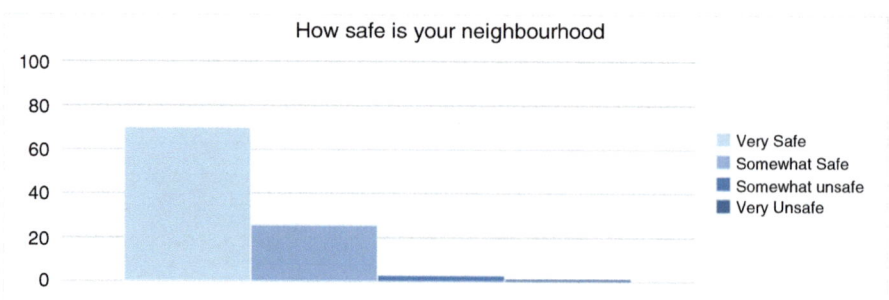

Note: All figures are in percentages

Source: KCVS 2018-19, Azim Premji University

Fig. 5.6 Perception of neighborhood safety

Fig. 5.7 Traveling on public transport at night by gender

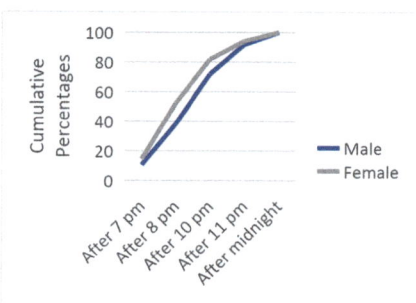

Note: All figures are in percentages

Source: KCVS 2018-19, Azim Premji University

It is safe to travel by:

Note: All figures are in percentages

Source: KCVS 2018-19, Azim Premji University

Fig. 5.8 Safe to travel by public transport

People worry more about being victims of crime than would actually experience it. People were mostly worried about experiencing property offenses (~65%) – mainly, theft and robbery, followed by offenses against the body (30%) like physical assault, murder, and suicide. This corresponds to the official crime figures released by the National Crime Records Bureau. SATARC also reported similar result and identified theft as being the most prevalent crime across the four Indian cities surveyed: Delhi, Mumbai, Bangalore, and Chennai. In our survey, only 5% worried about law and order offenses such as gang violence and caste violence; and crimes by government servants in their area. Most people felt comfortable leaving their home locked for a few days while they were outside their neighborhood or city. These results were observed in each of the six police ranges we studied – despite the higher prevalence of theft offenses that respondents reported to us, more than seven out of every ten respondents in every range found that their neighborhood was safe enough to leave their house locked for a few days.

People's responses to their notion of "seriousness" of the offense are illuminating. Our survey found that more than 80% of incidents involving property and economic offenses and offenses against the body were classified by people as "very serious" or "somewhat serious". This ties in with the actual victimization rates of people by these crimes. Calculated on the basis of the incidents of crime, we find that property offenses were the most prevalent, followed by law and order offenses. These together account for close to 80% of all incidents that were reported to us.

These observations point to an interesting fact: contrary to the expected results, we note that safety perception and fear of crime among people are different constructs. As Hinkle (2015) observes, this can be explained by looking at the types of items used to measure fear, particularly obvious from the questions used in most large-crime victimization surveys such as the NCVS in the US. Questions like "*How safe do you feel waking alone at night in your neighborhood?*" (as we ask in our survey) or "*How likely do you think that you will be a victim of (crime type) in the next 6 months?*", etc. do not draw a clear connection to being emotionally afraid of being a victim of crime. He points to studies in the United Kingdom (Farrall et al., 2008) showing that measures of perceived risk, fear or worry about crime may overstate the level of fear in society as people may be more likely to report feeling unsafe or perceiving personal victimization risk than they are to report feeling "emotionally afraid" of crime (p. 148).

From our survey, we observe that in Karnataka, people perceived that they are safe despite their observation that crime is a problem in their neighborhoods. Victimization from individual crimes or seriousness of the offenses, did not match their idea of feeling safe. External indicators of safety, such as the presence of police patrols and people's awareness of the nearest police station and its facilities, did not seem to influence their perception of safety.

4 Learning and Way Forward

KCVS has been designed as a pilot for India's first national crime victimization survey (the "All India Citizens Survey of Police Services") being conducted by the Bureau of Police Research and Development and National Council of Applied Economic Research. The entire process - from survey design, execution to data collection and analysis, offered useful training and practical field experience to the academics and students involved. Such a detailed study on the social and empirical basis of crime had not been conducted in India so far. This serves as an important instrument to carry out systemic and substantive legal reform and police reform. Findings from KCVS can be used to inform the process adopted for the national survey and interpret the results emerging from this to understand the national trends on crime victimization better. Our survey can serve as a consistent measure of a selected range of crimes experienced by households and of the likelihood of them being victims of crime. This is because, unlike official crime statistics, the information self-reported by victims in CVS covers their "[individual] experiences before, during, and after the offense has occurred" (Chockalingam, 2003).

KCVS provides an empirical basis for understanding why victims of crime engage or disengage with the criminal justice system and how this affects society. It can serve as an important tool for policy makers and civil society to build awareness of who the victims are, the spread of crime, circumstances in which victimization takes place, and measures that can be taken to curb crime. It also serves as a fair reflection of the capability of and people's confidence and trust in the police.

Some results that emerge from our survey go against the observations made in the other crime victimization surveys conducted so far in India. This is particularly noticeable in the variance we observe in the experiences of victimization by people based on their gender, caste, and geography which we described in the earlier section of this chapter. Further research needs to be done to examine the relationship between these variables and victimization in various regions across the country.

Private surveys such as ours are limited in their coverage owing to budgetary constraints. State-run surveys like periodic crime victim surveys conducted internationally, have the advantage of not being limited by similar resources and other constraints. They operate at scale and establish adequate safeguards to ensure the safety and security of persons involved. This includes setting up central units staffed by subject experts who can monitor the progress of the survey and evaluate results in time. KCVS covered the Police Ranges of Karnataka, but data at the district/ police station level collated by the NCRB "Crime in India" reports are essential for administrative planning and priorities assessment.

Further, as we experienced, surveyors may face local resistance to the process in a diverse and politically volatile country like India, issues which can be managed better in a state supported public opinion survey. The KCVS questionnaire was lengthy with several sections requiring people to provide diverse information, some questions could appear complicated and survey respondents may have experienced trouble in responding to them. Higher budgets and other resources could improve questionnaire design and be used to train surveyors for better execution of the survey. In order to obtain a true picture of victimization from crimes, crime categories should be expanded. Crimes against women and children are of a highly sensitive nature, and separate and detailed ethical protocols need to be put in place.

More generally, crime victimization surveys like the KCVS are not equipped to provide insights into lower volume-higher harm violence faced by society such as homicides, use of firearms, and crimes involving knives or sharp instruments. The time lag between occurrence of crime and collection of data about the crime does not make these surveys a reliable measure of emerging trends in crime in a region. They use correlation not causation, and so, cannot be effective in understanding the impact of specific interventions or targeted measures for reform.

Official statistics of crime provided by the NCRB cover a broader range of crimes since they includes seriously violent crimes like murder, homicide, domestic violence, and sexual assault. Crime rates are also calculated differently. The NCRB report breaks down self-identified instances of crime using specific characteristics like the age of the victim (as crimes against children, juveniles, adults, and senior citizens) and specifically classifies the data recorded in metropolitan or nonmetropolitan areas (defined as cities with a population of more than 20,00,000). These features are absent in a survey like ours.

Despite certain practical problems with data gathering and survey management, victim surveys are immensely valuable. They are a necessary supplement to official crime statistics since they look beyond the institutions, processes, and professionals and cover problems that people usually ignore or deal with informally. They provide the "big picture" on crime. Quantifying victimization across the general population of a state, mapping patterns and attitudes toward the system, examining the behavior of state actors, assessing their capability, and identifying obstacles to providing expected policing services to the community are the other advantages of a survey like this.[8]

They are a strong tool to provide useful inputs for designing and implementation of reforms. "Surveys can be used within a variety of research design frameworks and alongside other forms of data collection as part of a triangulated research design, in which multiple methods are used to obtain 'a more detailed and balanced picture of the situation'" (Altrichter et al., 2008, p.147). Regularly organized crime victimization surveys conducted in the same geographies and representative of a large national sample are a good indicator of longer term trends in crime, particularly for the common types of crimes experienced by the general population and even specific population groups. These surveys may not be definite reports of the incidence of crime *per se* but reveal the underlying concealed operation of social and economic power and violence in society, and changes in people's behavior over time and so, serve as powerful tools for analysis. They yield data that can be acted upon in a visible and tangible way and serve to better direct and strengthen police response and behavior. Such good quality data are critical for making improvements and evaluating effectiveness of the justice system.

---

[8] Explained in the context of legal needs surveys in OECD/Open Society (2019), "Legal Needs Surveys and Access to Justice" OECD Publishing: Paris https://www.oecd-ilibrary.org/docserver/g2g9a36c-en.pdf?expires=1616733247&id=id&accname=guest&checksum=85D057F1C6662 2C672F8D8BD103360F8 last accessed March 26, 2021.

Survey Questionnaire (English and Kannada)

KARNATAKA CRIME VICTIMISATION SURVEY	QUESTIONNAIRE ಪ್ರಶ್ನಾವಳಿ	March/ 2017/ SRC

Police Division ಪೊಲೀಸ್ ವಿಭಾಗ	
District: ಜಿಲ್ಲೆ	
City/Block (Taluk): ನಗರ/ ಬ್ಲಾಕು (ತಾಲ್ಲೂಕು)	
Police Station (Thana) ಪೊಲೀಸ್ ಠಾಣೆ	
Type of locality: ಸ್ಥಳದ ವಿಧ	Village_____ ಹಳ್ಳಿ Town / City_____ ನಗರ /ಪಟ್ಟಣ Metropolitan city _____ ಮಹಾನಗರ
Locality (Ward/Village): ಸ್ಥಳ (ವಾರ್ಡ್/ ಹಳ್ಳಿ)	
Polling Station No ಮತಗಟ್ಟೆ ಸಂಖ್ಯೆ	
Name of respondent ಉತ್ತರ ನೀಡುವವರ ಹೆಸರು	
Address ವಿಳಾಸ	_____ _____
Sex ಲಿಂಗ	Male 1 Female 2 ಗಂಡು ಹೆಣ್ಣು
Household Id ಮನೆ ಐಡಿ	

Name of Interviewer (INT): _____
ಸಂದರ್ಶಕರ ಹೆಸರು

Name of Supervisor (SUP): _____
ಸೂಪರ್ ವೈಸರ್ ಹೆಸರು

FIELD CONTROL INFORMATION											
	D	D	M	M	Y	Y	START TIME				
FIRST VISIT INTV DATE					1	7	END TIME				
SECOND VISIT INTV DATE					1	7	START TIME				
							END TIME				
SUPV.CODE			INV.CODE				CHECKED CODE				
ACCOMPANIED CALL	Y 1	N 2	BY:CODE				SIGN				
SPOT CHECK	Y 1	N 2	BY:CODE				SIGN				
BACK CHECK	Y 1	N 2	BY:CODE				SIGN				
SCRUTINY:FIELD	Y 1	N 2	BY:CODE				SIGN				
ANALYSIS OBSERVATION: EXTENT OF PROBLEM					NO /MINOR 1 MILD 2 SEVERE 3						
SCRUTINY : ANALYSIS				YES ....1 NO.........2			BY :				

STATEMENT OF INFORMED CONSENT
ವಿಷಯ ಅರ್ಥಮಾಡಿಕೊಂಡು ಸಮ್ಮತಿ ನೀಡಿರುವ ಬಗ್ಗೆ ಹೇಳಿಕೆಪತ್ರ

My name is _____ and I have come on behalf of Azim Premji University, Bangalore and Sigma Research, Bangalore. We are conducting a state survey on people's experience with crime. We will be interviewing hundreds of people across the Karnataka. We are doing a research on prevalence of crime, experience of the victim and interaction with police. Every person over the age of 18 has an equal chance of being included in this study. You have been selected by chance. There is no risk in participating in this survey. If you are uncomfortable about any question, you need not answer.

But if you answer our questions, you will help us in understanding the state of crime in Karnataka. This survey is an independent study and is not linked to any political party or government agency. Whatever information you provide will be kept strictly confidential. The findings of this survey will be used for research and writing articles in newspaper, books and journals. Participation in this survey is voluntary.

We hope that you will take part in this survey since your participation is important. It usually takes 30 to 35 minutes to complete this interview. Please spare some time for the interview and help me in successfully completing the survey.

ನನ್ನ ಹೆಸರು---------- ನಾನು ಬೆಂಗಳೂರಿನ ಅಜೀಂ ಪ್ರೇಂಜಿ ವಿಶ್ವವಿದ್ಯಾಲಯ ಮತ್ತು ಸಿಗ್ಮ ರೀಸರ್ಚ್ ಅವರ ಪರವಾಗಿ ಬಂದಿದ್ದೇನೆ. ನಾವು ಅಪರಾಧದ ಸಂಬಂಧದಲ್ಲಿ ಜನರ ಅನುಭವದ ಬಗ್ಗೆ ರಾಜ್ಯದಲ್ಲಿ ಸಮೀಕ್ಷೆ ಮಾಡುತ್ತಿದ್ದೇವೆ. ನಾವು ಕರ್ನಾಟಕದಾದ್ಯಂತ ನೂರಾರು ಜನರನ್ನು ಸಂದರ್ಶನ ಮಾಡಲಿದ್ದೇವೆ. ಅಪರಾಧದ ಮಟ್ಟ ಎಷ್ಟಿದೆ? ಬಲಿಯಾದವರ ಅನುಭವವೇನು? ಮತ್ತು ಪೊಲೀಸರ ಜೊತೆ ಮಾತುಕತೆ ಅನುಭವದ ಬಗ್ಗೆ ನಾವು ಸಂಶೋಧನೆ ಮಾಡುತ್ತಿದ್ದೇವೆ. 18 ವರ್ಷ ವಯಸ್ಸು ಮೀರಿದ ಪ್ರತಿಯೊಬ್ಬ ವ್ಯಕ್ತಿಗೂ ಈ ಅಧ್ಯಯನದಲ್ಲಿ ಪಾಲ್ಗೊಳ್ಳುವ ಸಮಾನ ಅವಕಾಶವಿದೆ. ನಿಮ್ಮನ್ನು ಅಕಸ್ಮಾತ್ ಆಗಿ ಆರಿಸಲಾಗಿದೆ. ಈ ಸಮೀಕ್ಷೆಯಲ್ಲಿ ಭಾಗಿಯಾದರೆ ನಿಮಗೆ ಯಾವ ಅಪಾಯವೂ ಇಲ್ಲ. ಯಾವುದೇ ಪ್ರಶ್ನೆ ನಿಮಗೆ ಹಿಡಿಸದಿದ್ದರೆ ನೀವು ಉತ್ತರಿಸಬೇಕಾಗಿಲ್ಲ.

ನಮ್ಮ ಪ್ರಶ್ನೆಗಳಿಗೆ ನೀವು ಉತ್ತರ ನೀಡಿದರೆ ಇಡೀ ಕರ್ನಾಟಕದಲ್ಲಿ ಅಪರಾಧದ ಸ್ಥಿತಿ ಗತಿ ಹೇಗಿದೆ ಎಂದು ತಿಳಿಯಲು ನೀವು ನಮಗೆ ನೆರವು ನೀಡಿದಂತಾಗುತ್ತದೆ. ಈ ಸಮೀಕ್ಷೆಯು ಸ್ವತಂತ್ರ ಅಧ್ಯಯನವಾಗಿದೆ ಮತ್ತು ಯಾವುದೇ ರಾಜಕೀಯ ಪಕ್ಷ ಅಥವಾ ಸರ್ಕಾರಿ ಏಜೆನ್ಸಿಗೆ ಸಂಬಂಧಿಸಿರುವುದಿಲ್ಲ. ನೀವು ಒದಗಿಸುವ ಯಾವುದೇ ಮಾಹಿತಿಯನ್ನು ರಹಸ್ಯವಾಗಿ ಇಡಲಾಗುತ್ತದೆ. ಈ ಸಮೀಕ್ಷೆಯ ಆಧಾರದ ಮೇಲೆ ಕಂಡುಕೊಂಡ ತೀರ್ಮಾನಗಳನ್ನು ನಮ್ಮ ಸಂಶೋಧನೆಗಳಿಗೆ ಮತ್ತು ವೃತ್ತಪತ್ರಿಕೆಗಳು, ಪುಸ್ತಕಗಳು ಮತ್ತು ಜರ್ನಲ್‌ಗಳಲ್ಲಿ ಲೇಖನಗಳನ್ನು ಬರೆಯಲು ಬಳಸಲಾಗುತ್ತದೆ. ಈ ಸಮೀಕ್ಷೆಯಲ್ಲಿ ಭಾಗಿಯಾಗಲೇ ಬೇಕೆಂಬ ಒತ್ತಾಯವಿಲ್ಲ. ನೀವು ಸ್ವಪ್ರೇರಣೆಯಿಂದ ಭಾಗವಹಿಸಬಹುದು.

ಈ ಸಮೀಕ್ಷೆಯಲ್ಲಿ ನೀವು ಭಾಗಿಯಾಗುವುದು ಮುಖ್ಯ. ಅದನ್ನು ಮನಗಂಡು ನೀವು ಸಮೀಕ್ಷೆಯಲ್ಲಿ ಪಾಲ್ಗೊಳ್ಳುತ್ತೀರೆಂದು ಆಶಿಸುತ್ತೇವೆ. ಸಂದರ್ಶನಕ್ಕೆ 30-35 ನಿಮಿಷಗಳ ಅವಧಿ ಬೇಕಾಗುತ್ತದೆ. ದಯವಿಟ್ಟು ಸ್ವಲ್ಪ ಕಾಲಾವಕಾಶ ಮಾಡಿಕೊಂಡು ಈ ಸಮೀಕ್ಷೆಯನ್ನು ಯಶಸ್ವಿಯಾಗಿ ಮುಗಿಸಲು ನೆರವು ನೀಡಬೇಕೆಂದು ಕೋರುತ್ತೇನೆ.

May I begin the interview now? ಈಗ ಸಂದರ್ಶನ ಆರಂಭಿಸೋಣವೇ?

Respondent agrees to be interviewed   1
ಸಂದರ್ಶನಕ್ಕೆ ಉತ್ತರ ನೀಡುವವರು ಒಪ್ಪಿದ್ದಾರೆ.
Respondent does not agree to be interviewed   2
ಸಂದರ್ಶನಕ್ಕೆ ಉತ್ತರ ನೀಡುವವರು ಒಪ್ಪಿರುವುದಿಲ್ಲ

	DEMOGRAPHIC INFORMATION ವ್ಯಕ್ತಿವಿವರ ಮಾಹಿತಿ	Skip
D1	Gender ಲಿಂಗ	Male ಗಂಡು ....1 Female ಹೆಣ್ಣು ....2 Other ಇತರ 3	
D2	What is your Religion? ನಿಮ್ಮ ಧರ್ಮ ಯಾವುದು	Hindu ಹಿಂದು ....1 Muslim ಮುಸ್ಲಿಂ ....2 Christian ಕ್ರೈಸ್ತ...3 Sikh ಸಿಖ್...4 Buddhist/Neo Buddhist ಬೌದ್ಧ/ನವಬೌದ್ಧ ....5 Jain ಜೈನ ....6 No religion ಯಾವ ಧರ್ಮವೂ ಇಲ್ಲ......................7 Others (Record response) ———————— 98 ಇತರ(ಉತ್ತರ ದಾಖಲಿಸಿ)	
D3	What are the languages spoken at home? MULTIPLE RESPONSE ನಿಮ್ಮ ಮನೆಯಲ್ಲಿ ಯಾವ ಯಾವ ಭಾಷೆಗಳನ್ನು ಮಾತನಾಡುತ್ತೀರಿ? ಒಂದಕ್ಕಿಂತ ಹೆಚ್ಚು ಭಾಷೆಗಳನ್ನು ಹೇಳಬಹುದು	Kannada ಕನ್ನಡ ....1 Tamil ತಮಿಳು ....2 Telugu ತೆಲುಗು ....3 Malayalam ಮಲಯಾಳಂ ....4 Hindi ಹಿಂದಿ ....5 English ಇಂಗ್ಲಿಷ್ ....6 Others (Record the response):_____ 98 ಇತರ(ಉತ್ತರ ದಾಖಲಿಸಿ)	
D4	What is your caste category ನಿಮ್ಮ ಜಾತಿ ಯಾವ ಪ್ರವರ್ಗ ದಲ್ಲಿ ಬರುತ್ತದೆ?	General ಸಾಮಾನ್ಯ ....1 Scheduled Caste ಪರಿಶಿಷ್ಟ ಜಾತಿ............................2 Schedule Tribe ಪರಿಶಿಷ್ಟ ಪಂಗಡ ....3 OBC ಇತರ ಹಿಂದುಳಿದ ಜಾತಿ ....4 Don't know/Can't Say ಗೊತ್ತಿಲ್ಲ/ಹೇಳಲಾಗದು 99	
D4a	Please Specify your Caste/Jati/Biradari: ನಿಮ್ಮ ಜಾತಿ ಯಾವುದು ನಿರ್ದಿಷ್ಟವಾಗಿ ತಿಳಿಸಿರಿ.	————————	
D5	What is your primary occupation: ನಿಮ್ಮ ಮೂಲ ಉದ್ಯೋಗ ಯಾವುದು?	Self-employed in agriculture.........................1 ಕೃಷಿ ಸ್ವಯಂ ಉದ್ಯೋಗಿ Self-employed in business/trade ....2 ಸ್ವಯಂ ಉದ್ಯೋಗಿ ವ್ಯಾಪಾರ Regular salaried employee ....3 ನಿಯತ ಸಂಬಳದ ಉದ್ಯೋಗಿ Casual wage labourer......................................4 ಸಾಂದರ್ಭಿಕ ಮಜೂರಿ ಕಾರ್ಮಿಕ Not working now, but is seeking and/or available for work ....5 ಈಗ ಕೆಲಸಮಾಡುತ್ತಿಲ್ಲ, ಆದರೆ ಕೆಲಸ ಹುಡುಕುತ್ತಿದ್ದೇನೆ Not able to work due to disability/old age .....6 ಕೆಲಸ ಮಾಡಲಾಗುವುದಿಲ್ಲ ಅಂಗವಿಕಲತೆ/ವಯಸ್ಸಾಗಿದೆ Attends educational institution ....7 ——————— ವಿದ್ಯಾ ಸಂಸ್ಥೆಗೆ ವಿದ್ಯಾರ್ಥಿಯಾಗಿ ಹೋಗುತ್ತಿದ್ದೇನೆ. Attends domestic duties for the household....8 ಕುಟುಂಬದಲ್ಲೇ ಮನೆಕೆಲಸಗಳನ್ನು ಮಾಡುತ್ತಿದ್ದೇನೆ Rent recipient, pensioner, remittance recipient, etc...9 ಮನೆ ಬಾಡಿಗೆ ಪಡೆಯುತ್ತಿದ್ದೇನೆ, ಪಿಂಚಣಿದಾರ, ಹಣ ಪಾವತಿ ಪಡೆಯುತ್ತಿದ್ದೇನೆ, ಇತ್ಯಾದಿ Others (Record response) ———————— 98 ಇತರ(ಉತ್ತರ ಬರೆದುಕೊಳ್ಳಿ) Can't Say ಹೇಳಲಾಗದು 99	
D6	What is your approximate Annual Household	Below 50,000 1	

	Income? ಅಂದಾಜಾಗಿ ನಿಮ್ಮ ಮನೆಯ ವಾರ್ಷಿಕ ಆದಾಯವೇನು?	ರೂ 50,000ಕ್ಕೆ ಕಡಿಮೆ	
		Between 50,000 and 1,00,000 .... 2 ರೂ 50,000 ಮತ್ತು 1,00,000ರ ನಡುವೆ	
		Between 1,00,000 and 3,00,000 .... 3 ರೂ 1,00,000 ಮತ್ತು 3,00,000 ನಡುವೆ	
		Between 3,00,000 and 10,00,000................. 4 ರೂ 3,00,000 ಮತ್ತು 10,00,000 ನಡುವೆ	
		Above 10,00,000 .... 5 ರೂ10,00,000 ಕ್ಕೂ ಮೇಲ್ಪಟ್ಟು	
D7a	Please provide the following details of your household ನಿಮ್ಮ ಕುಟುಂಬದ ವಿವರ ನೀಡುತ್ತೀರಾ?	Total number of individuals in the household: ಕುಟುಂಬದಲ್ಲಿರುವ ಒಟ್ಟು ವ್ಯಕ್ತಿಗಳ ಸಂಖ್ಯೆ	
D7b	Please tell the number of individuals who are ಕುಟುಂಬದ ಸದಸ್ಯರಲ್ಲಿ ಎಷ್ಟು ಜನರು	1. Males ಗಂಡಸರು : _____ 2. Females ಹೆಂಗಸರು: _____ 3. Others ಇತರೆ : _____	
D7c	Please tell me how many individuals in your household are in the following age groups ನಿಮ್ಮ ಕುಟುಂಬದ ಸದಸ್ಯರಲ್ಲಿ ಎಷ್ಟು ಜನರು ಈ ವಯಸ್ಸಿನ ಗುಂಪಿಗೆ ಸೇರುತ್ತಾರೆ?	1. 0 to 10 years 0 – 10 ವರ್ಷ	
		2. 11 to 18 years 11 – 18 ವರ್ಷ	
		3. 19 to 30 years 19 – 30 ವರ್ಷ	
		4. 31 to 45years 31 – 45 ವರ್ಷ	
		5. 46 to 60 years 46 to 60 ವರ್ಷ	
		6. >60 years: 60 ವರ್ಷ ಕ್ಕೂ ಮೇಲ್ಪಟ್ಟು	
D7d	Please tell me the number of earning members of the family who are: ನಿಮ್ಮ ಕುಟುಂಬದ ಸಂಪಾದಿಸುವ ಸದಸ್ಯರ ಸಂಖ್ಯೆ ತಿಳಿಸಿ	1. Males ಗಂಡಸರು : _____ 2. Females ಹೆಂಗಸರು: _____ 3. Others ಇತರೆ : _____	
D7e	Please tell me the number of individuals of 6+ years in the household who have ನಿಮ್ಮ ಕುಟುಂಬದ ಸದಸ್ಯರಲ್ಲಿ ಮುಂದಿನಿಂತೆ ವಿದ್ಯಾಭ್ಯಾಸ ಆಗಿರುವ 6 ವರ್ಷಕ್ಕೂ ಮೇಲ್ಪಟ್ಟು ವಯಸ್ಸಿನ ಸದಸ್ಯರ ಸಂಖ್ಯೆ ಎಷ್ಟು?	1. No formal schooling/Non Literate ಶಾಲಾ ಶಿಕ್ಷಣ ಇಲ್ಲ/ಅನಕ್ಷರಸ್ಥ	
		2. Below Primary schooling ಪ್ರಾಥಮಿಕ ಶಾಲೆಗಿಂತ ಕಡಿಮೆ	
		3. Primary Pass/Middle Fail ಪ್ರಾಥಮಿಕ ಶಾಲೆಯಲ್ಲಿ ಉತ್ತೀರ್ಣ/ಮಾಧ್ಯಮಿಕಶಾಲೆ ನಪಾಸು	
		4. Middle Pass/Matriculation Fail ಮಾಧ್ಯಮಿಕ ಶಾಲೆ ಪಾಸು / ಎಸ್ಎಸ್ಎಲ್ ಸಿ ನಪಾಸು	
		5. Completed Matriculation ಎಸ್ಎಸ್ಎಲ್ ಸಿ ಮುಗಿಸಿದ್ದಾರೆ.	
		6. Completed Class XII or PUC 12ನೇ ತರಗತಿ/ಪಿಯುಸಿ ಮುಗಿಸಿದ್ದಾರೆ.	
		7.Completed Bachelors/Undergraduate ಬ್ಯಾಚುಲರ್ ಪದವಿ ಮುಗಿಸಿದ್ದಾರೆ	
		8. Completed Post-Graduate (MA, M.Sc., M.Com., B. Ed., M. Ed., LLB, PGDM) ಸ್ನಾತಕೋತ್ತರ ಪದವಿ ಮುಗಿಸಿದ್ದಾರೆ. (ಎಂಎ, ಎಂ.ಎಸ್.ಸಿ, ಎಂ .ಕಾಂ, ಬಿ ಎಡ್., ಎಂ ಎಡ್., ಎಲ್ಎಲ್ಬಿ, ಪಿಜಿಡಿಎಂ)	
D8	How long have you lived in Karnataka? ಎಷ್ಟು ವರ್ಷದಿಂದ ಕರ್ನಾಟಕದಲ್ಲಿದ್ದೀರಿ?	0 – 2 years ವರ್ಷ .... 1 2 – 4 years ವರ್ಷ .... 2 4 – 6 years ವರ್ಷ .... 3 6 – 8 years ವರ್ಷ .... 4 8 – 10 years ವರ್ಷ .... 5 10 – 15 years ವರ್ಷ .... 6 More than 15 years 15 ವರ್ಷಕ್ಕಿಂತ ಹೆಚ್ಚು 7	
D8a	How long have you been living in this locality?	0 – 2 years ವರ್ಷ 1	

	ಎಷ್ಟು ವರ್ಷಗಳಿಂದ ಈ ಪ್ರದೇಶದಲ್ಲಿದ್ದೀರಿ?	2 - 4 years ವರ್ಷ .... 2 4 - 6 years ವರ್ಷ .... 3 6 – 8 years ವರ್ಷ .... 4 8 – 10 years ವರ್ಷ .... 5 10 – 15 years ವರ್ಷ .... 6 More than 15 years 15 ವರ್ಷಕ್ಕಿಂತ ಹೆಚ್ಚು 7	
D8b	Is your house ನಿಮ್ಮ ಮನೆ	Rented ಬಾಡಿಗೆ ಮನೆಯೇ ....1 Own ಸ್ವಂತದ್ದೋ.. 2	
D8c	How many times have you shifted residence in the past 5 years? ಕಳೆದ 5 ವರ್ಷದಲ್ಲಿ ನೀವು ಎಷ್ಟು ಬಾರಿ ಮನೆ ಬದಲಿಸಿದ್ದೀರಿ?	Haven't moved in the last 5 years .... 1 ಕಳೆದ 5 ವರ್ಷದಲ್ಲಿ ಮನೆ ಬದಲಿಸಿಲ್ಲ Moved once ಒಮ್ಮೆ ಬದಲಿಸಿದ್ದೇವೆ .... 2 Moved two times ಎರಡು ಬಾರಿ ಬದಲಿಸಿದ್ದೇವೆ.......... 3 Moved three times ಮೂರು ಬಾರಿ ಬದಲಿಸಿದ್ದೇವೆ ...... 4 Moved four times ನಾಲ್ಕುಬಾರಿ ಬದಲಿಸಿದ್ದೇವೆ .... 5 Moved five times ಐದು ಬಾರಿ ಬದಲಿಸಿದ್ದೇವೆ .... 6 More than five times ಐದು ಬಾರಿಗಿಂತ ಹೆಚ್ಚು ಸಲ ಬದಲಿಸಿದ್ದೇವೆ.. 7	
D9	Type of Dwelling ಮನೆ ಎಧ	Bungalow/Independent house with more than one floor .... 1 ಬಂಗಲೆ/ ಒಂದು ಮಹಡಿಗಿಂತ ಹೆಚ್ಚಿರುವ ಸ್ವತಂತ್ರ ಮನೆ Flat/Apartment in a gated community with Security.. 2 ಗೇಟೆಡ್ ಕಮುನಿಟಿ ಯಲ್ಲಿ ಫ್ಲಾಟ್/ಅಪಾರ್ಟ್ ಮೆಂಟ್, ಸೆಕ್ಯುರಿಟಿ ಇದೆ Flat/Apartment in a non-gated community... 3 ಫ್ಲಾಟ್/ಅಪಾರ್ಟ್ ಮೆಂಟ್ ಆದರೆ ಗೇಟೆಡ್ ಕಮುನಿಟಿ ಅಲ್ಲ Mainly kuccha house .... 4 ಬಹುಪಾಲು ಕಚ್ಚಾ ಮನೆ Slum/Jhugi/Jhopri. Pukka (both wall and roof made of pukka material) .... 5 ಕೊಳಗೇರಿ/ಜೋಪಡಿ. ಪಕ್ಕಾ ಮನೆ(ಗೋಡೆ ಮತ್ತು ಚಾವಣಿ ಸ್ಥಿರ ವಸ್ತುವಿಂದ ಮಾಡಿದ್ದು) Pukka-Kutcha (Either wall or roof is made of pukka material and other of kutcha material)6 ಪಕ್ಕಾ-ಕಚ್ಚಾ(ಗೋಡೆ ಅಥವಾ ಚಾವಣಿ ಪಕ್ಕಾ ವಸ್ತುವಿಂದ ಮಾಡಿದ್ದು ಮತ್ತು ಉಳಿದದ್ದು ಕಚ್ಚಾ ವಸ್ತುವಿಂದ ಮಾಡಿದ್ದು) Kutcha/Mud houses (both wall and roof are made of kutcha material) .... 7 ಕಚ್ಚಾ/ಮಣ್ಣಿನ ಮನೆ(ಗೋಡೆ ಮತ್ತು ಚಾವಣಿ ಕಚ್ಚಾ ವಸ್ತುವಿಂದ ಮಾಡಿದ್ದು) Hut (both wall and roof made of grass, leaves, Un-burnt brick or bamboo). .... 8 ಗುಡಿಸಲು (ಗೋಡೆ ಮತ್ತು ಚಾವಣಿ ಹುಲ್ಲು,ಎಲೆ, ಹಸಿ ಇಟ್ಟಿಗೆ, ಬಿದಿರಿನಿಂದ ಮಾಡಿದ್ದು)	

			Yes	No
D10	Do you have the following ಇವುಗಳಲ್ಲಿ ಯಾವುದನ್ನು ಹೊಂದಿದ್ದೀರಿ? **READOUT OR SHOW CARD** ಓದಿ ಹೇಳಿ ಅಥವಾ ಕಾರ್ಡ್ ತೋರಿಸಿ			
		A. Aadhar Card ಆಧಾರ್ ಕಾರ್ಡ್	1	2
		B. ATM Card ಎಟಿಎಂ ಕಾರ್ಡ್	1	2
		C. Bank Account ಬ್ಯಾಂಕ್ ಅಕೌಂಟ್	1	2
		D. PAN card ಪ್ಯಾನ್ ಕಾರ್ಡ್	1	2
		E. Ration card-BPL APL Card ರೇಷನ್ ಕಾರ್ಡ್-ಬಿಪಿಎಲ್ ಎಪಿಎಲ್ ಕಾರ್ಡ್	1	2
		F. Passport ಪಾಸ್ಪೋರ್ಟ್	1	2
		G. Driver's license ಡ್ರೈವರ್ಸ್ ಲೈಸೆನ್ಸ್	1	2
		H. Voter ID ಮತದಾರ ಚೀಟಿ	1	2
		I. NREGA Card .ಗ್ನಾ.ಉ. ಗ್ನಾ.ಕಾರ್ಡ್	1	2

			Yes	No	
D11	Total land and buildings including orchard and plantation owned by your household as of the date of the survey (Ask in local units, but record in standard acres): ತೋಟ ಮತ್ತು ನೆಡುತೋಟಗಳನ್ನು ಸೇರಿಸಿ ಈ ಸಮೀಕ್ಷೆ ನಡೆಸಿದ ದಿನದಂದು ನಿಮ್ಮ ಕುಟುಂಬ ಹೊಂದಿರುವ ಒಟ್ಟು ಭೂಮಿ ಮತ್ತು ಕಟ್ಟಡಗಳು ಎಷ್ಟು ತಿಳಿಸಿ (ಸ್ಥಳೀಯ ಮಾಪನಗಳ ಪ್ರಕಾರ ಕೇಳಿ ಮತ್ತು ಎಕರೆಗಳಲ್ಲಿ ಬರೆದುಕೊಳ್ಳಿ)	A. Agricultural Land ಕೃಷಿ ಭೂಮಿ: _____ B. Other Land ಇತರ ಭೂಮಿ:_____ C. No of Commercial buildings: _____ ವಾಣಿಜ್ಯ ಕಟ್ಟಡಗಳ ಸಂಖ್ಯೆ D. No of Residential buildings: _____ ವಸತಿ ಕಟ್ಟಡಗಳ ಸಂಖ್ಯೆ E. Total area ಒಟ್ಟು ವಿಸ್ತೀರ್ಣ: _____ F. Total area ಒಟ್ಟು ವಿಸ್ತೀರ್ಣ: _____			
D12	Do you or members of your household have the following ನೀವಾಗಲಿ ಅಥವಾ ನಿಮ್ಮ ಮನೆಯವರಾಗಲಿ ಈ ಯಾವುದನ್ನು ಹೊಂದಿದ್ದೀರಾ? **READOUT** ಓದಿಹೇಳಿ	A. Ceiling fan ಸೀಲಿಂಗ್ ಫ್ಯಾನ್	1	2	
		B. Air conditioner ಏರ್ ಕಂಡೀಷನರ್	1	2	
		C. LPG stove ಎಲ್ ಪಿ ಜಿ ಒಲ	1	2	
		D. Mobile phone ಮೊಬೈಲ್ ಫೋನ್	1	2	
		E. T.V ಟಿವಿ	1	2	
		F. Refrigerator ಫ್ರಿಜ್	1	2	
		G. Personal computer/laptop ಪಿಸಿ/ಲ್ಯಾಪ್ ಟಾಪ್	1	2	
		H. Scooter/Motorcycle/Moped ಸ್ಕೂಟರ್/ಮೋಟಾರು ಸೈಕಲ್	1	2	
		I. Car/Jeep/Van ಕಾರು/ಜೀಪು/ವ್ಯಾನು	1	2	
		J. Bicycle ಸೈಕಲ್	1	2	
		K. Watch ವಾಚು	1	2	
		L. Gold jewellery ಚಿನ್ನದ ಒಡವೆ	1	2	
		M. Tractor ಟ್ರಾಕ್ಟರ್	1	2	
		N. Motorized pumping set for irrigation ನೀರಾವರಿಗೆ ಮೋಟಾರ್ ಪಂಪ್ ಸೆಟ್	1	2	
D13	Please specify the number of livestock you own ನೀವು ಹೊಂದಿರುವ ಜಾನುವಾರುಗಳ ಸಂಖ್ಯೆ ತಿಳಿಸಿ	A. Goat/sheep/pig:_____ ಮೇಕೆ/ಕುರಿ/ಹಂದಿ B. Cow/Oxen/Buffalo: _____ ಹಸು/ಎತ್ತು/ಎಮ್ಮೆ C. Any other: _____ ಇತರ			
D14	Do you and your family usually deposit your savings in ಸಾಮಾನ್ಯವಾಗಿ ನಿಮ್ಮ ಕುಟುಂಬ ಉಳಿತಾಯಹಣವನ್ನು ಎಲ್ಲಿ ಠೇವಣಿ ಮಾಡುತ್ತದೆ? **READOUT** ಓದಿಹೇಳಿ		Yes	No	
		A. Banks ಬ್ಯಾಂಕು	1	2	
		B. Post Office ಅಂಚೆ ಕಚೇರಿ	1	2	
		C. Government Scheme ಸರ್ಕಾರಿ ಯೋಜನೆ	1	2	
		D. Chit funds ಚಿಟ್ ಫಂಡ್	1	2	
		F. Others (please specify) ಇತರ(ನಿರ್ದಿಷ್ಟ ಉತ್ತರ ದಾಖಲಿಸಿ) _____	1	2	
D15	What is your **primary** mode of transport to get around the locality? ನಿಮ್ಮ ಪ್ರದೇಶದಲ್ಲಿ ಓಡಾಡಲು ಮುಖ್ಯವಾಗಿ ಯಾವ ಸಾರಿಗೆ	Public Transport ....1 ಸಾರ್ವಜನಿಕರ ಸಾರಿಗೆ Privately hired transport including auto, taxi,			

Q No	Question	Coding Category	Skip
Q13.	Do you know where your nearest police station or chowki is? ನಿಮ್ಮ ಹತ್ತಿರದ ಪೋಲೀಸ್ ಠಾಣೆ/ ಚೌಕಿ ಎಲ್ಲಿದೆ ಗೊತ್ತಾ?	Yes ಹೌದು ....1 No ಇಲ್ಲ 2	
Q14.	How safe you think your neighbourhood is? ನಿಮ್ಮ ನೆರೆಹೊರೆ ಎಷ್ಟು ಸುರಕ್ಷಿತ ಅನಿಸುತ್ತದೆ?	Very safe ಬಹಳ ಸುರಕ್ಷಿತ ....1 Somewhat safe ಸುಮಾರಾಗಿ ಸುರಕ್ಷಿತ ....2 Somewhat unsafe ಸುಮಾರಾಗಿ ಅಸುರಕ್ಷಿತ ....3 Very unsafe ಬಹಳ ಅಸುರಕ್ಷಿತ ....4 Don't know/Can't say ಗೊತ್ತಿಲ್ಲ/ಹೇಳಲಾಗದು........99	
Q15.	How often do police patrol this area? ಈ ಪ್ರದೇಶದಲ್ಲಿ ಎಷ್ಟು ಬಾರಿ ಪೋಲೀಸ್ ಗಸ್ತು ನಡೆಯುತ್ತದೆ?	Daily ಪ್ರತಿದಿನ ....1 Bi-weekly ವಾರಕ್ಕೆ ಎರಡು ಬಾರಿ........................2 Weekly ವಾರಕ್ಕೆ ಒಮ್ಮೆ...............................3 Fortnightly ಹದಿನ್ನೆದು ದಿನಕ್ಕೊಮ್ಮೆ...................4 Monthly ತಿಂಗಳಿಗೊಮ್ಮೆ...............................5 Yearly ವರ್ಷಕ್ಕೊಮ್ಮೆ..................................6 Don't know / Can't say ಗೊತ್ತಿಲ್ಲ/ಹೇಳಲಾಗದು 99	
	CRIME AND VICTIMS ಅಪರಾಧ ಮತ್ತು ಅಪರಾಧದ ಆಹುತಿ		
Q16.	During the last one year, has anything been stolen or attempted to be stolen from your possession or from the possession of any member of your family? (house/ vehicles/ phones/household appliances/ goods/ jewellery) ಕಳೆದ ಒಂದು ವರ್ಷದಲ್ಲಿ ನಿಮ್ಮಲ್ಲಿರುವ ಅಥವಾ ನಿಮ್ಮ ಮನೆಯವರ ಯಾವುದೇ ವಸ್ತು ಕಳವಾಗಿದೆಯೇ/ ಕದಿಯುವ ಪ್ರಯತ್ನವಾಯಿತೇ(ಮನೆ/ವಾಹನ/ಫೋನ್/ಮನೆ ವಸ್ತು/ ಸರಕುಗಳು/ಒಡವೆ)	Yes ....1 ಹೌದು No ....2 ಇಲ್ಲ	If YES, Go to Incident Report Part 1, Page 13
Q17	During the last one year, has anyone damaged or tried to cause damage to your property (house/ vehicles/phones/household appliances/ goods/jewellery)? ಕಳೆದ ಒಂದು ವರ್ಷದಲ್ಲಿ ನಿಮ್ಮ ಆಸ್ತಿಗೆ ಯಾರಾದರೂ ಹಾನಿ ಮಾಡಿದರಾ ಅಥವಾ ಹಾನಿ ಮಾಡುವ ಪ್ರಯತ್ನವಾಯಿತೇ(ಮನೆ/ವಾಹನ/ಫೋನ್/ ಮನೆ ವಸ್ತು/ಸರಕುಗಳು/ಒಡವೆ)	Yes ....1 ಹೌದು No ....2 ಇಲ್ಲ	If YES, Go to Incident Report Part 2, Page 17
Q18.	During the last one year, have you or your family members lost money due to fraud in a chit fund, property deal or any other investment scheme? ಕಳೆದ ಒಂದು ವರ್ಷದಲ್ಲಿ ನೀವು ಅಥವಾ ನಿಮ್ಮ ಮನೆಯವರು ಚೀಟ್ ಫಂಡ್, ಆಸ್ತಿ ವ್ಯವಹಾರ ಅಥವಾ ಹೂಡಿಕೆ ಯೋಜನೆಯಿಂದ ಹಣ ಕಳೆದುಕೊಂಡಿರಾ?	Yes ....1 ಹೌದು No ....2 ಇಲ್ಲ	If YES, Go to Incident Report Part 3, Page 21
Q19.	Has any member of the family been victim of debit card, online or ATM frauds and has lost money? ನಿಮ್ಮ ಮನೆಯಲ್ಲಿ ಯಾರಾದರೂ ಡೆಬಿಟ್ ಕಾರ್ಡ್, ಆನ್ ಲೈನ್/ ಎಟಿಎಂ ಮೋಸಗಳಿಗೆ ಬಲಿಯಾಗಿ ಹಣ ಕಳೆದುಕೊಂಡರಾ?	Yes ....1 ಹೌದು No ....2 ಇಲ್ಲ	If YES, Go to Incident Report Part 4, Page 24
Q20.	During the last one year, have you or anyone in your family faced any physical assault or threat of physical assault in any way including through grabbing, slapping, shoving, punching or by guns, knives and other dangerous objects? ಕಳೆದ ಒಂದು ವರ್ಷದಲ್ಲಿ ನೀವು ಅಥವಾ ನಿಮ್ಮ ಮನೆಯವರು ಯಾರಾದರೊಬ್ಬರು ಎಳೆದಾಡುವುದು, ಕಪಾಳಕ್ಕೆಹೊಡೆತ, ತಳ್ಳುವುದು ,ಗುಸಾ ಮುಂತಾದ ಅಥವಾ ಬಂದೂಕು, ಚಾಕು ಅಥವಾ ಅಪಾಯಕಾರಿ ವಸ್ತುಗಳಿಂದ ದೈಹಿಕ ಹಲ್ಲೆ ಅಥವಾ ದೈಹಿಕ ಹಲ್ಲೆಯ ಬೆದರಿಕೆಗೆ ಒಳಗಾಗಿರುವಿರಾ?	Yes ....1 ಹೌದು No ....2 ಇಲ್ಲ	If Yes, Go to Incident Report Part 5, Page 27

Q21.	During the last one year has any person you know faced: READ OUT OR SHOW CARD ಕಳೆದ ಒಂದು ವರ್ಷದಲ್ಲಿ ನಿಮಗೆ ತಿಳಿದ ವ್ಯಕ್ತಿ ಇದನ್ನು		Yes	No	If yes for any of these, Go to
		A. Verbal lewd comments on appearance: ನಿಮ್ಮನ್ನು ನೋಡಿ ಹೇಗೆ	1	2	

	ಬಳಸುತ್ತೀರಿ? **SINGLE CODE**	carpool etc..2 ಆಟೋ, ಟಾಕ್ಸಿ, ಕಾರ್ ಪೂಲ್ ಇತ್ಯಾದಿ ಸೇರಿದಂತ ಖಾಸಗಿ ಬಾಡಿಗೆಗೆ ವಾಹನ Two-wheeler..3 2-ವೀಲರ್ Four-wheeler..4 4 ವೀಲರ್ Other (Please Specify): _____ .98 ಇತರ(ನಿರ್ದಿಷ್ಟ ವಾಹನಹೇಳಿರಿ)	
FEAR AND SAFETY ಭಯ ಮತ್ತು ಭದ್ರತೆ			
Q No	Question	Coding Category	Skip
Q1.	What time would you start worrying about safety of an adult male member of your household who is out alone at night? ನಿಮ್ಮ ಮನೆಯ ವಯಸ್ಸ ಗಂಡಸು ರಾತ್ರಿಯಲ್ಲಿ ಮನೆಯಿಂದ ಹೊರಗೆ ಹೋದಾಗ ಯಾವ ಸಮಯದಲ್ಲಿ ನಿಮಗೆ ಅವರ ರಕ್ಷಣೆ ಬಗ್ಗೆ ಚಿಂತೆ ಆಗುತ್ತದೆ?	After 7 pm ಸಂಜೆ 7 ಗಂಟೆ ನಂತರ...........................1 After 8 pm ರಾತ್ರಿ 8 ಗಂಟೆ ನಂತರ ....2 After 10 pm ರಾತ್ರಿ 10 ಗಂಟೆ ನಂತರ ....3 After 11 pm ರಾತ್ರಿ 11 ಗಂಟೆ ನಂತರ ....4 After midnight ಮಧ್ಯರಾತ್ರಿ ನಂತರ.................5 Would not worry ಚಿಂತೆಯಿಲ್ಲ .... 6 Don't know / Can't say ಗೊತ್ತಿಲ್ಲ/ಹೇಳಲಾಗದು 99	
Q2	What time would you start worrying about safety of an adult female member of your household who is out alone at night? ನಿಮ್ಮ ಮನೆಯ ವಯಸ್ಸ ಹೆಂಗಸು ರಾತ್ರಿಯಲ್ಲಿ ಮನೆಯಿಂದ ಹೊರಗೆ ಹೋದಾಗ ಯಾವ ಸಮಯದಲ್ಲಿ ನಿಮಗೆ ಅವರ ರಕ್ಷಣೆ ಬಗ್ಗೆ ಚಿಂತೆ ಆಗುತ್ತದೆ?	After 7 pm ಸಂಜೆ 7 ಗಂಟೆ ನಂತರ...........................1 After 8 pm ರಾತ್ರಿ 8 ಗಂಟೆ ನಂತರ ....2 After 10 pm ರಾತ್ರಿ 10 ಗಂಟೆ ನಂತರ ....3 After 11 pm ರಾತ್ರಿ 11 ಗಂಟೆ ನಂತರ ....4 After midnight ಮಧ್ಯರಾತ್ರಿ ನಂತರ.................5 Would not worry ಚಿಂತೆಯಿಲ್ಲ .... 6 Don't know / Can't say ಗೊತ್ತಿಲ್ಲ/ಹೇಳಲಾಗದು99	
Q3	Do you feel safe leaving your home locked for many days? ಬಹಳ ದಿನ ಮನೆಗೆ ಬೀಗ ಹಾಕಿ ಹೊರಗೆ ಹೋದರೆ ಸುರಕ್ಷಿತ ಎಂದು ಅನಿಸುತ್ತದೆಯೇ?	Yes ಹೌದು ....1 No ಇಲ್ಲ ....2 Don't know / Can't say ....99 ಗೊತ್ತಿಲ್ಲ/ಹೇಳಲಾಗದು	
Q4	Do you feel safe travelling using public transport alone during the day? ಹಗಲಲ್ಲಿ ಒಂಟೆಯಾಗಿ ಯಾವ ಸಾರ್ವಜನಿಕ ಸಾರಿಗೆಯಲ್ಲಿ ಪ್ರಯಾಣ ಮಾಡಿದರೆ ನಿಮಗೆ ಸುರಕ್ಷಿತ ಅನಿಸುತ್ತದೆ?	<table><tr><td></td><td>Yes</td><td>No</td><td>Don't know ಗೊತ್ತಿಲ್ಲ</td></tr><tr><td>A. KSRTC Bus ಕೆಎಸ್ಆರ್ ಟಿಸಿ ಬಸ್</td><td>1</td><td>2</td><td>99</td></tr><tr><td>B. Private Bus ಖಾಸಗಿ ಬಸ್</td><td>1</td><td>2</td><td>99</td></tr><tr><td>C. Train ರೈಲು</td><td>1</td><td>2</td><td>99</td></tr><tr><td>D. Auto ಆಟೋ</td><td>1</td><td>2</td><td>99</td></tr><tr><td>E. Taxi ಟಾಕ್ಸಿ</td><td>1</td><td>2</td><td>99</td></tr><tr><td>F.(If city) Metro ನಗರದಲ್ಲಿ ಮೆಟ್ರೊ</td><td>1</td><td>2</td><td>99</td></tr></table>	
Q5	At what time in the evening will you stop feeling safe while traveling using public transport? ಸಂಜೆ ಯಾವ ಸಮಯದಲ್ಲಿ ನಿಮಗೆ ಸಾರ್ವಜನಿಕ ಸಾರಿಗೆಯಲ್ಲಿ ಪ್ರಯಾಣ ಮಾಡುವಾಗ ಸುರಕ್ಷಿತ ಅನಿಸುವುದಿಲ್ಲ?	After 7 pm ಸಂಜೆ 7 ಗಂಟೆ ನಂತರ...........................1 After 8 pm ರಾತ್ರಿ 8 ಗಂಟೆ ನಂತರ ....2 After 10 pm ರಾತ್ರಿ 10 ಗಂಟೆ ನಂತರ ....3 After 11 pm ರಾತ್ರಿ 11 ಗಂಟೆ ನಂತರ ....4 After midnight ಮಧ್ಯರಾತ್ರಿ ನಂತರ.................5 Would not worry ಚಿಂತೆಯಿಲ್ಲ .... 6 Don't know/Can't say ಗೊತ್ತಿಲ್ಲ/ಹೇಳಲಾಗದು........ 99	
Q6.	At what time in the evening would you stop feeling safe while traveling in your personal transport? ಸಂಜೆ ಯಾವ ಸಮಯದಲ್ಲಿ ನಿಮಗೆ ನಿಮ್ಮ ಸ್ವಂತ ವಾಹನದಲ್ಲಿ	After 7 pm ಸಂಜೆ 7 ಗಂಟೆ ನಂತರ...........................1 After 8 pm ರಾತ್ರಿ 8 ಗಂಟೆ ನಂತರ ....2 After 10 pm ರಾತ್ರಿ 10 ಗಂಟೆ ನಂತರ ....3 After 11 pm ರಾತ್ರಿ 11 ಗಂಟೆ ನಂತರ 4	

Q No	Question	Coding Category	Skip
	ಪ್ರಯಾಣ ಮಾಡುವಾಗ ಸುರಕ್ಷಿತ ಅನಿಸುವುದಿಲ್ಲ ?	After midnight ಮಧ್ಯರಾತ್ರಿ ನಂತರ...........5 Would not worry ಚಿಂತೆಯಿಲ್ಲ...........6 Don't know/Can't say ಗೊತ್ತಿಲ್ಲ/ಹೇಳಲಾಗದು........99	
Q7.	Do you feel safe walking around in your neighbourhood during the day? ಹಗಲಲ್ಲಿ ನಿಮ್ಮ ನೆರೆಹೊರೆಯಲ್ಲಿ ಓಡಾಡುವಾಗ ಸುರಕ್ಷಿತ ಎನಿಸುತ್ತದೆಯೇ?	Yes ಹೌದು ....1 No ಇಲ್ಲ ....2 Don't know/Can't Say...........99 ಗೊತ್ತಿಲ್ಲ/ಹೇಳಲಾಗದು	
Q8.	Do you feel safe walking around in your neighbourhood in the evening? ಸಂಜೆ ನಿಮ್ಮ ನೆರೆಹೊರೆಯಲ್ಲಿ ಓಡಾಡುವಾಗ ಸುರಕ್ಷಿತ ಎನಿಸುತ್ತದೆಯೇ?	Yes ಹೌದು ....1 No ಇಲ್ಲ ....2 Don't know/Can't Say ಗೊತ್ತಿಲ್ಲ/ಹೇಳಲಾಗದು 99	
Q9.	At what time in the evening would you stop feeling safe walking around the neighbourhood? ಸಂಜೆ ಯಾವ ಸಮಯದಲ್ಲಿ ನಿಮಗೆ ನಿಮ್ಮ ನೆರೆಹೊರೆಯಲ್ಲಿ ಓಡಾಡುವಾಗ ಸುರಕ್ಷಿತವಲ್ಲ ಎನಿಸುತ್ತದೆ?	After 7 pm ಸಂಜೆ 7 ಗಂಟೆ ನಂತರ...........1 After 8 pm ರಾತ್ರಿ, 8 ಗಂಟೆ ನಂತರ ....2 After 10 pm ರಾತ್ರಿ, 10 ಗಂಟೆ ನಂತರ...........3 After 11 pm ರಾತ್ರಿ, 11 ಗಂಟೆ ನಂತರ ....4 After midnight ಮಧ್ಯರಾತ್ರಿ ನಂತರ...........5 Would not worry ಚಿಂತೆಯಿಲ್ಲ...........6 Don't know/Can't say ಗೊತ್ತಿಲ್ಲ/ಹೇಳಲಾಗದು........99	
Q10.	At what time in the evening would you stop feeling safe withdrawing money from your neighbourhood ATM? ಸಂಜೆ ಯಾವ ಸಮಯದಲ್ಲಿ ನಿಮಗೆ ನಿಮ್ಮ ಮನೆ ಹತ್ತಿರದ ಎಟಿಎಂನಿಂದ ಹಣ ತೆಗೆಯುವಾಗ ಸುರಕ್ಷಿತವಲ್ಲ ಎನಿಸುತ್ತದೆ?	After 7 pm ಸಂಜೆ 7 ಗಂಟೆ ನಂತರ...........1 After 8 pm ರಾತ್ರಿ, 8 ಗಂಟೆ ನಂತರ ....2 After 10 pm ರಾತ್ರಿ, 10 ಗಂಟೆ ನಂತರ...........3 After 11 pm ರಾತ್ರಿ, 11 ಗಂಟೆ ನಂತರ ....4 After midnight ಮಧ್ಯರಾತ್ರಿ ನಂತರ...........5 Would not worry ಚಿಂತೆಯಿಲ್ಲ...........6 Don't know/Can't say ಗೊತ್ತಿಲ್ಲ/ಹೇಳಲಾಗದು........99	
Q11.	How much of a problem do you think crime is in your area? ನೀವಿರುವ ಪ್ರದೇಶದಲ್ಲಿ ಅಪರಾಧ ಎಷ್ಟು ದೊಡ್ಡ ಸಮಸ್ಯೆ ಅನಿಸುತ್ತದೆ?	Big problem ದೊಡ್ಡ ಸಮಸ್ಯೆ...........1 Somewhat of a problem ಸುಮಾರಾಗಿ ಸಮಸ್ಯೆ.......2 Not much of a problem ದೊಡ್ಡ ಸಮಸ್ಯೆಯಲ್ಲ ....3 Not a problem at all ಸಮಸ್ಯೆಯೇ ಅಲ್ಲ ....4 Don't know ಗೊತ್ತಿಲ್ಲ 99	
Q12.	What do you think is the single most prevalent crime in this residential area? (Do not prompt. Record the respondent's answer) ಈ ವಾಸ ಪ್ರದೇಶದಲ್ಲಿ ಬಹಳ ನಡೆಯುವ ಒಂದು ಅಪರಾಧ ಯಾವುದು ಎನಿಸುತ್ತದೆ? (ಪರ್ಯಾಯ ಹೇಳಬೇಡಿ, ಉತ್ತರದಾರರ ಉತ್ತರ ದಾಖಲಿಸಿ)	Burglary ಕನ್ನಗಳ್ಳತನ ....1 Robbery ಕಳ್ಳತನ ....2 Physical Assault ದೈಹಿಕ ಹಲ್ಲೆ ....3 Sexual Assault/Harassment ಲೈಂಗಿಕ ಹಲ್ಲೆ/ ಕಿರುಕುಳ..... Fraud in chit fund, investment scheme, property deal ....5 ಚೀಟ್ ಫಂಡ್, ಹಣ ಹೂಡಿಕೆ ಸ್ಕೀಮ್, ಆಸ್ತಿ ವ್ಯವಹಾರದಲ್ಲಿ ಮೋಸ Fraud in debit/credit/ATM/online ....6 ಡೆಬಿಟ್/ಕ್ರೆಡಿಟ್/ಎಟಿಎಂ/ಆನ್ ಲೈನ್ ಮೋಸ Abduction/Kidnapping ಅಪಹರಣ...........7 Murder ಕೊಲೆ ....8 Suicide ಆತ್ಮಹತ್ಯೆ ....9 Road accidents ರಸ್ತೆ ಅಪಘಾತ...........10 Custodial Death ರಾಜಿ ಸಾವು ....11 Medical negligence ವೈದ್ಯಕೀಯ ನಿರ್ಲಕ್ಷ್ಯ...........12 Alcohol Poisoning ಮದ್ಯಪಾನದ ನಂಜು ....13 Vandalism ದಾಂಧಲೆ ....14 Religious/Caste violence ಧರ್ಮ/ಜಾತಿ ಹಿಂಸೆ.......15 Gang violence ಗುಂಪು ಹಿಂಸೆ...........16 Terrorism ಭಯೋತ್ಪಾದನೆ ....17 Social Exclusion ಸಮಾಜದಿಂದ ಬಹಿಷ್ಕಾರ...........18 Bribery ಲಂಚ...........19 Others (Please Specify): ....98 ಇತರ(ನಿರ್ದಿಷ್ಟ ಉತ್ತರ ಬರೆದುಕೊಳ್ಳಿ) Don't know ಗೊತ್ತಿಲ್ಲ 99	

.

Q No	Question	Coding Category	Skip
Q13.	Do you know where your nearest police station or chowki is? ನಿಮ್ಮ ಹತ್ತಿರದ ಪೊಲೀಸ್ ಠಾಣೆ/ ಚೌಕಿ ಎಲ್ಲಿದೆ ಗೊತ್ತಾ?	Yes ಹೌದು ....1 No ಇಲ್ಲ 2	
Q14.	How safe you think your neighbourhood is? ನಿಮ್ಮ ನೆರೆಹೊರೆ ಎಷ್ಟು ಸುರಕ್ಷಿತ ಅನಿಸುತ್ತದೆ?	Very safe ಬಹಳ ಸುರಕ್ಷಿತ ....1 Somewhat safe ಸುಮಾರಾಗಿ ಸುರಕ್ಷಿತ ....2 Somewhat unsafe ಸುಮಾರಾಗಿ ಅಸುರಕ್ಷಿತ ....3 Very unsafe ಬಹಳ ಅಸುರಕ್ಷಿತ ....4 Don't know/Can't say ಗೊತ್ತಿಲ್ಲ/ಹೇಳಲಾಗದು.......99	
Q15.	How often do police patrol this area? ಈ ಪ್ರದೇಶದಲ್ಲಿ ಎಷ್ಟು ಬಾರಿ ಪೊಲೀಸ್ ಗಸ್ತು ನಡೆಯುತ್ತದೆ?	Daily ಪ್ರತಿದಿನ ....1 Bi-weekly ವಾರಕ್ಕೆ ಎರಡು ಬಾರಿ.............................2 Weekly ವಾರಕ್ಕೆ ಒಮ್ಮೆ.......................................3 Fortnightly ಹದಿನ್ಯೆದು ದಿನಕ್ಕೊಮ್ಮೆ.........................4 Monthly ತಿಂಗಳಿಗೊಮ್ಮೆ.....................................5 Yearly ವರ್ಷಕ್ಕೊಮ್ಮೆ... 6 Don't know / Can't say ಗೊತ್ತಿಲ್ಲ/ಹೇಳಲಾಗದು 99	
	CRIME AND VICTIMS ಅಪರಾಧ ಮತ್ತು ಅಪರಾಧದ ಆಹುತಿ		
Q16.	During the last one year, has anything been stolen or attempted to be stolen from your possession or from the possession of any member of your family? (house/ vehicles/ phones/household appliances/ goods/ jewellery) ಕಳೆದ ಒಂದು ವರ್ಷದಲ್ಲಿ ನಿಮ್ಮಲ್ಲಿರುವ ಅಥವಾ ನಿಮ್ಮ ಮನೆಯವರ ಯಾವುದೇ ವಸ್ತು ಕಳವಾಗಿದೆಯೇ/ ಕದಿಯುವ ಪ್ರಯತ್ನ ವಾಯಿತೇ(ಮನೆ/ವಾಹನ/ಫೋನ್/ಮನೆ ವಸ್ತು/ ಸರಕುಗಳು/ಒಡವೆ)	Yes ....1 ಹೌದು No ....2 ಇಲ್ಲ	If YES, Go to Incident Report Part 1, Page 13
Q17	During the last one year, has anyone damaged or tried to cause damage to your property (house/ vehicles/phones/household appliances/ goods/jewellery)? ಕಳೆದ ಒಂದು ವರ್ಷದಲ್ಲಿ ನಿಮ್ಮ ಆಸ್ತಿಗೆ ಯಾರಾದರೂ ಹಾನಿ ಮಾಡಿದರಾ ಅಥವಾ ಹಾನಿ ಮಾಡುವ ಪ್ರಯತ್ನ ವಾಯಿತೇ(ಮನೆ/ವಾಹನ/ಫೋನ್/ ಮನೆ ವಸ್ತು/ಸರಕುಗಳು/ಒಡವೆ)	Yes ....1 ಹೌದು No ....2 ಇಲ್ಲ	If YES, Go to Incident Report Part 2, Page 17
Q18.	During the last one year, have you or your family members lost money due to fraud in a chit fund, property deal or any other investment scheme? ಕಳೆದ ಒಂದು ವರ್ಷದಲ್ಲಿ ನೀವು ಅಥವಾ ನಿಮ್ಮ ಮನೆಯವರು ಚಿಟ್ ಫಂಡ್, ಆಸ್ತಿ ವ್ಯವಹಾರ ಅಥವಾ ಹೂಡಿಕೆ ಯೋಜನೆಯಿಂದ ಹಣ ಕಳೆದುಕೊಂಡಿರಾ?	Yes ....1 ಹೌದು No ....2 ಇಲ್ಲ	If YES, Go to Incident Report Part 3, Page 21
Q19.	Has any member of the family been victim of debit card, online or ATM frauds and has lost money? ನಿಮ್ಮ ಮನೆಯಲ್ಲಿ ಯಾರಾದರೂ ಡೆಬಿಟ್ ಕಾರ್ಡ್, ಆನ್ ಲ್ಯನ್/ ಎಟಿಎಂ ಮೋಸಗಳಿಗೆ ಬಲಿಯಾಗಿ ಹಣ ಕಳೆದುಕೊಂಡರಾ?	Yes ....1 ಹೌದು No ....2 ಇಲ್ಲ	If YES, Go to Incident Report Part 4, Page 24
Q20.	During the last one year, have you or anyone in your family faced any physical assault or threat of physical assault in any way including through grabbing, slapping, shoving, punching or by guns, knives and other dangerous objects? ಕಳೆದ ಒಂದು ವರ್ಷದಲ್ಲಿ ನೀವು ಅಥವಾ ನಿಮ್ಮ ಮನೆಯವರ ಯಾರಾದರೂಬ್ಬರು ಎಳೆದಾಡುವುದು, ಕಪಾಳಕ್ಕೆಹೊಡೆತ, ತಳ್ಳುದುವುದು ,ಗುಸಾ ಮುಂತಾದ ಅಥವಾ ಬಂದೂಕು, ಚಾಕು ಅಥವಾ ಅಪಾಯಕಾರಿ ವಸ್ತುಗಳಿಂದ ದೈಕಿ ಹಲ್ಲೆ ಅಥವಾ ದೈಹಿಕ ಹಲ್ಲೆಯ ಬೆದರಿಕೆಗೆ ಒಳಗಾಗಿರುವಿರಾ?	Yes ....1 ಹೌದು No ....2 ಇಲ್ಲ	If Yes, Go to Incident Report Part 5, Page 27

Q21.	During the last one year has any person you know faced: READ OUT OR SHOW CARD ಕಳೆದ ಒಂದು ವರ್ಷದಲ್ಲಿ ನಿಮಗೆ ತಿಳಿದ ವ್ಯಕ್ತಿ ಇದನ್ನು		Yes	No	If yes for any of these, Go to
		A. Verbal lewd comments on appearance: ನಿಮ್ಮನ್ನು ನೋಡಿ ಹೇಗೆ	1	2	

Q No	Question	Coding Category			Skip
	ಎದುರಿಸಿದರಾ? ಕಾರ್ಡ್ ತೋರಿಸಿ ಅಥವಾ ಓದಿ ಹೇಳಿರಿ.	ಕಾಮುಕ್ತೆರೆಂದು ಟುಬ್ಬಾ ಮಾತುಗಳು ಆಡಿರುವುದು			Incident Report Part 6, Page 30
		B. Stared at indecently that made them feel uncomfortable ಕೆಟ್ಟದಾಗಿ ದಿಟ್ಟಿಸಿ ನೋಡಿದ್ದು ಅವರಿಗೆ ಅಹಿತವೆನಿಸಿತು?	1	2	
		C. Touched indecently, pinched, groped ಕೆಟ್ಟದಾಗಿ ಮುಟ್ಟಿದರು, ಚಿವುಟಿದರು, ಹಿಡಿದರು	1	2	
		D. Followed by people that made them uncomfortable ಅಹಿತವೆನಿಸುವಂತ ಜನರು ಅವರನ್ನು ಹಿಂಬಾಲಿಸಿದರು	1	2	
		E. Lewd vulgar, unwanted messages via SMS or Internet ಎಸ್ ಎಂ ಎಸ್/ ಇಂಟರ್ ನೆಟ್ ಮೂಲಕ ಕೆಟ್ಟ ಅಶ್ಲೀಲ, ಬೇಡದ ಮೆಸೇಜುಗಳು ಬಂದದ್ದು	1	2	
		F. Others: (Record the response) ಇತರ(ಉತ್ತರ ಬರೆದುಕೊಳ್ಳಿ)_____	1	2	
Q22.	Has any member of the family gone missing in past one year? ಕಳೆದ ಒಂದು ವರ್ಷದಲ್ಲಿ ನಿಮ್ಮ ಮನೆ ಸದಸ್ಯರಲ್ಲಿ ಯಾರಾದರೂ ಕಳೆದುಹೋಗಿದ್ದಾರಾ?	Yes ....1 ಹೌದು No ಇಲ್ಲ 2			If YES, Go to Incident Report Part 7, Page 34
Q23.	During the last one year, has there been any unnatural deaths in the family including through ಕಳೆದ ಒಂದು ವರ್ಷದಲ್ಲಿ ಈ ಮುಂದಿನವ ಸೇರಿದಂತ ನಿಮ್ಮ ಕುಟುಂಬದಲ್ಲಿ ಯಾವುದೇ ಅಸಹಜ ಸಾವು ಆಗಿತ್ತೇ?		Yes	No	If yes for any of these, Go to Incident Report Part 8, Page 38
		A. Murder ಕೊಲೆ	1	2	
		B. Suicide ಆತ್ಮಹತ್ಯೆ	1	2	
		C. Custodial death ರಾಜಿ ಸಾವು	1	2	
		D. Medical negligence ವೈದ್ಯಕೀಯ ನಿರ್ಲಕ್ಷತೆ	1	2	
		E. Road accidents, train Accidents ರಸ್ತೆ , ರೈಲು ಅಪಘಾತ	1	2	
		F. Alcohol poisoning ಮದ್ಯ ನಂಜು	1	2	
		G. Others: (Record the response) ಇತರ(ಉತ್ತರ ಬರೆದುಕೊಳ್ಳಿ)	1	2	
Q24.	Have any of the following incidents occurred in your village/locality in past year? READ OUT OR SHOW CARD ಕಳೆದ ಒಂದು ವರ್ಷದಲ್ಲಿ ನಿಮ್ಮ ಹಳ್ಳಿ/ಪ್ರದೇಶದಲ್ಲಿ ಈ ಯಾವುದೇ ಘಟನೆ ನಡೆದಿತ್ತೇ? ಕಾರ್ಡ್ ತೋರಿಸಿ ಅಥವಾ ಓದಿ ಹೇಳಿರಿ		Yes	No	If yes for any of these, Go to Incident Report Part 9, Page 41
		A. Bandhs or Hartals ಬಂದ್/ ಹರತಾಳ	1	2	
		B. Farmer protest ರೈತರ ಪ್ರತಿಭಟನೆ	1	2	
		C. Labour and student agitations ಕಾರ್ಮಿಕರ ಮತ್ತು ವಿದ್ಯಾರ್ಥಿಗಳ ಹೋರಾಟ	1	2	
		D. Violence due to religion ಧರ್ಮದ ಹೆಸರಿನಲ್ಲಿ ಹಿಂಸೆ	1	2	
		E. Violence due to caste ಜಾತಿಹೆಸರಿನಲ್ಲಿ ಹಿಂಸೆ	1	2	
		F. Violence due to language ಭಾಷೆಯ ಹೆಸರಿನಲ್ಲಿ ಹಿಂಸೆ	1	2	
		G. Terrorist attacks/incidents like bomb blast or shootings ಭಯೋತ್ಪಾದಕ ದಾಳಿ/ಬಾಂಬುದಾಳಿ ಅಥವಾ ಗುಂಡು ಹಾರಿಸುವಿಕೆಯಂತಹ ಘಟನೆ	1	2	
		H. Gang violence ಗುಂಪು ಹಿಂಸೆ	1	2	
		I. Any other similar incidents of group violence (Record the response) ಗುಂಪು ಹಿಂಸೆಯಂತಹ ತರಹದ ಯಾವುದೇ ಘಟನೆ (ಉತ್ತರ	1	2	

Q No	Question	Coding Category			Skip
		ಬರೆದುಕೊಳ್ಳಿ)_____			
Q25.	During the last one year, have you or any person in your family been denied access to: ಕಳೆದ ಒಂದು ವರ್ಷದಲ್ಲಿ ನಿಮ್ಮ ಕುಟುಂಬದ ಸದಸ್ಯರಿಗೆ ಅಥವಾ ನಿಮಗೆ ಈ ಯಾವುದೇ ಸೌಕರ್ಯದ ಬಳಕೆ ನಿರಾಕರಿಸಲಾಯಿತೇ?		Yes	No	If yes for any of these, Go to Incident Report Part 10, Page 44
		A. Public Well/Hand Pump/Other Water Resource ಸಾರ್ವಜನಿಕ ಬಾವಿ/ಕೈ ಪಂಪು/ಇತರ ನೀರು ಮೂಲ	1	2	
		B. Public Transport ಸಾರ್ವಜನಿಕ ಸಾರಿಗೆ	1	2	
		C. Places of Worship ಪೂಜಾ ಸ್ಥಳ	1	2	
		D. Government Buildings ಸರ್ಕಾರಿ ಕಟ್ಟಡಗಳು	1	2	
		E. Gram Sabha/Ward committee ಗ್ರಾಮ ಸಭೆ/ವಾರ್ಡ್ ಸಮಿತಿ	1	2	
		F. Public Schools/Educational Institutions ಸಾರ್ವಜನಿಕ ಶಾಲೆ/ ವಿದ್ಯಾ ಸಂಸ್ಥೆಗಳು	1	2	
		G. Hospitals/Clinics ಆಸ್ಪತ್ರೆ/ಕ್ಲಿನಿಕ್	1	2	
Q26.	During the last one year, have you or anyone in your family faced ಕಳೆದ ಒಂದು ವರ್ಷದಲ್ಲಿ ನಿಮ್ಮ ಕುಟುಂಬದ ಸದಸ್ಯರು ಅಥವಾ ನೀವು ಈ ಯಾವುದನ್ನಾದರೂ ಎದುರಿಸಿದಿರಾ?		Yes	No	If yes for any of these, Go to Incident Report Part 11, Page 47
		A. Physical Assault ದೈಹಿಕ ಹಲ್ಲೆ	1	2	
		B. Social Exclusion ಸಾಮಾಜಿಕ ಬಹಿಷ್ಕಾರ	1	2	
		C. Untouchability ಅಸ್ಪೃಶ್ಯತೆ	1	2	
		D. Verbal Abuse ಬೈಗುಳ	1	2	
		E. Public humiliation including being made fun of in public ಸಾರ್ವಜನಿಕವಾಗಿ ಹೀನಾಯ ಮಾಡುವುದೂ ಸೇರಿದಂತೆ ಅಪಮಾನ	1	2	
Q27.	During the last one year, has any public servant, government employee or police asked you for a bribe? ಕಳೆದ ಒಂದು ವರ್ಷದಲ್ಲಿ ನಿಮಗೆ ಯಾವುದೇ ಸಾರ್ವಜನಿಕ ನೌಕರ, ಸರ್ಕಾರಿ ಉದ್ಯೋಗಿ ಅಥವಾ ಪೋಲೀಸ್ ಸಿಬ್ಬಂದಿ ಲಂಚ ಕೇಳಿದರಾ?	Yes ....1 ಹೌದು No ....2 ಇಲ್ಲ			
Q28	During the last one year, do you know of any person who has been assaulted by any public servant, government employee or police? ಕಳೆದ ಒಂದು ವರ್ಷದಲ್ಲಿ ನಿಮಗೆ ಯಾವುದೇ ವ್ಯಕ್ತಿ ಯನ್ನು ಸಾರ್ವಜನಿಕ ನೌಕರ, ಸರ್ಕಾರಿ ಉದ್ಯೋಗಿ ಅಥವಾ ಪೋಲೀಸರು ಹಲ್ಲೆ ಮಾಡಿದ್ದು ಗೊತ್ತಾ?	Yes ....1 ಹೌದು No ....2 ಇಲ್ಲ			
	TO BE FILLED BY SURVEYOR, AFTER COMPLETION OF SURVEY				
S1	Were there any other people immediately present who might be listening during the interview? ಸಂದರ್ಶನದ ಕಾಲದಲ್ಲಿ ಅಲ್ಲಿದ್ದು ಕೇಳಿಸಿಕೊಂಡ ವ್ಯಕ್ತಿಗಳು ಇನ್ಯಾರಾದರೂ ಇದ್ದರಾ?	No one ಯಾರೂ ಇಲ್ಲ ....1 Husband ಗಂಡ ....2 Other adult male family members ....3 ಕುಟುಂಬದ ಇತರ ವಯಸ್ಕ ಗಂಡಸು Adult female family members ....4 ಕುಟುಂಬದ ಇತರ ವಯಸ್ಕ ಹೆಂಗಸು Any male from neighbourhood ....5 ನೆರೆಮನೆಯ ಯಾವುದೇ ಗಂಡಸು Any female from neighbourhood ....6 ನೆರೆಮನೆಯ ಯಾವುದೇ ಹೆಂಗಸು Small crowd ಚಿಕ್ಕ ಗುಂಪು ....7 Other ಇತರ ....8 Children ಮಕ್ಕಳು 9			
S2	Did the respondent consult with others for information to answer questions? ಉತ್ತರಗಳನ್ನು ನೀಡಲು ಮಾಹಿತಿಗಾಗಿ ಉತ್ತರ ನೀಡಿದವರು	Yes ಹೌದು.......................................1			

Q No	Question	Coding Category		Skip
	ಬೇರೆಯವರನ್ನು ಕೇಳಿದರಾ?	No ಇಲ್ಲ 2		
S3	At some stage did you notice something that made you feel that the respondent was answering under some fear or pressure? ಯಾವುದೋ ಹಂತದಲ್ಲಿ ಉತ್ತರ ನೀಡಿದವರು ಯಾವುದೋ ಭಯ ಅಥವಾ ಒತ್ತಡದಲ್ಲಿ ಉತ್ತರಿಸುತ್ತಿದ್ದಾರೆಂದು ಏನಾದರೂ ನಿಮ್ಮ ಗಮನಕ್ಕೆ ಬಂತೆ?	Yes .... 1 ಹೌದು No ಇಲ್ಲ .... 2 Don't know .... 99 ಗೊತ್ತಿಲ್ಲ		
S4	Language of the interview: _____ (Code accordingly) ಸಂದರ್ಶನದ ಭಾಷೆ (ಉತ್ತರಕ್ಕೆ ಅನುಗುಣವಾಗಿ ಕೋಡ್ ಬರೆಯಿರಿ)	Kannada ಕನ್ನಡ	1	
		Tamil ತಮಿಳು	2	
		Telugu ತೆಲುಗು	3	
		Malayalam ಮಲಯಾಳಂ	4	
		Tulu ತುಳು	5	
		Urdu ಉರ್ದು	6	
		Marathi ಮರಾಠಿ	7	
		Hindi ಹಿಂದಿ	8	
		Konkani ಕೊಂಕಣಿ	9	
		English ಇಂಗ್ಲಿಷ್	10	
		Other ಇತರ	11	

	INCIDENT REPORT ಘಟನೆಯ ವರದಿ			
Q16.	Part 1			
16A.	How many times has the incident occurred in the last one year? ಕಳೆದ ಒಂದು ವರ್ಷದಲ್ಲಿ ಎಷ್ಟು ಬಾರಿ ಈ ಘಟನೆ ನಡೆಯಿತು?	Once ಒಮ್ಮೆ .... 1 Twice ಎರಡು ಬಾರಿ .... 2 Thrice ಮೂರು ಬಾರಿ .... 3 More than thrice in the last year .... 4 ಕಳೆದ ಒಂದು ವರ್ಷದಲ್ಲಿ ಮೂರು ಬಾರಿಗಿಂತ ಹೆಚ್ಚು		
16B.	Time of occurrence of the most recent incident: ತೀರಾ ಇತ್ತೀಚಿನ ಘಟನೆ ನಡೆದಾಗ ಸಮಯ	Early Morning (5am to 10am) .... 1 ಮುಂಜಾನೆ Late Morning (10 am to 12pm) ಬೆಳಿಗ್ಗೆ .... 2 Early Afternoon (12pm to 3pm) .... 3 ಮಧ್ಯಾಹ್ನಕ್ಕೆ ಮುಂಚೆ Late Afternoon (3pm to 5pm) ಮಧ್ಯಾಹ್ನದ ನಂತರ .... Early Evening (5pm to 7pm) ಮುಸ್ಸಂಜೆ .... 5 Late Evening (7pm to 9pm) ಸಂಜೆ ನಂತರ .... 6 Early Night (9pm to 12am) ರಾತ್ರಿಗೆಮುಂಚೆ .... 7 Late Night (12am to 5am) ತಡ ರಾತ್ರಿ .... 8 Don't Know/Can't Say ಗೊತ್ತಿಲ್ಲ/ಹೇಳಲಾಗದು 99		
,16C	Was the attempt successful? ಪ್ರಯತ್ನ ಯಶಸ್ವಿಯಾಗಿತ್ತೇ?	Yes ಹೌದು .... 1 No ಇಲ್ಲ 2		If No, skip to 16E
16D.	If 16C is yes, what was type of the property? (Don't read out the options. Mark multiple options as respondents replies) 16C ಗೆ ಉತ್ತರ ಹೌದಾದರೆ, ಯಾವ ವಿಧದ ಆಸ್ತಿ (ಆಯ್ಕೆ ಓದಬೇಡಿ, ಬಹುಆಯ್ಕೆಗಳನ್ನು ಉತ್ತರದಾರರು ಹೇಳುತ್ತಿದ್ದಂತ ಗುರುತಿಸಿ) **CIRCLE ALL MENTIONED BY THE RESPONDENT** ಉತ್ತರದಾರರು ಹೇಳಿದವುಗಳ ಸುತ್ತ ಸುತ್ತುಗೆರೆ ಹಾಕಿರಿ.	Luggage ಲಗ್ಗೇಜು	1	
		Wallet ಹಣದ ಚೀಲ	2	
		Credit card / ATM card ಕ್ರೆಡಿಟ್ ಕಾರ್ಡ್/ಎಟಿಎಂ ಕಾರ್ಡ್	3	
		Jewellery ಆಭರಣ	4	
		T.V ಟಿವಿ	5	
		Mobile phone ಮೊಬೈಲ್ ಫೋನ್	6	
		Laptop ಲ್ಯಾಪ್ ಟಾಪ್	7	
		Cash ಹಣ	8	
		Four-wheeler 4-ವೀಲರ್	9	
		Two-wheeler 2ವೀಲರ್	10	
		Livestock ಜಾನುವಾರು	11	
		Other: (please specify) ಇತರ(ನಿರ್ದಿಷ್ಟವಾಗಿ ಹೇಳಿ)	98	

| 16E | What was approximate value of property? ಆಸ್ತಿಯ ಅಂದಾಜು ಮೊತ್ತ? | 0 –5000...1
5001 –10,000..2
10,001 –15,000 3
15,001 –20,000..4
20,001 –25,000 5
25,001 –30,000 6
30,001 –35,000 7
40,001 –45,000 8
50,001 –55,000 9
55,001 –60,000 10
60,001 –65,000 11
65,001 –70,000 12
70,001 –75,000 13
75,001 –80,000 14
80,001 –85,000 15
85,001 –90,000 16
Over90,000 ರೂ90,000 ವನ್ನೂ ಮೀರಿ.................17
Don't Know/Can't Say ಗೊತ್ತಿಲ್ಲ/ಹೇಳಲಾಗದು.......99 | |

16F	What was the location of the theft? ಕಳ್ಳತನ ನಡೆದಸ್ಥಳ ಇವುಗಳಲ್ಲಿ ಯಾವುದು? **Do not prompt** (ಪರ್ಯಾಯಗಳನ್ನು ಹೇಳಿಕೊಡಬೇಡಿ ಅವರೇ ಉತ್ತರಿಸಲಿ)	Home ಮನೆ .... 1 Friends house ಸ್ನೇಹಿತರ ಮನೆ .... 2 Work Place ಕೆಲಸದಸ್ಥಳ .... 3 On the street ಬೀದಿಯಲ್ಲಿ .... 4 Public transport ಸಾರ್ವಜನಿಕ ಸಾರಿಗೆ .... 5 Commercial place (Malls, Theatre, Restaurant)................ 6 ವಾಣಿಜ್ಯ ಸ್ಥಳ (ಮಾಲ್, ಥಿಯೇಟರ್, ಹೋಟೆಲ್) Place of worship ಪೂಜಾ ಸ್ಥಳ ....7 Neighbourhood area ನೆರೆಹೊರೆ ಪ್ರದೇಶ .... 8 Educational Institutes ವಿದ್ಯಾ ಸಂಸ್ಥೆ.................. 9 Playgrounds ಆಟದ ಮೈದಾನ .... 10 Hospitals ಆಸ್ಪತ್ರೆ .... 11 Police Stations ಪೊಲೀಸ ಠಾಣೆ .... 12 Other places: (PLEASE SPECIFY) ಇತರ(ನಿರ್ದಿಷ್ಟವಾಗಿ ಹೇಳಿ) _____ ....98 Don't Know/Can't Say ಗೊತ್ತಿಲ್ಲ/ಹೇಳಲಾಗದು.......99	
16G	Did you/your family member see the perpetrator of the theft? ಕಳ್ಳತನ ಮಾಡಿದವರನ್ನು ನೀವು/ನಿಮ್ಮ ಕುಟುಂಬದವರು ನೋಡಿದಿರಾ?	Yes ಹೌದು .... 1 No ಇಲ್ಲ 2	**If No go to 16 J.**
16H	If 16G is **yes**, do they know who the perpetrator of the crime is? 16ಜಿ ಗೆ ಉತ್ತರ ಹೌದು ಎಂದಾದರೆ ಕಳ್ಳತನ ಮಾಡಿದವರು ನಿಮಗೆ ಗೊತ್ತಾ?	Yes ಹೌದು .... 1 No ಇಲ್ಲ 2	
16I	If 16H is **yes**, who was it: (Do not prompt) 16ಎಚ್ ಗೆ ಉತ್ತರ ಹೌದು ಎಂದಾದರೆ ಕಳ್ಳತನ ಮಾಡಿದವರು ಯಾರು? (ಪರ್ಯಾಯಗಳನ್ನು ಹೇಳಿಕೊಡಬೇಡಿ ಅವರೇ ಉತ್ತರಿಸಲಿ)	Family ಕುಟುಂಬ .... 1 Friend ಸ್ನೇಹಿತ.. 2 Colleague ಸಹೋದ್ಯೋಗಿ............................ 3 Member of the locality ಪ್ರದೇಶದ ಸದಸ್ಯ .... 4 Acquaintance ಪರಿಚಯದವರು........................5 Member of your caste group/jati/biradari ..... 6 ನಿಮ್ಮ ಜಾತಿಯವರು Member of your religion ನಿಮ್ಮ ಧರ್ಮದವರು 7 Others: (Please Specify)_____ 98 ಇತರ(ನಿರ್ದಿಷ್ಟವಾಗಿ ಹೇಳಿ)	
16J	Why do you think that your property was stolen? (Do not prompt the answers) ನಿಮ್ಮ ಆಸ್ತಿ ಏಕೆ ಕಳ್ಳತನ ಮಾಡಲಾಯಿತನಿಸುತ್ತದೆ? (ಪರ್ಯಾಯಗಳನ್ನು ಹೇಳಿಕೊಡಬೇಡಿ ಅವರೇ ಉತ್ತರಿಸಲಿ)	Previous enmity ಹಿಂದಿನ ವೈರತ್ವ .... 1 Land related disputes ಭೂಮಿ ಸಂಬಂಧಿಸಿದ ವಿವಾದ 2 Family property disputes ಕುಟುಂಬದ ಆಸ್ತಿ ವಿವಾದ 3 Due to my caste ನನ್ನ ಜಾತಿ ಕಾರಣದಿಂದ ..... 4 Due to my religion ನನ್ನ ಧರ್ಮದ ಕಾರಣದಿಂದ .... 5 Due to my gender ನನ್ನ ಲಿಂಗದ ಕಾರಣದಿಂದ .... 6 Due to my mother-tongue ನನ್ನ ಮಾತೃಭಾಷೆಯಿಂದ....... Due to my native state ನನ್ನ ಹುಟ್ಟು ರಾಜ್ಯದಿಂದ ..... 8 Due to my sexual orientation ....9 ನನ್ನ ಲೈಂಗಿಕ ಪ್ರವೃತ್ತಿಯಿಂದ Due to my disability ನನ್ನ ವಿಕಲತೆಯಿಂದ .... 10 Due to my skin colour ನನ್ನ ಮೈ ಬಣ್ಣದಿಂದ .... 11 Due to other reasons: (PLEASE SPECIFY) _____ 98 ಇತರ ಕಾರಣಗಳು(ನಿರ್ದಿಷ್ಟವಾಗಿ ತಿಳಿಸಿ) Do not know ಗೊತ್ತಿಲ್ಲ/ಹೇಳಲಾಗದು.................... 99	
16K	Was any physical force or threats used while trying to steal the property? ಆಸ್ತಿ ಕದಿಯುವಾಗ ದೈಹಿಕ ಬಲ ಪ್ರಯೋಗ ಅಥವಾ ಬೆದರಿಕೆ ಒಡ್ಡಲಾಯಿತೇ?	Yes ಹೌದು .... 1 No ಇಲ್ಲ 2	
16L	Did anyone get hurt during the incident?	Yes ಹೌದು 1	

	ಘಟನೆಯಲ್ಲಿ ಯಾರಿಗಾದರೂ ಪೆಟ್ಟು ಆಯಿತೇ?	No ಇಲ್ಲ 2		
16M	Did you feel threatened? ನಿಮಗೆ ಹೆದರಿಕೆಯಾಯಿತೇ?	Yes ಹೌದು .... 1 No ಇಲ್ಲ 2		
16N	If 16L is yes, was any weapon used in the theft? 16 ಎಲ್ ಗೆ ಉತ್ತರ ಹೌದೆಂದರೆ ಕಳ್ಳತನಕ್ಕೆ ಯಾವುದೇ ಆಯುಧ ಬಳಸಿದರಾ?	Yes ಹೌದು .... 1 No ಇಲ್ಲ 2		
16O	If 16M is yes, did you/your family member resist the theft? 16 ಎಂ ಗೆ ಉತ್ತರ ಹೌದೆಂದರೆ ಕಳ್ಳತನವನ್ನು ನೀವು/ ನಿಮ್ಮ ಕುಟುಂಬದವರು ತಡೆದಿರಾ?	Yes ಹೌದು .... 1 No ಇಲ್ಲ 2		
16P	Did you report the incident to the police ಘಟನೆ ಬಗ್ಗೆ ಪೊಲೀಸರಿಗೆ ವರದಿ ಮಾಡಿದಿರಾ?	Yes ಹೌದು .... 1 No ಇಲ್ಲ 2		**If YES, skip to 16R**
16Q	If 16P is No, Why did you not report? (Do not prompt) 16 ಪಿ ಗೆ ಉತ್ತರ ಇಲ್ಲ ಎಂದಾದರೆ ವರದಿ ಏಕೆ ಮಾಡಲಿಲ್ಲ? (ಪರ್ಯಾಯಗಳನ್ನು ಹೇಳಿಕೊಡಬೇಡಿ ಅವರೇ ಉತ್ತರಿಸಲಿ) **CIRCLE ALL MENTIONED BY THE RESPONDENT** ಉತ್ತರದಾರರು ಹೇಳಿದವುಗಳ ಸುತ್ತ ಸುತ್ತುಗೆರೆ ಹಾಕಿರಿ	Fear of retaliation ತಿರುಗಿ ಸೇಡು ತೀರಿಸಿ ಕೊಳ್ಳುತ್ತಾರೆಂಬ ಭಯ	1	**After circling answers ,** **Skip to 16X**
		Lack of evidence ಸಾಕ್ಷಿಯಿರಲಿಲ್ಲ	2	
		Didn't know where to report ಎಲ್ಲಿ ವರದಿ ಮಾಡುವುದು ಗೊತ್ತಿಲ್ಲ	3	
		Didn't know helpline number ಸಹಾಯವಾಣಿ ನಂಬರ್ ಗೊತ್ತಿಲ್ಲ	4	
		Did not want to get stuck in police/court matters ಪೊಲೀಸ್/ ಕೋರ್ಟು ವ್ಯವಹರಿಸಿಗೆ ಸಿಕ್ಕಿಹಾಕಿಕೊಳ್ಳುವುದು ಇಷ್ಟವಿರಲಿಲ್ಲ	5	
		Uncomfortable to go to Police Station ಪೊಲೀಸ್ ಠಾಣೆಗೆ ಹೋಗುವುದು ಅಹಿತವಾಗಿತ್ತು	6	
		Did not think the police would be able to do anything about the case ಪ್ರಕರಣದ ಬಗ್ಗೆ ಪೊಲೀಸರು ಏನಾದರೂ ಮಾಡುತ್ತಾರೆ ಅನಿಸುವುದಿಲ್ಲ	7	
		Did not think police would entertain the case ಪೊಲೀಸರು ಕೇಸನ್ನು ತೆಗೆದುಕೊಳ್ಳುತ್ತಾರೆ ಅನಿಸಲಿಲ್ಲ	8	
		Police is unfair ಪೊಲೀಸರು ನ್ಯಾಯಪರರಲ್ಲ	9	
		Family matters need not be reported ಕುಟುಂಬ ವಿಷಯ ವರದಿಮಾಡಬಾರದು	10	
		This is better settled outside the police station ಪೊಲೀಸ್ ಠಾಣೆಯ ಹೊರಗೆ ಇತ್ಯರ್ಥ ಉತ್ತಮ	11	
		Bad past experience with reporting to Police ಹಿಂದೆ ಪೊಲೀಸ್ ಗೆ ವರದಿ ಮಾಡಿದ ಕೆಟ್ಟ ಅನುಭವವಿದೆ	12	
		Others: Please specify ಇತರ: ದಯವಿಟ್ಟು ನಿರ್ದಿಷ್ಟವಾಗಿ ಹೇಳಿ)_____	98	
		Don't Know/Can't Say ಗೊತ್ತಿಲ್ಲ/ ಹೇಳಲಾಗದು	99	
16R	If 16P is Yes, why did you report? 16 ಪಿ ಗೆ ಉತ್ತರ ಹೌದೆಂದರೆ ಏಕೆ ವರದಿ ಮಾಡಿದಿರಿ? **DO NOT PROMPT** ಪರ್ಯಾಯಗಳನ್ನು ಹೇಳಿಕೊಡಬೇಡಿ ಅವರೇ ಉತ್ತರಿಸಲಿ	To recover property/person .... 1 ಆಸ್ತಿ/ವ್ಯಕ್ತಿಯನ್ನು ಮರುಪಡೆಯಲು For insurance reasons ವಿಮೆ ಕಾರಣಗಳಿಗೆ .... 2 Crime should be reported .... 3 ಅಪರಾಧಗಳನ್ನು ವರದಿಮಾಡಬೇಕು It was a serious event ಇದು ಗಂಭೀರ ವಿಷಯ .... 4 Wanted offender to be caught and punished .5 ಅಪರಾಧಿಯನ್ನು ಹಿಡಿದು ಶಿಕ್ಷೆ ನೀಡಬೇಕು....................... To stop it from happening again/to get help .6 ಮತ್ತೆ ಇದು ಆಗದಂತೆ ನಿಲ್ಲಿಸಲು/ ಸಹಾಯ ಪಡೆಯಲು Other: (Please specify)_____ .. ಇತರ(ನಿರ್ದಿಷ್ಟವಾಗಿ ಹೇಳಿ)		
16S	If 16P is Yes, how did you report the above crime?	Called 100 ನಂ100ಕ್ಕೆ ಕರೆಮಾಡಿದೆ .... 1 Called other police helpline 2		

		16 ಪಿ ಗೆ ಉತ್ತರ ಹೌದೆಂದರೆ ಹೇಗೆ ವರದಿ ಮಾಡಿದಿರಿ?	ಇತರ ಪೊಲೀಸ್ ಸಹಾಯವಾಣಿಗೆ ಕರೆಮಾಡಿದೆ		
		DO NOT PROMPT ಪರ್ಯಾಯಗಳನ್ನು ಹೇಳಿಕೊಡಬೇಡಿ ಅವರೇ ಉತ್ತರಿಸಲಿ	Went to police station ಪೊಲೀಸ್ ಠಾಣೆಗೆ ಹೋದೆ 3		
			Approached a Police Officer ....4 ಪೊಲೀಸ್ ಆಫೀಸರನ್ನು ಭೇಟಿ ಮಾಡಿದೆ		
			Don't Remember ನೆನಪಿಲ್ಲ 99		
16T	If 16P is Yes, what did the police do upon hearing your complaint? (Don't read out the options. Mark multiple options as respondents replies) 16 ಪಿ ಗೆ ಉತ್ತರ ಹೌದೆಂದರೆ ನಿಮ್ಮ ದೂರು ಕೇಳಿದ ಮೇಲೆ ಪೊಲೀಸ್ ಏನು ಮಾಡಿದರು? (ಆಯ್ಕೆ ಓದಬೇಡಿ, ಉತ್ತರದಾರರು ಹೇಳುತ್ತಿದ್ದಂತ ಬಹುಆಯ್ಕೆಗಳನ್ನು ಗುರುತಿಸಿ) CIRCLE ALL MENTIONED BY THE RESPONDENT ಉತ್ತರದಾರರು ಹೇಳಿದವುಗಳ ಸುತ್ತ ಸುತ್ತುಗೆರೆ ಹಾಕಿರಿ.	File a complaint ದೂರು ದಾಖಲಿಸಿದರು	1	
			Register an FIR ಎಫ್ ಐ ಆರ್ ದಾಖಲಿಸಿದರು	2	
			Despatched a PCR vehicle ಪಿಸಿ ಆರ್ ಗಾಡಿ ಕಳುಹಿಸಿದರು	3	
			Took any injured persons for medical assistance ಗಾಯಗೊಂಡ ವ್ಯಕ್ತಿಯನ್ನು ವೈದ್ಯಕೀಯ ಚಿಕಿತ್ಸೆಗೆ ಕರೆದೊಯ್ಯರು	4	
			Asked you to go to another police station ಬೇರೆ ಪೊಲೀಸ್ ಠಾಣೆಗೆ ಹೋಗುವಂತೆ ನನಗೆ ಹೇಳಿದರು	5	
			Came to the spot and investigated ಸ್ಥಳಕ್ಕೆ ಬಂದು ತನಿಖೆಮಾಡಿದರು	6	
			Asked you not to file the complaint ದೂರು ದಾಖಲಿಸಬಾರದೆಂದು ಹೇಳಿದರು	7	
			Did not do anything ಏನೂ ಮಾಡಲಿಲ್ಲ	8	
			Other: (Please specify) ಇತರ(ನಿರ್ದಿಷ್ಟವಾಗಿ ಹೇಳಿ)	9 8	
16U	If 16P is Yes, Were you satisfied by the action of the police? 16 ಪಿ ಗೆ ಉತ್ತರ ಹೌದೆಂದರೆ ಪೊಲೀಸ್ ಕಾರ್ಯದ ಬಗ್ಗೆ ನಿಮಗೆ ತೃಪ್ತಿ ಇದೆಯೇ?	Yes ....1 ಹೌದು		If NO, skip to 16W
			No ಇಲ್ಲ 2		
16V	If 16U is Yes, Why are you satisfied by the police? (Don't read out the options. Mark multiple options as respondents replies) 16 ಯು ಗೆ ಉತ್ತರ ಹೌದೆಂದರೆ ಪೊಲೀಸ್ ತೆಗೆದುಕೊಂಡ ಕ್ರಮದ ಬಗ್ಗೆ ನಿಮಗೆ ಏಕೆ ತೃಪ್ತಿ ಇದೆ ? (ಆಯ್ಕೆ ಓದಬೇಡಿ, ಬಹುಆಯ್ಕೆಗಳನ್ನು ಸಂಬಂಧಪಟ್ಟವನ್ನು ಉತ್ತರದಾರರು ಹೇಳುತ್ತಿದ್ದಂತೆ ಗುರುತಿಸಿ) CIRCLE ALL MENTIONED BY THE RESPONDENT ಉತ್ತರದಾರರು ಹೇಳಿದವುಗಳ ಸುತ್ತ ಸುತ್ತುಗೆರೆ ಹಾಕಿರಿ.	They listened to the complaint ದೂರು ಕೇಳಿದರು	1	
			They registered the complaint accurately ನಿಖರವಾಗಿ ದೂರು ದಾಖಲಿಸಿದರು	2	
			They registered the complaint quickly ದೂರನ್ನು ಬೇಗ ದಾಖಲಿಸಿದರು	3	
			They explained the action that they will take ತೆಗೆದುಕೊಳ್ಳುವ ಕ್ರಮದ ಬಗ್ಗೆ ವಿವರಿಸಿದರು	4	
			They solved the problem ಸಮಸ್ಯೆ ಪರಿಹಾರ ಮಾಡಿದರು	5	
			Other: (please specify) ಇತರ (ನಿರ್ದಿಷ್ಟವಾಗಿ ಹೇಳಿ)	98	
16W	If 16U is No, Why are you not satisfied by the police? (Don't read out the options. Mark multiple options as respondents replies) 16 ಯು ಗೆ ಉತ್ತರ ಇಲ್ಲ ಎಂದಾದರೆ ಪೊಲೀಸ್ ತೆಗೆದುಕೊಂಡ ಕ್ರಮದ ಬಗ್ಗೆ ನಿಮಗೆ ಏಕೆ ತೃಪ್ತಿ ಇಲ್ಲ ? (ಆಯ್ಕೆ ಓದಬೇಡಿ, ಬಹುಆಯ್ಕೆಗಳನ್ನು ಉತ್ತರದಾರ ಹೇಳುತ್ತಿದ್ದಂತೆ ಗುರುತಿಸಿ) CIRCLE ALL MENTIONED BY THE RESPONDENT ಉತ್ತರದಾರರು ಹೇಳಿದವುಗಳ ಸುತ್ತ ಸುತ್ತುಗೆರೆ ಹಾಕಿರಿ.	They were not interested ಅವರಿಗೆ ಆಸಕ್ತಿಯಿರಲಿಲ್ಲ)	1	
			They were rude and impolite ಅವರು ಒರಟಾಗಿ ಮತ್ತು ಸೌಜನ್ಯವಿಲ್ಲದೆ ವರ್ತಿಸಿದರು,	2	
			They did not do enough ಬೇಕಾದಷ್ಟು ಮಾಡಲಿಲ್ಲ	3	
			They refused to file the FIR ಎಫ್ ಐ ಆರ್ ದಾಖಲಿಸಲು ನಿರಾಕರಿಸಿದರು	4	
			They tried to persuade me not to register an FIR ಎಫ್ ಐ ಆರ್ ದಾಖಲಿಸದಂತೆ ನನಗೆ ಒಪ್ಪಿಸಲು ಪ್ರಯತ್ನ ಮಾಡಿದರು	5	
			They took a long time to register my FIR ನನ್ನ ಎಫ್ ಐ ಆರ್ ದಾಖಲಿಸಲು ಬಹಳ ಕಾಲ ತೆಗೆದುಕೊಂಡರು	6	
			They told me to go away from the police station ಪೊಲೀಸ್ ಠಾಣೆಯಿಂದ ಹೋಗುವಂತ ಹೇಳಿದರು	7	
			They put me at fault ನನ್ನದೇ ತಪ್ಪುಎಂದು ಹೇಳಿದರು	8	
			They wanted a bribe ಲಂಚ ಕೇಳಿದರು	9	
			They physically assaulted me ದೈಹಿಕವಾಗಿ ಹಲ್ಲೆ ಮಾಡಿದರು	10	

		They verbally abused me ನನ್ನನ್ನು ಬೈದರು	11	
		They didn't find or apprehend the offender ಅಪರಾಧಿಯನ್ನು ಹುಡುಕಲಿಲ್ಲ/ ದಸ್ತಗಿರಿ ಮಾಡಲಿಲ್ಲ	12	
		They didn't recover my property (goods) ನನ್ನ ಆಸ್ತಿ (ಸರಕು) ಪತ್ತೆಹಚ್ಚಿಕೊಡಲಿಲ್ಲ	13	
		They didn't keep me properly informed ನನಗೆ ಸರಿಯಾಗಿ ಮಾಹಿತಿ ನೀಡಲಿಲ್ಲ	14	
		They were slow to arrive ಬಹಳ ತಡವಾಗಿ ಬಂದರು	15	
		Other: (please specify) ಇತರ(ನಿರ್ದಿಷ್ಟವಾಗಿ ಹೇಳಿ) _____	98	
16X	Was any person arrested due to the incident? ಘಟನೆಯಿಂದ ಯಾವುದೇ ವ್ಯಕ್ತಿಯನ್ನು ದಸ್ತಗಿರಿ ಮಾಡಿದರಾ?	Yes ಹೌದು ....1 No ಇಲ್ಲ 2		
16Y	How serious was the incident to you and your household? ನಿಮಗೆ ಮತ್ತು ನಿಮ್ಮ ಮನೆಗೆ ಈ ಘಟನೆ ಎಷ್ಟು ಗಂಭೀರವಾದುದು?	Very serious ಬಹಳ ಗಂಭೀರ...............................1 Somewhat serious ಸುಮಾರಾಗಿ ಗಂಭೀರ.............2 Not very serious ಬಹಳ ಗಂಭೀರವಲ್ಲ ....3 Not serious at all ಗಂಭೀರವೇ ಅಲ್ಲ.........................4 Don't know ಗೊತ್ತಿಲ್ಲ 99		
Q17 Part II				
17A	How many times has the incident occurred in the last one year? ಕಳೆದ ಒಂದು ವರ್ಷದಲ್ಲಿ ಎಷ್ಟು ಬಾರಿ ಘಟನೆ ನಡೆಯಿತು?	Once ಒಮ್ಮೆ..1 Twice ಎರಡು ಬಾರಿ ....2 Thrice ಮೂರು ಬಾರಿ ....3 More than thrice in the last year...................4 ಕಳೆದ ಒಂದು ವರ್ಷದಲ್ಲಿ ಮೂರು ಬಾರಿಗಿಂತ ಹೆಚ್ಚು		
17B	Time of occurrence of the most recent incident: ತೀರಾ ಇತ್ತೀಚಿನ ಘಟನೆಯ ಸಮಯ	Early Morning (5am to 10am) ....1 ಮುಂಜಾನೆ Late Morning (10 am to 12pm) ....2 ಬೆಳಿಗ್ಗೆ Early Afternoon (12pm to 3pm)......................3 ಮಧ್ಯಾಹ್ನಕ್ಕೆ ಮುಂಚೆ Late Afternoon (3pm to 5pm) ....4 ಮಧ್ಯಾಹ್ನದ ನಂತರ Early Evening (5pm to 7pm)...........................5 ಮುಸ್ಸಂಜೆ Late Evening (7pm to 9pm) ....6 ಸಂಜೆ ನಂತರ Early Night (9pm to 12am) ....7 ರಾತ್ರಿಗೆಮುಂಚೆ Late Night (12am to 5am) ....8 ತಡ ರಾತ್ರಿ Don't Know/Can't Say ಗೊತ್ತಿಲ್ಲ/ಹೇಳಲಾಗದು.......99		
17C	Was the attempt successful? ಪ್ರಯತ್ನ ಯಶಸ್ವಿಯಾಗಿತ್ತೇ?	Yes ಹೌದು ....1 No ಇಲ್ಲ 2		If NO, skip to 17E
17D	If 17C if yes, what was type of the property? (Don't read out the options. Mark multiple options as respondents replies) 17ಸಿ ಗೆ ಉತ್ತರ ಹೌದಾದರೆ, ಯಾವ ವಿಧದ ಆಸ್ತಿ (ಆಯ್ಕೆ ಓದಬೇಡಿ, ಬಹುಆಯ್ಕೆಗಳನ್ನು ಉತ್ತರದಾರ ಹೇಳುತ್ತಿದ್ದಂತೆ ಗುರುತಿಸಿ) **CIRCLE ALL MENTIONED BY THE RESPONDENT** ಉತ್ತರದಾರರು ಹೇಳಿದವುಗಳ ಸುತ್ತ ಸುತ್ತುಗೆರೆ ಹಾಕಿರಿ.	House ಮನೆ	1	
		Jewellery ಆಭರಣ	2	
		T.V ಟಿವಿ	3	
		Mobile phone ಮೊಬೈಲ್ ಫೋನ್	4	
		Laptop ಲ್ಯಾಪ್ ಟಾಪ್	5	
		Four-wheeler 4-ವೀಲರ್	6	
		Two-wheeler 2ವೀಲರ್	7	
		Other: (please specify) ಇತರ(ನಿರ್ದಿಷ್ಟವಾಗಿ ಹೇಳಿ) _____	98	

17E	What was approximate value of property? : ಆಸ್ತಿಯ ಅಂದಾಜು ಮೌಲ್ಯ ಎಷ್ಟು? _____	0 −5000...1 5001 − 10,000 ....2 10,001 −15,000 ....3 15,001 −20,000 ....4 20,001 −25,000 ....5 25,001 −30,000 ....6 30,001 −35,000 ....7 40,001 −45,000 ....8 50,001 −55,000 ....9 55,001 −60,000 ....10 60,001 −65,000 ....11 65,001 −70,000 ....12 70,001 −75,000 ....13 75,001 −80,000 ....14 80,001 −85,000 ....15 85,001 −90,000 ....16 Over 90,000 ರೂ90,000 ಮೀರಿ ....17 Don't Know/Can't Say ಗೊತ್ತಿಲ್ಲ/ಹೇಳಲಾಗದು.......99	
17F	What was the location when the damage was done? ಕಳ್ಳತನ ನಡೆದ ಸ್ಥಳ ಯಾವುದಾಗಿತ್ತು?	Home ಮನೆ ....1 Friends house ಸ್ನೇಹಿತರ ಮನೆ ....2 Work Place ಕೆಲಸದಸ್ಥಳ ....3 On the street ಬೀದಿಯಲ್ಲಿ ....4 Public transport ಸಾರ್ವಜನಿಕ ಸಾರಿಗೆ ....5 Commercial place (Malls, Theatre, Restaurant)............................6 ವಾಣಿಜ್ಯ ಸ್ಥಳ(ಮಾಲ್, ಥಿಯೇಟರ್, ಹೋಟೆಲ್) Place of worship ಪೂಜಾ ಸ್ಥಳ............................7 Neighbourhood area ನೆರೆಹೊರೆ ಪ್ರದೇಶ ....8 Educational Institutes ವಿದ್ಯಾ ಸಂಸ್ಥೆಗಳು.............9 Playgrounds ಆಟದ ಮೈದಾನ ....10 Hospitals ಆಸ್ಪತ್ರೆ..11 Police Stations ಪೋಲಿಸು ಠಾಣೆಗಳು ....12 Other places: (PLEASE SPECIFY) ಇತರ (ನಿರ್ದಿಷ್ಟವಾಗಿ ಹೇಳಿ) _____ ....98 Don't Know/Can't Say ಗೊತ್ತಿಲ್ಲ/ಹೇಳಲಾಗದು 99	
17G	Did you or your family member see the perpetrator of the damage? ಕಳ್ಳತನ ಮಾಡಿದವರನ್ನು ನೀವು/ನಿಮ್ಮ ಕುಟುಂಬದವರು ನೋಡಿದಿರಾ?	Yes ಹೌದು ....1 No ಇಲ್ಲ 2	If NO, skip to 17J
17H	If 17G in yes, do you know who they perpetrator of the crime is? 17ಜಿ ಗೆ ಉತ್ತರ ಹೌದು ಎಂದಾದರೆ ಕಳ್ಳತನ ಮಾಡಿದವರು ನಿಮಗೆ ಗೊತ್ತಾ?	Yes ಹೌದು ....1 No ಇಲ್ಲ 2	
17I	If 17H in yes, who was it: (Do not prompt) 17ಎಚ್ ಗೆ ಉತ್ತರ ಹೌದು ಎಂದಾದರೆ ಕಳ್ಳತನ ಮಾಡಿದವರು ಯಾರು? (ಪರ್ಯಾಯ ಹೇಳಿಕೊಡಬೇಡಿ ಅವರೇ ಹೇಳಲಿ)	Family ಕುಟುಂಬ ....1 Friend ಸ್ನೇಹಿತ...2 Colleague ಸಹೋದ್ಯೋಗಿ............................3 Member of the locality ಪ್ರದೇಶದ ಸದಸ್ಯ ....4 Acquaintance ಪರಿಚಯದವರು..........................5 Member of your caste group/jati/biradari .....6 ನಿಮ್ಮ ಜಾತಿಯವರು/ನೆಂಟರು Member of your religion ನಿಮ್ಮ ಧರ್ಮದವರು 7 Others: (Please Specify)_____ 98 ಇತರ(ನಿರ್ದಿಷ್ಟವಾಗಿ ಹೇಳಿ)	

17J	Why do you think that your property was damaged? (do not prompt) ನಿಮ್ಮ ಆಸ್ತಿ ಏಕೆ ಕಳ್ಳತನ ಮಾಡಲಾಯಿತೆನಿಸುತ್ತದೆ? (ಪರ್ಯಾಯ ಹೇಳಿಕೊಡಬೇಡಿ ಅವರೇ ಹೇಳಲಿ)	Previous enmity ಹಿಂದಿನ ವೈರತ್ವ ....1 Land related disputes ಭೂಮಿಗೆ ಸಂಬಂಧಿಸಿದ ವಿವಾದ .... Family property disputes ಕುಟುಂಬದ ಆಸ್ತಿ ವಿವಾದ 3 Due to my caste ನನ್ನ ಜಾತಿಕಾರಣದಿಂದ ....4 Due to my religion ನನ್ನ ಧರ್ಮದ ಕಾರಣದಿಂದ ......5 Due to my gender ನನ್ನ ಲಿಂಗದ ಕಾರಣದಿಂದ ....6 Due to my mother-tongue ನನ್ನ ಮಾತೃಭಾಷೆಯಿಂದ....... Due to my native state ನನ್ನ ಹುಟ್ಟು ರಾಜ್ಯದಿಂದ .....8 Due to my sexual orientation ....9 ನನ್ನ ಲೈಂಗಿಕ ಪ್ರವೃತ್ತಿಯಿಂದ Due to my disability ನನ್ನ ಏಕಲತೆಯಿಂದ ....10 Due to my skin colour ನನ್ನ ಮೈ ಬಣ್ಣದಿಂದ ....11 Due to other reasons: (PLEASE SPECIFY) _____ 98 ಇತರ ಕಾರಣಗಳು(ನಿರ್ದಿಷ್ಟವಾಗಿ ಹೇಳಿ) Do not know ಗೊತ್ತಿಲ್ಲ/ಹೇಳಲಾಗದು......................99	
17K	Did you report the incident to the police: ಘಟನೆ ಬಗ್ಗೆ ನೀವು ಪೊಲೀಸರಿಗೆ ವರದಿ ಮಾಡಿದಿರಾ?	Yes ಹೌದು ....1 No ಇಲ್ಲ 2	If yes, skip to 17M
17L	If 17K is No, Why did you not report? (Do not prompt) 17ಕೆ ಗೆ ಉತ್ತರ ಇಲ್ಲ ಎಂದಾದರೆ ವರದಿ ಏಕೆ ಮಾಡಲಿಲ್ಲ? **CIRCLE ALL MENTIONED BY THE RESPONDENT** ಉತ್ತರದಾರರು ಹೇಳಿದವುಗಳ ಸುತ್ತ ಸುತ್ತುಗೆರೆ **ಹಾಕಿರಿ**	Fear of retaliation ತಿರುಗಿ ಸೇಡು ತೀರಿಸಿ ಕೊಳ್ಳುತ್ತಾರೆಂಬ ಭಯ — 1 Lack of evidence ಸಾಕ್ಷಿಯಿರಲಿಲ್ಲ — 2 Didn't know where to report ಎಲ್ಲಿ ವರದಿ ಮಾಡುವುದು ಗೊತ್ತಿಲ್ಲ — 3 Didn't know helpline number ಸಹಾಯವಾಣಿ ನಂಬರ್ ಗೊತ್ತಿಲ್ಲ — 4 Did not want to get stuck in police/court matters ಪೊಲೀಸ್/ ಕೋರ್ಟು ವ್ಯವಹರಣೆಗೆ ಸಿಕ್ಕಿಹಾಕಿಕೊಳ್ಳುವುದು ಇಷ್ಟವಿರಲಿಲ್ಲ — 5 Uncomfortable to go to Police Station ಪೊಲೀಸ್ ಠಾಣೆಗೆ ಹೋಗುವುದು ಅಹಿತವಾಗಿತ್ತು — 6 Did not think the police would be able to do anything about the case ಈ ಪ್ರಕರಣದ ಬಗ್ಗೆ ಪೊಲೀಸರು ಏನಾದರೂ ಮಾಡುತ್ತಾರೆ ಅನಿಸಲಿಲ್ಲ — 7 Did not think police would entertain the case ಪೊಲೀಸರು ಕೇಸನ್ನು ತೆಗೆದುಕೊಳ್ಳುತ್ತಾರೆ ಅನಿಸಲಿಲ್ಲ — 8 Police is unfair ಪೊಲೀಸರು ನ್ಯಾಯಪರವಲ್ಲ — 9 Family matters need not be reported ಕುಟುಂಬ ವಿಷಯ ವರದಿಮಾಡಬಾರದು. — 10 This is better settled outside the police station ಪೊಲೀಸ್ ಠಾಣೆಯ ಹೊರಗೆ ಇತ್ಯರ್ಥ ಉತ್ತಮ. — 11 Bad past experience with reporting to Police ಪೊಲೀಸ್ ಗೆ ವರದಿ ಮಾಡಿದ ಕೆಟ್ಟ ಅನುಭವವಿದೆ — 12 Others: (Please specify)_____ ಇತರ(ನಿರ್ದಿಷ್ಟವಾಗಿ ದಾಖಲಿಸಿ) — 98 Don't Know/Can't Say ಗೊತ್ತಿಲ್ಲ/ಹೇಳಲಾಗದು — 99	**After circling answers, SKIP TO 17S**
17M	If 17K is Yes, why did you report? 17 ಕೆ ಗೆ ಉತ್ತರ ಹೌದೆಂದರೆ ಏಕೆ ವರದಿ ಮಾಡಿದಿರಿ?	To recover property/person ....1 ಆಸ್ತಿ/ವ್ಯಕ್ತಿಯನ್ನು ಮರುಪಡೆಯಲು For insurance reasons ಎಮ ಕಾರಣಗಳಿಗೆ............2 Crime should be reported ....3 ಅಪರಾಧಗಳನ್ನು ವರದಿಮಾಡಬೇಕು It was a serious event ....4 ಇದು ಗಂಭೀರ ವಿಷಯ Wanted offender to be caught and punished .5	

		ಅಪರಾಧಿಯನ್ನು ಹಿಡಿದು ಶಿಕ್ಷೆ ನೀಡಬೇಕು........................	
		To stop it from happening again/to get help/others..................6 ಮತ್ತೆ ಇದು ಆಗದಂತೆ ನಿಲ್ಲಿಸಲು/ ಸಹಾಯ ಪಡೆಯಲು	
		Other: (Please specify) _____ ಇತರೆ(ನಿರ್ದಿಷ್ಟವಾಗಿ ಹೇಳಿ) 98	
17N	If 17K is Yes, how did you report the above crime? 17 ಕೆ ಗೆ ಉತ್ತರ ಹೌದೆಂದರೆ ಹೇಗೆ ವರದಿ ಮಾಡಿದಿರಿ?	Called 100 ನಂ.100ಕ್ಕೆ ಕರೆಮಾಡಿದೆ 1	
		Called other police helpline ....2 ಪೋಲೀಸ್ ಸಹಾಯವಾಣಿಗೆ ಕರೆಮಾಡಿದೆ	
		Went to police station ಪೊಲೀಸ್ ಠಾಣೆಗೆ ಹೋದೆ 3	
		Approached a Police Officer ....4 ಪೊಲೀಸ್ ಆಫೀಸರನ್ನು ಭೇಟಿ ಮಾಡಿದೆ	
		Don't Remember ನೆನಪಿಲ್ಲ 99	
17O	If 17K is Yes, what did the police do upon hearing your complaint? (Don't read out the options. Mark multiple options as respondents replies) 17ಕೆ ಹೌದೆಂದರೆ ನಿಮ್ಮ ದೂರು ಕೇಳಿ ಪೊಲೀಸ್ ಏನು ಮಾಡಿದರು? (ಆಯ್ಕೆ ಓದಬೇಡಿ, ಬಹುಆಯ್ಕೆಗಳನ್ನು ಉತ್ತರದಾರ ಹೇಳುತ್ತಿದ್ದಂತೆ ಗುರುತಿಸಿ) **CIRCLE ALL MENTIONED BY THE RESPONDENT** ಉತ್ತರದಾರರು ಹೇಳಿದವುಗಳ ಸುತ್ತ ಸುತ್ತುಗೆರೆ ಹಾಕಿರಿ.	File a complaint ದೂರು ದಾಖಲಿಸಿದರು	1
		Register an FIR ಎಫ್ ಐ ಆರ್ ದಾಖಲಿಸಿದರು	2
		Despatched a PCR vehicle ಪಿಸಿ ಆರ್ ಗಾಡಿ ಕಳುಹಿಸಿದರು	3
		Took any injured persons for medical assistance ಗಾಸಿಗೊಂಡ ವ್ಯಕ್ತಿಯನ್ನು ವೈದ್ಯಕೀಯ ಚಿಕಿತ್ಸೆಗೆ ಕರೆದೊಯ್ದರು	4
		Asked you to go to another police station ಬೇರೆ ಪೊಲೀಸ್ ಠಾಣೆಗೆ ಹೋಗುವಂತೆ ನನಗೆ ಹೇಳಿದರು	5
		Came to the spot and investigated ಸ್ಥಳಕ್ಕೆ ಬಂದು ತನಿಖೆಮಾಡಿದರು	6
		Asked you not to file the complaint ದೂರು ದಾಖಲಿಸಬಾರದೆಂದು ಹೇಳಿದರು	7
		Did not do anything ಏನೂ ಮಾಡಲಿಲ್ಲ	8
		Other: (Please specify) ಇತರೆ(ನಿರ್ದಿಷ್ಟವಾಗಿ ದಾಖಲಿಸಿ)	98
17P	If 17K is Yes, Were you satisfied by the action of the police? 17 ಕೆ ಗೆ ಉತ್ತರ ಹೌದೆಂದರೆ ಪೊಲೀಸ್ ತೆಗೆದುಕೊಂಡ ಕ್ರಮದ ಬಗ್ಗೆ ನಿಮಗೆ ತೃಪ್ತಿ ಇದೆಯೇ?	Yes ....1 ಹೌದು	
		No ಇಲ್ಲ 2	
17Q	If 17P is Yes, Why are you satisfied by the police? (Don't read out the options. Mark multiple options as respondents replies) 17 ಪಿ ಗೆ ಉತ್ತರ ಹೌದೆಂದರೆ ಪೊಲೀಸ್ ತೆಗೆದುಕೊಂಡ ಕ್ರಮದ ಬಗ್ಗೆ ನಿಮಗೆ ಏಕೆ ತೃಪ್ತಿ ಇದೆ ? (ಆಯ್ಕೆ ಓದಬೇಡಿ, ಬಹುಆಯ್ಕೆಗಳನ್ನು ಉತ್ತರದಾರ ಹೇಳುತ್ತಿದ್ದಂತೆ ಗುರುತಿಸಿ) **CIRCLE IF RESPONDENT MENTIONS** ಉತ್ತರದಾರರು ಹೇಳಿದವುಗಳ ಸುತ್ತ ಸುತ್ತುಗೆರೆ ಹಾಕಿರಿ.	They listened to the complaint ದೂರು ಕೇಳಿದರು	1
		They registered the complaint accurately ಸರಿಯಾಗಿ ದೂರು ದಾಖಲಿಸಿದರು	2
		They registered the complaint quickly ದೂರುನ್ನು ಬೇಗ ದಾಖಲಿಸಿದರು	3
		They explained the action that they will take ಅವರು ತೆಗೆದುಕೊಳ್ಳುವ ಕ್ರಮದ ಬಗ್ಗೆ ವಿವರಿಸಿದರು	4
		They solved the problem ಸಮಸ್ಯೆ ಪರಿಹಾರ ಮಾಡಿದರು	5
		Other: (please specify) ಇತರೆ(ನಿರ್ದಿಷ್ಟವಾಗಿ ಹೇಳಿ)	98
17R	If 17P is No, Why are you not satisfied by the police? (Don't read out the options. Mark multiple options as respondents replies) 17 ಪಿ ಗೆ ಉತ್ತರ ಇಲ್ಲ ಎಂದಾದರೆ ಪೊಲೀಸ್ ಕಾರ್ಯದ ಬಗ್ಗೆ ನಿಮಗೆ ಏಕೆ ತೃಪ್ತಿ ಇಲ್ಲ ? (ಆಯ್ಕೆಗಳನ್ನು ಓದಬೇಡಿ, ಬಹುಆಯ್ಕೆಗಳನ್ನು ಉತ್ತರದಾರ ಹೇಳುತ್ತಿದ್ದಂತೆ ಗುರುತಿಸಿ) **CIRCLE IF RESPONDENT MENTIONS** ಉತ್ತರದಾರರು ಹೇಳಿದವುಗಳ ಸುತ್ತ ಸುತ್ತುಗೆರೆ ಹಾಕಿರಿ.	They were not interested ಅವರಿಗೆ ಆಸಕ್ತಿಯಿರಲಿಲ್ಲ	1
		They were rude and impolite ಅವರು ಒರಟಾಗಿ, ತಾಳ್ಮೆಯಿಲ್ಲದೆ ಮಾತನಾಡಿದರು.	2
		They did not do enough ಬೇಕಾದಷ್ಟು ಮಾಡಲಿಲ್ಲ.	3
		They refused to file the FIR ಎಫ್ ಐ ಆರ್ ದಾಖಲಿಸಲು ನಿರಾಕರಿಸಿದರು .	4
		They tried to persuade me not to register an FIR ಎಫ್ ಐ ಆರ್ ದಾಖಲಿಸದಂತೆ ನನಗೆ ಒಪ್ಪಿಸಲು ಪ್ರಯತ್ನ ಮಾಡಿದರು	5

		They took a long time to register my FIR ನನ್ನ ಎಫ್ ಐ ಆರ್ ದಾಖಲಿಸಲು ಬಹಳ ಕಾಲ ತೆಗೆದುಕೊಂಡರು.	6
		They told me to go away from the police station ಪೊಲೀಸ್ ಠಾಣೆಯಿಂದ ಹೋಗುವಂತೆ ಹೇಳಿದರು.	7
		They put me at fault ನನ್ನ ಮೇಲೇ ತಪ್ಪು ಹಾಕಿದರು	8
		They wanted a bribe ಲಂಚ ಕೇಳಿದರು	9
		They physically assaulted me ದೈಹಿಕವಾಗಿ ಹಲ್ಲೆ ಮಾಡಿದರು	10
		They verbally abused me ನನ್ನನ್ನು ಬೈದರು	11
		They didn't find or apprehend the offender ಅಪರಾಧಿಯನ್ನು ಹುಡುಕಲಿಲ್ಲ/ ದಸ್ತಗಿರಿ ಮಾಡಲಿಲ್ಲ	12
		They didn't recover my property (goods) ನನ್ನ ಆಸ್ತಿ (ಸರಕು) ಕಂಡುಹಿಡಿದುಕೊಡಲಿಲ್ಲ	13
		They didn't keep me properly informed ನನಗೆ ಸರಿಯಾಗಿ ಮಾಹಿತಿ ನೀಡಲಿಲ್ಲ	14
		They were slow to arrive ಅವರು ಬಹಳ ತಡವಾಗಿ ಬಂದರು	15
		Other: (please specify) ಇತರ(ನಿರ್ದಿಷ್ಟವಾಗಿ ಹೇಳಿರಿ)	98
17S	Was any person arrested due to the incident? ಘಟನೆಸಂಬಂಧದಲ್ಲಿ ಯಾವುದೇ ವ್ಯಕ್ತಿಯನ್ನು ದಸ್ತಗಿರಿ ಮಾಡಿದರಾ?	Yes ಹೌದು ....1 No ಇಲ್ಲ 2	
17T	How serious was the incident to you and your household? ನಿಮಗೆ ಮತ್ತು ನಿಮ್ಮ ಮನೆಗೆ ಈ ಘಟನೆ ಎಷ್ಟು ಗಂಭೀರವಾದುದು?	Very serious ಬಹಳ ಗಂಭೀರ..................................1 Somewhat serious ಸುಮಾರಾಗಿ ಗಂಭೀರ ....2 Not very serious ಬಹಳ ಗಂಭೀರವಲ್ಲ ....3 Not serious at all ಗಂಭೀರವೇ ಅಲ್ಲ........................4 Don't know ಗೊತ್ತಿಲ್ಲ 99	
Q18	**PART III**		
18A	How many times has the incident occurred in the last one year? ಕಳೆದ ಒಂದು ವರ್ಷದಲ್ಲಿ ಎಷ್ಟು ಬಾರಿ ಇಂಥ ಘಟನೆ ನಡೆಯಿತು?	Once ಒಮ್ಮೆ...1 Twice ಎರಡು ಬಾರಿ ....2 Thrice ಮೂರು ಬಾರಿ ....3 More than thrice in the last year.....................4 ಕಳೆದ ಒಂದು ವರ್ಷದಲ್ಲಿ ಮೂರು ಬಾರಿಗಿಂತ ಹೆಚ್ಚು	
18B	Time of occurrence of the most recent incident ತೀರಾ ಇತ್ತೀಚೆನ ಘಟನೆಯು ನಡೆದ ಸಮಯ	Early Morning (5am to 10am) ....1 ಮುಂಜಾನೆ Late Morning (10 am to 12pm) ....2 ಬೆಳಿಗ್ಗೆ Early Afternoon (12pm to 3pm).....................3 ಮಧ್ಯಾಹ್ನಕ್ಕೆ ಮುಂಚೆ Late Afternoon (3pm to 5pm) ....4 ಮಧ್ಯಾಹ್ನದ ಅನಂತರ Early Evening (5pm to 7pm) ....5 ಮುಸ್ಸಂಜೆ Late Evening (7pm to 9pm) ....6 ಸಂಜೆ ನಂತರ Early Night (9pm to 12am) ....7 ರಾತ್ರಿಗೆಮುಂಚೆ Late Night (12am to 5am) ತಡ ರಾತ್ರಿ................8 Don't Know/Can't Say ....99 ಗೊತ್ತಿಲ್ಲ/ಹೇಳಲಾಗದು	
18C	What kind of investment scheme did you lose money in? ಯಾವ ವಿಧದ ಹೂಡಿಕೆ ಯೋಜನೆಯಲ್ಲಿ ಹಣ ಕಳೆದುಕೊಂಡಿರಿ?	Property ಆಸ್ತಿ ....1 Chit fund ಚೀಟ್ ಫಂಡ್ ....2 Consumer fraud ....3 ಗ್ರಾಹಕ ಮೋಸ	

18D	Approximately how much money did you lose in this incident? ಅಂದಾಜಾಗಿ ಈ ಘಟನೆಯಲ್ಲಿ ಎಷ್ಟು ಹಣ ಕಳೆದುಕೊಂಡಿರಿ?	0 –5000..1 5001 –10,000..2 10,001 –15,000......................................3 15,001 –20,000......................................4 20,001 –25,000......................................5 25,001 –30,000......................................6 30,001 –35,000......................................7 40,001 –45,000......................................8 50,001 –55,000......................................9 55,001 –60,000.....................................10 60,001 –65,000.....................................11 65,001 –70,000.....................................12 70,001 –75,000.....................................13 75,001 –80,000.....................................14 80,001 –85,000.....................................15 85,001 –90,000.....................................16 Over90,000 ರೂ90,000 ಮೀರಿ.................17 Don't Know/Can't Say ಗೊತ್ತಿಲ್ಲ/ಹೇಳಲಾಗದು.......99		
18E	Was the money recovered? ಹಣ ವಾಪಸ್ಸು ಸಿಕ್ಕಿತೇ?	Yes ಹೌದು ....1 No ಇಲ್ಲ 2		
18F	Did you report the incident to the police ಘಟನೆ ಬಗ್ಗೆ ನೀವು ಪೊಲೀಸರಿಗೆ ವರದಿ ಮಾಡಿದಿರಾ?	Yes ಹೌದು ....1 No ಇಲ್ಲ 2		If YES, skip to **18H**
18G	If **18F is No**, Why did you not report? (Do not prompt) 18 ಎಫ್ ಗೆ ಉತ್ತರ ಇಲ್ಲ ಎಂದಾದರೆ ವರದಿ ಏಕೆ ಮಾಡಲಿಲ್ಲ? (ಪರ್ಯಾಯ ಹೇಳಿಕೊಡಬೇಡಿ ಅವರೇ ಹೇಳಿ) **CIRCLE ALL MENTIONED BY THE RESPONDENT** ಉತ್ತರದಾರರು ಹೇಳಿದವುಗಳ ಸುತ್ತ ಸುತ್ತುಗೆರೆ ಹಾಕಿರಿ	Fear of retaliation ತಿರುಗಿ ಸೇಡು ತೀರಿಸಿಕೊಳ್ಳುತ್ತಾರೆಂಬ ಭಯ	1	**After circling the answers, SKIP TO 18N**
		Lack of evidence ಸಾಕ್ಷಿಯರಲ್ಲಿ	2	
		Didn't know where to report ಎಲ್ಲಿ ವರದಿ ಮಾಡುವುದು ಗೊತ್ತಿರಲಿಲ್ಲ	3	
		Didn't know helpline number ಸಹಾಯವಾಣಿ ನಂಬರ್ ಗೊತ್ತಿಲ್ಲ	4	
		Did not want to get stuck in police/court matters ಪೊಲೀಸ್/ ಕೋರ್ಟಿನ ವ್ಯವಹಾರಕ್ಕೆ ಸಿಕ್ಕಿಹಾಕಿಕೊಳ್ಳುವುದು ಇಷ್ಟವಿರಲಿಲ್ಲ	5	
		Uncomfortable to go to Police Station ಪೊಲೀಸ್ ಠಾಣೆಗೆ ಹೋಗುವುದು ಅಹಿತವಾಗಿತ್ತು	6	
		Did not think the police would be able to do anything about the case ಪೊಲೀಸರು ಏನಾದರೂ ಮಾಡುತ್ತಾರೆ ಅನಿಸಲಿಲ್ಲ	7	
		Did not think police would entertain the case ಪೊಲೀಸರು ಕೇಸನ್ನು ತೆಗೆದುಕೊಳ್ಳುತ್ತಾರೆ ಅನಿಸಲಿಲ್ಲ	8	
		Police is unfair ಪೊಲೀಸರು ನ್ಯಾಯಪರರಲ್ಲ	9	
		Family matters need not be reported ಕುಟುಂಬ ವಿಷಯ ವರದಿಮಾಡಬಾರದು	10	
		This is better settled outside the police station ಪೊಲೀಸ್ ಠಾಣೆಗೆ ಹೊರಗೆ ಇತ್ಯರ್ಥ ಉತ್ತಮ	11	
		Bad past experience with reporting to Police ಪೊಲೀಸ್ ಗೆ ವರದಿ ಮಾಡಿ ಕೆಟ್ಟ ಅನುಭವವಿದೆ	12	
		Others: (Please specify)_____ ಇತರೆ(ಉತ್ತರ ನಿರ್ದಿಷ್ಟವಾಗಿ ಹೇಳಿರಿ)	98	
		Don't Know/Can't Say ಗೊತ್ತಿಲ್ಲ/ಹೇಳಲಾಗದು	99	
18H	If 18F is Yes, why did you report? 18ಎಫ್ ಗೆ ಉತ್ತರ ಹೌದೆಂದರೆ ಏಕೆ ವರದಿ ಮಾಡಿದಿರಿ?	To recover property/person ....1 ಆಸ್ತಿ/ವ್ಯಕ್ತಿಯನ್ನು ಮರುಪಡೆಯಲು For insurance reasons ....2 ಏಮೆ ಕಾರಣಗಳಿಗೆ Crime should be reported 3		

		ಅಪರಾಧಗಳನ್ನು ವರದಿಮಾಡಬೇಕು It was a serious event ....4 ಇದು ಗಂಭೀರ ವಿಷಯ Wanted offender to be caught and punished . 5 ಅಪರಾಧಿಯನ್ನು ಹಿಡಿದು ಶಿಕ್ಷೆ ನೀಡಬೇಕು........................ To stop it from happening again/to get help/others...6 ಮತ್ತೆ ಇದು ಆಗದಂತೆ ನಿಲ್ಲಿಸಲು/ ಸಹಾಯ ಪಡೆಯಲು Others: (Please specify) _____ 98 ಇತರೆ(ನಿರ್ದಿಷ್ಟವಾಗಿ ಹೇಳಿ)	
18I	If 18F Yes, how did you report the above crime? 18 ಎಫ್‌ ಗೆ ಉತ್ತರ ಹೌದೆಂದರೆ ಹೇಗೆ ವರದಿ ಮಾಡಿದಿರಿ?	Called 100 ನಂ.100 ಕ್ಕೆಕರೆಮಾಡಿದೆ ....1 Called other police helpline ....2 ಪೊಲೀಸ್ ಸಹಾಯವಾಣಿಗೆ ಕರೆಮಾಡಿದೆ Went to police station.......................................3 ಪೊಲೀಸ್ ಠಾಣೆಗೆ ಹೋದೆ Approached a Police Officer ....4 ಪೊಲೀಸ್ ಆಫೀಸರನ್ನು ಭೇಟಿ ಮಾಡಿದೆ Don't Remember ನೆನಪಿಲ್ಲ 99	

18J	If18F is Yes, what did the police do upon hearing your complaint? (Don't read out the options. Mark multiple options as respondents replies) 18 ಎಫ್ ಗೆ ಉತ್ತರ ಹೌದೆಂದರೆ ನಿಮ್ಮ ದೂರು ಕೇಳಿ ಪೊಲೀಸ್ ಏನು ಮಾಡಿದರು? (ಆಯ್ಕೆ ಓದಬೇಡಿ, ಬಹುಆಯ್ಕೆಗಳನ್ನು ಉತ್ತರದಾರ ಹೇಳುತ್ತಿದ್ದಂತೆ ಗುರುತಿಸಿ) **CIRCLE ALL MENTIONED BY THE RESPONDENT** ಉತ್ತರದಾರರು ಹೇಳಿದವುಗಳ ಸುತ್ತ ಸುತ್ತುಗೆರೆ ಹಾಕಿರಿ.	File a complaint ದೂರು ದಾಖಲಿಸಿದರು	1	
		Register an FIR ಎಫ್ ಐ ಆರ್ ದಾಖಲಿಸಿದರು	2	
		Despatched a PCR vehicle ಪಿಸಿ ಆರ್ ಗಾಡಿ ಕಳುಹಿಸಿದರು	3	
		Took any injured persons for medical assistance ಗಾಸಿಗೊಂಡ ವ್ಯಕ್ತಿಯನ್ನು ವೈದ್ಯಕೀಯ ಚಿಕಿತ್ಸೆಗೆ ಕರೆದೊಯ್ಯರು	4	
		Asked you to go to another police station ಬೇರೆ ಪೊಲೀಸ್ ಠಾಣೆಗೆ ಹೋಗುವಂತೆ ನಗನಗ ಹೇಳಿದರು	5	
		Came to the spot and investigated ಸ್ಥಳಕ್ಕೆ ಬಂದು ತನಿಖೆಮಾಡಿದರು	6	
		Asked you not to file the complaint ದೂರು ದಾಖಲಿಸಬಾರದೆಂದು ಹೇಳಿದರು	7	
		Did not do anything ಏನೂ ಮಾಡಲಿಲ್ಲ	8	
		Other: (Please specify) ಇತರೆ(ನಿರ್ದಿಷ್ಟವಾಗಿ ಹೇಳಿ)	98	
18K	If 18F is Yes, Were you satisfied by the action of the police? 18ಎಫ್ ಗೆ ಉತ್ತರ ಹೌದೆಂದರೆ ಪೊಲೀಸ್ ತೆಗೆದುಕೊಂಡ ಕ್ರಮದ ಬಗ್ಗೆ ನಿಮಗೆ ತೃಪ್ತಿ ಇದೆಯೇ?	Yes ಹೌದು ....1 No ಇಲ್ಲ..2		→18M
18L	If 18K is Yes, Why are you satisfied by the police? (Don't read out the options. Mark multiple options as respondents replies) 18ಕೆ ಎಂದರೆ ಪೊಲೀಸ್ ತೆಗೆದುಕೊಂಡ ಕ್ರಮದ ಬಗ್ಗೆ ನಿಮಗೆ ಏಕೆ ತೃಪ್ತಿ ಇದೆ ? (ಆಯ್ಕೆ ಓದಬೇಡಿ, ಬಹುಆಯ್ಕೆಗಳನ್ನು ಉತ್ತರದಾರರು ಹೇಳುತ್ತಿದ್ದಂತೆ ಗುರುತಿಸಿ) **CIRCLE IF RESPONDENT MENTIONS** ಉತ್ತರದಾರರು ಹೇಳಿದವುಗಳ ಸುತ್ತ ಸುತ್ತುಗೆರೆ ಹಾಕಿರಿ.	They listened to the complaint ದೂರು ಕೇಳಿದರು	1	**SKIP TO 18N**
		They registered the complaint accurately ಸರಿಯಾಗಿ ದೂರು ದಾಖಲಿಸಿದರು	2	
		They registered the complaint quickly ದೂರನ್ನು ಬೇಗ ದಾಖಲಿಸಿದರು	3	
		They explained the action that they will take ಅವರು ತೆಗೆದುಕೊಳ್ಳುತ್ತ ಕ್ರಮದ ಬಗ್ಗೆ ವಿವರಿಸಿದರು	4	
		They solved the problem ಸಮಸ್ಯೆ ಪರಿಹಾರ ಮಾಡಿದರು	5	
		Other: (please specify) ಇತರೆ(ನಿರ್ದಿಷ್ಟವಾಗಿ ಹೇಳಿ)	98	
18M	If 18K is No, Why are you not satisfied by the police? (Don't read out the options. Mark multiple options as respondents 18ಎಫ್ ಇಲ್ಲ ಎಂದರೆ ಪೊಲೀಸ್ ತೆಗೆದುಕೊಂಡ ಕ್ರಮದ ಬಗ್ಗೆ ನಿಮಗೆ ಏಕೆ ತೃಪ್ತಿ ಇಲ್ಲ ? (ಆಯ್ಕೆಗಳನ್ನು ಓದಬೇಡಿ, ಬಹುಆಯ್ಕೆಗಳನ್ನು ಉತ್ತರದಾರ ಹೇಳುತ್ತಿದ್ದಂತೆ ಗುರುತಿಸಿ) **CIRCLE ALL MENTIONED BY THE RESPONDET**	They were not interested ಅವರಿಗೆ ಆಸಕ್ತಿಯಿರಲಿಲ್ಲ	1	
		They were rude and impolite ಅವರು ಒರಟಾಗಿ ಸೌಜನ್ಯವಿಲ್ಲದೆ ವರ್ತಿಸಿದರು.	2	
		They did not do enough ಬೇಕಾದಷ್ಟು ಮಾಡಲಿಲ್ಲ	3	
		They refused to file the FIR ಎಫ್ ಐ ಆರ್ ದಾಖಲಿಸಲು ನಿರಾಕರಿಸಿದರು	4	
		They tried to persuade me not to register an FIR ಎಫ್ ಐ ಆರ್ ದಾಖಲಿಸದಂತೆ ನನಗೆ ಒಡ್ಡಿಸಲು ಪ್ರಯತ್ನ ಮಾಡಿದರು	5	

	ಉತ್ತರದಾರರು ಹೇಳಿದವುಗಳ ಸುತ್ತ ಸುತ್ತುಗೆರೆ ಹಾಕಿರಿ.	They took a long time to register my FIR ನನ್ನ ಎಫ್ ಐ ಆರ್ ದಾಖಲಿಸಲು ಬಹಳ ಕಾಲ ತೆಗೆದುಕೊಂದರು	6
		They told me to go away from the police station ಪೋಲೀಸ್ ಠಾಣೆಯಿಂದ ಹೋಗುವಂತ ಹೇಳಿದರು	7
		They put me at fault ನನ್ನ ಮೇಲೆ ತಪ್ಪು ಹಾಕಿದರು	8
		They wanted a bribe ಲಂಚ ಕೇಳಿದರು	9
		They physically assaulted me ಧೈಹಿಕವಾಗಿ ಹಲ್ಲೆ ಮಾಡಿದರು	10
		They verbally abused me ನನ್ನನ್ನು ಬೈದರು	11
		They didn't find or apprehend the offender ಅಪರಾಧಿಯನ್ನು ಹುಡುಕಲಿಲ್ಲ/ ದಸ್ತಗಿರಿ ಮಾಡಲಿಲ್ಲ	12
		They didn't recover my property (goods) ನನ್ನ ಆಸ್ತಿ (ಸರಕು) ಹುದುಕಿಕೊಡಲಿಲ್ಲ.	13
		They didn't keep me properly informed ನನಗೆ ಸರಿಯಾಗಿ ಮಾಹಿತಿ ನೀಡಲಿಲ್ಲ	14
		They were slow to arrive ಅವರು ಬಹಳ ತಡವಾಗಿ ಬಂದರು	15
		Other: (please specify) ಇತರ(ನಿದಿಷ್ಟವಾಗಿ ಹೇಳಿ)	98
18N	Was any person arrested due to the incident? ಘಟನೆಯಿಂದ ಯಾವುದೇ ವ್ಯಕ್ತಿಯನ್ನು ದಸ್ತಗಿರಿ ಮಾಡಿದರಾ?	Yes ಹೌದು .... 1 No ಇಲ್ಲ.. 2	
18O	How serious was the incident to you and your household? ನಿಮಗೆ ಮತ್ತು ನಿಮ್ಮ ಮನೆಗೆ ಈ ಘಟನೆ ಎಷ್ಟು ಗಂಭೀರವಾದುದು?	Very serious ಬಹಳ ಗಂಭೀರ ....1 Somewhat serious ಸುಮಾರಾಗಿ ಗಂಭೀರ...............2 Not very serious ಬಹಳ ಗಂಭೀರವಲ್ಲ ....3 Not serious at all ಗಂಭೀರವೇ ಅಲ್ಲ..........................4 Don't know ಗೊತ್ತಿಲ್ಲ....................................... 99	
Q19	**Part IV**		
19A	How many times has the incident occurred in the last one year? ಕಳೆದ ಒಂದು ವರ್ಷದಲ್ಲಿ ಎಷ್ಟು ಬಾರಿ ಘಟನೆ ನಡೆಯಿತು?	Once ಒಮ್ಮೆ...1 Twice ಎರಡು ಬಾರಿ ....2 Thrice ಮೂರು ಬಾರಿ ....3 More than thrice in the last year.....................4 ಕಳೆದ ಒಂದು ವರ್ಷದಲ್ಲಿ ಮೂರು ಬಾರಿಗಿಂತ ಹೆಚ್ಚು	
19B	Time of occurrence of the most recent incident ತೀರಾ ಇತ್ತೀಚಿನ ಘಟನೆಯ ಸಮಯ	Early Morning (5am to 10am) ಮುಂಜಾನೆ ....1 Late Morning (10 am to 12pm) ಬೆಳಿಗ್ಗೆ ....2 Early Afternoon (12pm to 3pm).....................3 ಮಧ್ಯಾಹ್ಕಕ್ಕೆ ಮುಂಚೆ Late Afternoon (3pm to 5pm) ಮಧ್ಯಾಹ್ಷದ ಅನಂತರ..... Early Evening (5pm to 7pm) ಮುಸ್ಸಂಜೆ ....5 Late Evening (7pm to 9pm) ಸಂಜೆ ನಂತರ ....6 Early Night (9pm to 12am) ರಾತ್ರಿಗೆ ಮುಂಚೆ ....7 Late Night (12am to 5am) ತಡ ರಾತ್ರಿ ....8 Don't Know/Can't Say ಗೊತ್ತಿಲ್ಲ/ಹೇಳಲಾಗದು.......99	
19C	What kind of debit card/ATM/online fraud did you face? ಯಾವ ರೀತಿಯಲ್ಲಿ ಡೆಬಿಟ್ ಕಾರ್ಡ್/ಎಟಿಎಂ/ ಆನ್ ಲೈನ್ ಮೋಸವನ್ನು ನೀವು ಎದುರಿಸಿದಿರಿ?	Online password theft ....1 ಆನ್ ಲೈನ್ ಪಾಸ್ ವರ್ಡ್ ಕಳ್ಳತನ ATM pin theft from public machine ....2 ಎಟಿಎಂ ಪಿನ್ ಕಳ್ಳತನ ಪಬ್ಲಿಕ್ ಮಷೀನಿನಲ್ಲಿ Phishing ಫಿಶಿಂಗ್ ....3 Callers asking for pins ....4 ಕರಮಾಡುವವರು ಪಿನ್ ಕೇಳಿದರು Other (please specify): _____ ....98 ಇತರ(ನಿದಿಷ್ಟವಾಗಿ ಹೇಳಿ) Don't Know/Can't Say ಗೊತ್ತಿಲ್ಲ/ಹೇಳಲಾಗದು	99
19D	Approximately, how much money did you lose in this incident? ಈ ಘಟನೆಯಲ್ಲಿ ಕಳೆದುಕೊಂಡ ಅಂದಾಜು ಹಣ ಎಷ್ಟು?	0 –5000...1 5001 –10,000...2 10,001 –15,000..3 15,001 –20,000..4	

		20,001 −25,000 ....5 25,001 −30,000 ....6 30,001 −35,000 ....7 40,001 −45,000 ....8 50,001 −55,000 ....9 55,001 −60,000 ....10 60,001 −65,000 ....11 65,001 −70,000 ....12 70,001 −75,000 ....13 75,001 −80,000 ....14 80,001 −85,000 ....15 85,001 −90,000 ....16 Over90,000 ರೂ90,000 ಮೀರಿ ..... 17 Don't Know/Can't Say ಗೊತ್ತಿಲ್ಲ/ಹೇಳಲಾಗದು 99		
19E	Was the money recovered? ಹಣ ವಾಪಸ್ಸು ಸಿಕ್ಕಿತೇ?	Yes ಹೌದು ....1 No ಇಲ್ಲ 2		
19F	Did you report the incident to the police: ಘಟನೆ ಬಗ್ಗೆ ನೀವು ಪೊಲೀಸರಿಗೆ ವರದಿ ಮಾಡಿದಿರಾ?	Yes ಹೌದು ....1 No ಇಲ್ಲ 2		If YES, skip to 19H
19G	If 19F is No, Why did you not report? (Do not prompt) 19 ಎಫ್ ಇಲ್ಲ ಎಂದರೆ ವರದಿ ಏಕೆ ಮಾಡಲಿಲ್ಲ?	Fear of retaliation retaliation ತಿರುಗಿ ಸೇಡು ತೀರಿಸಿಕೊಳ್ಳುತ್ತಾರೆಂಬ ಭಯ	1	SKIP TO 19N
		Lack of evidence ಸಾಕ್ಷಿಯಿರಲಿಲ್ಲ	2	
		Didn't know where to report ಎಲ್ಲಿ ವರದಿ ಮಾಡುವುದು ಗೊತ್ತಿಲ್ಲ	3	
		Didn't know helpline number ಸಹಾಯವಾಣಿ ನಂಬರ್ ಗೊತ್ತಿಲ್ಲ	4	
		Did not want to get stuck in police/court matters ಪೊಲೀಸ್/ ಕೋರ್ಟು ವ್ಯವಹರಣೆಗೆ ಸಿಕ್ಕಿಹಾಕಿಕೊಳ್ಳುವುದು ಇಷ್ಟವಿರಲಿಲ್ಲ	5	
		Uncomfortable to go to Police Station ಪೊಲೀಸ್ ಠಾಣೆಗೆ ಹೋಗುವುದು ಅಹಿತವಾಗಿತ್ತು	6	
		Did not think the police would be able to do anything about the case ಪೊಲೀಸರು ಏನಾದರೂ ಮಾಡುತ್ತಾರೆ ಅನಿಸಲಿಲ್ಲ	7	
		Did not think police would entertain the case ಪೊಲೀಸರು ಕೇಸನ್ನು ತೆಗೆದುಕೊಳ್ಳುತ್ತಾರೆ ಅನಿಸಲಿಲ್ಲ	8	
		Police is unfair ಪೊಲೀಸರು ನ್ಯಾಯಪರರಲ್ಲ	9	
		Family matters need not be reported ಕುಟುಂಬದ ವಿಷಯ ವರದಿಮಾಡಬಾರದು	10	
		This is better settled outside the police station ಪೊಲೀಸ್ ಠಾಣೆಯ ಹೊರಗೆ ಇತ್ಯರ್ಥ ಉತ್ತಮ	11	
		Bad past experience with reporting to Police ಪೊಲೀಸ್ ಗೆ ವರದಿ ಮಾಡಿದ ಕೆಟ್ಟ ಅನುಭವವಿದೆ	12	
		Others: (Please specify)_____ ಇತರ(ನಿರ್ದಿಷ್ಟವಾಗಿ ಹೇಳಿ)	98	
		Don't Know/Can't Say ಗೊತ್ತಿಲ್ಲ/ಹೇಳಲಾಗದು	99	
19H	If 19F is Yes, why did you report? 19ಎಫ್ ಗೆ ಉತ್ತರ ಹೌದೆಂದರೆ ಏಕೆ ವರದಿ ಮಾಡಿದಿರಿ?	To recover property/person ....1 ಆಸ್ತಿ/ವ್ಯಕ್ತಿಯನ್ನು ಮತ್ತೆ ಪಡೆಯಲು For insurance reasons ಏಮೆ ಕಾರಣಗಳಿಗೆ ....2 Crime should be reported................................3 ಅಪರಾಧಗಳನ್ನು ವರದಿಮಾಡಬೇಕು It was a serious event ಇದು ಗಂಭೀರ ವಿಷಯ ....4 Wanted offender to be caught and punished . 5 ಅಪರಾಧಿಯನ್ನು ಹಿಡಿದು ಶಿಕ್ಷೆ ನೀಡಬೇಕು .... To stop it from happening again/to get help/others ....6 ಮತ್ತೆ ಇದು ಆಗದಂತೆ ನಿಲ್ಲಿಸಲು/ ಸಹಾಯ ಪಡೆಯಲು Others: (Please specify) _____ ....98 ಇತರೆ(ನಿರ್ದಿಷ್ಟವಾಗಿ ಹೇಳಿ)		
19I	If 19F is Yes, how did you report the above crime?	Called 100 ನಂ.100ಕ್ಕೆ ಕರೆಮಾಡಿದೆ......................1		

	19 ಎಫ್ ಗೆ ಉತ್ತರ ಹೌದೆಂದರೆ ಹೇಗೆ ವರದಿ ಮಾಡಿದಿರಿ?	Called other police helpline............................ 2 ಪೊಲೀಸ್ ಸಕಾಯವಾಣಿಗೆ ಕರೆಮಾಡಿದೆ Went to police station ಪೊಲೀಸ್ ರಾಣಿಗೆ ಹೋದೆ .... 3 Approached a Police Officer............................ 4 ಪೊಲೀಸ್ ಆಫೀಸರನ್ನು ಭೇಟಿ ಮಾಡಿದೆ Don't Remember ನೆನಪಿಲ್ಲ.................................. 99	

19J	If 19F is Yes, what did the police do upon hearing your complaint? (Don't read out the options. Mark multiple options as respondents replies) 19ಎಫ್ ಹೌದೆಂದರೆ ನಿಮ್ಮ ದೂರು ಕೇಳಿ ಪೊಲೀಸ್ ಏನು ಮಾಡಿದರು? (ಆಯ್ಕೆ ಓದಬೇಡಿ, ಬಹುಆಯ್ಕೆಗಳನ್ನು ಉತ್ತರದಾರರು ಹೇಳುತ್ತಿದ್ದಂತೆ ಗುರುತಿಸಿ) CIRCLE ALL MENTIONED BY THE RESPONDENT ಉತ್ತರದಾರರು ನೀಡಿದ ಉತ್ತರದ ಸುತ್ತ ಸುತ್ತು ಗೆರೆ ಹಾಕಿರಿ	File a complaint ದೂರು ದಾಖಲಿಸಿದರು	1	
		Register an FIR ಎಫ್ ಐ ಆರ್ ದಾಖಲಿಸಿದರು	2	
		Despatched a PCR vehicle ಪಿ ಸಿ ಆರ್ ಗಾಡಿ ಕಳುಹಿಸಿದರು	3	
		Took any injured persons for medical assistance ಗಾಸಿಗೊಂಡ ವ್ಯಕ್ತಿಯನ್ನು ವೈದ್ಯಕೀಯ ಚಿಕಿತ್ಸೆಗೆ ಕರೆದೊಯ್ಯರು	4	
		Asked you to go to another police station ಬೇರೆ ಪೊಂಲೀಸ್ ರಾಣಿಗೆ ಹೋಗುವಂತೆ ನನಗೆ ಹೇಳಿದರು	5	
		Came to the spot and investigated ಸ್ಥಳಕ್ಕೆ ಬಂದು ತನಿಖೆಮಾಡಿದರು	6	
		Asked you not to file the complaint ದೂರು ದಾಖಲಿಸಬಾರದೆಂದು ಹೇಳಿದರು	7	
		If missing person, filed a missing person report ಕಳೆದುಹೋದ ವ್ಯಕ್ತಿಯಾದರೆ, ಕಳೆದುಹೋದ ವರದಿ ದಾಖಲಿಸಿದರು	8	
		Did not do anything ಏನೂ ಮಾಡಲಿಲ್ಲ	9	
		Other: (Please specify) ಇತರ(ನಿರ್ದಿಷ್ಟವಾಗಿ ಹೇಳಿ)	98	
19K	If 19F is Yes, Were you satisfied by the action of the police? 19ಎಫ್ ಗೆ ಉತ್ತರ ಹೌದೆಂದರೆ ಪೊಲೀಸ್ ತೆಗೆದುಕೊಂಡ ಕ್ರಮದ ಬಗ್ಗೆ ನಿಮಗೆ ತೃಪ್ತಿ ಇದೆಯೇ?	Yes ಹೌದು .... 1 No ಇಲ್ಲ.. 2		If NO, skip to 19M
19L	If 19K is Yes, Why are you satisfied by the police? (Don't read out the options. Mark multiple options as respondents replies) 19ಕೆ ಹೌದೆಂದರೆ ಪೊಲೀಸ್ ತೆಗೆದುಕೊಂಡ ಕ್ರಮದ ಬಗ್ಗೆ ನಿಮಗೆ ಏಕೆ ತೃಪ್ತಿ ಇದೆ ? (ಆಯ್ಕೆ ಓದಬೇಡಿ, ಬಹುಆಯ್ಕೆಗಳನ್ನು ಉತ್ತರದಾರ ಹೇಳುತ್ತಿದ್ದಂತೆ ಗುರುತಿಸಿ) CIRCLE IF RESPONDENT MENTIONS ಉತ್ತರದಾರರು ನೀಡಿದ ಉತ್ತರದ ಸುತ್ತ ಸುತ್ತು ಗೆರೆ ಹಾಕಿರಿ	They listened to the complaint ದೂರು ಕೇಳಿದರು	1	SKIP TO 19N
		They registered the complaint accurately ಸರಿಯಾಗಿ ದೂರು ದಾಖಲಿಸಿದರು	2	
		They registered the complaint quickly ದೂರನ್ನು ಬೇಗ ದಾಖಲಿಸಿದರು	3	
		They explained the action that they will take ಅವರು ತೆಗೆದುಕೊಳ್ಳುವ ಕ್ರಮದ ಬಗ್ಗೆ ವಿವರಿಸಿದರು	4	
		They solved the problem ಸಮಸ್ಯೆ ಪರಿಹಾರ ಮಾಡಿದರು	5	
		Other: (please specify) ಇತರ(ನಿರ್ದಿಷ್ಟವಾಗಿ ಹೇಳಿ)	98	
19M	If 19K is No, Why are you not satisfied by the police? (Don't read out the options. Mark multiple options as respondents replies) 19ಕೆ ಇಲ್ಲ ಎಂದರೆ ಪೊಲೀಸ್ ತೆಗೆದುಕೊಂಡ ಕ್ರಮದ ಬಗ್ಗೆ ನಿಮಗೆ ಏಕೆ ತೃಪ್ತಿ ಇಲ್ಲ ? (ಆಯ್ಕೆಗಳನ್ನು ಓದಬೇಡಿ, ಬಹುಆಯ್ಕೆಗಳನ್ನು ಉತ್ತರದಾರ ಹೇಳುತ್ತಿದ್ದಂತೆ ಗುರುತಿಸಿ) CIRCLE ALL MENTIONED BY THE RESPONDENT ಉತ್ತರದಾರರು ಹೇಳಿದವುಗಳ ಸುತ್ತ ಸುತ್ತುಗೆರೆ ಹಾಕಿರಿ.	They were not interested ಅವರಿಗೆ ಆಸಕ್ತಿಯಿರಲಿಲ್ಲ	1	
		They were rude and impolite ಅವರು ಒರಟಾಗಿ ಮಾತನಾಡಿದರು ತಾಳ್ಮೆ ತೋರಲಿಲ್ಲ	2	
		They did not do enough ಬೇಕಾದಷ್ಟು ಮಾಡಲಿಲ್ಲ	3	
		They refused to file the FIR ಎಫ್ ಐ ಆರ್ ದಾಖಲಿಸಲು ನಿರಾಕರಿಸಿದರು	4	
		They tried to persuade me not to register an FIR ಎಫ್ ಐ ಆರ್ ದಾಖಲಿಸದಂತೆ ನನಗೆ ಒಡ್ಡಿಸಲು ಪ್ರಯತ್ನ ಮಾಡಿದರು	5	
		They took a long time to register my FIR	6	

		ನನ್ನ ಎಫ್ ಐ ಆರ್ ದಾಖಲಿಸಲು ಬಹಳ ಕಾಲ ತೆಗೆದುಕೊಂಡರು	
		They told me to go away from the police station ಪೊಲೀಸ್ ಠಾಣೆಯಿಂದ ಹೊಗುವಂತೆ ಹೇಳಿದರು	7
		They put me at fault ನನ್ನ ಮೇಲೆಯೇ ತಪ್ಪು ಹಾಕಿದರು	8
		They wanted a bribe ಲಂಚ ಕೇಳಿದರು	9
		They physically assaulted me ದೈಹಿಕವಾಗಿ ಹಲ್ಲೆ ಮಾಡಿದರು	10
		They verbally abused me ನನ್ನನ್ನು ಬೈದರು	11
		They didn't find or apprehend the offender ಅಪರಾಧಿಯನ್ನು ಹುಡುಕಲಿಲ್ಲ/ ದಸ್ತಗಿರಿ ಮಾಡಲಿಲ್ಲ	12
		They didn't recover my property (goods) ನನ್ನ ಆಸ್ತಿ (ಸರಕು) ಹುಡುಕಿಕೊಡಲಿಲ್ಲ	13
		They didn't keep me properly informed ನನಗೆ ಸರಿಯಾಗಿ ಮಾಹಿತಿ ನೀಡಲಿಲ್ಲ	14
		They were slow to arrive ಅವರು ಬಹಳ ತಡವಾಗಿ ಬಂದರು	15
		Other: (please specify) _ ಇತರ(ನಿರ್ದಿಷ್ಟವಾಗಿ ಹೇಳಿ)	98
19N	Was any person arrested due to the incident? ಘಟನೆಯಿಂದ ಯಾವುದೇ ವ್ಯಕ್ತಿಯನ್ನು ದಸ್ತಗಿರಿ ಮಾಡಿದರಾ?	Yes ಹೌದು .... 1 No ಇಲ್ಲ.. 2	
19O	How serious was the incident to you and your household? ನಿಮಗೆ ಮತ್ತು ನಿಮ್ಮ ಮನೆಗೆ ಈ ಘಟನೆ ಎಷ್ಟು ಗಂಭೀರವಾದುದು?	Very serious ಬಹಳ ಗಂಭೀರ .... 1 Somewhat serious ಸುಮಾರಾಗಿ ಗಂಭೀರ............. 2 Not very serious ಬಹಳ ಗಂಭೀರವಲ್ಲ .... 3 Not serious at all ಗಂಭೀರವೇ ಅಲ್ಲ........................ 4 Don't know ಗೊತ್ತಿಲ್ಲ... 99	
Q20	Part V		
20A	How many times has the incident occurred in the last one year? ಕಳೆದ ಒಂದು ವರ್ಷದಲ್ಲಿ ಎಷ್ಟು ಬಾರಿ ಘಟನೆ ನಡೆಯಿತು?	Once ಒಮ್ಮೆ.. 1 Twice ಎರಡು ಬಾರಿ... 2 Thrice ಮೂರು ಬಾರಿ... 3 More than thrice in the last year .... 4 ಕಳೆದ ಒಂದು ವರ್ಷದಲ್ಲಿ ಮೂರು ಬಾರಿಗಿಂತ ಹೆಚ್ಚು	
20B	Time of occurrence of the most recent incident ತೀರಾ ಇತ್ತೀಚೆಗೆ ನಡೆದ ಘಟನೆಯ ಸಮಯ	Early Morning ಮುಂಜಾನೆ(5am to 10am) .... 1 Late Morning ಬೆಳಿಗ್ಗೆ(10 am to 12pm) .... 2 Early Afternoon (12pm to 3pm) .... 3 ಮಧ್ಯಾಹ್ನಕ್ಕೆ ಮುಂಚೆ Late Afternoon (3pm to 5pm)......................... 4 ಮಧ್ಯಾಹ್ನದ ನಂತರ Early Evening ಮುಸ್ಸಂಜೆ (5pm to 7pm)............. 5 Late Evening ಸಂಜೆ ನಂತರ (7pm to 9pm) .... 6 Early Night ರಾತ್ರಿಗೆ ಮುಂಚೆ (9pm to 12am)........ 7 Late Night ನಡು ರಾತ್ರಿ(12am to 5am)................. 8 Don't Know/Can't Say .... 99 ಗೊತ್ತಿಲ್ಲ/ಹೇಳಲಾಗದು	
20C	What was the kind of assault ಅದು ಎಂತಹ ಹಲ್ಲೆ	Threat of physical violence .... 1 ದೈಹಿಕ ಹಿಂಸೆಯ ಬೆದರಿಕೆ Threat of attack with gun, knives and other weapons .... 2 ಬಂದೂಕು, ಚಾಕು ಮತ್ತು ಇತರೆ ಆಯುದಗಳಿಂದ ದಾಳಿಯ ಬೆದರಿಕೆ Grabbed, Shoved, Slapped or punched .... 3 ಹಿಡಿದರು, ದಬ್ಬಿದರು, ಕೆನ್ನೆಗೆ ಹೊಡೆದರು ಅಥವಾ ಗುದ್ದಿದರು Attacked by throwing some dangerous object like stones .... 4 ಕಲ್ಲುಗಳಂತಹ ಕೆಲವು ಅಪಾಯಕಾರಿ ವಸ್ತುಗಳಿಂದ ದಾಳಿ ಮಾಡಿದರು Attacked with gun, knives and	

		other weapons...5 ಬಂದೂಕು, ಚಾಕು ಮತ್ತು ಇತರ ಆಯುಧಗಳಿಂದ ದಾಳಿ ಮಾಡಿದರು Other (please specify): _____ 98 ಇತರ(ನಿರ್ದಿಷ್ಟವಾಗಿ ಹೇಳಿ) Don't Know/Can't Say.....................................99 ಗೊತ್ತಿಲ್ಲ/ಹೇಳಲಾಗದು	
20D	How many people were involved and ಎಷ್ಟು ಜನರು ಭಾಗಿಯಾಗಿದ್ದರು?	One ಒಬ್ಬರು ....1 Two ಇಬ್ಬರು ....2 Three ಮೂವರು ....3 More than three ಮೂವರಿಗಿಂತ ಹೆಚ್ಚು ....4 Don't Know/Can't Say ಗೊತ್ತಿಲ್ಲ/ಹೇಳಲಾಗದು 99	
20E	Gender of the perpetrators ಹಲ್ಲೆಗಾರರ ಲಿಂಗ	Male ಗಂಡಸು ....1 Female ಹೆಂಗಸು ....2 Other ಇತರ..3 Don't Know/Can't Say ಗೊತ್ತಿಲ್ಲ/ಹೇಳಲಾಗದು.......99	
20F	Do you know who they perpetrator of the crime is? ಅಪರಾಧ ಮಾಡಿದವರು ಯಾರೆಂದು ನಿಮಗೆ ಗೊತ್ತಾ?	Yes ಹೌದು ....1 No ಇಲ್ಲ..2	If NO, skip to 20H
20G	If 20F yes, who was it: (Do not prompt) 20ಎಫ್ ಗೆ ಉತ್ತರ ಹೌದು ಎಂದಾದರೆ ಅವರು ಯಾರು ? (ಉತ್ತರ ಹೇಳಿಕೊಡಬೇಡಿ ಅವರೇ ಹೇಳಲಿ)	Family ಕುಟುಂಬ ....1 Friend ಸ್ನೇಹಿತ..2 Colleague ಸಹೋದ್ಯೋಗಿ.....................................3 Member of the locality ....4 Acquaintance ಆ ಪ್ರದೇಶದ ಪರಿಚಯದವರು ....5 Member of your caste group/jati/biradari ..... 6 ನಿಮ್ಮ ಜಾತಿಯವರು/ನಂಟರು Member of your religion ನಿಮ್ಮ ಧರ್ಮದವರು 7 Others: (Please Specify)_____ 98 ಇತರ(ನಿರ್ದಿಷ್ಟವಾಗಿ ಹೇಳಿ)	
20H	Why do you think you were attacked? (Do not prompt the answers) ನಿಮಗೆ ಏಕೆ ದಾಳಿ ಮಾಡಲಾಯಿತೆನಿಸುತ್ತದೆ? (ಉತ್ತರ ಹೇಳಿಕೊಡಬೇಡಿ ಅವರೇ ಹೇಳಲಿ)	Previous enmity ಹಿಂದಿನ ವೈರತ್ವ ....1 Land related disputes ಭೂಮಿಗೆ ಸಂಬಂಧಿಸಿದ ವಿವಾದ...... Family property disputes ಕುಟುಂಬದ ಆಸ್ತಿ ವಿವಾದ 3 Due to my caste ನನ್ನ ಜಾತಿಯ ಕಾರಣದಿಂದ ....4 Due to my religion ನನ್ನ ಧರ್ಮದ ಕಾರಣದಿಂದ ......5 Due to my gender ನನ್ನ ಲಿಂಗದ ಕಾರಣದಿಂದ........6 Due to my mother-tongue ನನ್ನ ಮಾತೃಭಾಷೆಯ ಕಾರಣದಿಂದ ....7 Due to my native state ನಾನು ಹುಟ್ಟಿದ ರಾಜ್ಯದ ಕಾರಣದಿಂದ ....8 Due to my sexual orientation.........................9 ನನ್ನ ಲೈಂಗಿಕ ಪ್ರವೃತ್ತಿ ಕಾರಣದಿಂದ Due to my disability ನನ್ನ ವಿಕಲತೆ ಕಾರಣದಿಂದ .....10 Due to my skin colour ನನ್ನ ಮೈ ಬಣ್ಣದಿಂದ..........11 Due to other reasons: (PLEASE SPECIFY) _____ 98 ಇತರ ಕಾರಣಗಳು(ನಿರ್ದಿಷ್ಟವಾಗಿ ಹೇಳಿ) Do not know ಗೊತ್ತಿಲ್ಲ...99	
20I	Did you report the incident to the police ಘಟನೆ ಬಗ್ಗೆ ನೀವು ಪೊಲೀಸರಿಗೆ ವರದಿ ಮಾಡಿದಿರಾ?	Yes ಹೌದು ....1 No ಇಲ್ಲ..2	If NO, skip to 20K
20J	If 20I is No, Why did you not report? (Do not prompt)	Fear of retaliation retaliation ತಿರುಗಿ ಸೇಡು ತೀರಿಸಿಕೊಳ್ತಾರಂಬ ಭಯ	1	After circling

	20.ಐ ಗೆ ಉತ್ತರ ಇಲ್ಲ ಎಂದಾದರೆ ವರದಿ ಏಕೆ ಮಾಡಲಿಲ್ಲ?	Lack of evidence ಸಾಕ್ಷ್ಯಿರಲಿಲ್ಲ	2	**the answers**, **SKIP TO 20Q**
		Didn't know where to report ಎಲ್ಲಿ ವರದಿ ಮಾಡುವುದು ಗೊತ್ತಿಲ್ಲ	3	
		Didn't know helpline number ಸಹಾಯವಾಣಿ ನಂಬರ್ ಗೊತ್ತಿಲ್ಲ	4	
		Did not want to get stuck in police/court matters ಪೊಲೀಸ್/ ಕೋರ್ಟು ವ್ಯವಹರಣೆಗೆ ಸಿಕ್ಕಿಹಾಕಿಕೊಳ್ಳುವುದು ಇಷ್ಟವಿರಲಿಲ್ಲ	5	
		Uncomfortable to go to Police Station ಪೊಲೀಸ್ ಠಾಣೆಗೆ ಹೋಗುವುದು ಅಹಿತವಾಗಿತ್ತು	6	
		Did not think the police would be able to do anything about the case ಪೊಲೀಸರು ಏನಾದರೂ ಮಾಡುತ್ತಾರೆ ಅನಿಸಲಿಲ್ಲ	7	
		Did not think police would entertain the case ಪೊಲೀಸರು ಕೇಸನ್ನು ತೆಗೆದುಕೊಳ್ಳುತ್ತಾರೆ ಅನಿಸಲಿಲ್ಲ	8	
		Police is unfair ಪೊಲೀಸರು ನ್ಯಾಯಪರರಲ್ಲ	9	
		Family matters need not be reported ಕುಟುಂಬದ ವಿಷಯ ವರದಿಮಾಡಬಾರದು	10	
		This is better settled outside the police station ಪೊಲೀಸ್ ಠಾಣೆಯ ಹೊರಗೆ ಇತ್ಯರ್ಥ ಉತ್ತಮ	11	
		Bad past experience with reporting to Police ಪೊಲೀಸ್ ಗೆ ವರದಿ ಮಾಡಿದ ಕೆಟ್ಟ ಅನುಭವವಿದೆ	12	
		Others: (Please specify)_____ ಇತರೆ(ನಿರ್ದಿಷ್ಟವಾಗಿ ಹೇಳಿ)	98	
		Don't Know/Can't Say ಗೊತ್ತಿಲ್ಲ/ಹೇಳಲಾಗದು	99	
20K	If 20I is Yes, why did you report? 20 ಐ ಗೆ ಉತ್ತರ ಹೌದೆಂದರೆ ಏಕೆ ವರದಿ ಮಾಡಿದಿರಿ?	To recover property/person ....1 ಆಸ್ತಿ/ವ್ಯಕ್ತಿಯನ್ನು ಮರು ಪಡೆಯಲು		
		For insurance reasons ವಿಮೆ ಕಾರಣಗಳಿಗೆ 2		
		Crime should be reported....................................3 ಅಪರಾಧಗಳನ್ನು ವರದಿಮಾಡಬೇಕು		
		It was a serious event ....4 ಇದು ಗಂಭೀರ ವಿಷಯ		
		Wanted offender to be caught and punished . 5 ಅಪರಾಧಿಯನ್ನು ಹಿಡಿದು ಶಿಕ್ಷೆ ನೀಡಬೇಕು		
		To stop it from happening again/to get help/others ....6 ಮತ್ತೆ ಇದು ಆಗದಂತೆ ನಿಲ್ಲಿಸಲು/ ಸಹಾಯ ಪಡೆಯಲು		
		Others: (Please specify) _____ ..... 98 ಇತರೆ(ನಿರ್ದಿಷ್ಟವಾಗಿ ಹೇಳಿ)		
20L	If 20I is Yes, how did you report the above crime? 20 ಐ ಗೆ ಉತ್ತರ ಹೌದೆಂದರೆ ಮೇಲಿನ ಅಪರಾಧದ ಬಗ್ಗೆ ಹೇಗೆ ವರದಿ ಮಾಡಿದಿರಿ?	Called 100 ....1 ನಾ 100ಕ್ಕೆ ಕರೆಮಾಡಿದ		
		Called other police helpline...............................2 ಪೊಲೀಸ್ ಸಹಾಯವಾಣಿಗೆ ಕರೆಮಾಡಿದೆ		
		Went to police station ....3 ಪೊಲೀಸ್ ಠಾಣೆಗೆ ಹೋದೆ		
		Approached a Police Officer...............................4 ಪೊಲೀಸ್ ಆಫೀಸರನ್ನು ಭೇಟಿ ಮಾಡಿದೆ		
		Don't Remember .... 99 ನೆನಪಿಲ್ಲ		
20M	If 20I is Yes, what did the police do upon hearing your complaint? (Don't read out the options. Mark multiple options as respondents replies) 20 ಐ ಗೆ ಉತ್ತರ ಹೌದೆಂದರೆ ನಿಮ್ಮ ದೂರು ಕೇಳಿ ಪೊಲೀಸ್ ಏನು ಮಾಡಿದರು? (ಆಯ್ಕೆ ಓದಬೇಡಿ, ಬಹುಆಯ್ಕೆಗಳನ್ನು ಉತ್ತರದಾರರು ಹೇಳುತ್ತಿದ್ದಂತೆ ಗುರುತಿಸಿ) **CIRCLE ALL MENTIONED BY THE RESPONDENT** ಉತ್ತರದಾರರು ಹೇಳಿದವುಗಳ ಸುತ್ತ ಸುತ್ತುಗೆರೆ ಹಾಕಿರಿ.	File a complaint ದೂರು ದಾಖಲಿಸಿದರು	1	
		Register an FIR ಎಫ್ ಐ ಆರ್ ದಾಖಲಿಸಿದರು	2	
		Despatched a PCR vehicle ಪಿ ಸಿ ಆರ್ ಗಾಡಿ ಕಳುಹಿಸಿದರು	3	
		Took any injured persons for medical assistance ಗಾಸಿಗೊಂಡ ವ್ಯಕ್ತಿಯನ್ನು ವೈದ್ಯಕೀಯ ಚಿಕಿತ್ಸೆಗೆ ಕರೆದೊಯ್ದರು	4	
		Asked you to go to another police station ಬೇರೆ ಪೊಲೀಸ್ ಠಾಣೆಗೆ ಹೋಗುವಂತೆ ನನಗೆ ಹೇಳಿದರು	5	

		Came to the spot and investigated ಸ್ಥಳಕ್ಕೆ ಬಂದು ತನಿಖೆಮಾಡಿದರು	6	
		Asked you not to file the complaint ದೂರು ದಾಖಲಿಸಬಾರದೆಂದು ಹೇಳಿದರು	7	
		If missing person, filed a missing person report ಕಳೆದುಹೋದದ್ದು ವ್ಯಕ್ತಿಯಾದರೆ, ವ್ಯಕ್ತಿ ಕಳೆದುಹೋದ ವರದಿ ದಾಖಲಿಸಿದರು	8	
		Did not do anything ಏನೂ ಮಾಡಲಿಲ್ಲ	9	
		Other: (Please specify) ಇತರ(ನಿರ್ದಿಷ್ಟವಾಗಿ ಹೇಳಿ)	98	
20N	If 20I is Yes, Were you satisfied by the action of the police? 20 ಐ ಗೆ ಉತ್ತರ ಹೌದೆಂದರೆ ಪೊಲೀಸ್ ತೆಗೆದುಕೊಂಡ ಕ್ರಮದ ಬಗ್ಗೆ ನಿಮಗೆ ತೃಪ್ತಿ ಇದೆಯೇ?	Yes ಹೌದು .... 1 No ಇಲ್ಲ... 2	If NO, skip to 20P
20O	20N is Yes, Why are you satisfied by the police? (Don't read out the options. Mark multiple options as respondents replies) 20ಎನ್ ಗೆ ಉತ್ತರ ಹೌದೆಂದರೆ ಪೊಲೀಸ್ ತೆಗೆದುಕೊಂಡ ಕ್ರಮದ ಬಗ್ಗೆ ನಿಮಗೆ ಏಕೆ ತೃಪ್ತಿ ಇದೆ ? (ಆಯ್ಕೆ ಓದಬೇಡಿ, ಬಹುಆಯ್ಕೆಗಳನ್ನು ಉತ್ತರದಾರ ಹೇಳುತ್ತಿದ್ದಂತೆ ಗುರುತಿಸಿ) **CIRCLE IF RESPONDENT MENTIONS** ಉತ್ತರದಾರರು ಹೇಳಿದವುಗಳ ಸುತ್ತ ಸುತ್ತುಗೆರೆ ಹಾಕಿರಿ.	They listened to the complaint ದೂರು ಕೇಳಿದರು	1	**SKIP TO 20Q**
		They registered the complaint accurately ಸರಿಯಾಗಿ ದೂರು ದಾಖಲಿಸಿದರು	2	
		They registered the complaint quickly ದೂರನ್ನು ಬೇಗ ದಾಖಲಿಸಿದರು	3	
		They explained the action that they will take ಅವರು ತೆಗೆದುಕೊಳ್ಳುವ ಕ್ರಮದ ಬಗ್ಗೆ ವಿವರಿಸಿದರು	4	
		They solved the problem ಸಮಸ್ಯೆ ಪರಿಹಾರ ಮಾಡಿದರು	5	
		Other: (please specify) ಇತರ(ನಿರ್ದಿಷ್ಟವಾಗಿ ಹೇಳಿ)	98	
20P	If 20N is No, Why are you not satisfied by the police? (Don't read out the options. Mark multiple options as respondents replies) 20 ಎನ್ ಗೆ ಉತ್ತರ ಇಲ್ಲ ಎಂದರೆ ಪೊಲೀಸ್ ತೆಗೆದುಕೊಂಡ ಕ್ರಮದ ಬಗ್ಗೆ ನಿಮಗೆ ಏಕೆ ತೃಪ್ತಿ ಇಲ್ಲ ? (ಆಯ್ಕೆಗಳನ್ನು ಓದಬೇಡಿ, ಬಹುಆಯ್ಕೆಗಳನ್ನು ಉತ್ತರದಾರ ಹೇಳುತ್ತಿದ್ದಂತೆ ಗುರುತಿಸಿ) **CIRCLE ALL MENTIONED BY THE RESPONDENT** ಉತ್ತರದಾರರು ಹೇಳಿದವುಗಳ ಸುತ್ತ ಸುತ್ತುಗೆರೆ ಹಾಕಿರಿ.	They were not interested ಅವರಿಗೆ ಆಸಕ್ತಿಯಿರಲಿಲ್ಲ	1	
		They were rude and impolite ಅವರು ಒರಟಾಗಿ ಸೌಜನ್ಯವಿಲ್ಲದೆ ವರ್ತಿಸಿದರು,	2	
		They did not do enough ಬೇಕಾದಷ್ಟು ಮಾಡಲಿಲ್ಲ	3	
		They refused to file the FIR ಎಫ್ ಐ ಆರ್ ದಾಖಲಿಸಲು ನಿರಾಕರಿಸಿದರು	4	
		They tried to persuade me not to register an FIR ಎಫ್ ಐ ಆರ್ ದಾಖಲಿಸದಂತೆ ನನಗೆ ಒಪ್ಪಿಸಲು ಪ್ರಯತ್ನ ಮಾಡಿದರು	5	
		They took a long time to register my FIR ನನ್ನ ಎಫ್ ಐ ಆರ್ ದಾಖಲಿಸಲು ಬಹಳ ಕಾಲ ತೆಗೆದುಕೊಂಡರು	6	
		They told me to go away from the police station ಪೊಲೀಸ್ ಠಾಣೆಯಿಂದ ಹೋಗುವಂತೆ ಹೇಳಿದರು	7	
		They put me at fault ನನ್ನ ಮೇಲೇ ತಪ್ಪು ಹಾಕಿದರು	8	
		They wanted a bribe ಲಂಚ ಕೇಳಿದರು	9	
		They physically assaulted me ದೈಹಿಕವಾಗಿ ಹಲ್ಲೆ ಮಾಡಿದರು	10	
		They verbally abused me ನನ್ನ ಬೈದರು	11	
		They didn't find or apprehend the offender ಅಪರಾಧಿಯನ್ನು ಹುಡುಕಲಿಲ್ಲ/ ದಸ್ತಗಿರಿ ಮಾಡಲಿಲ್ಲ	12	
		They didn't recover my property (goods) ನನ್ನ ಆಸ್ತಿ (ಸರಕು) ಹುಡುಕಿಕೊಡಲಿಲ್ಲ.	13	
		They didn't keep me properly informed ನನಗೆ ಸರಿಯಾಗಿ ಮಾಹಿತಿ ನೀಡಲಿಲ್ಲ	14	
		They were slow to arrive ಅವರು ಬಹಳ ತಡವಾಗಿ ಬಂದರು	15	
		Other: (please specify)ಇತರ(ನಿರ್ದಿಷ್ಟವಾಗಿ	98	

		ಹೇಳಿ)		
20Q	Was any person arrested due to the incident? ಘಟನೆಯಿಂದ ಯಾವುದೇ ವ್ಯಕ್ತಿಯನ್ನು ದಸ್ತಗಿರಿ ಮಾಡಿದರಾ?	Yes ಹೌದು .... 1 No ಇಲ್ಲ.. 2		
20R	How serious was the incident to you and your household? ನಿಮಗೆ ಮತ್ತು ನಿಮ್ಮ ಮನೆಗೆ ಈ ಘಟನೆ ಎಷ್ಟು ಗಂಭೀರವಾದುದು?	Very serious ಬಹಳ ಗಂಭೀರ .... 1 Somewhat serious ಸುಮಾರಾಗಿ ಗಂಭೀರ .... 2 Not very serious ಬಹಳ ಗಂಭೀರವಲ್ಲ .... 3 Not serious at all ಗಂಭೀರವೇ ಅಲ್ಲ........................ 4 Don't know ಗೊತ್ತಿಲ್ಲ................................ 99		
Q21 Part VI				
21A	How many times has the incident occurred in the last one year? ಕಳೆದ ಒಂದು ವರ್ಷದಲ್ಲಿ ಎಷ್ಟು ಬಾರಿ ಘಟನೆ ನಡೆಯಿತು?	Once .... 1 ಒಮ್ಮೆ Twice .... 2 ಎರಡು ಬಾರಿ Thrice .... 3 ಮೂರು ಬಾರಿ More than thrice in the last year .... 4 ಕಳೆದ ಒಂದು ವರ್ಷದಲ್ಲಿ ಮೂರು ಬಾರಿಗಿಂತ ಹೆಚ್ಚು		
21B	Time of occurrence of the most recent incident ತೀರಾ ಇತ್ತೀಚಿನ ಘಟನೆಯ ಸಮಯ	Early Morning ಮುಂಜಾನೆ (5am to 10am) .... 1 Late Morning ಬೆಳಿಗ್ಗೆ (10 am to 12pm) .... 2 Early Afternoon (12pm to 3pm) .... 3 ಮಧ್ಯಾಹ್ನಕ್ಕೆ ಮುಂಚೆ Late Afternoon (3pm to 5pm)......................... 4 ಮಧ್ಯಾಹ್ನದ ನಂತರ Early Evening ಮುಸ್ಸಂಜೆ (5pm to 7pm)............. 5 Late Evening ಸಂಜೆ ನಂತರ (7pm to 9pm)......... 6 Early Night ರಾತ್ರಿಗೆಮುಂಚೆ (9pm to 12am) .... 7 Late Night ತಡ ರಾತ್ರಿ (12am to 5am) .... 8 Don't Know/Can't Say ಗೊತ್ತಿಲ್ಲ/ಹೇಳಲಾಗದು....... 99		
21C	Age of the victim ಸಂತ್ರಸ್ತರ ವಯಸ್ಸು	1 – 6 yrs ವರ್ಷಗಳು............................ 1 6-12 yrs ವರ್ಷಗಳು............................ 2 12-18 yrs ವರ್ಷಗಳು........................... 3 18-25 yrs ವರ್ಷಗಳು. .... 4 25-40 yrs ವರ್ಷಗಳು........................... 5 40-59 yrs ವರ್ಷಗಳು........................... 6 60 and above................................. 7 60ವರ್ಷಗಳು ಮತ್ತು ಅದಕ್ಕೂ ಮೀರಿ		
21D	Gender of the victim ಸಂತ್ರಸ್ತರ ಲಿಂಗ	Male ಗಂಡಸು .... 1 Female ಹೆಂಗಸು................................ 2 Other ಇತರೆ .... 3 Can't Say ಹೇಳಲಾಗದು 99		
21E	Do you know where did the incident occurred ಘಟನೆ ನಡೆದ ಸ್ಥಳ ಯಾವುದಾಗಿತ್ತು ನಿಮಗೆ ಗೊತ್ತೆ?	Home ಮನೆ .... 1 Friends house ಸ್ನೇಹಿತರ ಮನೆ .... 2 Work Place ಕೆಲಸದಸ್ಥಳ .... 3 On the street ಬೀದಿಯಲ್ಲಿ .... 4 Public transport ಸಾರ್ವಜನಿಕ ಸಾರಿಗೆ .... 5 Commercial place (Malls, Theatre, Restaurant)....................... 6 ವಾಣಿಜ್ಯ ಸ್ಥಳ(ಮಾಲ್, ಥಿಯೇಟರ್, ಹೋಟೆಲ್) Neighbourhood area ನೆರೆಹೊರೆ ಪ್ರದೇಶ.............. 7 Educational Institutes ವಿದ್ಯಾ ಸಂಸ್ಥೆಗಳು .... 8 Playgrounds ಆಟದ ಮೈದಾನ .... 9 Hospitals ಆಸ್ಪತ್ರೆ .... 10 Police Stations ಪೋಲೀಸ್ ಠಾಣೆ.................... 11 Place of worship ಪೂಜಾ ಸ್ಥಳ.................... 12 Other (please specify): _____ .... 98 ಇತರೆ(ನಿರ್ದಿಷ್ಟವಾಗಿ ಹೇಳಿ)		

		Don't Know/Can't Say ಗೊತ್ತಿಲ್ಲ/ಹೇಳಲಾಗದು...... 99		
21F	Did the victim know the perpetrator? ಸಂತ್ರಸ್ತರಿಗೆ ಅಪರಾಧ ಎಸಗಿದವರು ಗೊತ್ತಿತ್ತಾ?	Yes ಹೌದು 1		**Skip to 21J**
		No ಇಲ್ಲ.. 2		
		Don't Know/Can't Say .... 99 ಗೊತ್ತಿಲ್ಲ/ಹೇಳಲಾಗದು		
21G	If 21F yes, was it: (Do not prompt) 21.ಎಫ್ ಗೆ ಉತ್ತರ ಹೌದು ಎಂದರೆ ಅದು ಯಾರು? (ಉತ್ತರ ಹೇಳಿಕೊಡಬೇಡಿ ಅವರೇ ಉತ್ತರಿಸಲಿ)	Member of Family ಕುಟುಂಬದ ಸದಸ್ಯ 1		
		Friend ಸ್ನೇಹಿತ 2		
		Colleague or co-worker ಸಹೋದ್ಯೋಗಿ 3		
		Member of the locality ಪ್ರದೇಶದ ನಿವಾಸಿ 4		
		Acquaintance .... 5 ಪರಿಚಯದವರು		
		Member of your caste group/jati/biradari..... 6 ನಿಮ್ಮ ಜಾತಿಯವರು		
		Member of your religion .... 7 ನಿಮ್ಮ ಧರ್ಮದವರು		
		Stranger ಅಪರಿಚಿತರು 8		
		Group of unknown people ಗೊತ್ತಿಲ್ಲದ ಗುಂಪು 9		
		Teacher ಉಪಾಧ್ಯಾಯರು 10		
		Co-worker ಜೊತೆ ಕೆಲಸಗಾರರು 11		
		Doctor-Nurse ಡಾಕ್ಟರ್-ನರ್ಸ್ 12		
		Police ಪೋಲೀಸ್... 13		
		Neighbours in locality ನೆರೆಹೊರೆಯವರು 14		
		Family member ಕುಟುಂಬದ ಸದಸ್ಯ...................... 15		
		Others: (Please Specify ಇತರೆ(ನಿರ್ದಿಷ್ಟವಾಗಿ ಹೇಳಿ)_____ 98		
		Do not know ಗೊತ್ತಿಲ್ಲ/ಹೇಳಲಾಗದು 99		
21H	If 21F is yes, what was the gender of perpetrator 21 ಎಫ್ ಗೆ ಉತ್ತರ ಹೌದೆಂದರೆ ಅಪರಾಧ ಎಸಗಿದವರ ಲಿಂಗ ಯಾವುದು?	Male ಗಂಡಸು 1		
		Female ಹೆಂಗಸು 2		
		Other ಇತರೆ 3		
21I	If 21F is yes, please specify the number of perpetrators 21 ಎಫ್ ಗೆ ಉತ್ತರ ಹೌದೆಂದರೆ ಅಪರಾಧ ಎಸಗಿದವರು ಎಷ್ಟು ಮಂದಿ ಇದ್ದರು?	One ಒಬ್ಬರು 1		
		Two ಇಬ್ಬರು 2		
		Three ಮೂವರು 3		
		More than three ಮೂವರಿಗಿಂತ ಹೆಚ್ಚು 4		
		Don't Know/Can't Say ಗೊತ್ತಿಲ್ಲ/ಹೇಳಲಾಗದು 99		
21J	Did you report the incident to the police: ಘಟನೆ ಬಗ್ಗೆ ನೀವು ಪೊಲೀಸರಿಗೆ ವರದಿ ಮಾಡಿದಿರಾ?	Yes ಹೌದು 1		If YES, skip to 21L
		No ಇಲ್ಲ.. 2		
21K	If 21J is No, Why did you not report? (Do not prompt) 21ಜೆ ಇಲ್ಲ ಎಂದರೆ ಏಕೆ ವರದಿ ಮಾಡಿಲ್ಲ?(ಉತ್ತರ ಹೇಳಿಕೊಡಬೇಡಿ ಅವರೇ ಉತ್ತರಿಸಲಿ)	Fear of retaliation retaliation ತಿರುಗಿ ಸೇಡು ತೀರಿಸಿಕೊಳ್ಳುತ್ತಾರೆಂಬ ಭಯ	1	**SKIP TO 21R**
		Lack of evidence ಸಾಕ್ಷಿಯಿರಲಿಲ್ಲ	2	
		Didn't know where to report ಎಲ್ಲಿ ವರದಿ ಮಾಡುವುದು ಗೊತ್ತಿಲ್ಲ	3	
		Didn't know helpline number ಸಹಾಯವಾಣಿ ನಂಬರ್ ಗೊತ್ತಿಲ್ಲ	4	
		Did not want to get stuck in police/court matters ಪೊಲೀಸ್/ ಕೋರ್ಟು ವ್ಯವಹರಣೆಗೆ ಸಿಕ್ಕಿಹಾಕಿಕೊಳ್ಳುವುದು ಇಷ್ಟವಿರಲಿಲ್ಲ	5	
		Uncomfortable to go to Police Station ಪೊಲೀಸ್ ಠಾಣೆಗೆ ಹೋಗುವುದು ಅಹಿತವಾಗಿತ್ತು	6	
		Did not think the police would be able to do anything about the case ಪೊಲೀಸರು ಏನಾದರೂ ಮಾಡುತ್ತಾರೆ ಅನಿಸಲಿಲ್ಲ	7	
		Did not think police would entertain the case ಪೊಲೀಸರು ಕೇಸನ್ನು ತೆಗೆದುಕೊಳ್ಳುತ್ತಾರೆ ಅನಿಸಲಿಲ್ಲ	8	
		Police is unfair ಪೊಲೀಸರು ನ್ಯಾಯಪರರಲ್ಲ	9	
		Family matters need not be reported	10	

		ಕುಟುಂಬದ ವಿಷಯ ವರದಿಮಾಡಬಾರದು	
		This is better settled outside the police stationಪೊಲೀಸ್ ಠಾಣೆಯ ಹೊರಗೆ ಇತ್ಯರ್ಥ ಉತ್ತಮ	11
		Bad past experience with reporting to Police ಪೊಲೀಸ್ ಗೆ ವರದಿ ಮಾಡಿದ ಕೆಟ್ಟ ಅನುಭವವಿದೆ	12
		Others: (Please specify) ಇತರ(ನಿರ್ದಿಷ್ಟವಾಗಿ ಹೇಳಿ)_____	98
		Don't Know/Can't Say ಗೊತ್ತಿಲ್ಲ/ಹೇಳಲಾಗದು	99
21L	If 21J is Yes, why did you report? 21 ಜೆ ಗೆ ಉತ್ತರ ಹೌದೆಂದರೆ ಏಕೆ ವರದಿ ಮಾಡಿದಿರಿ?	For insurance reasons .... 2 ವಿಮೆ ಕಾರಣಗಳಿಗೆ Crime should be reported .... 3 ಅಪರಾಧಗಳನ್ನು ವರದಿಮಾಡಬೇಕು It was a serious event .... 4 ಇದು ಗಂಭೀರ ವಿಷಯ Wanted offender to be caught and punished. 5 ಅಪರಾಧಿಯನ್ನು ಹಿಡಿದು ಶಿಕ್ಷೆ ನೀಡಬೇಕು To stop it from happening again/to get help/others .... 6 ಮತ್ತೆ ಇದು ಆಗದಂತೆ ನಿಲ್ಲಿಸಲು/ ಸಹಾಯ ಪಡೆಯಲು Others: (Please specify) _____ ..... 98 ಇತರ(ನಿರ್ದಿಷ್ಟವಾಗಿ ಹೇಳಿ)	
21M	If 21J is Yes, how did you report the above crime? 21 ಜೆ ಗೆ ಉತ್ತರ ಹೌದೆಂದರೆ ಹೇಗೆ ವರದಿ ಮಾಡಿದಿರಿ?	Called 100 .... 1 ನಂ 100ಕ್ಕೆ ಕರೆಮಾಡಿದೆ Called other police helpline............... 2 ಪೊಲೀಸ್ ಸಹಾಯವಾಣಿಗೆ ಕರೆಮಾಡಿದೆ Went to police station .... 3 ಪೊಲೀಸ್ ಠಾಣೆಗೆ ಹೋದೆ Approached a Police Officer............... 4 ಪೊಲೀಸ್ ಆಫೀಸರನ್ನು ಭೇಟಿ ಮಾಡಿದೆ Don't Remember .... 99 ನೆನಪಿಲ್ಲ	
21N	If 21J is Yes, what did the police do upon hearing your complaint? (Don't read out the options. Mark multiple options as respondents replies) 21 ಜೆ ಹೌದೆಂದರೆ ನಿಮ್ಮ ದೂರು ಕೇಳಿ ಪೊಲೀಸ್ ಏನು ಮಾಡಿದರು? (ಆಯ್ಕೆ ಓದಬೇಡಿ, ಬಹುಆಯ್ಕೆಗಳನ್ನು ಉತ್ತರದಾರ ಹೇಳುತ್ತಿದ್ದಂತೆ ಗುರುತಿಸಿ) **CIRCLE ALL MENTIONED BY THE RESPONDENT** ಉತ್ತರದಾರರು ಹೇಳಿದವುಗಳ ಸುತ್ತ ಸುತ್ತುಗೆರೆ ಹಾಕಿರಿ.	File a complaint ದೂರು ದಾಖಲಿಸಿದರು	1
		Register an FIR ಎಫ್ ಐ ಆರ್ ದಾಖಲಿಸಿದರು	2
		Despatched a PCR vehicle ಪಿಸಿ ಆರ್ ಗಾಡಿ ಕಳುಹಿಸಿದರು	3
		Took any injured persons for medical assistance ಗಾಸಿಗೊಂಡ ವ್ಯಕ್ತಿಯನ್ನು ವೈದ್ಯಕೀಯ ಚಿಕಿತ್ಸೆಗೆ ಕರೆದೊಯ್ದರು	4
		Asked you to go to another police station ಬೇರೆ ಪೊಲೀಸ್ ಠಾಣೆಗೆ ಹೋಗುವಂತೆ ನನಗೆ ಹೇಳಿದರು	5
		Came to the spot and investigated ಸ್ಥಳಕ್ಕೆ ಬಂದು ತನಿಖೆಮಾಡಿದರು	6
		Asked you not to file the complaint ದೂರು ದಾಖಲಿಸಬಾರದೆಂದು ಹೇಳಿದರು	7
		If missing person, filed a missing person report ಕಳೆದುಹೋದದ್ದು ವ್ಯಕ್ತಿಯಾದರೆ, ವ್ಯಕ್ತಿ ಕಳೆದುಹೋದ ವರದಿಯನ್ನು ದಾಖಲಿಸಿದರು	8
		Did not do anything ಏನೂ ಮಾಡಿಲ್ಲ	9
		Other: (Please specify) ಇತರ(ನಿರ್ದಿಷ್ಟವಾಗಿ ಹೇಳಿ)	98
21O	If 20J is Yes, Were you satisfied by the action of the police? 21ಜೆ ಗೆ ಉತ್ತರ ಹೌದೆಂದರೆ ಪೊಲೀಸ್ ತೆಗೆದುಕೊಂಡ ಕ್ರಮದ ಬಗ್ಗೆ ನಿಮಗೆ ತೃಪ್ತಿ ಇದೆಯೇ?	Yes ಹೌದು .... 1 No ಇಲ್ಲ.. 2	**If NO, skip to 21Q**
21P	If 21O is Yes, Why are you satisfied by the police? (Don't read out the options. Mark multiple options as respondents replies)	They listened to the complaint ದೂರು ಕೇಳಿದರು	1	**SKIP TO 21R**
		They registered the complaint accurately ಸರಿಯಾಗಿ ದೂರು ದಾಖಲಿಸಿದರು	2	

		ಕುಟುಂಬದ ವಿಷಯ ವರದಿಮಾಡಬಾರದು	
		This is better settled outside the police stationಪೋಲೀಸ್ ಠಾಣೆಯ ಹೊರಗೆ ಇತ್ಯರ್ಥ ಉತ್ತಮ	11
		Bad past experience with reporting to Police ಪೋಲೀಸ್ ಗೆ ವರದಿ ಮಾಡಿದ ಕೆಟ್ಟ ಅನುಭವವಿದೆ	12
		Others: (Please specify) ಇತರ(ನಿರ್ದಿಷ್ಟವಾಗಿ ಹೇಳಿ)_____	98
		Don't Know/Can't Say ಗೊತ್ತಿಲ್ಲ/ಹೇಳಲಾಗದು	99
21L	If 21J is Yes, why did you report? 21 ಜೆ ಗೆ ಉತ್ತರ ಹೌದೆಂದರೆ ಏಕೆ ವರದಿ ಮಾಡಿದಿರಿ?	For insurance reasons .... 2 ಏಮೆ ಕಾರಣಗಳಿಗೆ Crime should be reported .... 3 ಅಪರಾಧಗಳನ್ನು ವರದಿಮಾಡಬೇಕು It was a serious event .... 4 ಇದು ಗಂಭೀರ ವಿಷಯ Wanted offender to be caught and punished. 5 ಅಪರಾಧಿಯನ್ನು ಹಿಡಿದು ಶಿಕ್ಷೆ ನೀಡಬೇಕು To stop it from happening again/to get help/others .... 6 ಮತ್ತೆ ಇದು ಆಗದಂತೆ ನಿಲ್ಲಿಸಲು/ ಸಹಾಯ ಪಡೆಯಲು Others: (Please specify) _____ ..... 98 ಇತರ(ನಿರ್ದಿಷ್ಟವಾಗಿ ಹೇಳಿ)	
21M	If 21J is Yes, how did you report the above crime? 21 ಜೆ ಗೆ ಉತ್ತರ ಹೌದೆಂದರೆ ಹೇಗೆ ವರದಿ ಮಾಡಿದಿರಿ?	Called 100 .... 1 ನಂ 100ಕ್ಕೆ ಕರೆಮಾಡಿದೆ Called other police helpline...................... 2 ಪೋಲೀಸ್ ಸಹಾಯವಾಣಿಗೆ ಕರೆಮಾಡಿದೆ Went to police station .... 3 ಪೋಲೀಸ್ ಠಾಣೆಗೆ ಹೋದೆ Approached a Police Officer....................... 4 ಪೋಲೀಸ್ ಆಫೀಸರನ್ನು ಭೇಟಿ ಮಾಡಿದೆ Don't Remember .... 99 ನೆನಪಿಲ್ಲ	
21N	If 21J is Yes, what did the police do upon hearing your complaint? (Don't read out the options. Mark multiple options as respondents replies) 21 ಜೆ ಹೌದೆಂದರೆ ನಿಮ್ಮ ದೂರು ಕೇಳಿ ಪೋಲೀಸ್ ಏನು ಮಾಡಿದರು? (ಆಯ್ಕೆ ಓದಬೇಡಿ, ಬಹುಆಯ್ಕೆಗಳನ್ನು ಉತ್ತರದಾರ ಹೇಳುತ್ತಿದ್ದಂತೆ ಗುರುತಿಸಿ) **CIRCLE ALL MENTIONED BY THE RESPONDENT** ಉತ್ತರದಾರರು ಹೇಳಿದವುಗಳ ಸುತ್ತ ಸುತ್ತುಗೆರೆ ಹಾಕಿರಿ.	File a complaint ದೂರು ದಾಖಲಿಸಿದರು	1
		Register an FIR ಎಫ್ ಐ ಆರ್ ದಾಖಲಿಸಿದರು	2
		Despatched a PCR vehicle ಪಿ.ಸಿ ಆರ್ ಗಾಡಿ ಕಳುಹಿಸಿದರು	3
		Took any injured persons for medical assistance ಗಾಸಿಗೊಂಡ ವ್ಯಕ್ತಿಯನ್ನು ವೈದ್ಯಕೀಯ ಚಿಕಿತ್ಸೆಗೆ ಕರೆದೊಯ್ದರು	4
		Asked you to go to another police station ಬೇರೆ ಪೋಲೀಸ್ ಠಾಣೆಗೆ ಹೋಗುವಂತೆ ನನಗೆ ಹೇಳಿದರು	5
		Came to the spot and investigated ಸ್ಥಳಕ್ಕೆ ಬಂದು ತನಿಖೆಮಾಡಿದರು	6
		Asked you not to file the complaint ದೂರು ದಾಖಲಿಸಬಾರದೆಂದು ಹೇಳಿದರು	7
		If missing person, filed a missing person report ಕಳೆದುಹೋದದ್ದು ವ್ಯಕ್ತಿಯಾದರೆ, ವ್ಯಕ್ತಿ ಕಳೆದುಹೋದ ವರದಿಯನ್ನು ದಾಖಲಿಸಿದರು	8
		Did not do anything ಏನೂ ಮಾಡಲಿಲ್ಲ	9
		Other: (Please specify) ಇತರ(ನಿರ್ದಿಷ್ಟವಾಗಿ ಹೇಳಿ)	98
21O	If 20J is Yes, Were you satisfied by the action of the police? 21ಜೆ ಗೆ ಉತ್ತರ ಹೌದೆಂದರೆ ಪೋಲೀಸ್ ತೆಗೆದುಕೊಂಡ ಕ್ರಮದ ಬಗ್ಗೆ ನಿಮಗೆ ತೃಪ್ತಿ ಇದೆಯೇ?	Yes ಹೌದು .... 1 No ಇಲ್ಲ 2	**If NO, skip to 21Q**
21P	If 21O is Yes, Why are you satisfied by the police? (Don't read out the options. Mark multiple options as respondents replies)	They listened to the complaint ದೂರು ಕೇಳಿದರು	1	**SKIP TO 21R**
		They registered the complaint accurately ಸರಿಯಾಗಿ ದೂರು ದಾಖಲಿಸಿದರು	2	

	21ಬ ಗೆ ಉತ್ತರ ಹೌದೆಂದರೆ ಪೋಲೀಸ್ ತೆಗೆದುಕೊಂಡ ಕ್ರಮದ ಬಗ್ಗೆ ನಿಮಗೆ ಏಕೆ ತೃಪ್ತಿ ಇದೆ ? (ಆಯ್ಕೆ ಓದಬೇಡಿ, ಬಹು ಆಯ್ಕೆಗಳನ್ನು ಉತ್ತರದಾರ ಹೇಳುತ್ತಿದ್ದಂತೆ ಗುರುತಿಸಿ) **CIRCLE IF RESPONDENT MENTIONS** ಉತ್ತರದಾರರು ಹೇಳಿದವುಗಳ ಸುತ್ತ ಸುತ್ತುಗೆರೆ ಹಾಕಿರಿ.	They registered the complaint quickly ದೂರನ್ನು ಬೇಗ ದಾಖಲಿಸಿದರು	3	
		They explained the action that they will take ಅವರು ತೆಗೆದುಕೊಳ್ಳುತ್ತ ಕ್ರಮದ ಬಗ್ಗೆ ವಿವರಿಸಿದರು	4	
		They solved the problem ಸಮಸ್ಯೆ ಪರಿಹಾರ ಮಾಡಿದರು	5	
		Other: (please specify) ಇತರ(ನಿರ್ದಿಷ್ಟವಾಗಿ ಹೇಳಿ)	98	
21Q	If 21O is No, Why are you not satisfied by the police? (Don't read out the options. Mark multiple options as respondents replies) 21ಬ ಗೆ ಉತ್ತರ ಇಲ್ಲ ಎಂದಾದರೆ ಪೋಲೀಸ್ ತೆಗೆದುಕೊಂಡ ಕ್ರಮದ ಬಗ್ಗೆ ನಿಮಗೆ ಏಕೆ ತೃಪ್ತಿ ಇಲ್ಲ ? (ಆಯ್ಕೆಗಳನ್ನು ಓದಬೇಡಿ, ಬಹುಆಯ್ಕೆಗಳನ್ನು ಉತ್ತರದಾರ ಹೇಳುತ್ತಿದ್ದಂತೆ ಗುರುತಿಸಿ) **CIRCLE ALL MENTIONED BY THE RESPONDENT** ಉತ್ತರದಾರರು ಹೇಳಿದವುಗಳ ಸುತ್ತ ಸುತ್ತುಗೆರೆ ಹಾಕಿರಿ.	They were not interested ಅವರಿಗೆ ಆಸಕ್ತಿಯಿರಲಿಲ್ಲ	1	
		They were rude and impolite ಅವರು ಒರಟಾಗಿ ವರ್ತಿಸಿದರು, ತಾಳ್ಮೆತೋರಲಿಲ್ಲ	2	
		They did not do enough ಬೇಕಾದಷ್ಟು ಮಾಡಲಿಲ್ಲ	3	
		They refused to file the FIR ಎಫ್ ಐ ಆರ್ ದಾಖಲಿಸಲು ನಿರಾಕರಿಸಿದರು	4	
		They tried to persuade me not to register an FIR ಎಫ್ ಐ ಆರ್ ದಾಖಲಿಸದಂತೆ ನನಗೆ ಒಪ್ಪಿಸಲು ಪ್ರಯತ್ನ ಮಾಡಿದರು	5	
		They took a long time to register my FIR ನನ್ನ ಎಫ್ ಐ ಆರ್ ದಾಖಲಿಸಲು ಬಹಳ ಕಾಲ ತೆಗೆದುಕೊಂಡರು	6	
		They told me to go away from the police station ಪೋಲೀಸ್ ಠಾಣೆಯಿಂದ ಹೋಗುವಂತೆ ಹೇಳಿದರು	7	
		They put me at fault ನನ್ನ ಮೇಲೇ ತಪ್ಪು ಹಾಕಿದರು	8	
		They wanted a bribe ಲಂಚ ಕೇಳಿದರು	9	
		They physically assaulted me ನನಗೆ ದೈಹಿಕವಾಗಿ ಹಲ್ಲೆ ಮಾಡಿದರು	10	
		They verbally abused me ನನ್ನನ್ನು ಬೈದರು	11	
		They didn't find or apprehend the offender ಅಪರಾಧಿಯನ್ನು ಹುಡುಕಲಿಲ್ಲ/ ದಸ್ತಗಿರಿ ಮಾಡಲಿಲ್ಲ	12	
		They didn't recover my property (goods) ನನ್ನ ಆಸ್ತಿ (ಸರಕು) ಹುಡುಕಿಕೊಡಲಿಲ್ಲ	13	
		They didn't keep me properly informed ನನಗೆ ಸರಿಯಾಗಿ ಮಾಹಿತಿ ನೀಡಲಿಲ್ಲ	14	
		They were slow to arrive ಅವರು ಬಹಳ ತಡವಾಗಿ ಬಂದರು	15	
		Other: (please specify) ಇತರ(ನಿರ್ದಿಷ್ಟವಾಗಿ ಹೇಳಿ)	98	
21R	Was any person arrested due to the incident? ಘಟನೆಯಿಂದ ಯಾವುದೇ ವ್ಯಕ್ತಿಯನ್ನು ದಸ್ತಗಿರಿ ಮಾಡಿದರಾ?	Yes ಹೌದು ....1 No ಇಲ್ಲ 2		
21S	How serious was the incident to you and your household? ನಿಮಗೆ ಮತ್ತು ನಿಮ್ಮ ಮನೆಗೆ ಈ ಘಟನೆ ಎಷ್ಟು ಗಂಭೀರವಾದುದು?	Very serious ಬಹಳ ಗಂಭೀರ ....1 Somewhat serious ಸುಮಾರಾಗಿ ಗಂಭೀರ ....2 Not very serious ಬಹಳ ಗಂಭೀರವಲ್ಲ.....................3 Not serious at all ಗಂಭೀರವೇ ಅಲ್ಲ........................4 Don't know ಗೊತ್ತಿಲ್ಲ................................99		
Q22 Part VII				
22A	How many times has the incident occurred in the last one year? ಕಳೆದ ಒಂದು ವರ್ಷದಲ್ಲಿ ಎಷ್ಟು ಬಾರಿ ಈ ಘಟನೆ ನಡೆಯಿತು?	Once ಒಮ್ಮೆ.........1 Twice ಎರಡು ಬಾರಿ......................2 Thrice ಮೂರು ಬಾರಿ ....3 More than thrice in the last year ....4 ಕಳೆದ ಒಂದು ವರ್ಷದಲ್ಲಿ ಮೂರು ಬಾರಿಗಿಂತ ಹೆಚ್ಚು		
22B	Time of occurrence of the most recent incident:	Early Morning ಮುಂಜಾನೆ (5am to 10am)........1		

	ತೀರಾ ಇತ್ತೀಚಿನ ಘಟನೆಯ ಸಮಯ	Late Morning ಬೆಳಿಗ್ಗೆ (10 am to 12pm)............... 2 Early Afternoon (12pm to 3pm) .... 3 Late Afternoon (3pm to 5pm)......................... 4 ಮಧ್ಯಾಹ್ನದ ನಂತರ Early Evening ಮುಸ್ಸಂಜೆ (5pm to 7pm)............ 5 Late Evening ಸಂಜೆ ನಂತರ (7pm to 9pm)......... 6 Early Night ರಾತ್ರಿಗೆ ಮುಂಚೆ (9pm to 12am)........ 7 Late Night ತಡ ರಾತ್ರಿ (12am to 5am) .... 8 Don't Know/Can't Say ಗೊತ್ತಿಲ್ಲ/ಹೇಳಲಾಗದು 99	
22CA	Please tell me the name, age, gender of the member of the family gone missing in past one year ಕಳೆದ ಒಂದು ವರ್ಷದಲ್ಲಿ ಕಳೆದುಹೋದ ನಿಮ್ಮ ಮನೆ ಸದಸ್ಯರ ಹೆಸರು , ವಯಸ್ಸು, ಲಿಂಗ ತಿಳಿಸಿ	Name: _____ ಹೆಸರು	
22CB	Gender ಲಿಂಗ	Male ಗಂಡಸು .... 1 Female ಹೆಂಗಸು .... 2 Other ಇತರೆ .... 3 Can't Say ಹೇಳಲಾಗದು 99	
22CC	Age ವಯಸ್ಸು	1 – 6 yrs. ವರ್ಷಗಳು .... 1 6-12 yrs ವರ್ಷಗಳು.. 2 12-18 yrs ವರ್ಷಗಳು .... 3 18-25 yrs ವರ್ಷಗಳು. .... 4 25-40 yrs ವರ್ಷಗಳು. .... 5 40-59 yrs ವರ್ಷಗಳು. .... 6 60 and above.. 7 60ವರ್ಷಗಳು ಮತ್ತು ಅದಕ್ಕೂ ಮೇರಿ Can't Say.. 99 ಹೇಳಲಾಗದು	
22D	Relationship to the respondent ಉತ್ತರದಾರರೊಂದಿಗೆ ಸಂಬಂಧ	Son ಮಗ.. 1 Daughter ಮಗಳು .... 2 Mother ತಾಯಿ .... 3 Father ತಂದೆ... 4 Brother ಸಹೋದರ .... 5 Sister ಸಹೋದರಿ .... 6 Grandfather ತಾತ .... 7 Grandmother ಅಜ್ಜಿ...................................... 8 Uncle ಅಂಕಲ್ .... 9 Aunt ಆಂಟಿ... 10 Friend ಸ್ನೇಹಿತ .... 11 Can't Say ಹೇಳಲಾಗದು 99	
22E	Did the family receive any calls for extortion (kidnapping) ಒತ್ತೆ ಹಣಕ್ಕಾಗಿ (ಅಪಹರಣಕ್ಕೆ) ಏನಾದರೂ ಕರೆಗಳು ಕುಟುಂಬದವರಿಗೆ ಬಂದಿತೇ?	Yes ಹೌದು .... 1 No ಇಲ್ಲ .... 2 Don't know ಗೊತ್ತಿಲ್ಲ... 99	22G
22F	If 22E yes, did the family pay the extortion 22ಇ ಗೆ ಉತ್ತರ ಹೌದು ಎಂದಾದರೆ ಕುಟುಂಬ ಹಣ ನೀಡಿತೇ?	Yes ಹೌದು .... 1 No ಇಲ್ಲ .... 2 Don't Know/Can't Say ಗೊತ್ತಿಲ್ಲ/ಹೇಳಲಾಗದು 99	
22G	Was the person found? ವ್ಯಕ್ತಿ ಸಿಕ್ಕರೇ?	Yes ಹೌದು .... 1 No ಇಲ್ಲ .... 2 Don't Know/Can't Say ಗೊತ್ತಿಲ್ಲ/ಹೇಳಲಾಗದು 99	22J
22H	If 22G is yes, was the person found 22ಜಿ ವ್ಯಕ್ತಿ ಎಲ್ಲಿ ಸಿಕ್ಕಿದರು	Home ಮನೆ .... 1 Friends house ಸ್ನೇಹಿತರ ಮನೆ .... 2 At a relative's house ನೆಂಟರ ಮನೆ .... 3 At work place ಕೆಲಸದ ಸ್ಥಳ .... 4 On the street ಬೀದಿಯಲ್ಲಿ .... 5 On public transport ಸಾರ್ವಜನಿಕ ಸಾರಿಗೆ .... 6 At a commercial place	

		(Malls, Theatre, Restaurant)............................ 7 ವಾಣಿಜ್ಯ ಸ್ಥಳ(ಮಾಲ್, ಥಿಯೇಟರ್, ಹೋಟೆಲ್) In the neighbourhood area ನೆರೆಹೊರೆ ಪ್ರದೇಶ..... 8 At an educational institutes ವಿದ್ಯಾ ಸಂಸ್ಥೆಗಳು 9 At a playgrounds... 10 ಆಟದ ಮೈದಾನ At a hospitals .... 11 ಆಸ್ಪತ್ರೆ At a police stations .... 12 ಪೊಲೀಸ್ ಠಾಣೆ At a place of worship .... 13 ಪೂಜಾ ಸ್ಥಳ In a different city/town/village .... 14 ನಗರ/ಪಟ್ಟಣ/ಹಳ್ಳಿ Other places (please specify): _____ 98 ಇತರ(ಹೆಸರಿಸಿ) Don't Know/Can't Say..................................... 99 ಗೊತ್ತಿಲ್ಲ/ಹೇಳಲಾಗದು	
22I	The place from which the person is reported to be missing: ವ್ಯಕ್ತಿಯು ಕಾಣೆಯಾಗಿದ ಸ್ಥಳದ ವರದಿ?	Home ಮನೆ .... 1 Friends house ಸ್ನೇಹಿತರ ಮನೆ .... 2 Work Place ಕೆಲಸದಸ್ಥಳ .... 3 On the street .... 4 ಬೀದಿಯಲ್ಲಿ Public transport .... 5 ಸಾರ್ವಜನಿಕ ಸಾರಿಗೆ Commercial place (Malls, Theatre, Restaurant)........................ 6 ವಾಣಿಜ್ಯ ಸ್ಥಳ(ಮಾಲ್, ಥಿಯೇಟರ್, ಹೋಟೆಲ್) Neighbourhood area ನೆರೆಹೊರೆ ಪ್ರದೇಶ .... 7 Educational Institutes .... 8 ವಿದ್ಯಾ ಸಂಸ್ಥೆಗಳು Playgrounds .... 9 ಆಟದ ಮೈದಾನ Hospitals .... 10 ಆಸ್ಪತ್ರೆ Police Stations ಪೊಲೀಸ್ ಠಾಣೆ.......................... 11 Place of worship ಪೂಜಾ ಸ್ಥಳ............................ 12 Other places (please specify): _____ 98 ಇತರ(ನಿರ್ದಿಷ್ಟವಾಗಿ ಹೇಳಿ) Don't Know/Can't Say..................................... 99 ಗೊತ್ತಿಲ್ಲ/ಹೇಳಲಾಗದು	
22J	If 22G is No, How much time since when the person went missing 22ಜೆ ಇಲ್ಲ ಎಂದರೆ ಎಷ್ಟು ಕಾಲದಿಂದ ವ್ಯಕ್ತಿ ಕಾಣೆಯಾಗಿದ್ದಾರೆ?	1-2 days .... 1 1-2ದಿನಗಳು Less than a week.. 2 1 ವಾರಕ್ಕಿಂತ ಕಡಿಮೆ A week .... 3 ಒಂದು ವಾರ 2 weeks .... 4 2ವಾರ More than 2 weeks but less than a month ..... 5 2 ವಾರಕ್ಕಿಂತ ಹೆಚ್ಚು ಆದರೆ ಒಂದು ತಿಂಗಳಿಗಿಂತ ಕಡಿಮೆ A month .... 6 1ತಿಂಗಳು 1-6 months .... 7 1-6ತಿಂಗಳು More than 6 months but less than a year....... 8 6ತಿಂಗಳಿಗಿಂತ ಹೆಚ್ಚು ಆದರೆ ಒಂದು ವರ್ಷಕ್ಕಿಂತ ಕಡಿಮೆ A year .... 9 ಒಂದು ವರ್ಷ More than a year.. 10 ಒಂದು ವರ್ಷಕ್ಕಿಂತ ಹೆಚ್ಚು	

		Don't Know/Can't Say.......................99 ಗೊತ್ತಿಲ್ಲ/ಹೇಳಲಾಗದು		
22K	Did you report the incident to the police: ಘಟನೆ ಬಗ್ಗೆ ನೀವು ಪೋಲೀಸರಿಗೆ ವರದಿ ಮಾಡಿದಿರಾ?	Yes ....1 ಹೌದು No ....2 ಇಲ್ಲ		If YES, skip to **22M**
22L	If 22K is No, Why did you not report? (Do not prompt) 22ಕೆ ಇಲ್ಲ ಎಂದರೆ ವರದಿ ಏಕೆ ಮಾಡದಿಲ್ಲ?	Fear of retaliation retaliation ತಿರುಗಿ ಸೇಡು ತೀರಿಸಿಕೊಳ್ಳುತ್ತಾರಂಬ ಭಯ	1	**SKIP TO 22S**
		Lack of evidence ಸಾಕ್ಷಿಯಿರಲಿಲ್ಲ	2	
		Didn't know where to report ಎಲ್ಲಿ ವರದಿ ಮಾಡುವುದು ಗೊತ್ತಿರಲಿಲ್ಲ	3	
		Didn't know helpline number ಸಹಾಯವಾಣಿ ನಂಬರ್ ಗೊತ್ತಿರಲಿಲ್ಲ	4	
		Did not want to get stuck in police/court matters ಪೋಲೀಸ್/ ಕೋರ್ಟು ವ್ಯವಹರಣೆಗೆ ಸಿಕ್ಕಿಹಾಕಿಕೊಳ್ಳುವುದು ಇಷ್ಟವಿರಲಿಲ್ಲ	5	
		Uncomfortable to go to Police Station ಪೋಲೀಸ್ ಠಾಣೆಗೆ ಹೋಗುವುದು ಅಹಿತವಾಗಿತ್ತು	6	
		Did not think the police would be able to do anything about the case ಪೋಲೀಸರು ಏನಾದರೂ ಮಾಡುತ್ತಾರೆ ಅನಿಸಲಿಲ್ಲ	7	
		Did not think police would entertain the case ಪೋಲೀಸರು ಕೇಸನ್ನು ತಗೆದುಕೊಳ್ಳುತ್ತಾರ ಅನಿಸಲಿಲ್ಲ	8	
		Police is unfair ಪೋಲೀಸರು ನ್ಯಾಯಪರರಲ್ಲ	9	
		Family matters need not be reported ಕುಟುಂಬದ ವಿಷಯ ವರದಿಮಾಡಬಾರದು	10	
		This is better settled outside the police station ಪೋಲೀಸ್ ಠಾಣೆಗೆ ಹೊರಗೆ ಇತ್ಯರ್ಥ ಉತ್ತಮ	11	
		Bad past experience with reporting to Police ಪೋಲೀಸ್ ಗೆ ವರದಿ ಮಾಡಿ ಕೆಟ್ಟ ಅನುಭವವಿದೆ	12	
		Others: (Please specify)_____ ಇತರೆ(ನಿರ್ದಿಷ್ಟವಾಗಿ ಹೇಳಿ)	98	
		Don't Know/Can't Say ಗೊತ್ತಿಲ್ಲ/ಹೇಳಲಾಗದು	99	
22M	If 22K is Yes, why did you report? 22 ಕೆ ಗೆ ಉತ್ತರ ಹೌದೆಂದರೆ ಏಕೆ ವರದಿ ಮಾಡಿದಿರಿ?	To recover property/person ....1 ಆಸ್ತಿ/ವ್ಯಕ್ತಿಯನ್ನು ಮರುಪಡೆಯಲು For insurance reasons ....2 ಏಮೆ ಕಾರಣಗಳಿಗೆ Crime should be reported ....3 ಅಪರಾಧಗಳನ್ನು ವರದಿಮಾಡಬೇಕು It was a serious event ....4 ಇದು ಗಂಭೀರ ವಿಷಯ Wanted offender to be caught and punished.5 ಅಪರಾಧಿಯನ್ನು ಹಿಡಿದು ಶಿಕ್ಷೆ ನೀಡಬೇಕು .... To stop it from happening again/to get help/others ....6 ಮತ್ತೆ ಇದು ಆಗದಂತೆ ನಿಲ್ಲಿಸಲು/ ಸಹಾಯ ಪಡೆಯಲು Others: (Please specify) _____ .....98 ಇತರೆ(ನಿರ್ದಿಷ್ಟವಾಗಿ ಹೇಳಿ)		
22N	If 22K is Yes, how did you report the above crime? 22ಕೆ ಗೆ ಉತ್ತರ ಹೌದೆಂದರೆ ಹೇಗೆ ವರದಿ ಮಾಡಿದಿರಿ?	Called 100 ....1 ನಂ 100ಕ್ಕೆ ಕರೆಮಾಡಿದೆ Called other police helpline............................2 ಪೋಲೀಸ್ ಸಹಾಯವಾಣಿಗೆ ಕರೆಮಾಡಿದೆ Went to police station ....3 ಪೋಲೀಸ್ ಠಾಣೆಗೆ ಹೋದೆ Approached a Police Officer............................4 ಪೋಲೀಸ್ ಆಫೀಸರನ್ನು ಭೇಟಿ ಮಾಡಿದೆ Don't Remember ....99 ನೆನಪಿಲ್ಲ		
22O	If 22K is Yes, what did the police do upon hearing your complaint?	File a complaint ದೂರು ದಾಖಲಿಸಿದರು	1	
		Register an FIR ಎಫ್ ಐ ಆರ್ ದಾಖಲಿಸಿದರು	2	

	(Don't read out the options. Mark multiple options as respondents replies) 22ಕೆ ಗೆ ಉತ್ತರ ಹೌದೆಂದರೆ ನಿಮ್ಮ ದೂರು ಕೇಳಿ ಪೊಲೀಸ್ ಏನು ಮಾಡಿದರು? (ಆಯ್ಕೆ ಓದಬೇಡಿ, ಬಹುಆಯ್ಕೆಗಳನ್ನು ಉತ್ತರದಾರ ಹೇಳುತ್ತಿದ್ದಂತ ಗುರುತಿಸಿ) **CIRCLE ALL MENTIONED BY THE RESPONDENT** ಉತ್ತರದಾರರು ಹೇಳಿದವುಗಳ ಸುತ್ತ ಸುತ್ತುಗೆರೆ ಹಾಕಿರಿ.	Despatched a PCR vehicle ಪಿಸಿ ಆರ್ ಗಾಡಿ ಕಳುಹಿಸಿದರು	3
		Took any injured persons for medical assistance ಗಾಸಿಗೊಂಡ ವ್ಯಕ್ತಿಯನ್ನು ವೈದ್ಯಕೀಯ ಚಿಕಿತ್ಸೆಗೆ ಕರೆದೊಯ್ಯರು	4
		Asked you to go to another police station ಬೇರೆ ಪೊಲೀಸ್ ಠಾಣೆಗೆ ಹೋಗುವಂತ ನನಗೆ ಹೇಳಿದರು	5
		Came to the spot and investigated ಸ್ಥಳಕ್ಕೆ ಬಂದು ತನಿಖೆಮಾಡಿದರು	6
		Asked you not to file the complaint ದೂರು ದಾಖಲಿಸಬಾರದೆಂದು ಹೇಳಿದರು	7
		If missing person, filed a missing person report ಕಳೆದುಹೋದದ್ದು ವ್ಯಕ್ತಿಯಾದರೆ, ವ್ಯಕ್ತಿ ಕಳೆದುಹೋದ ವರದಿ ದಾಖಲಿಸಿದರು	8
		Did not do anything ಏನೂ ಮಾಡಲಿಲ್ಲ	9
		Other: (Please specify) ಇತರೆ(ನಿರ್ದಿಷ್ಟವಾಗಿ ಹೇಳಿ)	98
22P	If 21K is Yes, Were you satisfied by the action of the police? 22ಕೆ ಗೆ ಉತ್ತರ ಹೌದೆಂದರೆ ಪೊಲೀಸ್ ತೆಗೆದುಕೊಂಡ ಕ್ರಮದ ಬಗ್ಗೆ ನಿಮಗೆ ತೃಪ್ತಿ ಇದೆಯೇ?	Yes ಹೌದು ....1 No ಇಲ್ಲ 2	If NO, skip to 22R
22Q	If 22P is Yes, Why are you satisfied by the police? (Don't read out the options. Mark multiple options as respondents replies) 22ಪಿ ಗೆ ಉತ್ತರ ಹೌದೆಂದರೆ ಪೊಲೀಸ್ ತೆಗೆದುಕೊಂಡ ಕ್ರಮದ ಬಗ್ಗೆ ನಿಮಗೆ ಏಕೆ ತೃಪ್ತಿ ಇದೆ ? (ಆಯ್ಕೆ ಓದಬೇಡಿ, ಬಹುಆಯ್ಕೆಗಳನ್ನು ಉತ್ತರದಾರ ಹೇಳುತ್ತಿದ್ದಂತ ಗುರುತಿಸಿ) **CIRCLE IF RESPONDENT MENTIONS** ಉತ್ತರದಾರರು ಹೇಳಿದವುಗಳ ಸುತ್ತ ಸುತ್ತುಗೆರೆ ಹಾಕಿರಿ.	They listened to the complaint ದೂರು ಕೇಳಿದರು	1	**SKIP TO 22S**
		They registered the complaint accurately ಸರಿಯಾಗಿ ದೂರು ದಾಖಲಿಸಿದರು	2
		They registered the complaint quickly ದೂರನ್ನು ಬೇಗ ದಾಖಲಿಸಿದರು	3
		They explained the action that they will take ಅವರು ತೆಗೆದುಕೊಳ್ಳುವ ಕ್ರಮದ ಬಗ್ಗೆ ಏವರಿಸಿದರು	4
		They solved the problem ಸಮಸ್ಯೆ ಪರಿಹಾರ ಮಾಡಿದರು	5
		Other: (please specify) ಇತರ (ನಿರ್ದಿಷ್ಟವಾಗಿ ಹೇಳಿ)	98
22R	If 22P is No, Why are you not satisfied by the police? (Don't read out the options. Mark multiple options as respondents replies) 22ಪಿ ಗೆ ಉತ್ತರ ಇಲ್ಲ ಎಂದಾದರೆ ಪೊಲೀಸ್ ತೆಗೆದುಕೊಂಡ ಕ್ರಮದ ಬಗ್ಗೆ ನಿಮಗೆ ಏಕೆ ತೃಪ್ತಿ ಇಲ್ಲ ? (ಆಯ್ಕೆಗಳನ್ನು ಓದಬೇಡಿ, ಬಹುಆಯ್ಕೆಗಳನ್ನು ಉತ್ತರದಾರ ಹೇಳುತ್ತಿದ್ದಂತ ಗುರುತಿಸಿ) **CIRCLE ALL MENTIONED BY THE RESPONDENT** ಉತ್ತರದಾರರು ಹೇಳಿದವುಗಳ ಸುತ್ತ ಸುತ್ತುಗೆರೆ ಹಾಕಿರಿ.	They were not interested ಅವರಿಗೆ ಆಸಕ್ತಿಯಿರಲಿಲ್ಲ	1	
		They were rude and impolite ಅವರು ಒರಟಾಗಿ ವರ್ತಿಸಿದರು, ಸೌಜನ್ಯ ವಿರಲಿಲ್ಲ	2
		They did not do enough ಬೇಕಾದಷ್ಟು ಮಾಡಲಿಲ್ಲ	3
		They refused to file the FIR ಎಫ್ ಐ ಆರ್ ದಾಖಲಿಸಲು ನಿರಾಕರಿಸಿದರು	4
		They tried to persuade me not to register an FIR ಎಫ್ ಐ ಆರ್ ದಾಖಲಿಸದಂತ ನನಗೆ ಒಪ್ಪಿಸಲು ಪ್ರಯತ್ನ ಮಾಡಿದರು	5
		They took a long time to register my FIR ನನ್ನ ಎಫ್ ಐ ಆರ್ ದಾಖಲಿಸಲು ಬಹಳ ಕಾಲ ತೆಗೆದುಕೊಂಡರು	6
		They told me to go away from the police station ಪೊಲೀಸ್ ಠಾಣೆಯಿಂದ ಹೋಗುವಂತ ಹೇಳಿದರು	7
		They put me at fault ನನ್ನ ಮೇಲೆ ತಪ್ಪು ಹಾಕಿದರು	8
		They wanted a bribe ಲಂಚ ಕೇಳಿದರು	9
		They physically assaulted me ನನಗೆ ದೈಹಿಕವಾಗಿ ಹಲ್ಲೆ ಮಾಡಿದರು	10
		They verbally abused me ನನ್ನನ್ನು ಬೈದರು	11
		They didn't find or apprehend the offender ಅಪರಾಧಿಯನ್ನು ಹುಡುಕಲಿಲ್ಲ/ ದಸ್ತಗಿರಿ ಮಾಡಲಿಲ್ಲ	12
		They didn't recover my property (goods) ನನ್ನ ಆಸ್ತಿ (ಸರಕು) ಹುಡುಕಿ ಕೊಡಲಿಲ್ಲ	13

		They didn't keep me properly informed ನನಗೆ ಸರಿಯಾಗಿ ಮಾಹಿತಿ ನೀಡಲಿಲ್ಲ	14	
		They were slow to arrive ಅವರು ಬಹಳ ತಡವಾಗಿ ಬಂದರು	15	
		Other: (please specify) ಇತರ(ನಿರ್ದಿಷ್ಟವಾಗಿ ಹೇಳಿ)	98	
22S	Was any person arrested due to the incident? ಘಟನೆಯಿಂದ ಯಾವುದೇ ವ್ಯಕ್ತಿಯನ್ನು ದಸ್ತಗಿರಿ ಮಾಡಿದರಾ?	Yes ಹೌದು .... 1 No ಇಲ್ಲ 2		
22T	How serious was the incident to you and your household? ನಿಮಗೆ ಮತ್ತು ನಿಮ್ಮ ಮನೆಗೆ ಈ ಘಟನೆ ಎಷ್ಟು ಗಂಭೀರವಾದುದು?	Very serious ಬಹಳ ಗಂಭೀರ .... 1 Somewhat serious ಸುಮಾರಾಗಿ ಗಂಭೀರ............ 2 Not very serious ಬಹಳ ಗಂಭೀರವಲ್ಲ .... 3 Not serious at all ಗಂಭೀರವೇ ಅಲ್ಲ .... 4 Don't know ಗೊತ್ತಿಲ್ಲ 99		
Q23 Part VIII				
23A	How many times has the incident occurred in the last one year? ಕಳೆದ ಒಂದು ವರ್ಷದಲ್ಲಿ ಎಷ್ಟು ಬಾರಿ ಈ ಘಟನೆ ನಡೆಯಿತು?	Once ಒಮ್ಮೆ.. 1 Twice ಎರಡು ಬಾರಿ................................ 2 Thrice ಮೂರು ಬಾರಿ .... 3 More than thrice in the last year .... 4 ಕಳೆದ ಒಂದು ವರ್ಷದಲ್ಲಿ ಮೂರು ಬಾರಿಗಿಂತ ಹೆಚ್ಚು		
23B	Time of occurrence of the most recent incident ತೀರಾ ಇತ್ತೀಚಿನ ಘಟನೆಯ ಸಮಯ	Early Morning (5am to 10am) ಮುಂಜಾನ .... 1 Late Morning (10 am to 12pm) ಬೆಳಿಗ್ಗೆ .... 2 Early Afternoon ಮಧ್ಯಾಹ್ನಕ್ಕೆ ಮುಂಚೆ(12pm to 3pm) ..... 3 Late Afternoon ಮಧ್ಯಾಹ್ನಕ್ಕೆ ನಂತರ(3pm to 5pm)........ 4 Early Evening ಮುಸ್ಸಂಜೆ (5pm to 7pm)............ 5 Late Evening ಸಂಜೆ ನಂತರ (7pm to 9pm)........ 6 Early Night ರಾತ್ರಿಗೆ ಮುಂಚೆ (9pm to 12am)........ 7 Late Night ತಡ ರಾತ್ರಿ (12am to 5am) .... 8 Don't Know/Can't Say ಗೊತ್ತಿಲ್ಲ/ಹೇಳಲಾಗದು 99		
23C	Where did the incident occur: ಘಟನೆ ಎಲ್ಲಿ ನಡೆಯಿತು	Home ಮನೆ .... 1 Friends house ಸ್ನೇಹಿತರ ಮನೆ .... 2 Work Place ಕೆಲಸದಸ್ಥಳ .... 3 On the street ಬೀದಿಯಲ್ಲಿ .... 4 Public transport ಸಾರ್ವಜನಿಕ ಸಾರಿಗೆ .... 5 Commercial place (Malls, Theatre, Restaurant)........................ 6 ವಾಣಿಜ್ಯ ಸ್ಥಳ(ಮಾಲ್, ಥಿಯೇಟರ್, ಹೋಟೆಲ್) Neighbourhood area ನೆರೆಹೊರೆ ಪ್ರದೇಶ .... 7 Educational Institutes ವಿದ್ಯಾ ಸಂಸ್ಥೆಗಳು .... 8 Playgrounds ಆಟದ ಮೈದಾನ.......................... 9 Hospitals ಆಸ್ಪತ್ರೆ .... 10 Police Stations ಪೊಲೀಸ್ ಠಾಣೆ........................ 11 Place of worship ಪೂಜಾ ಸ್ಥಳ .... 12 Other places: (please specify) ಇತರ ಸ್ಥಳ (ನಿರ್ದಿಷ್ಟವಾಗಿ ಹೇಳಿ)........................ 98 Don't Know/Can't Say ಗೊತ್ತಿಲ್ಲ/ಹೇಳಲಾಗದು 99		
23D	If Q23 is (b) Suicide, was the suicide related to the following ಪ್ರ 23 (ಬಿ) ಆತ್ಮಹತ್ಯೆ ಆದರೆ , ಆ ಆತ್ಮಹತ್ಯೆಗೆ ಈ ಮುಂದಿನವುಗಳಲ್ಲಿ ಯಾವುದು ಕಾರಣ	Agricultural Debts ಕೃಷಿ ಸಾಲಗಳು .... 1 Drought ಬರ .... 2 Education related problems........................... 3 ಶಿಕ್ಷಣಕ್ಕೆ ಸಂಬಂಧಿಸಿದ ತೊಂದರೆಗಳು Mental Health ಮಾನಸಿಕ ಆರೋಗ್ಯ.................... 4 Family Issues ಕುಟುಂಬ ಸಮಸ್ಯೆ.......................... 5 Bullying ದಾದಾಗಿರಿ.................................. 6 Eve teasing ಹೆಣ್ಣುಮಕ್ಕಳಿಗೆ ಭೇದಿಸುವುದು .... 7 Others: (Please Specify)		

		ಇತರ (ನಿರ್ದಿಷ್ಟವಾಗಿ ಹೇಳಿ)		
		Don't Know/Can't Say ಗೊತ್ತಿಲ್ಲ/ಹೇಳಲಾಗದು	99	
23E	Did you report the incident to the police? ಘಟನೆ ಬಗ್ಗೆ ನೀವು ಪೊಲೀಸರಿಗೆ ವರದಿ ಮಾಡಿದಿರಾ?	Yes ಹೌದು 1		If YES, Skip to **23G**
		No ಇಲ್ಲ 2		
23F	If 23E is No, Why did you not report? (Do not prompt) 23 ಇ ಗೆ ಉತ್ತರ ಇಲ್ಲ ಎಂದಾದರೆ ವರದಿ ಏಕೆ ಮಾಡಲಿಲ್ಲ?	Fear of retaliation retaliation ತಿರುಗಿ ಸೇಡು ತೀರಿಸಿಕೊಳ್ಳುತ್ತಾರೆಂಬ ಭಯ	1	**SKIP TO 23M**
		Lack of evidence ಸಾಕ್ಷ್ಯಿರಲಿಲ್ಲ	2	
		Didn't know where to report ಎಲ್ಲಿ ವರದಿ ಮಾಡುವುದು ಗೊತ್ತಿಲ್ಲ	3	
		Didn't know helpline number ಸಹಾಯವಾಣಿ ನಂಬರ್ ಗೊತ್ತಿಲ್ಲ	4	
		Did not want to get stuck in police/court matters ಪೊಲೀಸ್/ ಕೋರ್ಟು ವ್ಯವಹರಿಸಿಗೆ ಸಿಕ್ಕಿಹಾಕಿಕೊಳ್ಳುವುದು ಇಷ್ಟವಿರಲಿಲ್ಲ	5	
		Uncomfortable to go to Police Station ಪೊಲೀಸ್ ಠಾಣೆಗೆ ಹೋಗುವುದು ಅಹಿತವಾಗಿತ್ತು	6	
		Did not think the police would be able to do anything about the case ಪೊಲೀಸರು ಏನಾದರೂ ಮಾಡುತ್ತಾರ ಅನಿಸಲಿಲ್ಲ	7	
		Did not think police would entertain the case ಪೊಲೀಸರು ಕೇಸನ್ನು ತೆಗೆದುಕೊಳ್ಳುತ್ತಾರ ಅನಿಸಲಿಲ್ಲ	8	
		Police is unfair ಪೊಲೀಸರು ನ್ಯಾಯಪರರಲ್ಲ	9	
		Family matters need not be reported ಕುಟುಂಬದ ವಿಷಯ ವರದಿಮಾಡಬಾರದು	10	
		This is better settled outside the police station ಪೊಲೀಸ್ ಠಾಣೆಯ ಹೊರಗೆ ಇತ್ಯರ್ಥ ಉತ್ತಮ	11	
		Bad past experience with reporting to Police ಪೊಲೀಸ್ ಗೆ ವರದಿ ಮಾಡಿದ ಕೆಟ್ಟ ಅನುಭವವಿದೆ	12	
		Others: (Please specify)_____ ಇತರ(ನಿರ್ದಿಷ್ಟವಾಗಿ ಹೇಳಿ)	98	
		Don't Know/Can't Say ಗೊತ್ತಿಲ್ಲ/ಹೇಳಲಾಗದು	99	
23G	If 23E is Yes, why did you report? 23ಇ ಗೆ ಉತ್ತರ ಹೌದೆಂದರೆ ಏಕೆ ವರದಿ ಮಾಡಿದಿರಿ?	To recover property/person ....1 ಆಸ್ತಿ/ವ್ಯಕ್ತಿಯನ್ನು ಮರು ಪಡೆಯಲು For insurance reasons ವಿಮೆ ಕಾರಣಗಳಿಗೆ .... 2 Crime should be reported ಅಪರಾಧಗಳನ್ನು ವರದಿಮಾಡಬೇಕು. 3 It was a serious event ಇದು ಗಂಭೀರ ವಿಷಯ .... 4 Wanted offender to be caught and punished .... 5 ಅಪರಾಧಿಯನ್ನು ಹಿಡಿದು ಶಿಕ್ಷೆ ನೀಡಬೇಕು To stop it from happening again/to get help/others ..... 6 ಮತ್ತೆ ಇದು ಆಗದಂತೆ ನಿಲ್ಲಿಸಲು/ ಸಹಾಯ ಪಡೆಯಲು Others: (Please specify) ಇತರ(ನಿರ್ದಿಷ್ಟವಾಗಿ ಹೇಳಿ)_____ 98		
23H	If 23E is Yes, how did you report the above crime? 23ಇ ಎ ಫ್ ಗೆ ಉತ್ತರ ಹೌದೆಂದರೆ ಹೇಗೆ ವರದಿ ಮಾಡಿದಿರಿ?	Called 100 ನಂ.100ಕ್ಕೆ ಕರೆಮಾಡಿದೆ .... 1 Called other police helpline ಪೊಲೀಸ್ ಸಹಾಯವಾಣಿಗೆ ಕರೆಮಾಡಿದೆ .... 2 Went to police station ಪೊಲೀಸ್ ಠಾಣೆಗೆ ಹೋದೆ .... 3 Approached a Police Officer ಪೊಲೀಸ್ ಆಫೀಸರನ್ನು ಭೇಟಿ ಮಾಡಿದೆ .... 4 Don't Remember ನೆನಪಿಲ್ಲ 99		
23I	If 23E is Yes, what did the police do upon hearing your complaint? (Don't read out the options. Mark multiple options as respondents replies) 23ಇ ಗೆ ಉತ್ತರ ಹೌದೆಂದರೆ ನಿಮ್ಮ ದೂರು ಕೇಳಿ ಪೊಲೀಸ್ ಏನು ಮಾಡಿದರು? (ಆಯ್ಕೆ ಓದಬೇಡಿ,	File a complaint ದೂರು ದಾಖಲಿಸಿದರು	1	
		Register an FIR ಎಫ್ ಐ ಆರ್ ದಾಖಲಿಸಿದರು	2	
		Despatched a PCR vehicle ಪಿಸಿ ಆರ್ ವಾಹನ ಕಳುಹಿಸಿದರು	3	
		Took any injured persons for medical assistance ಗಾಸಿಗೊಂಡ ವ್ಯಕ್ತಿಯನ್ನು ವೈದ್ಯಕೀಯ ಚಿಕಿತ್ಸೆಗೆ ಕರೆದೊಯ್ದರು	4	
		Asked you to go to another police station	5	

		ಬೇರೆ ಪೂಲೀಸ್ ಠಾಣೆಗೆ ಹೋಗುವಂತ ನನಗೆ ಹೇಳಿದರು		
	ಬಹುಆಯ್ಕೆಗಳನ್ನು ಉತ್ತರದಾರ ಹೇಳುತ್ತಿದ್ದಂತೆ ಗುರುತಿಸಿ) **CIRCLE ALL MENTIONED BY THE RESPONDENT** ಉತ್ತರದಾರರು ಹೇಳಿದವುಗಳ ಸುತ್ತ ಸುತ್ತುಗೆರ ಹಾಕಿರಿ.	Came to the spot and investigated ಸ್ಥಳಕ್ಕೆ ಬಂದು ತನಿಖೆಮಾಡಿದರು	6	
		Asked you not to file the complaint ದೂರು ದಾಖಲಿಸಬಾರದೆಂದು ಹೇಳಿದರು	7	
		If missing person, filed a missing person report ಕಳೆದುಹೋದದ್ದು ವ್ಯಕ್ತಿಯಾದರೆ, ವ್ಯಕ್ತಿ ಕಳೆದುಹೋದ ವರದಿ ದಾಖಲಿಸಿದರು	8	
		Did not do anything ಏನೂ ಮಾಡಲಿಲ್ಲ	9	
		Other: (Please specify) ಇತರ(ನಿರ್ದಿಷ್ಟವಾಗಿ ಹೇಳಿ)	98	
23J	If 23E is Yes, Were you satisfied by the action of the police? 23 ಇ ಹೌದೆಂದರೆ ಪೂಲೀಸ್ ತೆಗೆದುಕೊಂಡ ಕ್ರಮದ ಬಗ್ಗೆ ನಿಮಗೆ ತೃಪ್ತಿ ಇದೆಯೇ?	Yes ಹೌದು .... 1 No .... 2 ಇಲ್ಲ		If No, skip to 23L
23K	If 23J is Yes, Why are you satisfied by the police? (Don't read out the options. Mark multiple options as respondents replies) 23ಜೆ ಹೌದೆಂದರೆ ಪೂಲೀಸ್ ತೆಗೆದುಕೊಂಡ ಕ್ರಮದ ಬಗ್ಗೆ ನಿಮಗೆ ಏಕೆ ತೃಪ್ತಿ ಇದೆ ? (ಆಯ್ಕೆ ಓದಬೇಡಿ, ಬಹುಆಯ್ಕೆಗಳನ್ನು ಉತ್ತರದಾರ ಹೇಳುತ್ತಿದ್ದಂತೆ ಗುರುತಿಸಿ) **CIRCLE IF RESPONDENT MENTIONS** ಉತ್ತರದಾರರು ಹೇಳಿದವುಗಳ ಸುತ್ತ ಸುತ್ತುಗೆರ ಹಾಕಿರಿ.	They listened to the complaint ದೂರು ಕೇಳಿದರು	1	**SKIP TO 23M**
		They registered the complaint accurately ಸರಿಯಾಗಿ ದೂರು ದಾಖಲಿಸಿದರು	2	
		They registered the complaint quickly ದೂರನ್ನು ಬೇಗ ದಾಖಲಿಸಿದರು	3	
		They explained the action that they will take ಅವರು ತೆಗೆದುಕೊಳ್ಳುವ ಕ್ರಮದ ಬಗ್ಗೆ ವಿವರಿಸಿದರು	4	
		They solved the problem ಸಮಸ್ಯೆ ಪರಿಹಾರ ಮಾಡಿದರು	5	
		Other: (please specify) ಇತರೆ(ನಿರ್ದಿಷ್ಟವಾಗಿ ಹೇಳಿ)	98	
23L	If 23J is No, Why are you not satisfied by the police? (Don't read out the options. Mark multiple options as respondents replies) 23ಜೆ ಗೆ ಉತ್ತರ ಇಲ್ಲ ಎಂದರೆ ಪೂಲೀಸ್ ತೆಗೆದುಕೊಂಡ ಕ್ರಮದ ಬಗ್ಗೆ ನಿಮಗೆ ಏಕೆ ತೃಪ್ತಿ ಇಲ್ಲ ? (ಆಯ್ಕೆಗಳನ್ನು ಓದಬೇಡಿ, ಬಹುಆಯ್ಕೆಗಳನ್ನು ಉತ್ತರದಾರ ಹೇಳುತ್ತಿದ್ದಂತೆ ಗುರುತಿಸಿ) **CIRCLE ALL MENTIONED BY THE RESPONDENT** ಉತ್ತರದಾರರು ಹೇಳಿದವುಗಳ ಸುತ್ತ ಸುತ್ತುಗೆರ ಹಾಕಿರಿ.	They were not interested ಅವರಿಗೆ ಆಸಕ್ತಿಯಿರಲಿಲ್ಲ	1	
		They were rude and impolite ಅವರು ಒರಟಾಗಿ, ಸೌಜನ್ಯವಿಲ್ಲದೆ ವರ್ತಿಸಿದರು	2	
		They did not do enough ಮಾಡ ಬೇಕಾದಷ್ಟು ಮಾಡಲಿಲ್ಲ	3	
		They refused to file the FIR ಎಫ್ ಐ ಆರ್ ದಾಖಲಿಸಲು ನಿರಾಕರಿಸಿದರು	4	
		They tried to persuade me not to register an FIR ಎಫ್ ಐ ಆರ್ ದಾಖಲಿಸದಂತೆ ನನಗೆ ಒಡ್ಡಿಸಲು ಪ್ರಯತ್ನ ಮಾಡಿದರು	5	
		They took a long time to register my FIR ನನ್ನ ಎಫ್ ಐ ಆರ್ ದಾಖಲಿಸಲು ಬಹಳ ಕಾಲ ತೆಗೆದುಕೊಂಡರು	6	
		They told me to go away from the police station ಪೂಲೀಸ್ ಠಾಣೆಯಿಂದ ಹೋಗುವಂತ ಹೇಳಿದರು	7	
		They put me at fault ನನ್ನ ಮೇಲೆ ತಪ್ಪು ಹಾಕಿದರು	8	
		They wanted a bribe ಲಂಚ ಕೇಳಿದರು	9	
		They physically assaulted me ನನಗೆ ದೈಹಿಕವಾಗಿ ಹಲ್ಲೆ ಮಾಡಿದರು	10	
		They verbally abused me ನನ್ನ ಬೈದರು	11	
		They didn't find or apprehend the offender ಅಪರಾಧಿಯನ್ನು ಹುಡುಕಲಿಲ್ಲ/ ದಸ್ತಗಿರಿ ಮಾಡಲಿಲ್ಲ	12	
		They didn't recover my property (goods) ನನ್ನ ಆಸ್ತಿ (ಸರಕು) ಹುಡುಕಿಕೊಡಲಿಲ್ಲ	13	
		They didn't keep me properly informed ನನಗೆ ಸರಿಯಾಗಿ ಮಾಹಿತಿ ನೀಡಲಿಲ್ಲ	14	
		They were slow to arrive ಅವರು ಬಹಳ ತಡವಾಗಿ ಬಂದರು	15	
		Other: (please specify) ಇತರೆ(ನಿರ್ದಿಷ್ಟವಾಗಿ ಹೇಳಿ)_____	98	
23M	Was any person arrested due to the incident? ಘಟನೆಯಿಂದ ಯಾವುದೇ ವ್ಯಕ್ತಿಯನ್ನು ದಸ್ತಗಿರಿ ಮಾಡಿದರಾ?	Yes ಹೌದು .... 1 No ಇಲ್ಲ.. 2		

| 23N | How serious was the incident to you and your household?
ನಿಮಗೆ ಮತ್ತು ನಿಮ್ಮ ಮನೆಗೆ ಈ ಘಟನೆ ಎಷ್ಟು ಗಂಭೀರವಾದದ್ದು | Very serious ಬಹಳ ಗಂಭೀರ 1
Somewhat serious ಸುಮಾರಾಗಿ ಗಂಭೀರ 2
Not very serious ಬಹಳ ಗಂಭೀರವಲ್ಲ 3
Not serious at all ಗಂಭೀರವೇ ಅಲ್ಲ 4
Don't know ಗೊತ್ತಿಲ್ಲ ....99 | |

Q24 Part IX			
24A	How many times has the incident occurred in the last one year? ಕಳೆದ ಒಂದು ವರ್ಷದಲ್ಲಿ ಎಷ್ಟು ಬಾರಿ ಘಟನೆ ನಡೆಯಿತು?	Once ಒಮ್ಮೆ ....1 Twice ಎರಡು ಬಾರಿ ....2 Thrice ಮೂರು ಬಾರಿ ....3 More than thrice in the last year ....4 ಕಳೆದ ಒಂದು ವರ್ಷದಲ್ಲಿ ಮೂರು ಬಾರಿಗಿಂತ ಹೆಚ್ಚು	
24B	Time of occurrence of the most recent incident ತೀರಾ ಇತ್ತೀಚಿನ ಘಟನೆಯ ಸಮಯ	Early Morning ಮುಂಜಾನೆ (5am to 10am) ....1 Late Morning ಬೆಳಿಗ್ಗೆ (10 am to 12pm)...................2 Early Afternoon (12pm to 3pm) ....3 ಮಧ್ಯಾಹ್ನಕ್ಕೆ ಮುಂಚೆ Late Afternoon (3pm to 5pm) ....4 ಮಧ್ಯಾಹ್ನದ ನಂತರ Early Evening ಮುಸ್ಸಂಜೆ(5pm to 7pm)...................5 Late Evening ಸಂಜೆ ನಂತರ (7pm to 9pm) ....6 Early Night ರಾತ್ರಿಗೆ ಮುಂಚೆ (9pm to 12am) ....7 Late Night ತಡ ರಾತ್ರಿ (12am to 5am) ....8 Don't Know/Can't Say ....99 ಗೊತ್ತಿಲ್ಲ/ಹೇಳಲಾಗದು	

24C	Were you affected by the incident in any of the following ways? ಘಟನೆಯಿಂದ ಈ ಯಾವುದೇ ರೀತಿಯಲ್ಲಿ ನಿಮಗೆ ಪರಿಣಾಮ ಆಯಿತೇ?		Yes	No
		Deprivation of essential services such as rations, water, medicines ರೇಷನ್, ನೀರು, ಔಷಧಿಗಳಂತಹ ಅಗತ್ಯ ವಸ್ತುಗಳು ದೊರಕದಿರುವುದು.	1	2
		Forced not go to work ಕೆಲಸಕ್ಕೆ ಹೋಗದಿರಲು ಬಲತ್ಕಾರ	1	2
		Forced to participate in the bandh/hartal/agitation/unrest/violence ಬಂದ್/ ಹರತಾಳ/ ಹೋರಾಟದಲ್ಲಿ ಭಾಗಿಯಾಗಲು ಒತ್ತಡ	1	2
		Suffered physical harm ದೈಹಿಕ ಹಾನಿ ಉಂಟಾಯಿತು	1	2
		Suffered damage to property ಆಸ್ತಿ ಹಾನಿ ಉಂಟಾಯಿತು	1	2
		Other problems ಇತರ ಸಮಸ್ಯೆಗಳು	1	2

24D	Did the police take any action to restore normalcy in the area? ಪ್ರದೇಶದಲ್ಲಿ ಜನಜೀವನ ಸಾಮಾನ್ಯ ಸ್ಥಿತಿಗೆ ಬರಲು ಪೋಲೀಸರು ಏನಾದರೂ ಕ್ರಮ ತೆಗೆದುಕೊಂಡರಾ?	Yes ಹೌದು ....1 No ಇಲ್ಲ ....2 Don't Know/Can't Say ಗೊತ್ತಿಲ್ಲ/ಹೇಳಲಾಗದು 99	
24E	How long did it take before the situation to become normal? ಜನಜೀವನ ಸಾಮಾನ್ಯ ಸ್ಥಿತಿಗೆ ಬರಲು ಎಷ್ಟು ಕಾಲ ಹಿಡಿಯಿತು?	1-2 days 1-2 ದಿನಗಳು ....1 Less than a week ವಾರಕ್ಕಿಂತ ಕಮ್ಮಿ.......................2 A week ಒಂದುವಾರ ....3 2 weeks ಎರಡುವಾರಗಳು..................................4 More than 2 weeks but less than a month ......5 A month ಎರಡು ವಾರಕ್ಕಿಂತ ಹೆಚ್ಚು ಆದರೆ ತಿಂಗಳೆ ಗಿಂತ ಕಡಿಮೆ ....6 2-6 months 2-6 ತಿಂಗಳು...............................7 More than 6 months but less than a year ....8 A year2-6 ತಿಂಗಳಿಗಿಂತ ಹೆಚ್ಚು ಆದರೆ ವರ್ಷಕ್ಕಿಂತ ಕಡಿಮೆ 9 More than a year ವರ್ಷಕ್ಕಿಂತ ಹೆಚ್ಚು 10 Don't Know/Can't Say ಗೊತ್ತಿಲ್ಲ/ಹೇಳಲಾಗದು 99	
24F	Did you report the incident to the police: ಘಟನೆ ಬಗ್ಗೆ ನೀವು ಪೊಲೀಸರಿಗೆ ವರದಿ ಮಾಡಿದಿರಾ?	Yes ಹೌದು ....1 No ಇಲ್ಲ 2	If YES, skip to 24H
24G	If 24F is No, Why did you not report? (Do not	Fear of retaliation retaliation ತಿರುಗಿ ಸೇಡು 1	SKIP

	prompt) 24 ಎಫ್ ಗೆ ಉತ್ತರ ಇಲ್ಲ ಎಂದರೆ ವರದಿ ಏಕೆ ಮಾಡಲಿಲ್ಲ?	ತೆರಿಸಿಕೊಳ್ಳುತ್ತಾರೆಂಬ ಭಯ		TO 24N
		Lack of evidence ಸಾಕ್ಷಿಯಿರಲಿಲ್ಲ	2	
		Didn't know where to report ಎಲ್ಲಿ ವರದಿ ಮಾಡುವುದು ಗೊತ್ತಿರಲಿಲ್ಲ	3	
		Didn't know helpline number ಹೆಲ್ಪ್ ಲೈನ್ ನಂಬರ ಗೊತ್ತಿರಲಿಲ್ಲ	4	
		Did not want to get stuck in police/court matters ಪೂಲೀಸ್/ ಕೋರ್ಟಿಗೆ ಸಿಕ್ಕಿಹಾಕಿಕೊಳ್ಳುವುದು ಇಷ್ಟವಿರಲಿಲ್ಲ	5	
		Uncomfortable to go to Police Station ಪೂಲೀಸ್ ಠಾಣೆಗೆ ಹೋಗುವುದು ಅಹಿತವಾಗಿತ್ತು	6	
		Did not think the police would be able to do anything about the case ಪೂಲೀಸರು ಏನಾದರೂ ಮಾಡುತ್ತಾರೆ ಅನಿಸುವುದಿಲ್ಲ	7	
		Did not think police would entertain the case ಪೂಲೀಸರು ಕೇಸನ್ನು ತೆಗೆದುಕೊಳ್ಳುತ್ತಾರೆ ಅನಿಸುವುದಿಲ್ಲ	8	
		Police is unfair ಪೂಲೀಸರು ಅನ್ಯಾಯಯಿತರು	9	
		Family matters need not be reported ಕುಟುಂಬ ವಿಷಯ ವರದಿಮಾಡಬಾರದು	10	
		This is better settled outside the police station ಪೂಲೀಸ್ ಠಾಣೆಗೆ ಹೊರಗೆ ಇತ್ಯರ್ಥ ಉತ್ತಮ	11	
		Bad past experience with reporting to Police ಪೂಲೀಸ್ ಗೆ ವರದಿ ಮಾಡಿ ಕೆಟ್ಟ ಅನುಭವವಿದೆ	12	
		Others: (Please specify) ಇತರ(ನಿರ್ದಿಷ್ಟವಾಗಿ ಹೇಳಿ)	98	
		Don't Know/Can't Say ಗೊತ್ತಿಲ್ಲ/ಹೇಳಲಾಗದು	99	
24H	If 24F is Yes, why did you report? 24ಎಫ್ ಹೌದೆಂದರೆ ಏಕೆ ವರದಿ ಮಾಡಿದಿರಿ?	To recover property/person ಆಸ್ತಿ/ವ್ಯಕ್ತಿಯನ್ನು ಮರು ಪಡೆಯಲು ....1 For insurance reasons ಏಮೆ ಕಾರಣಗಳಿಗೆ ....2 Crime should be reported ಅಪರಾಧಗಳನ್ನು ವರದಿಮಾಡಬೇಕು ......3 It was a serious event ಇದು ಗಂಭೀರ ವಿಷಯ ....4 Wanted offender to be caught and punished..........5 ಅಪರಾಧಿಯನ್ನು ಹಿಡಿದು ಶಿಕ್ಷೆ ನೀಡಬೇಕು To stop it from happening again/to get help........ 6 ಮತ್ತೆ ಇದು ಆಗದಂತೆ ನಿಲ್ಲಿಸಲು/ ಸಹಾಯ ಪಡೆಯಲು Others: (Please specify) ಇತರ(ನಿರ್ದಿಷ್ಟವಾಗಿ ಹೇಳಿ) 98		
24I	If 24F is Yes, how did you report the above crime? 24ಎಫ್ ಗೆ ಉತ್ತರ ಹೌದೆಂದರೆ ಅಪರಾಧದ ಬಗ್ಗೆ ಹೇಗೆ ವರದಿ ಮಾಡಿದಿರಿ?	Called 100 ನಂ 100ಕ್ಕೆ ಕರೆಮಾಡಿದೆ...............1 Called other police helpline ....2 ಪೂಲೀಸ್ ಹೆಲ್ಪ್ ಲೇನ್ ಕರಮಾಡಿದೆ Went to police station ಪೂಲೀಸ್ ಠಾಣೆಗೆ ಹೋದೆ ....3 Approached a Police Officer.................................4 ಪೂಲೀಸ್ ಆಫೀಸರನ್ನು ಭೇಟಿ ಮಾಡಿದೆ Don't Remember ನೆನಪಿಲ್ಲ 99		
24J	If 24F is Yes, what did the police do upon hearing your complaint? (Don't read out the options. Mark multiple options as respondents replies) 24 ಎಫ್ ಗೆ ಉತ್ತರ ಹೌದೆಂದರೆ ನಿಮ್ಮ ದೂರು ಕೇಳಿ ಪೂಲೀಸ್ ಏನು ಮಾಡಿದರು? (ಆಯ್ಕೆ ಓದಬೇಡಿ, ಬಹುಆಯ್ಕೆಗಳನ್ನು ಪ್ರತಿಕ್ರಿಯೆದಾರ ಹೇಳುತ್ತಿದ್ದಂತೆ ಗುರುತಿಸಿ) **CIRCLE ALL MENTIONED BY THE RESPONDENT** ಉತ್ತರದಾರು ಹೇಳಿದವುಗಳ ಸುತ್ತ ಸುತ್ತುಗೆರೆ ಹಾಕಿರಿ.	File a complaint ದೂರು ದಾಖಲಿಸಿದರು	1	
		Register an FIR ಎಫ್ ಐ ಆರ್ ದಾಖಲಿಸಿದರು	2	
		Despatched a PCR vehicle ಪಿಸಿ ಆರ್ ವಾಹನ ಕಳುಹಿಸಿದರು	3	
		Took any injured persons for medical assistance ಗಾಸಿಗೊಂಡ ವ್ಯಕ್ತಿಯನ್ನು ವೈದ್ಯಕೀಯ ಚಿಕಿತ್ಸೆಗೆ ಕರೆದೊಯ್ದರು	4	
		Asked you to go to another police station ಬೇರೆ ಪೂಲೀಸ್ ಠಾಣೆಗೆ ಹೋಗುವಂತೆ ನನಗೆ ಹೇಳಿದರು	5	
		Came to the spot and investigated ಸ್ಥಳಕ್ಕೆ ಬಂದು ತನಿಖೆಮಾಡಿದರು	6	
		Asked you not to file the complaint ದೂರು ದಾಖಲಿಸಬಾರದೆಂದು ಹೇಳಿದರು	7	
		If missing person, filed a missing person report ಕಳೆದುಹೋದ್ದದು ವ್ಯಕ್ತಿಯಾದರೆ, ವ್ಯಕ್ತಿ ಕಳೆದುಹೋದ ವರದಿ	8	

\

		ದಾಖಲಿಸಿದರು		
		Did not do anything ಏನೂ ಮಾಡಿಲಿಲ್ಲ	9	
		Other: (Please specify) ಇತರ(ನಿರ್ದಿಷ್ಟವಾಗಿ ಹೇಳಿ)	98	
24K	If 24F is Yes, Were you satisfied by the action of the police? 24 ಎಫ್ ಉತ್ತರ ಹೌದೆಂದರ ಪೊಲೀಸ್ ಕಾರ್ಯದ ಬಗ್ಗೆ ನಿಮಗೆ ತೃಪ್ತಿ ಇದೆಯೇ?	Yes ಹೌದು...1 No ಇಲ್ಲ 2		If NO, skip to 24M
24L	If 24K is Yes, Why are you satisfied by the police? (Don't read out the options. Mark multiple options as respondents replies) 24 ಕೆ ಗೆ ಉತ್ತರ ಹೌದೆಂದರ ಪೊಲೀಸ್ ತೆಗೆದುಕೊಂಡ ಕ್ರಮದ ಬಗ್ಗೆ ನಿಮಗೆ ಏಕೆ ತೃಪ್ತಿ ಇದೆ ? (ಆಯ್ಕ ಓದಬೇಡಿ, ಬಹುಆಯ್ಕೆಗಳನ್ನು ಉತ್ತರದಾರ ಹೇಳುತ್ತಿದ್ದಂತೆ ಗುರುತಿಸಿ) **CIRCLE IF RESPONDENT MENTIONS** ಉತ್ತರದಾರರು ಹೇಳಿದವುಗಳ ಸುತ್ತ ಸುತ್ತುಗೆರ ಹಾಕಿರಿ.	They listened to the complaint ದೂರು ಕೇಳಿದರು	1	**SKIP TO 24N**
		They registered the complaint accurately ಸರಿಯಾಗಿ ದೂರು ದಾಖಲಿಸಿದರು	2	
		They registered the complaint quickly ದೂರನ್ನು ಬೇಗ ದಾಖಲಿಸಿದರು	3	
		They explained the action that they will take ಅವರು ತೆಗೆದುಕೊಳ್ಳುವ ಕ್ರಮದ ಬಗ್ಗೆ ವಿವರಿಸಿದರು	4	
		They solved the problem ಸಮಸ್ಯ ಪರಿಹಾರ ಮಾಡಿದರು	5	
		Other: (please specify) ಇತರ (ನಿರ್ದಿಷ್ಟವಾಗಿ ಹೇಳಿ)	98	
24M	If 24K is No, Why are you not satisfied by the police? (Don't read out the options. Mark multiple options as respondents replies) 24ಕೆ ಗೆ ಉತ್ತರ ಇಲ್ಲ ಎಂದಾದರೆ ಪೊಲೀಸ್ ತೆಗೆದುಕೊಂಡ ಕ್ರಮದ ಬಗ್ಗೆ ನಿಮಗೆ ಏಕೆ ತೃಪ್ತಿ ಇಲ್ಲ ? (ಆಯ್ಕೆಗಳನ್ನು ಓದಬೇಡಿ, ಬಹುಆಯ್ಕೆಗಳನ್ನು ಉತ್ತರದಾರ ಹೇಳುತ್ತಿದ್ದಂತೆ ಗುರುತಿಸಿ) **CIRCLE ALL MENTIONED BY THE RESPONDENT** ಉತ್ತರದಾರರು ಹೇಳಿದವುಗಳ ಸುತ್ತ ಸುತ್ತುಗೆರಿಗೆ ಹಾಕಿರಿ.	They were not interested ಅವರಿಗೆ ಆಸಕ್ತಿಯಿರಲಿಲ್ಲ	1	
		They were rude and impolite ಅವರು ಒರಟಾಗಿ, ಸೌಜನ್ಯ ಇಲ್ಲದೆ ವರ್ತಿಸಿದರು	2	
		They did not do enough ಮಾಡ ಬೇಕಾದಷ್ಟು ಮಾಡಲಿಲ್ಲ	3	
		They refused to file the FIR ಎಫ್ ಐ ಆರ್ ದಾಖಲಿಸಲು ನಿರಾಕರಿಸಿದರು	4	
		They tried to persuade me not to register an FIR ಎಫ್ ಐ ಆರ್ ದಾಖಲಿಸದಂತೆ ನನಗೆ ಒಪ್ಪಿಸಲು ಪ್ರಯತ್ನ ಮಾಡಿದರು	5	
		They took a long time to register my FIR ನನ್ನ ಎಫ್ ಐ ಆರ್ ದಾಖಲಿಸಲು ಬಹಳ ಕಾಲ ತೆಗೆದುಕೊಂಡರು	6	
		They told me to go away from the police station ಪೊಲೀಸ್ ಠಾಣೆಯಿಂದ ಹೋಗುವಂತೆ ಹೇಳಿದರು	7	
		They put me at fault ನನ್ನ ಮೇಲೆ ತಪ್ಪು ಹಾಕಿದರು	8	
		They wanted a bribe ಲಂಚ ಕೇಳಿದರು	9	
		They physically assaulted me ನನಗೆ ದೈಹಿಕವಾಗಿ ಹಲ್ಲ ಮಾಡಿದರು	10	
		They verbally abused me ನನ್ನನ್ನು ಬೈದರು	11	
		They didn't find or apprehend the offender ಅಪರಾಧಿಯನ್ನು ಹುಡುಕಲಿಲ್ಲ/ ದಸ್ತಗಿರಿ ಮಾಡಲಿಲ್ಲ	12	
		They didn't recover my property (goods) ನನ್ನ ಆಸ್ತಿ (ಸರಕು) ಒಪ್ಪಿಸಲಿಲ್ಲ	13	
		They didn't keep me properly informed ನನಗೆ ಸರಿಯಾಗಿ ಮಾಹಿತಿ ನೀಡಲಿಲ್ಲ	14	
		They were slow to arrive ಅವರು ಬಹಳ ತಡವಾಗಿ ಬಂದರು	15	
24N	Was any person arrested due to the incident? ಘಟನೆಯಿಂದ ಯಾವುದೇ ವ್ಯಕ್ತಿಯನ್ನು ದಸ್ತಗಿರಿ ಮಾಡಿದರಾ	Yes ಹೌದು ....1 No ಇಲ್ಲ 2		
24O	How serious was the incident to you and your household? ನಿಮಗೆ ಮತ್ತು ನಿಮ್ಮ ಮನೆಗೆ ಈ ಘಟನೆ ಎಷ್ಟು ಗಂಭೀರವಾದುದು?	Very serious ಬಹಳ ಗಂಭೀರ .... 1 Somewhat serious ಸುಮಾರಾಗಿ ಗಂಭೀರ .... 2 Not very serious ಬಹಳ ಗಂಭೀರವಲ್ಲ..................... 3 Not serious at all ಗಂಭೀರವೇ ಅಲ್ಲ .... 4 Don't know ಗೊತ್ತಿಲ್ಲ................................ 99		
Q25	**Part X**			
25A	How many times has the incident occurred in the last one year? ಕಳೆದ ಒಂದು ವರ್ಷದಲ್ಲಿ ಎಷ್ಟು ಬಾರಿ ಈ ಘಟನೆ ನಡೆಯಿತು?	Once ಒಮ್ಮೆ.. 1 Twice ಎರಡು ಬಾರಿ .... 2 Thrice ಮೂರು ಬಾರಿ................................ 3 More than thrice in the last year .... 4 ಕಳೆದ ಒಂದು ವರ್ಷದಲ್ಲಿ ಮೂರು ಬಾರಿಗಿಂತ ಹೆಚ್ಚು		
25B	Time of occurrence of the most recent incident: ತೀರಾ ಇತ್ತೀಚಿನ ಘಟನೆಯ ಸಮಯ	Early Morning ಮುಂಜಾನೆ (5am to 10am) .... 1 Late Morning ಬೆಳಿಗ್ಗೆ (10 am to 12pm) .... 2 Early Afternoon ಮಧ್ಯಾಹ್ನಕ್ಕೆ ಮುಂಚೆ (12pm to 3pm) 3		

		Late Afternoon ಮಧ್ಯಾಹ್ನದ ನಂತರ(3pm to 5pm) 4	
		Early Evening ಮುಸ್ಸಂಜೆ(5pm to 7pm)........................... 5	
		Late Evening ಸಂಜೆ ನಂತರ (7pm to 9pm) 6	
		Early Night ರಾತ್ರಿಗೆಮುಂಚೆ(9pm to 12am)...................... 7	
		Late Night ತಡ ರಾತ್ರಿ (12am to 5am)............................ 8	
		Don't Know/Can't Say ಗೊತ್ತಿಲ್ಲ/ಹೇಳಲಾಗದು 99	

25C	Why do you think you were denied access to these? (Don't read out the options. Mark multiple options as respondents replies) ಇವೆಲ್ಲದಕ್ಕೆ ನಿಮಗೆ ಏಕೆ ಅವಕಾಶವಿಲ್ಲ ಅನಿಸುತ್ತದೆ? (ಆಯ್ಕೆ ಓದಬೇಡಿ, ಬಹುಆಯ್ಕೆಗಳನ್ನು ಉತ್ತರದಾರ ಹೇಳುತ್ತಿದ್ದಂತೆ ಗುರುತಿಸಿ) **CIRCLE ALL MENTIONED BY THE RESPONDENT** ಉತ್ತರದಾರರು ಹೇಳಿದವುಗಳ ಸುತ್ತ ಸುತ್ತುಗೆರೆ ಹಾಕಿರಿ.	Feud with influential persons in the community ಸಮುದಾಯದ ಪ್ರಭಾವೀ ವ್ಯಕ್ತಿಗಳ ಜೊತೆ ಕಲಹ	1	
		Caste ಜಾತಿ	2	
		Religion ಧರ್ಮ	3	
		Gender ಲಿಂಗ	4	
		Mother-tongue ಮಾತೃಭಾಷೆ	5	
		Native State ಹುಟ್ಟಿದ ರಾಜ್ಯ	6	
		Sexual orientation ಲೈಂಗಿಕ ಪ್ರವೃತ್ತಿ	7	
		Skin colour ಮೈ ಬಣ್ಣ	8	
		Disability ಎಕಲತೆ	9	
		Other reasons: ಇತರೆ ಕಾರಣಗಳು	98	
25D	Did you report the incident to the police ಘಟನೆ ಬಗ್ಗೆ ನೀವು ಪೊಲೀಸರಿಗೆ ವರದಿ ಮಾಡಿದಿರಾ?	Yes ಹೌದು ....1 No ಇಲ್ಲ..2		If YES, skip to 25F
25E	If 25D is No, Why did you not report? (Do not prompt) 25 ಡಿ ಗೆ ಉತ್ತರ ಇಲ್ಲ ಎಂದಾದರೆ ವರದಿ ಏಕೆ ಮಾಡಿಲ್ಲ (ಉತ್ತರ ಸೂಚಿಸ ಬೇಡಿ ಅವರೇ ಹೇಳಲಿ)	Fear of retaliation ತಿರುಗಿ ಸೇಡು ತೀರಿಸಿ ಕೊಳ್ಳುತ್ತಾರೆಂಬ ಭಯ	1	**SKIP TO 25L**
		Lack of evidence ಸಾಕ್ಷಿಯಿರಲಿಲ್ಲ	2	
		Didn't know where to report ಎಲ್ಲಿ ವರದಿ ಮಾಡುವುದು ಗೊತ್ತಿರಲಿಲ್ಲ	3	
		Didn't know helpline number ಹೆಲ್ಪ್ ಲೈನ್ ನಂಬರ್ ಗೊತ್ತಿರಲಿಲ್ಲ	4	
		Did not want to get stuck in police/court matters ಪೊಲೀಸ್/ ಕೋರ್ಟು ವ್ಯವಹರಗಳಿಗೆ ಸಿಕ್ಕಿಹಾಕಿಕೊಳ್ಳುವುದು ಇಷ್ಟವಿರಲಿಲ್ಲ	5	
		Uncomfortable to go to Police Station ಪೊಲೀಸ್ ಠಾಣೆಗೆ ಹೋಗುವುದು ಅಹಿತವಾಗಿತ್ತು	6	
		Did not think the police would be able to do anything about the case ಪೊಲೀಸರು ಏನಾದರೂ ಮಾಡುತ್ತಾರ ಅನಿಸಲಿಲ್ಲ	7	
		Did not think police would entertain the case ಪೊಲೀಸರು ಕೇಸನ್ನು ತೆಗೆದುಕೊಳ್ಳುತ್ತಾರ ಅನಿಸಲಿಲ್ಲ	8	
		Police is unfair ಪೊಲೀಸರು ನ್ಯಾಯಪರರಲ್ಲ	9	
		Family matters need not be reported ಕುಟುಂಬ ವಿಷಯ ವರದಿಮಾಡಬಾರದು	10	
		This is better settled outside the police station ಪೊಲೀಸ್ ಠಾಣೆಯ ಹೊರಗೆ ಇತ್ಯರ್ಥ ಉತ್ತಮ	11	
		Bad past experience with reporting to Police ಪೊಲೀಸ್ ಗೆ ವರದಿ ಮಾಡಿದ ಕೆಟ್ಟ ಅನುಭವವಿದೆ	12	
		Others: (Please specify) ಇತರೆ(ನಿರ್ದಿಷ್ಟವಾಗಿ ಹೇಳಿ)_____	98	
		Don't Know/Can't Say ಗೊತ್ತಿಲ್ಲ/ಹೇಳಲಾಗದು	99	
25F	If 25D is Yes, why did you report? 25 ಡಿ ಗೆ ಉತ್ತರ ಹೌದು ಎಂದಾದರೆ ವರದಿ ಏಕೆ ಮಾಡಿದಿರಿ?	To recover property/person ಆಸ್ತಿ/ವ್ಯಕ್ತಿಯನ್ನು ಮರುಪಡೆಯಲು	1	
		For insurance reasons ವಿಮೆ ಕಾರಣಗಳಿಗೆ	2	
		Crime should be reported ಅಪರಾಧಗಳನ್ನು ವರದಿಮಾಡಬೇಕು	3	
		It was a serious event ಇದು ಗಂಭೀರ ವಿಷಯ	4	
		Wanted offender to be caught and punished ಅಪರಾಧಿಯನ್ನು ಹಿಡಿದು ಶಿಕ್ಷಿ ನೀಡಬೇಕು	5	
		To stop it from happening again/to get help ಮತ್ತೆ ಇದು ಆಗದಂತೆ ನಿಲ್ಲಿಸಲು/ ಸಹಾಯ ಪಡೆಯಲು	7	
		Others: (Please specify) ಇತರೆ(ಹೆಸರಿಸಿ)_____	98	
25G	If 25D is Yes, how did you report the	Called 100 ನಂ 100ಕ್ಕೆ ಕರೆಮಾಡಿದೆ 1		

	above crime? 25ಡಿ ಗೆ ಉತ್ತರ ಹೌದೆಂದರೆ ಹೇಗೆ ವರದಿ ಮಾಡಿದಿರಿ?	Called other police helpline .... 2 ಪೊಲೀಸ್ ಸಹಾಯವಾಣಿಗೆ ಕರಮಾಡಿದೆ Went to police station ಪೊಲೀಸ್ ಠಾಣೆಗೆ ಹೋದೆ .... 3 Approached a Police Officer .... 4 ಪೊಲೀಸ್ ಆಫೀಸರನ್ನು ಭೇಟಿ ಮಾಡಿದೆ Don't Remember ನೆನಪಿಲ್ಲ....................................... 99	
25H	If 25D is Yes, what did the police do upon hearing your complaint? (Don't read out the options. Mark multiple options as respondents replies) 25ಡಿ ಗೆ ಉತ್ತರ ಹೌದೆಂದರೆ ನಿಮ್ಮ ದೂರು ಕೇಳಿ ಪೊಲೀಸ್ ಏನು ಮಾಡಿದರು? (ಆಯ್ಕೆ ಓದಬೇಡಿ, ಬಹುಆಯ್ಕೆಗಳನ್ನು ಉತ್ತರದಾರ ಹೇಳುತ್ತಿದ್ದಂತೆ ಗುರುತಿಸಿ) **CIRCLE ALL MENTIONED BY THE RESPONDENT** ಉತ್ತರದಾರರು ಹೇಳಿದವುಗಳ ಸುತ್ತ ಸುತ್ತುಗೆರೆ ಹಾಕಿರಿ.	File a complaint ದೂರು ದಾಖಲಿಸಿದರು	1	
		Register an FIR ಎಫ್ ಐ ಆರ್ ದಾಖಲಿಸಿದರು	2	
		Despatched a PCR vehicle ಪಿ ಸಿ ಆರ್ ವಾಹನ ಕಳುಹಿಸಿದರು	3	
		Took any injured persons for medical assistance ಗಾಸಿಗೊಂಡ ವ್ಯಕ್ತಿಯನ್ನು ವೈದ್ಯಕೀಯ ಚಿಕಿತ್ಸೆಗೆ ಕರೆದೊಯ್ದರು	4	
		Asked you to go to another police station ಬೇರೆ ಪೊಲೀಸ್ ಠಾಣೆಗೆ ಹೋಗುವಂತೆ ನನಗೆ ಹೇಳಿದರು	5	
		Came to the spot and investigated ಸ್ಥಳಕ್ಕೆ ಬಂದು ತನಿಖೆಮಾಡಿದರು	6	
		Asked you not to file the complaint ದೂರು ದಾಖಲಿಸಬಾರದೆಂದು ಹೇಳಿದರು	7	
		If missing person, filed a missing person report ಕಳೆದುಹೋದ ವ್ಯಕ್ತಿಯಾದರೆ, ಕಳೆದುಹೋದ ವರದಿ ದಾಖಲಿಸಿದರು	8	
		Did not do anything ಏನೂ ಮಾಡಲಿಲ್ಲ	9	
		Other: (Please specify) ಇತರೆ(ನಿರ್ದಿಷ್ಟವಾಗಿ ಹೇಳಿ)	98	
25I	If 25D is Yes, Were you satisfied by the action of the police 25 ಡಿ ಗೆ ಉತ್ತರ ಹೌದೆಂದರೆ ಪೊಲೀಸ್ ತೆಗೆದುಕೊಂಡ ಕ್ರಮದ ಬಗ್ಗೆ ನಿಮಗೆ ತೃಪ್ತಿ ಇದೆಯೆ	Yes ಹೌದು .... 1 No ಇಲ್ಲ.. 2		→25K
25J	If 25I is Yes, Why are you satisfied by the police (Don't read out the options. Mark multiple options as respondents replies) 25 ಐಗೆ ಉತ್ತರ ಹೌದೆಂದರೆ ಪೊಲೀಸ್ ತೆಗೆದುಕೊಂಡ ಕ್ರಮದ ಬಗ್ಗೆ ನಿಮಗೆ ಏಕೆ ತೃಪ್ತಿ ಇದೆ ? (ಆಯ್ಕೆ ಓದಬೇಡಿ, ಬಹುಆಯ್ಕೆಗಳನ್ನು ಉತ್ತರದಾರ ಹೇಳುತ್ತಿದ್ದಂತೆ ಗುರುತಿಸಿ) **CIRCLE IF RESPONDENT MENTIONS** ಉತ್ತರದಾರರು ಹೇಳಿದವುಗಳ ಸುತ್ತ ಸುತ್ತುಗೆರೆ ಹಾಕಿರಿ.	They listened to the complaint ದೂರು ಕೇಳಿದರು	1	**SKIP TO 25L**
		They registered the complaint accurately ಸರಿಯಾಗಿ ದೂರು ದಾಖಲಿಸಿದರು	2	
		They registered the complaint quickly ದೂರನ್ನು ಬೇಗ ದಾಖಲಿಸಿದರು	3	
		They explained the action that they will take ಅವರು ತೆಗೆದುಕೊಳ್ಳುವ ಕ್ರಮದ ಬಗ್ಗೆ ವಿವರಿಸಿದರು	4	
		They solved the problem ಸಮಸ್ಯೆ ಪರಿಹಾರ ಮಾಡಿದರು	5	
		Other: (please specify) ಇತರೆ(ನಿರ್ದಿಷ್ಟವಾಗಿ ಹೇಳಿ)	98	
25K	If 25I is No, Why are you not satisfied by the police? (Don't read out the options. Mark multiple options as respondents replies) 25 ಐ ಗೆ ಉತ್ತರ ಇಲ್ಲ ಎಂದರೆ ಪೊಲೀಸ್ ತೆಗೆದುಕೊಂಡ ಕ್ರಮದ ಬಗ್ಗೆ ನಿಮಗೆ ಏಕೆ ತೃಪ್ತಿ ಇಲ್ಲ ? (ಆಯ್ಕೆಗಳನ್ನು ಓದಬೇಡಿ, ಬಹುಆಯ್ಕೆಗಳನ್ನು ಉತ್ತರದಾರ ಹೇಳುತ್ತಿದ್ದಂತೆ ಗುರುತಿಸಿ) **CIRCLE ALL MENTIONED BY THE RESPONDENT** ಉತ್ತರದಾರರು ಹೇಳಿದವುಗಳ ಸುತ್ತ ಸುತ್ತುಗೆರೆ ಹಾಕಿರಿ.	They were not interested ಅವರಿಗೆ ಆಸಕ್ತಿಯಿರಲಿಲ್ಲ	1	
		They were rude and impolite ಅವರು ಒರಟಾಗಿಸೌಜನ್ಯವಿಲ್ಲದೆ ವರ್ತಿಸಿದರು	2	
		They did not do enough ಬೇಕಾದಷ್ಟು ಮಾಡಲಿಲ್ಲ	3	
		They refused to file the FIR ಎಫ್ ಐ ಆರ್ ದಾಖಲಿಸಲು ನಿರಾಕರಿಸಿದರು	4	
		They tried to persuade me not to register an FIR ಎಫ್ ಐ ಆರ್ ದಾಖಲಿಸದಂತೆ ನನಗೆ ಒಪ್ಪಿಸಲು ಪ್ರಯತ್ನ ಮಾಡಿದರು	5	
		They took a long time to register my FIR ನನ್ನ ಎಫ್ ಐ ಆರ್ ದಾಖಲಿಸಲು ಬಹಳ ಕಾಲ ತೆಗೆದುಕೊಂಡರು	6	
		They told me to go away from the police station ಪೊಲೀಸ್ ಠಾಣೆಯಿಂದ ಹೋಗುವಂತೆ ಹೇಳಿದರು	7	
		They put me at fault ನನ್ನ ಮೇಲೇ ತಪ್ಪು ಹಾಕಿದರು	8	
		They wanted a bribe ಲಂಚ ಕೇಳಿದರು	9	
		They physically assaulted me ದೈಹಿಕವಾಗಿ ಹಲ್ಲೆ ಮಾಡಿದರು	10	
		They verbally abused me ನನ್ನನ್ನೇ ಬೈದರು	11	
		They didn't find or apprehend the offender ಅಪರಾಧಿಯನ್ನು ಹುಡುಕಲಿಲ್ಲ/ ದಸ್ತಗಿರಿ ಮಾಡಲಿಲ್ಲ	12	
		They didn't recover my property (goods) ನನ್ನ ಆಸ್ತಿ (ಸರಕು) ಹುಡುಕಿಕೊಡಲಿಲ್ಲ	13	
		They didn't keep me properly informed	14	

		ನನಗೆ ಸರಿಯಾಗಿ ಮಾಹಿತಿ ನೀಡಲಿಲ್ಲ	
		They were slow to arrive ಅವರು ಬಹಳ ತಡವಾಗಿ ಬಂದರು	15
		Other: (please specify) ಇತರ(ನಿರ್ದಿಷ್ಟವಾಗಿ ಹೇಳಿ)	98
25L	Was any person arrested due to the incident? ಘಟನೆಯಿಂದ ಯಾವುದೇ ವ್ಯಕ್ತಿಯನ್ನು ದಸ್ತಗಿರಿ ಮಾಡಿದರಾ?	Yes ಹೌದು ....1 No ಇಲ್ಲ...2	
25M	How serious was the incident to you and your household? ನಿಮಗೆ ಮತ್ತು ನಿಮ್ಮ ಮನೆಗೆ ಈ ಘಟನೆ ಎಷ್ಟು ಗಂಭೀರವಾದುದು?	Very serious ಬಹಳ ಗಂಭೀರ.........................1 Somewhat serious ಸುಮಾರಾಗಿ ಗಂಭೀರ.........................2 Not very serious ಬಹಳ ಗಂಭೀರವಲ್ಲ ....3 Not serious at all ಗಂಭೀರವೇ ಅಲ್ಲ...................4 Don't know ಗೊತ್ತಿಲ್ಲ 99	
Q26	**Part XI**		
26A	How many times has the incident occurred in the last one year? ಕಳೆದ ಒಂದು ವರ್ಷದಲ್ಲಿ ಎಷ್ಟು ಬಾರಿ ಈ ಘಟನೆ ನಡೆಯಿತು?	Once ಒಮ್ಮೆ ....1 Twice ಎರಡು ಬಾರಿ ....2 Thrice ಮೂರು ಬಾರಿ ....3 More than thrice in the last year ....4 ಕಳೆದ ಒಂದು ವರ್ಷದಲ್ಲಿ ಮೂರು ಬಾರಿಗಿಂತ ಹೆಚ್ಚು	
26B	Time of occurrence of the most recent incident: ತೀರಾ ಇತ್ತೀಚಿನ ಘಟನೆಯ ಸಮಯ	Early Morning ಮುಂಜಾನೆ (5am to 10am) ....1 Late Morning ಬೆಳಿಗ್ಗೆ (10 am to 12pm) ....2 Early Afternoon (12pm to 3pm) ....3 ಮಧ್ಯಾಹ್ನಕ್ಕೆ ಮುಂಚೆ Late Afternoon (3pm to 5pm) ....4 ಮಧ್ಯಾಹ್ನದ ನಂತರ Early Evening ಮುಸ್ಸಂಜೆ (5pm to 7pm) ....5 Late Evening ಸಂಜೆ ನಂತರ (7pm to 9pm) ....6 Early Night ರಾತ್ರಿಗೆಮುಂಚೆ (9pm to 12am) ......7 Late Night ತಡ ರಾತ್ರಿ (12am to 5am) ....8 Don't Know/Can't Say ಗೊತ್ತಿಲ್ಲ/ಹೇಳಲಾಗದು 99	
26C	Do you know who the perpetrator of the crime is? ಅಪರಾಧ ಮಾಡಿದವರು ಯಾರು ಗೊತ್ತಾ?	Yes ಹೌದು ....1 No ಇಲ್ಲ 2	If NO, skip to **25E**
26D	If 26C is yes, why do you think this happened 26 ಸಿ. ಗೆ ಉತ್ತರ ಹೌದೆಂದರೆ ಏಕೆ ಇದು ಆಯಿತೆನಿಸುತ್ತದೆ?	Previous enmity ಹಿಂದಿನ ವೈರತ್ವ..........................1 Land related disputes ಭೂಮಿಗೆ ಸಂಬಂಧಿಸಿದ ವಿವಾದ ....2 Family property disputes ಕುಟುಂಬದ ಆಸ್ತಿ ವಿವಾದ....................3 Due to my caste ನನ್ನ ಜಾತಿ ಕಾರಣದಿಂದ ....4 Due to my religion ನನ್ನ ಧರ್ಮದ ಕಾರಣದಿಂದ ....5 Due to my gender ನನ್ನ ಲಿಂಗದ ಕಾರಣದಿಂದ...............6 Due to my mother-tongue ನನ್ನ ಮಾತೃಭಾಷೆ ಕಾರಣದಿಂದ.......7 Due to my native state ನನ್ನ ಹುಟ್ಟು ರಾಜ್ಯದ ಕಾರಣದಿಂದ ....8 Due to my sexual orientation ನನ್ನ ಲೈಂಗಿಕ ಪ್ರವೃತ್ತಿಯಿಂದ.....9 Due to my disability ನನ್ನ ವಿಕಲತೆಯಿಂದ ....10 Due to my skin colour ನನ್ನ ಮೈಬಣ್ಣದಿಂದ.............11 Due to other reasons: (please specify) ....98 ಇತರ ಕಾರಣಗಳು(ನಿರ್ದಿಷ್ಟವಾಗಿ ಹೇಳಿ) Do not know ಗೊತ್ತಿಲ್ಲ/ಹೇಳಲಾಗದು................99	
26E	Did you report the incident to the police: ಘಟನೆ ಬಗ್ಗೆ ನೀವು ಪೊಲೀಸರಿಗೆ ವರದಿ ಮಾಡಿದಿರಾ	Yes ಹೌದು ....1 No ಇಲ್ಲ..2	If YES, skip to **26G**
26F	If 26E is No, Why did you not report? (Do not prompt) 26 ಇ ಗೆ ಉತ್ತರ ಇಲ್ಲ ಎಂದಾದರೆ ವರದಿ ಏಕೆ ಮಾಡಲಿಲ್ಲ?	Fear of retaliation retaliation ತಿರುಗಿ ಸೇಡು ತೀರಿಸಿಕೊಳ್ಳುತ್ತಾರೆಂಬ ಭಯ	1	**SKIP TO 26M**
		Lack of evidence ಸಾಕ್ಷಿಯರಲಿಲ್ಲ	2	
		Didn't know where to report ಎಲ್ಲಿ ವರದಿ ಮಾಡುವುದು ಗೊತ್ತಿಲ್ಲ	3	
		Didn't know helpline number ಸಹಾಯವಾಣಿ ನಂಬರ್ ಗೊತ್ತಿಲ್ಲ	4	
		Did not want to get stuck in police/court matters	5	

		ಪೊಲೀಸ್/ ಕೋರ್ಟು ವ್ಯವಹರಣಿಗೆ ಸಿಕ್ಕಿಹಾಕಿಕೊಳ್ಳುವುದು ಇಷ್ಟವಿರಲಿಲ್ಲ	
		Uncomfortable to go to Police Station ಪೊಲೀಸ್ ಠಾಣೆಗೆ ಹೋಗುವುದು ಅಹಿತವಾಗಿತ್ತು	6
		Did not think the police would be able to do anything about the case ಪೊಲೀಸರು ಏನಾದರೂ ಮಾಡುತ್ತಾರೆ ಅನಿಸರಲಿಲ್ಲ	7
		Did not think police would entertain the case ಪೊಲೀಸರು ಕೇಸನ್ನು ತೆಗೆದುಕೊಳ್ಳುತ್ತಾರೆ ಅನಿಸಲಿಲ್ಲ	8
		Police is unfair ಪೊಲೀಸರು ನ್ಯಾಯ ಪರರಲ್ಲ	9
		Family matters need not be reported ಕುಟುಂಬದ ವಿಷಯ ವರದಿಮಾಡುಬಾರದು	10
		This is better settled outside the police station ಪೊಲೀಸ್ ಠಾಣೆಯ ಹೊರಗೆ ಇತ್ಯರ್ಥ ಉತ್ತಮ	11
		Bad past experience with reporting to Police ಪೊಲೀಸ್ ಗೆ ವರದಿ ಮಾಡಿದ ಕೆಟ್ಟ ಅನುಭವವಿದೆ	12
		Others: (Please specify)_____ ಇತರೆ(ನಿರ್ದಿಷ್ಟವಾಗಿ ಹೇಳಿ)	98
		Don't Know/Can't Say ಗೊತ್ತಿಲ್ಲ/ಹೇಳಲಾಗದು	99
26G	If 26E is Yes, why did you report? 26 ಇ ಗೆ ಉತ್ತರ ಹೌದೆಂದರೆ ಏಕೆ ವರದಿ ಮಾಡಿದಿರಿ?	To recover property/person .... 1 ಆಸ್ತಿ/ವ್ಯಕ್ತಿಯನ್ನು ಮರುಪಡೆಯಲು	
		For insurance reasons .... 2 ವಿಮೆ ಕಾರಣಗಳಿಗೆ	
		Crime should be reported .... 3 ಅಪರಾಧಗಳನ್ನು ವರದಿಮಾಡಬೇಕು	
		It was a serious event .... 4 ಇದು ಗಂಭೀರ ವಿಷಯ	
		Wanted offender to be caught and punished .... 5 ಅಪರಾಧಿಯನ್ನು ಹಿಡಿದು ಶಿಕ್ಷೆ ನೀಡಬೇಕು	
		To stop it from happening again/to get help .... 6 ಮತ್ತೆ ಇದು ಆಗದಂತೆ ನಿಲ್ಲಿಸಲು/ ಸಹಾಯ ಪಡೆಯಲು	
		Others: (Please specify) ಇತರೆ(ಹೆಸರಿಸಿ)_____ ..98	
26H	If 26E is Yes, how did you report the above crime? 26ಇ ಗೆ ಉತ್ತರ ಹೌದೆಂದರೆ ಮೇಲಿನ ಅಪರಾಧದ ಬಗ್ಗೆ ಹೇಗೆ ವರದಿ ಮಾಡಿದಿರಿ?	Called 100 ನಂ100ಕ್ಕೆ ಕರೆಮಾಡಿದೆ 1	
		Called other police helpline .... 2 ಪೊಲೀಸ್ ಸಹಾಯವಾಣಿ ಕರೆಮಾಡಿದೆ	
		Went to police station ಪೊಲೀಸ್ ಠಾಣೆಗೆ ಹೋದೆ 3	
		Approached a Police Officer .... 4 ಪೊಲೀಸ್ ಆಫೀಸರನ್ನು ಭೇಟಿ ಮಾಡಿದೆ	
		Don't Remember ನೆನಪಿಲ್ಲ 99	
26I	If 26E is Yes, what did the police do upon hearing your complaint? (Don't read out the options. Mark multiple options as respondents replies) 26ಇ ಗೆ ಉತ್ತರ ಹೌದೆಂದರೆ ನಿಮ್ಮ ದೂರು ಕೇಳಿ ಪೊಲೀಸ್ ಏನು ಮಾಡಿದರು? (ಆಯ್ಕೆ ಓದಬೇಡಿ, ಬಹುಆಯ್ಕೆಗಳನ್ನು ಪ್ರತಿಕ್ರಿಯೆದಾರ ಹೇಳುತ್ತಿದ್ದಂತೆ ಗುರುತಿಸಿ **CIRCLE ALL MENTIONED BY THE RESPONDENT** ಉತ್ತರದಾರರು ಹೇಳಿದವುಗಳ ಸುತ್ತ ಸುತ್ತುಗೆರೆ ಹಾಕಿರಿ.	File a complaint ದೂರು ದಾಖಲಿಸಿದರು	1
		Register an FIR ಎಫ್ ಐ ಆರ್ ದಾಖಲಿಸಿದರು	2
		Despatched a PCR vehicle ಪಿಸಿ ಆರ್ ಗಾಡಿ ಕಳುಹಿಸಿದರು	3
		Took any injured persons for medical assistance ಗಾಸಿಗೊಂಡ ವ್ಯಕ್ತಿಯನ್ನು ವೈದ್ಯಕೀಯ ಚಿಕಿತ್ಸೆಗೆ ಕರೆದೊಯ್ದರು	4
		Asked you to go to another police station ಬೇರೆ ಪೊಲೀಸ್ ಠಾಣೆಗೆ ಹೋಗುವಂತೆ ನನಗೆ ಹೇಳಿದರು	5
		Came to the spot and investigated ಸ್ಥಳಕ್ಕೆ ಬಂದು ತನಿಖೆಮಾಡಿದರು	6
		Asked you not to file the complaint ದೂರು ದಾಖಲಿಸಬಾರದೆಂದು ಹೇಳಿದರು	7
		If missing person, filed a missing person report ಕಳೆದುಹೋದದ್ದು ವ್ಯಕ್ತಿಯಾದರೆ, ವ್ಯಕ್ತಿ ಕಳೆದುಹೋದ ವರದಿ ದಾಖಲಿಸಿದರು	8
		Did not do anything ಏನೂ ಮಾಡಲಿಲ್ಲ	9
		Other: (Please specify) ಇತರೆ(ನಿರ್ದಿಷ್ಟವಾಗಿ ಹೇಳಿ) _____	98
26J	If 26E is Yes, Were you satisfied by the action of the police? 26ಇ ಗೆ ಉತ್ತರ	Yes ಹೌದು 1	
		No ಇಲ್ಲ 2	If NO, skip to

	ಹೌದೆಂದರೆ ಪೊಲೀಸ್ ತೆಗೆದುಕೊಂಡ ಕ್ರಮದ ಬಗ್ಗೆ ನಿಮಗೆ ತೃಪ್ತಿ ಇದೆಯೇ			**26L**
26K	If 26J is Yes, Why are you satisfied by the police? (Don't read out the options. Mark multiple options as respondents replies) 26ಜೆ ಗೆ ಉತ್ತರ ಹೌದೆಂದರೆ ಪೊಲೀಸ್ ತೆಗೆದುಕೊಂಡ ಕ್ರಮದ ಬಗ್ಗೆ ನಿಮಗೆ ಏಕೆ ತೃಪ್ತಿ ಇದೆ ? (ಆಯ್ಕೆ ಓದಬೇಡಿ, ಬಹುಆಯ್ಕೆಗಳನ್ನು ಉತ್ತರದಾರ ಹೇಳುತ್ತಿದ್ದಂತೆ ಗುರುತಿಸಿ) **CIRCLE IF RESPONDENT MENTIONS** ಉತ್ತರದಾರರು ಹೇಳಿದವುಗಳ ಸುತ್ತ ಸುತ್ತುಗೆರೆ ಹಾಕಿರಿ.	They listened to the complaint ದೂರು ಕೇಳಿದರು	1	**SKIP TO 26M**
		They registered the complaint accurately ಸರಿಯಾಗಿ ದೂರು ದಾಖಲಿಸಿದರು	2	
		They registered the complaint quickly ದೂರನ್ನು ಬೇಗ ದಾಖಲಿಸಿದರು	3	
		They explained the action that they will take ಅವರು ತೆಗೆದುಕೊಳ್ಳುವ ಕ್ರಮದ ಬಗ್ಗೆ ವಿವರಿಸಿದರು	4	
		They solved the problem ಸಮಸ್ಯೆ ಪರಿಹಾರ ಮಾಡಿದರು	5	
		Other: (please specify) ಇತರೆ(ನಿರ್ದಿಷ್ಟವಾಗಿ ಹೇಳಿ)	98	
26L	If 26J is No, Why are you not satisfied by the police? (Don't read out the options. Mark multiple options as respondents replies) 26 ಜೆ ಗೆ ಉತ್ತರ ಇಲ್ಲ ಎಂದಾದರೆ ಪೊಲೀಸ್ ಕಾರ್ಯದ ಬಗ್ಗೆ ನಿಮಗೆ ಏಕೆ ತೃಪ್ತಿ ಇಲ್ಲ ? (ಆಯ್ಕೆಗಳನ್ನು ಓದಬೇಡಿ, ಬಹುಆಯ್ಕೆಗಳನ್ನು ಉತ್ತರ ಹೇಳುತ್ತಿದ್ದಂತೆ ಗುರುತಿಸಿ **CIRCLE ALL MENTIONED BY THE RESPONDENT**	They were not interested ಅವರಿಗೆ ಆಸಕ್ತಿಯಿರಲಿಲ್ಲ	1	
		They were rude and impolite ಅವರು ಒರಟಾಗಿ, ತಾಳ್ಮೆಯಿಲ್ಲದವರು	2	
		They did not do enough ಬೇಕಾದಷ್ಟು ಮಾಡಲಿಲ್ಲ	3	
		They refused to file the FIR ಎಫ್ ಐ ಆರ್ ದಾಖಲಿಸಲು ನಿರಾಕರಿಸಿದರು	4	
		They tried to persuade me not to register an FIR ಎಫ್ ಐ ಆರ್ ದಾಖಲಿಸದಂತೆ ನನಗೆ ಒಪ್ಪಿಸಲು ಪ್ರಯತ್ನ ಮಾಡಿದರು	5	
		They took a long time to register my FIR ನನ್ನ ಎಫ್ ಐ ಆರ್ ದಾಖಲಿಸಲು ಬಹಳ ಕಾಲ ತೆಗೆದುಕೊಂಡರು	6	
		They told me to go away from the police station ಪೊಲೀಸ್ ಠಾಣೆಯಿಂದ ಹೋಗುವಂತೆ ಹೇಳಿದರು	7	
		They put me at fault ನನ್ನ ಮೇಲೆ ತಪ್ಪು ಹಾಕಿದರು	8	
		They wanted a bribe ಲಂಚ ಕೇಳಿದರು	9	
		They physically assaulted me ದೈಹಿಕವಾಗಿ ಹಲ್ಲೆ ಮಾಡಿದರು	10	
		They verbally abused me ನನ್ನ ಬೈದರು	11	
		They didn't find or apprehend the offender ಅಪರಾಧಿಯನ್ನು ಹುಡುಕಲಿಲ್ಲ/ ದಸ್ಗಿರಿ ಮಾಡಲಿಲ್ಲ	12	
		They didn't recover my property (goods) ನನ್ನ ಆಸ್ತಿ (ಸರಕು) ಒಪ್ಪಿಸಲಿಲ್ಲ	13	
		They didn't keep me properly informed ನನಗೆ ಸರಿಯಾಗಿ ಮಾಹಿತಿ ನೀಡಲಿಲ್ಲ	14	
		They were slow to arrive ಅವರು ಬಹಳ ತಡವಾಗಿ ಬಂದರು	15	
		Other: (please specify) ಇತರೆ(ನಿರ್ದಿಷ್ಟವಾಗಿ ಹೇಳಿ)	98	
26M	Was any person arrested due to the incident? ಘಟನೆಯಿಂದ ಯಾವುದೇ ವ್ಯಕ್ತಿಯನ್ನು ದಸ್ಗಿರಿ ಮಾಡಿದರಾ?	Yes ಹೌದು ....1 No ಇಲ್ಲ.............................2		
26N	How serious was the incident to you and your household? ನಿಮಗೆ ಮತ್ತು ನಿಮ್ಮ ಮನೆಗೆ ಈ ಘಟನೆ ಎಷ್ಟು ಗಂಭೀರವಾದುದು?	Very serious ಬಹಳ ಗಂಭೀರ................. 1 Somewhat serious ಸುಮಾರಾಗಿ ಗಂಭೀರ .... 2 Not very serious ಬಹಳ ಗಂಭೀರವಲ್ಲ..................... 3 Not serious at all ಗಂಭೀರವೇ ಅಲ್ಲ........................ 4 Don't know ಗೊತ್ತಿಲ್ಲ..........................99		

THANK AND CLOSE
ಧನ್ಯವಾದ ಹೇಳಿ ಮುಕ್ತಾಯ ಮಾಡಿ

References

Alexander, M. (2012). New jim crow - Mass incarceration in the age of color blindness. New York: The New Press

Altrichter, H., Feldman, A., Posch, P., Somekh, B. (2008). Teachers investigate their work: An introduction to action research across the professions. New York: Routledge. https://doi.org/10.4324/9781315811918

Broadhurst, R., Bacon-Shone, J., Bouhours, B., Bouhours, T., & Kingwa, L. (Eds.). (2011). *Business and the risk of crime in China.* ANU.

Chockalingam, K. (2003). *Measures for crime victims in the Indian Criminal Justice System.* The 144th International Senior Seminar Visiting Experts' Papers, Resource Material Series No.81: https://www.unafei.or.jp/publications/pdf/RS_No81/No81_11VE_Chockalingam.pdf

Common Cause & Lokniti - Centre for the Study of Developing Societies. (2018). *Status of policing in India report, 2018: A study of performance and perceptions.* Common Cause.

Durani, A., Kumar, R., Sane, R., & Sinha, N. (2017) Safety trends and reporting of crime. Mumbai: IDFC Institute

Farrall, S., & Maruna, S. (2004). Desistance-focused criminal justice policy research: Introduction to a special issue on desistance from crime and public policy. *The Howard Journal of Criminal Justice.* https://doi.org/10.1111/j.1468-2311.2004.00335.x

Farrall, S., Jackson, J., & Gray, E. (2008). Reassessing the fear of crime. *European Journal of Criminology, 5*(3), 363–380. https://doi.org/10.1177/1477370808090834

Ferraro, K. F. (1995) Fear of crime: Interpreting victimization risk. SUNY Series in New Directions in Crime and Justice Studies New York: State University of New York Press

Harcourt, B. E. (2006). Against prediction: Profiling, policing, and punishing in an actuarial age. Chicago:University of Chicago Press. https://doi.org/10.7208/9780226315997

Hinkle, J. C. (2015). Emotional fear of crime Vs. perceived safety and risk: Implications for measuring "Fear" and testing the broken windows thesis. American Journal of Criminal Justice, 40(1), 147–168. https://doi.org/10.1007/s12103-014-9243-9

Lewis, D. A., & Salem, G. (1986). *Fear of crime: Incivility and the production of a social problem New Brunswick.* Transaction Publishers.

OECD/Open Society. (2019). *Legal needs surveys and access to justice.* OECD Publishing. https://www.oecd-ilibrary.org/docserver/g2g9a36c-en.pdf?expires=1616733247&id=id&accname=guest&checksum=85D057F1C66622C672F8D8BD103360F8

Ogneva-Himmelberger, Y., Ross, L., Caywood, T., Khananayev, M., & Starr, C. (2019). *Analyzing the relationship between perception of safety and reported crime in an urban neighborhood using GIS and sketch maps.* Special Issue Urban Crime Mapping and Analysis Using GIS (November 27, 2019).

Sarkar, A., Mukhopadhyay, D., Blake, C., & Prasad D. (2015). Crime victimisation and safety perception: A public survey of delhi and mumbai. New Delhi: Commonwealth Human Rights Initiative

Taylor, R. B. (2002) Fear of crime, social ties, and collective efficacy: Maybe masquerading measurement, maybe déj`a vu all over again. Justice Quarterly, 19(4), 773–792. https://doi.org/10.1080/07418820200095421

Yang, S.-M., & Hinkle, J. (2012). Issues in survey design: Using surveys of victimization and fear of crime as examples. In *Handbook of survey methodology for the social sciences.* https://doi.org/10.1007/978-1-4614-3876-2_25

Sudhir Krishnaswamy is the Vice-Chancellor of the National Law School of India University and Varsha Aithala is a doctoral candidate at the National Law School of India University.

This chapter mainly draws from our work on the Karnataka Crime Victimization Survey conducted by Azim Premji University, Bengaluru. Our thinking on this was greatly shaped by our research team on the Karnataka Crime Victimization Survey at Azim Premji University, particularly, Dr. Siddharth Swaminathan and Asha Venugopalan. Asha Venugopalan prepared the statistical analysis and provided preliminary drafts of the survey report.

All figures, tables, and charts in this chapter are drawn from the Karnataka Crime Victimization Survey conducted by Azim Premji University, Bengaluru in 2018–2019.

Index

© The Editor(s) (if applicable) and The Author(s), under exclusive license to
Springer Nature Switzerland AG 2022
S. Krishnaswamy et al. (eds.), *Crime Victimisation in India*, Springer Series on
Asian Criminology and Criminal Justice Research,
https://doi.org/10.1007/978-3-031-12251-4

Printed by Printforce, the Netherlands